Praise for *Abolishing Surveillance*

"*Abolishing Surveillance: Digital Media Activism and State Repression* gifts us with incredible insight into digital media as a constellation of struggle but also a channel of surveillance that functions as a toehold for state and capital to deactivate social movements. Through these rarely documented histories of repression against environmental activists, independent media makers, grassroots organizers, and working-class communities of color, Robé skillfully brings a constellation of practices together to draw an alarming portrait of the surveillance architecture in the United States. This essential history of compliance and control in the context of our contemporary democracy is essential reading for our unprecedented times."
—Angela J. Aguayo, associate professor at the University of Illinois, Urbana-Champaign, and author of *Documentary Resistance: Social Change and Participatory Media*

"A much-needed text in a world of unbridled state surveillance, Robé's follow-up to *Breaking the Spell* takes a deep dive into the dangerous world of copwatching in working-class communities of color, Muslim American countersurveillance collectives, the investigative work of animal rights activists, and the independent media produced by countersummit protesters. Once again Robé's work is informed by interviews with the grassroots media activists taking the risks necessary to protect and further their movements. But *Abolishing Surveillance* does not shy away from offering constructive critiques of the groups showcased and gives us insight to the way forward and on how to survive life under Big Brother now and for years to come."
—Franklin López, anarchist filmmaker, founder of sub.Media

"With his signature verve, commitments to media and activism, and close attention and connection to communities of practice and protest, Chris Robé details American mediated and embodied struggles against decades (eons?) of surveillance and policing. Connecting four social movement's media and grassroots resistance, *Abolishing Surveillance* draws on the histories and distinct struggles of animal rights activists, anarchists, cop-watchers, and Muslim and Arab Americans to contribute to autonomy and mutual awareness. From undercover video in the '80s, to algorithms and social media today, Robé tracks linked legacies of anti-racist violence and racial capitalism and our movements' resistance and solidarity. To read him is to learn, engage, and keep strong."

—Alexanra Juhasz, distinguished professor
of film, Brooklyn College, CUNY

"*Abolishing Surveillance* reads like an epic novel of revolution and resistance. It pulses with the excitement of community groups fighting back through any media necessary, from activist videos, YouTube postings, secret underground exposes, social media, websites, VR, police countersurveillance, and protests over commercial media representations. This exceptionally well-written, compelling book explains the intensification of state sponsored surveillance and infiltrations of the last fifty years in the entangled context of the rise of neoliberalism, racialized capitalism, policing, and the carceral state. But it also explodes with optimism as dynamic, innovative strategies of grassroots community media and organizing critique, intervene in, and dismantle these technologies of power by reinventing how digital media can be deployed and circulated to change power relations. A riveting read, this eye-opening book demands that digital media in all its forms and platforms be seen as essential tools entwined with on-the-ground organizing, remaking and reimagining oppositional media."

—Patricia R. Zimmermann, author of *Documentary Across Platforms: Reverse Engineering Media, Place, and Politics*

Abolishing Surveillance

Digital Media Activism
and State Repression

Chris Robé

ISBN: 978-1-62963-361-9 (paperback)
ISBN: 978-1-62963-691-7 (ebook)
Library of Congress Control Number: 2022942406

Cover design by John Yates/stealworks.com
Cover painting, "January 19th, 2015," by Leslie Barlow | lesliebarlowartist.com
Interior design by briandesign

10 9 8 7 6 5 4 3 2 1

PM Press
PO Box 23912
Oakland, CA 94623
www.pmpress.org

Printed in the USA.

Contents

ACKNOWLEDGMENTS   ix

INTRODUCTION   **"We Tell Ourselves Stories in Order to Live"**   1

CHAPTER 1   **Seeing Past the Walls of Slaughterhouses:** Animal Rights, Undercover Video, and Struggles over Visibility   17

CHAPTER 2   **Here Come the Anarchists:** State Repression, Video Activism, and Counter-summit Protesting   88

CHAPTER 3   **Documenting the Little Abuses:** Copwatching, Countersurveillance, and Community Organizing   126

CHAPTER 4   **Somali American Narratives and Suspect Communities:** Visibility, Representation, and Media Making in the Age of Islamophobia   183

CODA   261

NOTES   268

SELECTED BIBLIOGRAPHY   306

INDEX   311

ABOUT THE AUTHOR   320

Dedicated to Dana and Nora, who made yet another book possible in more ways than they will ever know

Acknowledgments

First and foremost, I would like to thank all of the activists, organizers, and other communities I encountered conducting research for this book, who made it possible. Their generosity of spirit and thoughtful reflection on the work they and others do was invaluable in writing this book. The willingness of others to offer their time and insights to explain to absolute strangers their activism and community organizing never ceases to amaze me.

Many friends have been invaluable in randomly discussing this project. Angela Aguayo, who engages in parallel work, has always been one of my most special of comrades. Julia Lesage has been incredibly supportive of my work and a source of inspiration with her own work and brilliance. My dear friend, John F. Lennon, assisted me in stumbling through many ideas found within this book while hiking through innumerable Florida woods and beaches. Friends and colleagues at Florida Atlantic University have unwittingly assisted me in this work simply through our nights out discussing our research over beers or after playing music together: Maria Fadiman, Carla Calargé, Stephen Charbonneau, Mark Harvey, Phil Lewin, and Phil Hough.

Florida Atlantic University made much of this research possible through a series of funding initiatives like the Peace, Justice, and Human Rights Faculty Research Grant, the Morrow Fund Research Grant, and the Distinguished Lecture Series Faculty Research Support Award. A Scholarly and Creative Accomplishment Fellowship provided me a semester off to conduct more in-depth interviews in Minneapolis. A sabbatical during the academic year of 2022–23 allowed me to fine-tune the manuscript for publication. Dr. Carol Mills, director of the School of Communication and Multimedia Studies, has been very supportive of my research. My students—particularly in my course Radical Film, New Media, and Social Movements—have been a valuable sounding board for much of this research as well.

I would like to thank all the good people at PM Press for their support and making such work possible. Independent publishers serve a vital role in providing affordable and accessible material of all variety to a wide readership. As an avid reader and a writer, I appreciate PM Press's impressive catalogue and their continuing support of politically engaged authors. Additionally, I would like to thank Jane Banks who edited the manuscript at an earlier stage.

My wife, Dana Eades, and daughter, Nora Ballantyne, mean everything to me and provide endless support for this work. They are often unwittingly conscripted during dinners to engage with the minutiae of this research that would bore other mere mortals to death.

"We Tell Ourselves Stories in Order to Live"

J oan Didion opens one of her most famous essays with these words as she considers the fissures exposed by the multiple social upheavals that splintered the 1960s and 1970s.[1] Her words do not just refer to the ways in which individuals impose narratives to add meaning to the random events, people, and places that we encounter throughout our lives. She also suggests a collective sense of storytelling, that is, the ways in which communities and nations arrange narrative details to not only present a coherent understanding of the world we occupy, but also to situate these narratives within sentimental and idealized frames.

"American exceptionalism" remains one of the most powerful collective sentimental narratives within the United States. We are "a city upon a hill," as Puritan leader John Winthrop famously said, quoting the Sermon on the Mount and blessing our earliest stages of conquest in the American colonies as nothing less than a covenant with God. The narrative catapults the founding of the United States from the context of ordinary history into the divine ledgers of manifest destiny. Like all nations, the United States was founded upon brute violence. Yet, "what is distinctively 'American,'" according to historian Richard Slotkin, "is not necessarily the amount or kind of violence that characterizes our history but the mythic significance" we imbue it with that variously justifies its existence or effaces it from full view.[2] As we will see in the forthcoming chapters, national crises create urgent moments for American exceptionalism to be resurrected and updated.

I write this introduction during the fall of 2021, the twentieth anniversary of the 9/11 attacks in the United States. Although 9/11 represents an undeniable tragedy, it has also become a strategy through which the US is able to further bury its history of violence. We are told that "everything changed" on 9/11. It serves as a pivot point of US history, enabling a new political trajectory that assumes some unique rupture from the sanguine ways of the past when the country supposedly aligned more closely with its ideals of equality and happiness, with only a brief historical aberration or two marring the path. Thus a day of tragedy provides cover for a deeper historical reckoning.

For example, in the recent five-part Netflix documentary *Turning Point* (2021) a bureaucrat from the National Security Agency (NSA) reflects, "There's before 9/11, and there's after 9/11" when it comes to governmental spying on its own population. A series of talking heads proclaim the importance of the Fourth Amendment against illegal search and seizure before concluding that the NSA's illegal wiretapping is unprecedented and nothing less than "an unauthorized government raid on your house."

However, this fiction only remains plausible if we conveniently overlook two facts. First, the United States government has routinely engaged in illegal search and seizures against any community that it has deemed suspect. The 1919–20 Palmer Raids targeted immigrant communities, arresting around ten thousand people and deporting another five hundred with feminist anarchist Emma Goldman being the most famous deportee.[3] COINTELPRO, the FBI's illegal targeting, harassment, and undermining of individuals and groups it deemed "un-American," ran from 1956 until 1971. These instances and countless others repeatedly expose the government's willingness to invade the privacy of those it considers at odds with American exceptionalism.

Moreover, to assume that post-9/11 wiretapping represents a blanket invasion of privacy upon all US citizens is to ignore the differential way in which such surveillance is applied, with working-class communities of color and immigrant groups often bearing the brunt of this overreach. The outrage behind "unprecedented" NSA spying can only be upheld if you occupy a seat in that mythical city upon a hill and belong to a community that has the privilege of remaining oblivious to the long history of government surveillance and violence on its own people. Of course, the NSA's spying practices should be condemned. But they do not represent any new historical trajectory, instead they indicate an extension of such firmly established practices into newer digital realms.

Boston University asked select faculty members to reflect upon "how 9/11 changed the world." A historian suggested that police militarization was "to a large extent, a response to Sept. 11."[4] Although 9/11 certainly assisted in accelerating the militarization of the police, the police and military have always mutually constituted one another. For example, the emergence of the sheriff in England "was responsible for enforcing the monarch's will in military, fiscal, and judicial matters, and for maintaining domestic peace."[5] Mark Neocleous notes that in the US "police power grew out of the slave patrol, which was itself conceived of as a militia force."[6]

This book and the movements addressed within it challenge notions of American exceptionalism by drawing attention to the bloody historical legacy that has defined the United States and targeted disenfranchised communities. Furthermore, the book examines how these movements, communities, and their allies are pushing back with grassroots and digital media activism to establish their autonomy and self-determination.

Before addressing specific movements, though, one must recognize that policing is an integral part of the modern-day nation-state that assisted the rise of capitalism. As Michel Foucault notes, capitalism was "exposed to a number of risks that previously were much more containable."[7] He contends that "the problem" for the state is how "to fix workers to the production apparatus, to establish them in one place or move them to another where they are needed, to subject them to its rhythm, to impose on them the constancy or regularity it requires, in short, to form them as a labor force."[8] Surveillance and policing serve as twin engines in disciplining the nation-state's inhabitants to ensure "that manners, behavior, propriety, an industry are all conducted properly."[9] The forms of surveillance and policing, however, take on different configurations as they respond to resistances at various historical moments.

The 1960s represent a unique crisis for capitalism and the United States. Domestic resistance took on myriad forms of urban rebellions, student upheavals, civil rights demonstrations, draft resistance, feminism, and gay liberation, to name only a few. These resistances were further emboldened and bulwarked by being threaded together with global revolts that similarly challenged militarism, capitalism, and hierarchy in general.[10] Furthermore, 1967–73 signaled the most intense strike wave within the United States since World War II.[11]

Although the Nixon administration is often held responsible for initiating the rise of the carceral state as it cracked down on domestic protests, historian Elizabeth Hinton convincingly locates its origins within Johnson administration policies arising from the war on crime and the war on poverty.[12] Subsequent administrations of both political parties capitalized on this turn in policy. Additionally, this work suggests that the rise of the carceral state was not in response to crime, but instead to quell those who challenged the status quo while simultaneously warehousing those ignored or discarded by capitalism.[13]

Not coincidentally, Donald Trump dusted off and resuscitated Nixon's hackneyed phrase, claiming to be the "law and order" president when responding to the nationwide revolts against the murder of George Floyd and police violence that occurred throughout the summer of 2020. Out of his growing frustration with governors and mayors he deemed "soft" against protesters, Trump threatened to deploy the military to quell such revolts. Although Trump was routinely dismissed by most as overreacting, his actions were not an anomaly. Previous presidents invoked the Insurrection Act multiple times, most recently during the 1960s to summon the National Guard to quell various rebellions across the United States.[14] But overall, Trump's blunt response reminds us how easily military and policing functions blur and how politicians call with impunity upon the police and military to suppress resistance.

Ultimately, surveillance and policing work to pacify populations. This pacification is most successful when no explicit violence is required. Instead, people consent to the state's actions by being convinced that it "is committed to their security" and welfare.[15] This book explores how four different contemporary social movements reject the notion of the benevolent state. I investigate how digital media making within the United States has been integrated into other activist practices against state repression and in support of self-determination. The book investigates a series of disparate social movements not often discussed in relationship with one another: animal rights activists, counter-summit protesters, Latinx copwatchers, and Muslim American community organizers. Although most social movements resist state repression through collective organizing and digital technology (from Indigenous water defenders to the far right in its own deeply problematic ways), I chose these four movements since together they illustrate a more comprehensive overview of various forms of digital and grassroots resistance against state repression.

Distinct Periods of Federal, State, and Local Repression against Activists

Each chapter examines a social movement that addresses a different instance of explicit state repression. The first chapter addresses how from the late 1980s to the first decade of the 2000s, the FBI targeted animal rights and environmental activists as "domestic terrorists."[16] Although the chapter primarily focuses on the use of undercover video by animal rights activists and the attempt by states to pass legislation criminalizing undercover footage on factory farms (called "ag-gag" laws by its critics), it also signals how the criminalization of animal rights and environmental activism by the federal government during the 1990s provided the foundations for later legislation to build upon.

Chapter 2 charts how law enforcement utilized the Patriot Act (2001) against protesters at the 2008 Republican National Convention (RNC) hosted in the Twin Cities. Law enforcement preemptively arrested independent media makers and grassroots organizers before the convention took place. In particular, a group of college-aged people who ironically named themselves the RNC Welcoming Committee and designed a webpage that archived and promoted protest actions were labeled "domestic terrorists." The group promoted themselves as "the RNC 8" and mobilized their defense through jail support and videos that challenged their being labeled as "dangerous anarchists" by law enforcement and commercial news.

Chapter 3 investigates state repression by zeroing in on New York City during the rise of "broken windows" policing in the early 1990s, which asserted that punishing minor infractions like drinking from open containers, jaywalking, and hopping subway turnstiles would reduce more significant crime like homicides. No substantive evidence has ever been provided to validate that broken windows policing led to such results. Nonetheless, it has spread its influence across the country for the last thirty years by predominantly targeting working-class communities of color through such disastrous policies as stop-and-frisk, which was declared unconstitutional in 2013 but continues in altered forms to the present day. Additionally, such policing has concretely led to the harassment of various working-class communities of color to clear the way for gentrification of their neighborhoods and to enforce evictions by often negligent landlords.

The final chapter explores how the Countering Violent Extremism (CVE) federal program, developed under the George W. Bush administration and enacted under the Obama administration, targeted Muslim American communities as sites of "domestic terrorism." I focus on the Cedar Riverside neighborhood of Minneapolis, the location of the largest Somali refugee community in the United States and one of the pilot cities for CVE. The Islamophobia marshalled by the country's response to 9/11 set the stage for daily harassment of Muslim American communities across the United States from both federal and local law enforcement and fed into the negative representations of such communities across commercial media.

The book does not just examine the actions of the state—all four chapters address the work of resistance movements against the smooth functioning of state repression and the circuits of capitalism as well. In many instances, animal rights activists have successfully challenged ag-gag laws while asserting the inherent right of other-than-human animals to not be subjected to short lives of misery and suffering as their bodies are rendered into meat, eggs, or dairy. Both Latinx copwatchers and Muslim American community organizers challenge the shredding of the social safety net under neoliberalism by asserting their own forms of mutual aid and the need for political representation within local and national elections while simultaneously demanding funding and support from the state in other than carceral directions. In other words, the current movement to defund the police advocates the channeling of those funds into social services which are better performed by others. Counter-summit protesters along with all the other groups discussed here assert their rights to both protest and film the police. Although not all those belonging to such movements see their actions as challenging neoliberal practices, a significant majority of the nearly one hundred movement leaders I interviewed for this book do.

The Racialized "Other"

Surveillance and policing do not simply work to ensure the smooth functioning of capitalism and the state, but have also been deeply intertwined with race, specifically with Black communities within the United States. The formation of slave patrols within the United States represents some of the earliest instances of surveillance and policing used to regulate the mobility of Black bodies.[17] According to Kristian Williams, these patrols mark "a transitional model in the development of policing" from a rural society to a more industrialized configuration.[18] Elizabeth Hinton concludes that slave patrols represent "the foundational logic of American policing: mandating social order through the surveillance and social control of people of color."[19]

Surveillance and its technology build from and promote racist visual regimes. John Fiske calls surveillance a "machine of whiteness" that assumes whiteness as the norm and views anything diverging from it as suspect, if not outright criminal.[20] Within the United States, early forms of surveillance intersect with slavery. For example, the lantern laws of the eighteenth-century surveilled and punished slaves discovered outside after dark. "We can think of the lantern as a prosthesis," notes Simone Browne, "a technology that made it possible for the black body to be constantly illuminated from dusk to dawn, made knowable, locatable, and contained."[21]

More than a century later, modern-day surveillance technologies like closed-circuit television serve as an extension of this racist visual regime. They are deployed predominantly within working-class communities of color, upholding whiteness as the norm. The technology might appear to be neutral, but the way in which it is deployed constantly reinforces racial hierarchies. As Fiske notes, "Surveillance allows different races to be policed differently."[22] It causes someone like Trayvon Martin to be killed for simply purchasing candy at a local convenience store while allowing his killer, George Zimmerman, to remain free. It enables the imprisonment of Marissa Alexander, a Black woman, for firing a warning shot at her abusive husband although she should have been protected by Florida's controversial stand-your-ground law.[23] We will see this racist visual regime operating in how broken windows policing targets working-class communities of color in the chapter on copwatching and the way in which CVE policy is deployed predominantly against Muslim American communities in the final chapter.

We tell ourselves stories in order to live.

The racialized "Other" has bulwarked the United States from its beginning, whether it be through the enforced extraction of labor through slavery or the forced occupation of Native American lands and the genocide of Indigenous peoples. These racist practices have been legitimated and reinforced through commercial media, education, and social policies that dehumanize various races or marginalize their historic contributions. Such practices safeguard what Cedric Robinson refers to as racial capitalism. "Capitalism," according to Robinson, "required racism in order to police and rationalize the exploitation of workers."[24] Racism reinforces capitalism by inhibiting solidarity between workers. The erection of racial barriers enables continuing economic exploitation by framing it as secondary to racial grievances.

Racial capitalism extends into the present and sets parameters for the ways in which working-class communities of color are policed and surveilled. Policing, gentrification, political disenfranchisement, and the evisceration of needed state resources are tightly intertwined and course through the Latinx communities and Muslim American communities discussed in the later pages of this book. Critically needed state resources are withheld from such communities while an increased amount of state and federal money flows into their policing and surveillance. This creates a vicious loop. As such communities become targeted for surveillance by law enforcement, crimes appear to increase because the obsessive vision of the state classifies more and more inhabitants' actions as suspect.[25] Simply put, the criminals you're watching are going to be the ones you catch.

The racial Other is associated in more subtle ways as well with the social movements discussed here. Bestial descriptions are often leveled against anarchist communities by the state. The RNC 8 in chapter 2, for example, is predominantly composed of white, college-aged individuals. As it has done to many anarchist communities before them, the state accused them of hoarding bottles of piss to lob at police officers during protests as well as defecating in buckets in the squats they occupy. Repeatedly, anarchists are described as unhygienic and slovenly, attributes that have initially been cast against communities of color. However, the problem for the state in the RNC 8's case is that they are predominantly white, so traditionally racist bestial imagery is difficult to use against these groups when other class and racial stereotypes directly contradict them.

Similarly, other-than-human animals on factory farms are associated with the racial Other in two predominant ways. First, there is a long tradition of associating communities of color as indistinguishable from other-than-human animals. Bestial imagery has been weaponized to distance people of color from their own humanity as well as to denigrate other-than-human animals within speciesist logic as beneath humans. Many Black animal rights activists hold that Black liberation depends on fighting both racism and speciesism. Marjorie Spiegel argues in *The Dreaded Comparison: Human and Animal Slavery* that despite different socioeconomic and political factors that support the subjugation of other-than-human animals and Black people, "they are built around the same basic relationship—that between oppressor and oppressed."[26] Claire Jean Kim notes, "By linking their cause to black liberation, animal liberationists can not only achieve a clearer understanding of the structures of power they are struggling against and the world they hope to create but in turn can radicalize abolition by questioning its continuing human assumptions."[27] Syl Ko notes, "Animals' fates and their situation are very much entangled with our own."[28] Because anti-Blackness and speciesism are so deeply connected, she asserts, "reevaluating our ideas about nonhuman animals is an essential ingredient in the project of black liberation."[29]

All of this is not to claim that humans and other-than-human animals occupy the same space or share identical struggles. But one must recognize that their struggles are related and address how speciesism feeds into racism and vice versa. This brings me to the second way in which the racial Other haunts struggles over factory farming: undocumented people of color make up a significant amount of its workforce. They occupy some of the most dangerous and exploitative working conditions with high injury and turnover rates. Their labor is predicated upon other-than-human animals' suffering and murder. In the factory farm system, the exploitation of people of color and other-than-human animals reinforce each other.

Digital Media as a Central Location of Struggle

Digital media is central to assisting on-the-ground organizing but simultaneously provides a toehold for the state and capital to neutralize social movements. This should not be surprising since visibility and surveillance have always been twin components of the state. As Foucault notes, disciplinary power, which the state in part embodies, "is exercised through its invisibility; at the same time it imposes on those whom it subjects a principle of compulsory visibility."[30] Electronic and digital technologies have been key in extending such surveillance.

The concept of sousveillance updates Foucault's notion of surveillance. Earlier models of surveillance originate from an invisible center of control to observe others, like Jeremy Bentham's panopticon. Sousveillance recognizes how digital technology has allowed all of us to surveil each other. Sousveillance doesn't eliminate older modes of surveillance but operates simultaneously with them.[31] In our current age, surveillance and spectacle converge—whether it be the ways in which we monitor each other over social media, or view Ring TV to watch surveillance doorbell footage of thieves stealing packages, or log into the Citizen Virtual Patrol Network in Newark, NJ, where sixty-two cameras are placed in high traffic areas for viewers to spot and report alleged crimes taking place.[32]

It is worth noting here that when I refer to surveillance, the state, policing, or carceral logic I mean a much broader terrain of power relations that extend beyond any specific institution. Foucault stresses that the state is less a transcendent reality than a body of disciplinary practices and power relations that run laterally between people.[33] The state must be understood,

FIGURE 0.1: Amazon's Ring doorbell provides access to any video shot through its device on its Ring TV platform, thus normalizing surveillance as another form of entertainment.

according to Brendan McQuade, as "a condensation of social relations" that "develops in interaction with ongoing conflicts both within the institutional apparatus of the state and apart from it."[34]

Likewise, carceral logic constitutes a "broader phenomenon than imprisonment" including "all the social controls that characterize societies like ours."[35] It dictates how we are treated at home, in school, at our jobs, and so forth. Power, as Foucault stresses, is constituted by knowledge. He observes, "There is no power relation without the correlative constitution of a field of knowledge, nor any knowledge that does not presuppose and constitute at the same time power relations."[36] This is why the ceaseless gathering of information, whether through explicit police surveillance, data mining over social media, tracking our credit card purchases, and pinging our cell phones plays into the practices of a surveillance-based society that can marshal such information against us at any given moment.

As many social theorists note, the rise of neoliberalism and the carceral state create new disciplinary practices that attempt to fundamentally alter how we conceive of ourselves. Neoliberalism is not simply an economic place but also a disciplinary regime to extend market relations into every aspect of our lives so that we conceptualize ourselves as entrepreneurs of ourselves, shredding any sense of solidarity or collective will.[37] Franco Berardi asks, "Privatization, competition, individualism—aren't these the consequences of a catastrophic overturning of the investments of collective desire? The loss of solidarity deprived workers of any political force and created the conditions for the hyper-exploitation of precarious labor, reducing the labor force to a condition of immaterial slavery."[38] Maurizio Lazzarato identifies debt as one of the core ingredients of neoliberal disciplinary practices that constantly annexes our futures to reproduce capitalist power relations in paying off debts for goods and services we couldn't afford in the first place.[39] This individualized and self-interested outlook creates the conditions for people to argue that wearing masks is a personal choice during a pandemic rather than a collective good needed for public health.

We tell ourselves stories in order to live.

Didion twisted this phrase in a mostly pessimistic direction, suggesting that stories swath ourselves and our collective consciousness in sentimental narratives that protect us from confronting our worst selves and smooth away the rough edges of a violent national history. She was no believer in collective movements, but instead a child of the 1950s where existential angst and ennui became her defining pose.

Yet this expression, despite Didion's intent, has its utopian leanings as well.

The social movements discussed in these pages challenge the ways of neoliberalism by asserting their collective will and solidarity against neoliberalism's atomistic practices. These groups attempt to seize back their own labor and collective and individual subjectivities from the circuits of capital to assert their own autonomy and desires. The media provide a central terrain for this struggle to take place, particularly in the twenty-first century where digital technology has saturated many areas of the Global North and has made increasing inroads into peripheral territories. The stories told by various social movements across numerous digital platforms assert nothing less than a forced recognition of their importance and will to live. They take Didion's assertion in a most literal fashion.

Similarly, though, repressive powers also use these platforms to contain movements against the status quo. Jacques Rancière argues that the police do not simply occupy a physical space but extend metaphorically into our very language and perceptions. The police order the ways in which we understand and experience our world in predictable ways that benefit the state and capitalism. The police create consensus through the management of our insecurities and fear within the "symbolic constitution of the social."[40] For example, the middle class increasingly occupies precarious employment that undermines any sense of security and autonomy. Instead of mobilizing for better conditions of employment, employees are instead encouraged to readjust their expectations and lifestyles to accept and accommodate these changes.

Popular culture represents a central terrain to establish this consensus as well as challenge it. Stuart Hall long ago stressed that "popular culture is one of the sites where the struggle for and against a culture of the powerful is engaged; it is also the stake to be won or lost in that struggle. It is the arena of consent and resistance."[41] We will observe this struggle at work throughout all the chapters of this book. Not only will we witness the creation of grassroots media organizations and alternative forms of representation to challenge dominant representations of popular culture, we will also see how these groups navigate commercial media making—from outright opposition, most dramatically seen in chapter 4 as Somali American youth protest an HBO-produced television series that feeds into Islamophobic stereotypes, to working with commercial media, as one copwatch group does in chapter 3, by creating a reality television series with Black Entertainment Network around their activism.

Activist media provide an invaluable function in not only representing alternative points of view, but also in establishing new subjectivities altogether. As Stuart Hall notes, alternative media making creates "a form of representation which is able to constitute us as new kinds of subjects, and thereby enable us to discover places from which to speak."[42] Additionally, as I and other scholars argue elsewhere, activist media-making practices feed into collective organizing, forming affective bonds of solidarity, and reshaping individual and collective identities. In other words, activist media making is not simply about representation, but also about the new forms of production, distribution, exhibition, and reception practices that feed into grassroots organizing in profound directions.[43]

The chapters of this book proceed chronologically in order to identify the growing centrality of online activism as well as to trace different formations it has taken across time. It reveals the gradual progression of how "social" media became an important platform for much activism at the start of the twenty-first century.[44] Contrary to lazy journalistic accounts of online activism as nothing more than "slacktivism," where online users virtue-signal their solidarity with social movements while failing to participate offline, online and offline activism constantly commingle. Paolo Gerbaudo documents how online activism complements on-the-ground mobilizing by creating emotional conduits that can assist in generating collective action.[45] Similarly, Peter Snowdon conceptualizes online video "as one vector among many for the ongoing work of mutual self-mobilization that makes radical political change possible, or, at least, conceivable."[46] The following chapters will document different campaigns' varying degrees of success in that regard.

Furthermore, one must analyze the videos discussed in this book not only on their own merits, but also as an extension of a wider set of activist practices. They belong to a larger constellation of media that define each movement. The videos are both singular and part of a collective archive relating to animal rights, counter-summit protesting, copwatching, and Muslim American resistance. Many videos do not simply function at one particular time or within a singular campaign. They can be repeatedly remixed and recirculated for various activist campaigns as necessary. This means we must balance individual analysis of the videos together with the contexts and practices they emerge from. The aesthetic forms the videos inhabit along with the practices that make them possible all provide concrete instances of engagement that must be accounted for.

Using various media platforms as a means of activism is not unequivocally beneficial. Employing social media and online spaces for grassroots activism produces its own distinct challenges. Unlike in the past when media activists struggled to have their work screened at all, they now contend with a supersaturated visual field where one's video or campaign can easily be lost among the white noise of innumerable social media productions. Even if a video does gain online traction, the threat of decontextualization always accompanies it whereby the original intent of the video or message might be lost or intentionally derailed by a troll or political opponent. We will see this occur repeatedly in the chapters concerning copwatching and Muslim American youth activism.

Additional questions arise regarding how working through the connective logic of social media might compromise one's on-the-ground activism. As Thomas Poell and José van Dijck note, "Social media impute their logic onto activist communication practices."[47] Online platforms often prioritize an individual, personalized voice over that of collective action. Such platforms produce a space for an aggregate of individuals to come together rather than a collective space.[48] In other words, users inhabit online space that either dampers or outright forecloses a more collective sense of identity that flows beyond individual concerns. What forms of solidarity and trust can arise out of such venues remains in question—particularly given law enforcement's ceaseless surveillance of online platforms and communities.[49]

Gaming algorithms, the programming social media sites use to promote certain content over others, pose additional obstacles to gaining visibility for one's cause on platforms that prioritize short-term events rather than the long-term struggles that most social movements require. We will examine how the various social movements discussed within these pages wrestle with these issues. Nevertheless, at least with the cases addressed within these pages, digital media activism alone does not make or break a well-organized grassroots campaign although it can hinder or amplify one's mobilization. The online world is not the entire story but only one fragment from a larger organizing strategy that encompasses both physical and virtual spaces.

Longer Histories and Wider Contexts Shaping Twenty-First Century (Media) Activism

None of the social movements discussed in this book emerged suddenly without precedent. They connect to much longer histories of community organizing and media activism. A longer historical context is essential to fully account for the formations of present-day media activism and social movements.

Although the first chapter predominantly focuses on "ag-gag" laws used against undercover animal rights activists in the twenty-first century, undercover videomaking stretches back to the 1980s during antivivisection campaigns against the lab testing of other-than-human animals. And, as indicated earlier, the rise of such laws occurred because environmental and animal rights activism had been targeted by federal legislation decades earlier.

The copwatching in chapter 3 being done by Latinx groups in NYC has origins that stretch back to the 1970s with the Young Lords and other anticolonial liberation struggles in Latin America and the Caribbean. The counter-summit protesting addressed in chapter 2 arises from the alterglobalization movement gaining traction throughout the 1990s.

Interestingly, chapters 2 and 4 complement each other as they both take place in Minneapolis during different times and focus on different groups. Still, historical threads interweave the two together. Although chapter 4 mainly addresses Muslim American youth resistance against CVE in Minneapolis and increasing Islamophobic hostility descending upon Muslim communities after the election of Trump, their resistance against repression and police brutality connects to chapter 2, which documents similar instances of brutality against counter-summit protesters. Both the RNC 8 and Muslim American communities have been designated as "domestic terrorists," although the sustained way in which Muslim American communities have had to endure the assault of being a suspect community is qualitatively different than that of a group of anarchists being labeled "terrorists" for a select amount of time. Such connections highlight the sustained police violence against marginal communities throughout both time periods and gestures toward the systemic problems of policing that haunt the Twin Cities. Journalist Luke Mogelson notes how a 2015 ACLU investigation found that "Black people in Minneapolis were nine times more likely than whites to be arrested for low-level offenses"[50] In 2007, five high-ranking Black police officers sued their employer for institutional racism.[51]

In a related fashion, chapter 4 addresses the emergence of the grassroots media organization Unicorn Riot in Minneapolis that has in part assisted in providing positive coverage of Muslim American youth activism. Although officially founded in 2015, the organization has roots that extend back to the 2008 RNC. Many of its members gained experience either by covering the protests for Twin Cities Indymedia or being in the streets witnessing firsthand the violence directed against independent media makers.

The relevancy of these two chapters unexpectedly extends into the present as protests erupted in Minneapolis and elsewhere in May 2020 over the murder of George Floyd. Unprecedented numbers of people across the racial spectrum mobilized against police violence. Although the effect of these mobilizations is far from clear, they nonetheless indicate the increasing distrust and unharnessed potential for collective organizing against the police. While there was a considerable amount of protest coverage, it largely ignored the longer histories of police brutality that have plagued Minneapolis, which both chapters 2 and 4 cover. The horrific 2016 live-streaming of Philando Castile's murder went unmentioned in most accounts. Moreover, completely absent from coverage was the 2015 killing of Jamar Clark that ignited two weeks of protests in the neighborhood surrounding the Fourth Precinct where Clark's murderer was stationed. Although the attention and mobilizing around George Floyd's death marks a unique instance of mass protest within US history, it belongs to a longer lineage of police brutality and mobilizing against it located in the Twin Cities.

We tell ourselves stories in order to live.

The value of providing histories of media activism and grassroots organizing in general is that they acknowledge specific and important historical moments and connections that can assist us in better situating and understanding future mobilizations both within and across social movements. By understanding the disparate struggles discussed in this book in relation to one another, we chart a wider mapping of their interconnections, their lineages, and the ways in which digital media activism relates to and assists on-the-ground organizing. We can observe both the limitations and potentials of these organizers while exploring the histories of the movements and struggles to which they are indebted. If this book encourages more mutual awareness across these struggles and potentially fosters some dialogue among them, it will be worth the effort.

There are concrete reasons social movements might remain unaware of one another. Lack of resources, harassment by law enforcement and others, and the pressing needs of immediate campaigns all limit social movements' full consideration of how their goals, tactics, and strategies might be related to other groups and organizations. Perhaps this book can provide a momentary respite to reflect on the ways in which these struggles are connected; how digital media activism can both assist and limit on-the-ground organizing; and, how the state and capitalism attempt to neutralize such movements not solely through brute force and reactionary legislation, but also by circulating their beliefs throughout commercial media, making media activism necessary. The groups discussed here represent various resistance movements against contemporary neoliberalism and the hierarchical, racist, speciesist, and classist disciplinary practices that allow for the state and capitalism to take their current forms. This book recognizes the vexed yet vital terrain that on-the-ground organizing and media activism occupies, and how the struggles documented here might lead to unprecedented future moments where the self-determination of all people and species become fully enshrined.

We tell ourselves stories in order to live.

CHAPTER 1

Seeing Past the Walls of Slaughterhouses

Animal Rights, Undercover Video, and Struggles over Visibility

A shaky image of a long red barn dominates the right side of the frame. To the left, smoke billows from some unseen opening, obscured by idling eighteen-wheelers. The snow-encrusted foothills of the Rockies loom behind the scene, and weathered prairie grass stretches out to the foreground. A yellow bulldozer slowly drifts across the frame.

Off-frame, a woman calmly notes that there is a cow at the front of the bulldozer, although we can't identify it because the camera is too distant.

A different off-frame female voice exclaims, "Oh my god! He's alive."

FIGURE 1.1: Amy Meyer became the first person charged with violating an ag-gag law as she filmed a downed cow being pushed by a bulldozer at a Utah factory farm. Authorities falsely claimed it was illegal for her to film. In 2017, Utah's ag-gag law was ruled unconstitutional.

FIGURE 1.2: The owner confronts Amy Meyer and casually lobs a series of false accusations that she trespassed on private property and had no right to film his farm. The awkward framing of the video is a result of Meyer attempting to film and reply to the owner simultaneously.

The scene becomes an impromptu call-and-response between the two women. One provides needed exposition in a calm voice for what the image itself cannot capture.

"He's probably a downed cow."

"The worker appears to be standing over where we saw the bulldozer dump the cow who is still alive."

Interspersed between these observations are the other woman's reactions her voice trembling, "Oh my god."

"Yes, he's alive!" The women's voices shift between reason and emotion as they confront animal cruelty.

The sequence abruptly cuts to a man in a red trucker's hat leaning from the driver's side of his truck to the open passenger window, intercepting the woman with the camera. The frame stumbles around, often losing focus on the man's face as the woman attempts to film him and simultaneously push back against his assertion that she trespassed on his property. He asserts a series of falsehoods while recording her in response on his cell phone: "You guys were on that property. If you read the rights here and the laws of Utah, you can't film an agricultural property without my consent."

The woman refutes his claim: "I am on a public easement," and says that the Utah law only applies if she were filming *on* his property.

He largely ignores her answers and asserts, "I'm going to hang up and call the cops."

FIGURE 1.3: Literally shooting from the hip, Amy Meyer slyly captures a sheriff badgering her with questions to tangle her up in self-incrimination. She wisely stops answering them.

As he drives off, she focuses on the license plate and reads it to the camera for documentation.

Another abrupt cut: the camera pivots to the side road she is standing on as two burly male sheriffs approach her. This final sequence comprises the video's remaining six-and-a-half minutes and could serve as a training video in how to avoid answering the roundabout badgering questions cops often employ to make people incriminate themselves:

"What's going on today?"

"Taking pictures?"

"Did you have a friend with you?"

The woman tentatively and curtly answers the first two questions, but then reverses course, asking the cop if she is standing on a public easement before finally stating repeatedly in various forms: "I don't want to answer any questions."

Despite her response, however, the cop still peppers her with questions:

"Was your friend trespassing on the property?"

"Just wondering how you got here."

"Where do you live?"

The woman responds, "I don't understand why I have to answer these questions if I am not suspected of a crime." She shoots from a low angle with the cop's face towering before the frame in silhouette with the sun bleeding through the clouds blocking it. Again, the frame shakily captures his image as she struggles simultaneously to document and resist his line of questioning. At one moment, he asks her, "Would you stop pointing that at me?" She ignores his request and continues filming. Near the end of the sequence, the sheriff tells her that she is free to leave but that he is going to "screen criminal charges of trespass on you since one of our witnesses said they saw you." She asks what that means. He explains that the state prosecutor will review the charges and determine if there is enough evidence to move forward on them. The video suddenly cuts out.

This video shot by Amy Meyer in 2013 documents the first instance of someone being charged using an "ag-gag" law, an informal term that lumps together a series of state laws that have criminalized various ways to document the conditions of factory farms and their impacts on the animals within them. When I spoke with Meyer, she told me that she left the encounter uncertain of where things stood. Then, a few weeks later, she recalls: "I got two letters from random attorneys saying they'll represent me. And I was like, what is this about? I didn't even know I was being charged with anything. But then I did get a letter saying I was being charged with 'agricultural operation interference.'"[1]

This video distills many of the central themes that guide this chapter. First, for the past forty years, video has served as a central medium within the animal rights movement in exposing animal cruelty. Yet despite the indexical nature of video, that is, its ability to provide the illusion of recording reality itself, the visual alone is not enough. Meyer's video exemplifies this. Without the two women's commentary, it would never be clear from the images alone that a bulldozer is pushing a downed cow. Instead, the audio track nudges us in that direction both through what they are saying along with the one woman's emotional response to it. More often than not, much animal rights footage is grainy, badly lit, or shaky. The context is not clear and the actions within the frame are not so easily interpreted. These videos rely heavily on voice-over and/or text to assist in deciphering the visual. As we will repeatedly witness throughout this chapter, a war between the state, the animal agriculture industry, and animal rights activists is fought over the meaning of images to determine how to interpret the living conditions and treatment of animals in a variety of scenarios.

Second, Meyer's video illustrates the collusion between law enforcement and the agricultural industry. Not surprisingly, all of these "ag-gag" laws have been implemented in states with heavy investment in animal agriculture. Although her video cuts abruptly between footage of the farm's owner and the sheriff, both stick to what is essentially the same script: she is trespassing, and she has no right to videotape them or the agricultural facility.[2] Will Potter, a journalist who covers animal rights and environmental activism, is not surprised at this alignment since he believes animal rights activists are "presented as this ideological threat to core concepts that underpin what some people think it means to be an American—defense of capitalism, a religiously aligned state, defense of industry, the belief that humans are exceptional."[3]

Third, the video hints at the troubled relationship between animal rights activists and the state. Tactics implemented by activists are countered by the state with new laws designed to criminalize their actions, which then lead animal rights activists to innovate new tactics that skirt these state laws until the state finally implements newer laws that criminalize these innovations. In more concrete terms, undercover video became a primary tactic for animal rights activists from the 1980s onward, causing the state and federal governments to pass a series of laws criminalizing their actions. This led to the gradual taming of many animal rights organizations to predominantly focus on animal welfare within the United States. In other words, rather than explicitly demanding the abolition of the agricultural industry altogether, they settled on creating better living conditions for other-than-human animals in such facilities. Nevertheless, a new group formed in 2013 called Direct Action Everywhere (DxE) that deployed more aggressive tactics like "open rescue" where activists enter farms in public view and remove animals that they consider are being mistreated. This has now caused states to level a series of felony accusations against those activists to suppress this tactic.

More importantly, this chapter raises bigger questions regarding the politics of visibility that guides much of animal rights activism, as it relates to much of the media activism documented throughout this book. Beatles member Paul McCartney once remarked: "If slaughterhouses had glass walls, everyone would be vegetarian." Animal rights activists have run with this idea by employing undercover video in locations where animals suffer: circuses, laboratories, puppy mills, and, most prevalently during the past twenty years, factory farms. It is not uncommon to hear animal rights activists praise the power of the image in advancing their cause. Scott David, a prior undercover investigator, told me: "I don't really think that we can convince people of much if we didn't have the video evidence that our investigators gathered."[4] Taylor Radig, another undercover investigator, had once believed, "If more people could see what I've seen, so many more people would, you know, make changes to their lifestyle and really put a stop to what's happening to animals."[5] Mary Beth Sweetland, a longtime animal rights activist and director of investigations for the Humane Society of the United States, stated in a 2012 interview: "I'd say that if they consider themselves a humane and compassionate person, they must force themselves to look, not just satisfy themselves with self-assurance that they know what it's like. They don't know what it's like, until they see it with their own eyes."[6]

Overwhelmingly, the image is assumed to most adequately relay the suffering of animals most directly to uninformed viewers. Secondarily, most animal rights activists assume that viewers' well-being is not a priority. Viewers need to endure other-than-human animal suffering and ignore their own discomfort in confronting these imagery and sounds. In addition, the animal rights movement, more than any other, believes that this singular focus on other-than-human animal suffering should take precedence in much of its video activism. Although videos might also emphasize other-than-human animals' autonomy after they are freed from oppressive conditions, one would be hard pressed to find a video where this suffering is not present at all. One cannot imagine any other social movement employing a video strategy where suffering takes such a foundational position. As a result, this chapter explores what is gained in such an approach as well as what it limits.

Often lost within discussions of animal rights video activism is that visibility itself belongs to wider disciplinary practices where speciesism—the belief that privileges humans over other-than-human animals—takes precedent by relegating the latter into an object for our consumption as food, clothing, entertainment, companionship, or the like. As Foucault stresses, these disciplinary practices should not be understood as limited to a specific institution. Instead, they represent a type of power that comprises "a whole set of instruments, techniques, procedures, levels of application, targets" that run throughout society.[7]

In regard to animal rights video activism, one might pause to consider if the videos remain too singularly focused on the slaughterhouse, the laboratory, or the puppy mill as the main sites of animal oppression. What do they enable viewers to see? But, also, what do they obscure in limiting our views to particular institutions while ignoring the more complex ways in which speciesism defines our daily lives and our language. As Timothy Pachirat, a political scientist who went undercover at a slaughterhouse, notes, there is a much more complex relationship between "sight and sequestration. . . .

And even when intended as a tactic of social and political transformation, the act of making the hidden visible may be equally likely to generate other, more effective ways of confining it."[8]

This chapter offers a critical genealogy of the role that video has played in animal rights campaigns over the last forty years in order to assess where it has advanced the movement and where it has not. It will investigate the complex workings between animal rights activists' use of video and animal agriculture's fixation on stopping this form of exposure with the support of the state apparatus. Tellingly, both sides see video as a central terrain for the fight; this makes sense to a certain extent, as visual culture and video in particular pervades more and more of our lives as smart phones and computers become more ubiquitous and social media websites facilitate the rapid circulation of videos.

As filmmaker Peter Snowdon observes, video activism no longer serves as an afterthought or a mere recording of much political activism, but instead represents an integral part of it.[9] During the planning stages of most actions, the event's translatability over video and its redistribution over social media and other news outlets constitute a core consideration. Whatever the drawbacks that might accompany animal rights activists' reliance upon video, one must acknowledge how they were at the vanguard of realizing video's potential in their activism, as this chapter will document. The question, however, remains: What balance should be struck between realizing the centrality of digital media technology in engaging in animal rights' activism and considering in what circumstances could this tactic impede other strategic actions?

Early Histories: 1980s and 1990s, Animal Liberation Front and PETA

The Animal Liberation Front's (ALF) roots stretch back to the Hunt Saboteur Association's founding in 1963 in England.[10] Some of its members split in 1972 to form the Band of Mercy. Two of its members, Ronnie Lee and Cliff Goodman, were arrested in 1974 for a raid on the Oxford Laboratory Animal Colonies in Bicester. After their release, Goodman became a police informer while Lee founded the Animal Liberation Front in 1976.[11]

The origins of ALF in the United States are a bit murkier. Some claim that a 1977 release of two dolphins from a research facility in Hawaii marks the first US ALF action. Others suggest that the 1979 raid that took place at New York University's Medical Center where activists disguised themselves as lab workers to smuggle out a cat, two dogs, and two guinea pigs was the first US-based ALF action. Ingrid Newkirk provides the most well-known US ALF origin story in her book *Free the Animals* where an ex-cop called "Valerie" led a 1982 Christmas Eve raid on a Howard University laboratory to release twenty-four cats that were being experimented upon.[12]

During the 1980s, ALF chapters within the US focused their energy primarily on vivisection occurring in laboratories. Either by shooting their own footage or stealing tapes recorded by lab workers, ALF would give the footage to People for the Ethical Treatment of Animals (PETA), whose personnel would then edit the footage into half-hour tapes which they would distribute during news conferences. By far the most famous animal rights tapes during the 1980s were ALF-PETA collaborations with *Unnecessary Fuss* (1984), *Britches* (1985), and *Breaking Barriers* (1986), which ignited a string of bad publicity for various primate labs across the United States.

Although all three videos garnered wide media attention, I will focus on the first, *Unnecessary Fuss*. It set the template for ALF-PETA collaborations, had a wide impact and longevity, and represents one of the most brutal of all animal rights undercover tapes ever produced. ALF members gained assistance from someone working at the Head Trauma Clinic at the University of Pennsylvania. Primates had their heads cemented in a metal box attached to a hydraulic pump that would then slam their heads against the box's interior walls. ALF snuck inside the lab and pilfered seventy hours of videotape shot by lab assistants documenting these experiments.[13]

Activists waded through all seventy hours of this brutal footage, and Alex Pacheco, one of the cofounders of PETA, assembled a twenty-four-minute documentary, called *Unnecessary Fuss*.[14] The brutal aesthetic of the video makes it one of the most difficult to watch of animal rights tapes and reflects the brutality that we witness occurring in the laboratory. Most animal rights tapes employ some kind of musical soundtrack that underlies the footage of animals suffering to provide at least some type of buffer between viewers and the images of animals in pain and their screams. *Unnecessary Fuss* provides none. Furthermore, the video uses the lab technicians' long takes of their experiments to situate the viewer uncomfortably within the lengthy procedures employed against the primates and the atmosphere of cruel indifference that surrounds them.

We learn that the video's title comes from a remark made by Thomas Gennarelli, one of the lead scientists of the lab. The opening prologue quotes him saying during an interview, "I am not willing to go on the record to discuss the laboratory studies…because it has potential to stir up all sorts of unnecessary fuss among those who are sensitive to those kinds of things." This tactic of appropriating Gennarelli's own words against him announces the overall tactic of the video, which redeploys the lab's own recordings against itself.

As Jaimie Baron notes, however, with utilizing the footage shot by perpetrators there is always a danger of unintentionally spreading their message. Instead, one must always contextualize and counterpoint such footage in order to distance viewers from the source's original purpose.[15] She notes that this is often achieved through narration, which is the strategy used in *Unnecessary Fuss*. Ingrid Newkirk narrates the documentary in an affectless tone. She contextualizes the material for viewers in a cold, clinical way. This tone serves two functions: first, it counters the notion that animal rights activists are victims of their emotions, unable to think critically, they are "good-hearted but soft-headed." In fact, Newkirk's voice eviscerates this notion as it states precisely and dispassionately what we are watching and how it connects to larger issues; and second, her tone stresses the clinical brutality we witness as the primates have their heads throttled in a mechanical apparatus, as lab workers employ a hammer and chisel to release the primates' heads from the contraption, and as we watch dazed primates suffer the aftereffects of brutal head trauma.

For example, in one scene we watch a lab worker extend and retract a dazed baboon's arm. All we see of the worker are his hands and lower torso. The shot centers around the baboon whose head shakes and is visibly disoriented while having her reflexes tested. Newkirk notes over this imagery: "This federally funded head injury clinic receives approximately one million tax dollars every year and is now in its thirteenth year. This baboon has suffered the infliction of severe brain damage, and she may receive as many as five more head injuries in the next nine months before she is killed. In the next sequences, you will see how she is injured in a hydraulic type of device called the Pen 2." Newkirk ingenuously ties the violence we witness on screen to federally funded taxpayer dollars, extending culpability to us since we fund it. Moreover, her narration predicts future violence against the baboon. Newkirk's voice-over serves multiple functions. It suggests that this is not an isolated instance or the work of an outlier but instead has taxpayer funded federal support. It also shifts temporal location in order to emphasize the repeated violence that this baboon has suffered and will suffer.

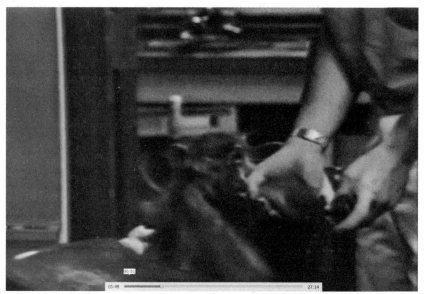

FIGURE 1.4: Released in 1984, *Unnecessary Fuss* gained significant traction by documenting the brutal treatment of baboons in a laboratory at the University of Pennsylvania.

Newkirk's affectless tone also emphasizes "the extractive gaze" of the video. Jaimie Baron defines this gaze as one that "seeks to transform human beings into information regardless of the consequences for the human beings themselves. This gaze evidences no sympathy or empathy."[16] Although Baron is referring to humans, this description nonetheless accurately describes the gaze that defines the entirety of *Unnecessary Fuss* and the way in which the lab workers treat the baboons.

As mentioned earlier, the rough aesthetic of the video mimics the brutality of the lab. Hard cuts define the video. There are no wipes, dissolves, or fade outs that ease the transitions between scenes of cruelty. Instead, we are jarred by the movement between them and are relentlessly shocked by each new manifestation of cruelty within the lab. For example, the image of the traumatized baboon in the aforementioned scene cuts to another baboon strapped by wrists and ankles to a lab table, its head completely encased in a metal apparatus as it struggles to free itself.

Likewise, the toggling of the video's audio between the diegetic sounds of the lab and Newkirk's voice-over is abrupt. An uncomfortable silence punctuates each moment when the lab noises drop out and voice-over suddenly intrudes and vice versa. Newkirk's voice stands alone, without context, removed from the sounds of the lab. Her every word stresses the

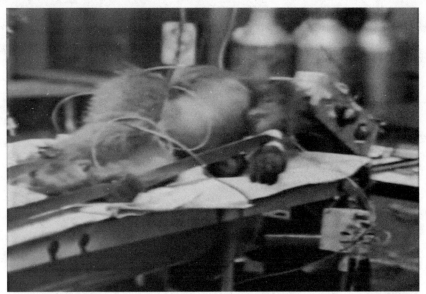

FIGURE 1.5: *Unnecessary Fuss* repurposes the footage taken by lab technicians to expose the brutality that the lab unleashed upon primates. Here we see a metal box placed around a baboon's head that is then throttled within it to cause a head injury.

pervasive and pointless cruelty of the lab. On the other hand, the ambient sounds of the lab and the casual speech of the lab workers we hear off camera emphasize the cavalier normalization of the abuse that permeates this workplace.

The video also employs what Jaimie Baron refers to as "the accusatory gaze," where footage is appropriated against itself to draw a critical gaze to the subjects within it who were not intended as the center of attention.[17] In the case of *Unnecessary Fuss*, this means drawing a critical gaze to the lab workers rather than the primates who are supposed to be the main subject of the footage. One section of the video quotes another lead investigator of the lab from a newspaper interview, "Researchers would never laugh at the apes." White words appear on a black background where the source and date of the quote are cited: *Philadelphia Daily News*, March 31, 1984.

The footage suddenly cuts to a close-up of a dazed baboon sitting on a lab table. A heavy incision runs along the center of his scalp. A tube emerges from the side of his body. The camera lingers on the baboon until zooming back to reveal a young woman holding him by his shoulders. Off-camera we hear a male coworker joke, "Here, kitty, kitty, kitty, look at the camera" as he attempts to draw the baboon to look towards the camera. In the meantime, the woman mugs and smiles before the camera. The

FIGURE 1.6: The lab technicians' casual attitude toward their animal cruelty is captured in this scene where a female worker teases a dazed baboon before the camera in *Unnecessary Fuss.*

baboon twitches at times and then rests his head back, gazing up to the female lab tech.

Interestingly, an off-frame male lab tech jokingly warns, "You better hope the antivivisection people don't get ahold of this film." The comment provides for a disturbingly self-reflexive moment that suggests some of the techs are aware of the cruelty they are inflicting and use jokes to distance themselves from fully acknowledging this reality. Another male voice comments on the baboon "He has the punk look," which causes the female lab worker to chuckle.

The video carries on for another painful thirty seconds. The entire sequence only lasts for a minute and fifty seconds, but the cold gaze of the camera and the cruel playfulness of the techs transform it into an excruciating moment in which we witness their objectification of and indifference to the primates. The casual joking and laughing that runs throughout it hammers home the idea that these are everyday people like ourselves, who are engaging in such cruel and relentless violence with only the alibi of "science" to shield them from the significance of their actions. Nevertheless, the raw footage relays a deeply disturbing environment where the torture of these primates has been normalized.

PETA cofounder Alex Pacheco held a news conference at the Hilton Hotel in Philadelphia on October 2, 1984, and he released the footage and provided an overview of the lab atrocities.[18] Although the footage shocked many, it also led to a futile hunt for the ALF raiders of the lab. PETA also submitted the tapes to the US Department of Agriculture, which launched an investigation into the lab and found several violations.[19] Despite the USDA findings, the National Institute of Health refused to cut the lab's funding, which led to a sit-in by activists in its main building. Finally, the video made its way to Margaret Heckler, secretary of Health and Human Services, who was so disturbed by the footage that she called on the NIH director, James Wyngaarden, to cease all funding, which he finally did.[20] The lab was then closed and its chief veterinarian was fired.[21] Despite the NIH's actions, Gennarelli, one of the scientists in charge of the lab, later received funding from them to experiment on rats and miniature pigs.[22]

The footage within the video continues to be repurposed in other animal rights campaigns. For example, when General Motors remained the only auto manufacturer using animals for its crash tests, *Unnecessary Fuss* was used in actions to disrupt auto exhibits and confront dealerships.[23] More recently in 2015, the USDA cited the University of Pennsylvania for more incidents of animal cruelty with traumatic brain injuries on pigs and a severe burn on a primate after surgery.[24] *Unnecessary Fuss* was used to document the long history of abusive practices that Penn researchers have engaged in.[25]

Rather than understanding *Unnecessary Fuss* or any animal rights video as freestanding entities, one should instead conceptualize them as a part of a larger constellation of videos comprising an ever-growing archive made to be constantly repurposed as footage from one video gets remixed into other videos. Perhaps the most famous instance of this is found in the 2015 film *Earthlings* (Shaun Monson), which relentlessly stitches together the most famous undercover animal rights videos into a feature-length film. These videos do not simply document past actions but are also often incorporated into newer ones. They are a part of a wider terrain of actions. They should be less conceptualized only as videos but instead as "one vector among many" in which animal rights campaigns operate.[26] These videos do not simply represent actions taking place but are also part of them and always hold the potential to inform and become a part of future actions. As a result, it is difficult to assess the impact of any one of these videos since they are often not working in isolation from one another but are a part of a larger campaign of tactics at the time of their release and might be harnessed later for future campaigns.

Breaking Free Video Magazine and the 1999 Animal Rights Conference

The camcorder revolution accompanied the growth of animal rights activism during the 1980s and 1990s. With the arrival of more affordable, consumer friendly equipment like 8 mm and SVHS camcorders during the 1980s, video activism proliferated. It became so prevalent by the mid-1990s that Thomas Harding, cofounder of Britain's first video magazine, *Undercurrents*, published *The Video Activist Handbook* in 1997 as a guide for activists.

Closer to home, a surge of media activism occurred in the Pacific Northwest where many animal rights and environmental activists were located. Eugene, Oregon, served as a hotbed of this media activism by the mid- to late-1990s. The *EarthFirst!* journal moved there in 1992. A cable access show called *Cascadia Alive!* aired from 1996 to 2005, covering many of the environmental actions occurring in North America. *Green Anarchy*, an anarcho-primitivist magazine, started publishing in Eugene in 2002, and the Cascadia Media Collective produced a *Video Guerrilla Primer* during the same year.[27]

Animal rights activism was also falling under the increasing scrutiny of the federal government. According to Will Potter, "After a 1987 arson at the University of California at Davis, the FBI labeled an animal rights crime 'domestic terrorism' for the first time."[28] In 1992, the US Congress passed the Animal Enterprise Protection Act (AEPA). It established the crime of animal enterprise terrorism for anyone who "intentionally causes physical disruption to the functioning of an animal enterprise by intentionally stealing, damaging, or causing the loss of property" with economic damage exceeding $10,000.[29] Although the act proved largely ineffectual in halting animal rights activism or even prosecuting it, it nonetheless signaled how the federal government increasingly targeted animal rights activism as deserving more severe punishment than other forms of activism.

During this time, the video magazine format became increasingly popular, eventually warranting a special section in *The Video Activist Handbook*. The format provided a series of advantages. It allowed media makers to establish a database of subscribers to distribute their work to. "More importantly," according to Thomas Harding, it "can be controlled entirely by the people who manage it. Unlike community television, cable or mainstream television, editorial control rests with the video activists. This is an exciting opportunity for people frustrated with the limitations imposed by other distribution outlets."[30]

Yet an accompanying problem with the video magazine was the amount of labor needed to create it. Harding warns in *The Video Activist Handbook*, "Now you have to do all the legwork—packaging tapes, maintaining a database, advertising, winning publicity, liaising with suppliers, and so on. Long hours are a norm. Pace yourself."[31] These requirements made such a format difficult to sustain since it was easy to burn out because collecting content was only part of the complicated and labor-intensive task of creating each issue.

Breaking Free Video Magazine marks the first animal rights video magazine to appear in the United States. There were only two issues: one in 1998 and another in 1999. Josh Harper and Joshua Kielas, longtime friends who lived in Eugene, Oregon, cocreated it. Early skateboarding video magazines like *411 Video Magazine*, founded in 1993, had inspired Harper. He explains, "This video magazine could show all the latest stuff that was happening because it was new content every couple of months."[32] Through crash editing on two VCRs, Harper created his own skateboarding video magazine in the mid-1990s with the unfortunate name of *Coolin'*. He was enamored with the affective power relayed by such video magazines: "What you're trying to evoke is you just want everyone to feel that stoked you feel. You want that adrenaline to make its way to people's living rooms." As Harper became increasingly involved with animal rights activism, he started wondering how the format and the feelings evoked by skateboarding video magazines could be translated into more political directions. He reflects, "I was like maybe this is the way I can get people to empathize with nonhumans, with ecosystems."

But Harper lacked the money and equipment to engage in such an enterprise. While he contemplated creating an animal rights video magazine, Kielas received an injury payment from a boating accident. Kielas is a musician who had always been interested in the newest forms of media technology. Although he shared veganism with Harper, Kielas objected to Harper's more radical ideas and forms of direct action. Regardless, Harper's concept of an animal rights video magazine appealed to Kielas, who subsequently bought all the equipment for transforming this idea into a reality. He purchased a Seagate Barracuda nine gigabyte hard drive, which at the time seemed to hold immense memory capability; a micro-JPG capture card; a high 8 camcorder; Adobe Premiere; an SVHS deck; and a few other items.

Harper had an outgoing personality and used his many connections with animal rights and environmental activists to obtain footage for the first two issues. Each issue would be built up article by article. Kielas recalls,

"We'd get some footage and we'd start working on something. And then, you know, as time went on, a little more footage would come in and we'd do another…that's when we decided to call it a video magazine."[33]

It was a labor-intensive endeavor, not helped by equipment that was barely capable of tackling the demands of the project. "I think we had every technical problem," notes Kielas. Seemingly simple tasks like rendering a title inserted in one of its sections would take all day. Harper laughs as he remembers, "the little Pentium 3 processor just couldn't handle mastering the material." When any serious technical problems arose, they would contact local video activist guru Tim Lewis to assist in troubleshooting the issue. They duplicated tapes by sending the master to a warehouse somewhere in Florida, making around two hundred copies, which was all they could afford.[34]

The first issue opened with a snarky disclaimer, embodying an irreverent punk rock ethos that Harper identified with: "We don't want to encourage, condone, advise, cheer, advocate, embolden, favor, incite, inspire, foster, promote or otherwise stimulate people to commit criminal or illegal acts such as locking down to doors, blockading roads, destroying machinery, painting on buildings, taking over offices, freeing animals, dismantling bulldozers, hanging banners from roofs, bridges, trees, or any other freestanding object or any other such action no matter how much positive change such an action may bring about." This disclaimer reveals the tape as more of a primer in direct action than about educating viewers on animal rights.

A surprisingly small amount of animal rights undercover footage made its way into the first issue. *Breaking Free Video Magazine* provides one of the rare instances where mobilization takes precedence over animal suffering. Its intended audience seems to be those already familiar with animal rights issues. Instead, the video magazine draws awareness to the various groups and actions viewers can get involved with to further their engagement. The magazine chronicles a series of actions occurring across the United States.

The opening montage of the first issue relays this call to action. Fast-paced, keyboard-heavy techno music, reflective of the alternative scene of the 1990s, plays over a series of clips from amateur activist footage: cops applying pepper spray directly to protesters' eyes, ALF members dressed in white lab coats and black balaclavas breaking into a lab, a forest defender precariously perched on the top of a wooden tripod, protesters marching down a street, heavily armed police with gas masks, a young white male resisting arrest trying to pull his arms free from two cops gripping either

FIGURE 1.7: *Breaking Free* (1998) is one of the first animal rights video magazines. It culled together activist footage from the United States, Canada, and Europe to document various resistance movements against animal and environmental exploitation.

side. Audio sampling of a male authority figure warning, "You will be gassed," repeats over the soundtrack. The style is very reminiscent of the Emergency Broadcast Network, a multimedia performance group from the early 1990s, where quick edits, heavy sampling, and an obnoxious synthetic soundtrack combine to overload viewers with information at a frenetic pace.

Following this, Josh Harper in voice-over explains different forms of direct action. When he mentions "symbolic" direct action, we see amateur footage of a banner drop over a building's facade with the words: "Tears Are Not Enough. Act in Defense of Animals." When he mentions "disruptive" direct action, we see forest protesters clashing with the police and an individual wearing a black balaclava overturning a table. Finally, when he mentions, "the most direct [forms of direct action]," we see ALF footage of activists breaking into a lab and a burned-out office, alluding to ALF's and ELF's support of arson against environmental polluters and animal exploiters.

Most sections of the video magazine chronicle different actions occurring across the United States with contact information often following at the

FIGURE 1.8: *Breaking Free* advocated for widespread direct action including marches, banner drops, and, ultimately, arson, which would eventually lead the FBI to identify environmental and animal rights activists as the most pressing forms of "domestic terrorism" during the 1990s and early 2000s.

end of each segment. To break up the monotony of protest footage, Kielas and Harper created a pseudocommercial for ALF showing a man wearing a red balaclava waking up, washing his hair through it in the shower, and subsequently going about his day masked as he picks up supplies like spray paint presumably for an action. When asked by a neighbor what he plans to do tonight, he hides a large paper bag full of supplies behind his back while replying, "Ummm, nothing." This is followed by footage of a busted security fence and a building on fire.[35]

Harper recalls that his announcement of the first issue over various activist listservs generated interest. "People started posting about it on email lists, and the orders just blew up and everyone wanted to see that thing," he remembers. Andy Stepanian, another animal rights activist who would become a member of the Stop Huntington Animal Cruelty (SHAC) campaign, recollects, "When *Breaking Free* came along, it was like all of a sudden you got to see what everybody was doing."[36] Keep in mind that access to the internet at this time was relatively limited.

The second issue presented some global actions and incorporated slightly more undercover footage, such as including a sequence from PETA's

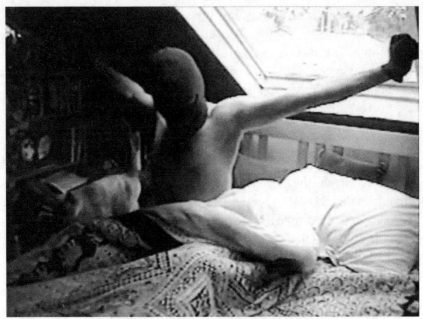

FIGURE 1.9: A commercial for the Animal Liberation Front within *Breaking Free*. A recurrent motif among humorous anarchist-inspired videos is having someone wear a balaclava in domestic situations. Like all good anarchists, he has a cat next to him.

Breaking Barriers video of animal abuse in a primate center in Maryland shot by ALF members. It also created international buzz with people in Spain and a couple other European countries wanting PAL formatted tapes to distribute. "We sent them their own master, which they put subtitles over, and then they distributed themselves," Harper told me. "And then like every three months, they cut us a check for some very nominal amount they sold. You know, I think we were asking for fifty cents US for each copy they sold or something."

The video magazine format became increasingly popular among animal rights activists from 2000 through 2010. The SHAC campaign, which targeted investors in Huntington Life Science, a notorious animal experimenter constantly being exposed for its cruelty, used the format within both its British-produced *Time for Action* series (2001–9) and its US-based videos like *This Means War* (2001) and *The Mandate* (2002). Not surprisingly, Josh Harper was involved in some of the US-based SHAC video magazines.[37]

Video had become such a popular medium in the animal rights movement by the late 1990s, that it occupied a central position in a conference organized by Karen Davis, founder of United Poultry Concerns, in June 26–27, 1999, as part of a debate on the merits of legal versus illegal direct action.[38]

Patty Mark, founder of Animal Liberation Victoria in Australia, introduced many US activists to the tactic of "open rescue," which her group had been practicing.[39] The idea was activists should not clandestinely enter animal facilities but instead visibly engage in such rescues without any disguise in order to be accountable and legitimate such actions. Many activists were skeptical over this approach. Yet groups like Mercy for Animals and Animal Equality began engaging in open rescues shortly thereafter.

Most relevant to this chapter, however, was the centrality that video activism took within the conference. Discussion revolved around two sets of videos: one shot by the ALF of undercover raids and footage shot by Animal Liberation Victoria (ALV) representing open rescue. According to Davis, the ALV videos presented a more nuanced style of animal liberation: "The Australian direct action shows suffering, compassion, a trained team, and the highly skilled use of a camera, the ALF video shows a posturing, self-centered rescue—despite the anonymity of the rescuers—in which empathy for the victims, however felt, is visibly lacking. Significantly, there is no involvement between the ALF rescuers and the animals they are liberating, as there is between the rescuers and the hens in the Australian video."[40] Sadly, I have not been able locate the exact videos that were screened during the conference, so I am unable to evaluate how accurate Davis's account is of the tapes screened. Nevertheless, regardless of the accuracy, it is important that such close attention was being paid to the framing each video provided of the other-than-human animals' relationship to their liberators.

According to Davis, empathy and the viewers' relationship to animals should take precedence. As we will see later in the chapter, empathy also holds a particularly central role in animal rights activists' use of virtual reality. It has also been increasingly theorized within the animal rights movement that a more complicated dynamic is at work than one might initially suspect.

Lori Gruen has developed the concept of "entangled empathy" to address empathy's multifarious processes. She emphasizes empathy's relational nature where it is not simply about our relationship with others, but that "our very selves are constituted by these relations."[41] In other words, she argues that empathy is not just something to be felt by humans toward other-than-human animals, but that it redefines the relations between the two and our very understanding of ourselves. Davis indicates this by emphasizing "the involvement" between rescuers and animals during her account of ALV videos.

This filmed relational attitude of empathy is also important in the ALV videos; they are not simply reproducing the narcissism that can often be found in much liberal documentary filmmaking. Elizabeth Cowie has stressed that many liberal documentaries can fulfill the viewer's ego ideal of being a "nice" person, "that we can be touched by human suffering, by the causes and claims of others."[42] Although Cowie is explicitly referring to human suffering, one can easily see how applicable this is toward other-than-human animal suffering as well in making viewers feel like a "moral" person in witnessing such footage.

Furthermore, Cowie emphasizes how such documentaries require that their filmed subjects "be properly helpless, as well as voiceless, or at least voicing only their plight, their suffering, and must not make any overt demands for help."[43] This provides a unique challenge for animal rights documentaries where suffering often takes precedence and casts animals as nothing more than as victims. Many within the animal rights community assert that they are "the voices for the voiceless," a problematic, self-serving assumption that similarly presents animals as victims. Although most other-than-human animals might not be speaking human languages, it doesn't necessarily mean that they are voiceless. But the question remains how one can move animal rights videos beyond this hierarchized relation between the beneficent viewer and the "helpless" animal. Davis at least indicates one solution in that we see some form of interactions between humans and other-than-human animals onscreen that moves beyond the heroic ideal of rescuers simply freeing the animals to validate viewers' conceit of being good people for witnessing such suffering.[44] For example, a video might show interactions between humans and other-than-human animals at a farm sanctuary that highlights the autonomy and agency of the latter running around, frolicking, or other such activities.

Davis also notes two other important points that are worth considering throughout this chapter when evaluating the effectiveness of the animal rights footage. First, she notes that other-than-human animals should be filmed in their singularity to counter the overwhelming nature of the vast suffering inflicted upon animals "that renders all of them invisible and unpersonable."[45]

Second, Davis notes "the emphasis of the story must remain on the animal."[46] But this is not as easy as it might first appear since there are subtle ways in which the videos still unconsciously bolster the viewer's ego at the expense of the other-than-human animals being filmed. Elizabeth Cowie writes that liberal documentaries do this in part by presenting subjects that are unable "to provide a sophisticated analysis of their circumstances and its cause, or else they will rival the spectator as knowing subject."[47] The documentarian with human subjects can encourage or assist their subjects in coming up with such an analysis, but that is not possible when the subjects are animals.

This is a difficult tendency to counter in animal rights videos where most other-than-human animals are incapable of providing a sophisticated analysis of their situations. So, one must accept that this narcissistic dynamic might inevitably be a part of most of these videos. Still, we need reminders that such activist footage does not simply benefit the other-than-human animals but also reinforces human viewers' sense that they are "good" and "enlightened." While it is not possible to completely eliminate this self-interested tendency of activist footage, it can be minimized by emphasizing the relational nature between human animals and other-than-humans that entangled empathy suggests.

Regardless of the difficulty in navigating which form animal rights activist videos should ultimately take, the 1999 conference represents a unique moment in the movement where the stylistic constraints and capabilities of these videos were being discussed and theorized. Material was not simply shown to represent various tactics of animal rights liberators, but aesthetics, framing, narrative, and other production values of the videos took center stage as well, which, among other things, indicates the importance video had upon the movement at the time.

Government Crackdowns on the Movement

By the twenty-first century, a whole set of reactionary federal legislation was passed that was either directed at animal rights activists or simply had negative repercussions for those involved in the movement. Most notoriously, the Patriot Act passed shortly after the 2001 9/11 attacks in the United States. While not specifically aimed at the animal rights movement, it had implications for it because the act removed the statute of limitations of certain terrorist offenses and expanded the notion of terrorism by establishing a new category of "domestic terrorism."[48] It also eroded many of the checks and balances of the US Constitution. For instance, it allowed the federal government to track people's library checkouts, spy on them without warrants, and monitor their phone and internet communications.[49]

The FBI launched Operation Backfire in 2004, which ultimately brought about the indictment of seventeen people engaged in ALF and ELF actions from 1995 to 2001.[50] Perhaps most devastatingly, the endeavor sowed distrust in animal rights and environmental activist communities by flipping fellow activists into informers and coercing some activists to disclose sensitive information that could lead to others' arrests as a way to reduce their own sentences.[51]

On May 24, 2004, seven animal rights activists of the SHAC campaign were indicted by a New Jersey grand jury for conspiring to violate the 1992 Animal Enterprise Protection Act.[52] Most troubling, the federal government not only went after activists engaged in animal rights' actions but also those who supported them. The SHAC website figured heavily in the government's prosecution of the SHAC 7, as the seven charged were called. Even though the SHAC website held disclaimers that those running it did not engage in illegal activities, the distribution of information regarding illegal activity was also considered criminal.[53]

The Animal Enterprise Terrorism Act (AETA) grew out of the agricultural industries' growing fear regarding the potential of the SHAC campaign to devastate corporate profits and the inability of the 1992 AEPA to curb animal rights activism. John E. Lewis, the deputy assistant director of the FBI's Counterterrorism Division, testified during a 2004 congressional hearing: "While the [1992] statute intended to provide a framework for the prosecution of individuals involved in animal rights extremism, it does not reach many of the criminal activities engaged in by SHAC in furtherance of its overall objective of shutting down Huntingdon Life Sciences."[54] SHAC was repeatedly named during this hearing by various industry and law enforcement figures as a looming threat.

Proindustry groups like the American Legislative Exchange Council (ALEC) had been working diligently behind the scenes in advocating for tougher federal legislation against animal rights groups. In 2003, ALEC drafted a report entitled, "Animal and Ecological Terrorism in America." According to Will Potter, the report advocated for three things: (1) expanding the notion of terrorism to include nonviolent civil disobedience; (2) outlawing any action that may "publicize, promote or aid an act of animal or ecological terrorism," an extremely vague definition that would criminalize almost all forms of protest; and (3) creating a terrorist registry to function as a political blacklist.[55]

The AETA was signed into law in 2006—though ALEC's demand for a terrorist registry never made it into the statute. The AETA expanded upon the AEPA by focusing on "secondary and tertiary targets, such as family members or any 'person' or entity having a connection to, or relationship with, or [business] transactions with an animal enterprise."[56] Additionally, it increases penalties and the labeling of animal rights activists as terrorists.

Due to this new onslaught of federal legislation, many animal rights groups within the United States tamed down their activism, focusing more on animal welfare issues than explicitly arguing for the wholesale abolition of animal agriculture. Likewise, undercover tactics became increasingly important since direct action and public forms of activism were coming under the scrutiny of law enforcement. The outcome was a wave of animal rights undercover footage taken during the first decade of the twenty-first century, some of which led to a significant overhaul of industrial agricultural practices.

The Rise of Undercover Video

As mentioned earlier, undercover animal rights video has been around since mid-1980s with the ALF-PETA collaborations. Much of this earlier footage focused around lab investigations with ALF members either secretly invading labs or posing as employees within them. By the late 1990s, employment-based undercover investigations increased. These types of investigations send someone to work for a company suspected or known to be animal abusers like circuses, puppy mills, or factory farms. The intent is to document animal cruelty or the failure to follow federal or state mandated procedures, or to simply record the miserable yet perfectly legal living conditions that other-than-human animals endure.

Factory farms became a central target around the mid- to late 1990s since they seemed to be activists' best bet in exposing conditions where the vast majority of other-than-human animal cruelty and death occurs. Compared to circuses, puppy mills, and laboratories, factory farms produce the greatest amount of visible animal suffering. Furthermore, they are easy targets in that the other-than-human animals' living conditions are nearly uniformly terrible. Keep in mind that the Humane Methods of Slaughter Act of 1958 provides very weak definitions of what constitutes "humane" slaughter, but worse, it excludes birds and fish from its purview, which means that it doesn't cover over 95 percent of all the animals slaughtered, since poultry far outnumbers any other group of animals killed.[57] Just to put this in perspective, as of 2020, 66 billion chickens are killed each year globally. The second most frequently other-than-human animal slaughtered is pigs, which comes to a mere 1.5 billion worldwide.[58]

Furthermore, the USDA works in conjunction with animal agriculture, the very industry it oversees. In addition to providing nutritional information and creating guidelines for public health, it is charged with the promotion of animal agriculture.[59] Likewise, by directing its attention toward quality control, the USDA naturalizes the violent work that defines all slaughterhouses and creates a very watered-down notion of what qualifies as "humane" conditions within animal agriculture that in any other environment would easily be classified as cruelty.[60] Add to all this that USDA inspectors only provide quick and infrequent inspections of facilities, and you have established the perfect conditions for widespread systemic violence and abuse to take place.

As one might imagine, it is difficult to interview employment-based undercover investigators. Most of those active in the field do not want to have their identities potentially compromised by a nosy researcher. Even those who have quit undercover investigations do not appreciate recollecting the horrors that they engaged in during the course of their careers. For over a year, I spoke with eight investigators and another person who oversees investigations but never served as an investigator herself. A majority of those I spoke with worked in the field for approximately two years, but two investigators had been engaging in undercover investigations for over fifteen years. I spoke with four women and five men. Five were in their late twenties or early thirties. The others were in their late thirties, late forties, and one who had overseen investigations was in her mid-sixties. Only two that I spoke with were people of color: Black/Latinx and Filipino. The undercover investigator community is relatively small, but I could never get a precise number of people involved because of concerns about secrecy. I should also mention that I had never experienced undercover training nor had I engaged in an investigation, so this section is perforce cobbled together from my interviews and other materials.

One of the most difficult things for me to understand was why anyone would be an undercover investigator in the first place. They are separated from family and friends for long periods of time, often isolated in rural communities, and engaged in backbreaking labor and practices that they vehemently oppose. Since investigators must participate in the slaughter and inhumane treatment of other-than-human animals in order to preserve their cover, this job would be untenable to the average animal activist.

First, undercover work attracts those who care deeply about other-than-human animals. Taylor Radig, a former investigator for Animal

Outlook (formerly known as Compassion Over Killing) explained how she had "grown up with animals my whole life."[61] "Pete," who had been in the field for over fifteen years, relayed how a Pomeranian he had failed to save from neglect motivated him to become involved in animal rights.[62] "Astrid," who worked for Animal Outlook, recalls intervening to stop her father's abuse of a puppy. Despite her father being much larger than her, she recalls, "I did get into some physical altercations protecting that puppy."[63]

Another reason was a certain idealism and ego believing that they could enact the change they wanted to see. Investigators are so committed to changing the circumstances of other-than-human animals that they are willing to participate in abuse to achieve the greater good. Astrid notes, "When I was younger, I always wanted to change the world." Scott David, a former investigator for Animal Outlook, remembers summoning up his idealism when reading an online advertisement for undercover investigators: "When I was young, I really liked superheroes and heroes in general and that sort of idea of being able to stand up and do something brave and adventurist and stuff like that for the sake of others. So when I saw that ad, even though, you know, everything in it was trying to convince me that, like, you shouldn't do this, it's going to be like a horrible time, I thought it was everything that I was looking for."[64]

Perhaps more surprisingly, several investigators parleyed their interest in law enforcement, the military, or some other related skill into undercover investigations. Bob Guilfoyle, an investigator with the Humane Society of the United States (HSUS), had been an undercover private investigator before joining animal rights.[65] Pete wanted to be a cop but admitted, "I just never got hired." During my talk with him, he repeatedly brought up the role of his martial arts training and work as a volunteer firefighter in informing his undercover work. For example, when I asked him about negotiating how he lives with the contradiction of caring for animals but having to hurt and kill them when going undercover, he cited the final chapter of Sun Tzu's *The Art of War* regarding spies: "There's a moral concept of saving people throughout the book. Except the last chapter. In the last chapter is the employment of secret agents. And in that chapter, there is no shred of morality that is hinted at. It is simply get shit done. And that does not mean that I should . . . be above accountability." Nevertheless, he continues, "I kill animals and I let animals die when I could save them constantly while undercover. And it is because that, you know, that specific element that unfortunately does have to have its own set of standards."

Not surprisingly, many undercover investigators are loners. When I asked Chrystal Ferber, a former investigator for Animal Outlook, how she adapted to being away from friends and family for so long, she quietly noted, "I'm truthfully not close to my family."[66] The investigators I spoke with generally avoided speaking about their families other to note that they disagreed with them on a number of issues in addition to the treatment of animals. *Barn 8*, a fictional account of an undercover raid based on numerous interviews with former and current investigators, provides an accurate summary of most investigators being "such loners, their absence was barely noticed."[67]

The interviewees were drawn to undercover investigation because they saw undercover footage themselves, were encouraged by a friend or colleague to apply, or stumbled upon an advertisement regarding it. Many of my interviewees cited *Earthlings* or PETA's 2002 undercover compilation *Meet Your Meat* as an influence. Ferber recalls, "For me, it was definitely undercover footage that pushed me from being a vegetarian to a vegan. I know that sometimes they resulted in rescues of animals, places getting shut down." Astrid recollects, "I got involved in the movement from watching documentaries on TV and streaming platforms like YouTube and Netflix." Cody Carlson, a former undercover investigator, mentioned being motivated by seeing *Meet Your Meat* during a punk show.[68]

Bob Guilfoyle and Scott David both came across online advertisements for undercover investigators. Mary Beth Sweetland, director of investigations for the Humane Society, stumbled across a PETA ad in the newspaper that led her down the route to animal rights activism.[69] Taylor Radig interned at Compassion Over Killing and was approached by Cody Carlson about becoming an investigator. Taylor Radig was friends with Chrystal Ferber, and encouraged her to get involved. Sean Thomas interned at PETA, where someone asked him if he would like to do investigations.[70] Steve Garrett, who worked at Last Chance for Animals, encouraged Pete to get involved in undercover work.[71]

The training to become an investigator varies from organization to organization. Again, I never directly observed such a training, so the following description is an amalgam of what I learned from my interviewees and patched together from other sources. An air of secrecy pervades the entire endeavor, with some of my interviewees being more circumspect than others since they didn't want to reveal trade secrets that the agricultural industry could exploit.

Such training is rigorous and demanding. Before engaging in it, one must pass an extensive background check and undergo an interview. The head of investigations would also scour the internet to see how traceable a future investigator's identity might be and identify any evidence that might disqualify someone from conducting undercover investigations.[72]

If a candidate passed the background check and interview, they were trained in several different areas. Physical training played a large role, since many of the jobs undercover investigators held required long hours on one's feet, repetitive movement, and considerable physical labor. This training could take various forms such as weight lifting, bending over cages, shoveling animal waste, or any other of the numerous tasks that such employment demands. Pete, who trained some of the earliest undercover investigators like Cody Carlson, emphasized, "It should never be an excuse that you can't physically do something and that's the reason you don't get the evidence. So always be prepared. I show people: here's the kinds of workouts that you can do to avoid injury and be prepared for even the toughest of jobs that are out there."[73]

Investigators also needed to be trained in how to work their cameras and shoot from their body. Cameras are typically located around the chest, decoyed as a button or hidden in a pocket with a cutout for the lens. Sean Thomas relays the difficulty in shooting in such a fashion: "There is a whole way of kind of reinterpreting your normal body movements. It can be very frustrating because, on one hand, I'm saying to them [trainees]: just move exactly naturally. Don't stand awkwardly and all that. But, at the same time, you have to be the tripod. You have to be creating these shots that are steady and show things clearly. And it can be very difficult for people to kind of normalize what is getting movement within their camera work."[74] Radig also emphasized the importance of getting clear and precise shots: "You just kind of have to learn to how to position yourself so you're getting the most information you can, not just like the hands of the person beating an animal but the actual person. It's very, very hard to convict animal cruelty. And you need, like, as much information as possible for a DA to even consider it."

Positioning yourself to get a good shot is not the only challenge. Investigators must multitask: maintaining their cover, perhaps performing some job, and then filming. As Radig relates: "You're thinking two things at once. You're trying to engage a person in a conversation and then essentially positioning your body in a way that it doesn't look awkward."

Not only do investigators have to think about getting one decent shot, but they must also consider how to capture an adequate variety of vantage points. Bob Guilfoyle instructs: "You want to get multiple angles of everything. I would get that shot from one angle. I would look at my lighting. I'd take like a five or six second snippet and move like four or five feet to the left or right to get another shot of a five or six second clip."

Pete differentiated between criminal shots and campaign shots. Criminal shots, according to him, are "evidence of any and all crimes that are going on. There's animal abuse, neglect, tax evasion, and all that shit." Campaign shots, on the other hand, Pete joked, "If you get this shot, then Sarah McLachlan will start fucking singing 'in the arms of the angel'…like a slow pan that looks dramatic." They are not easy to get. Pete adds drily, "I fucking forget to get those shots every fucking case."

The amount of coverage an investigator would shoot varied in terms of their filming skills along with the quality of the cameras they used. Some cameras, particularly during the late 1990s, were not easy to turn on and off. So, an investigator might shoot continuously throughout the day and mentally stockpile important moments where they recorded something of significance that they could then fast-forward to when they reviewed their footage later offsite. A more dexterous undercover investigator with better equipment might only film very few select moments that they considered notable.

Although undercover investigators have to use their real names, since lying on federal W-9s constitutes a felony, they nonetheless manufacture false backgrounds. During training, they engage in role-playing. Pete, for example, would place a trainee in a situation where he plays an employer accusing them of being an animal rights activist. He observes, "I want you to role play yelling back at me and convincing me, like, 'Shut the fuck up. I am not an activist.' If there's a tough situation that we're going to be in, we're going to simulate it or we're going to set it up and you're going to go into it."

Bob Guilfoyle recalls his investigation manager making him engage in talking drills. They would be walking around in public and the manager "would point to someone and be like, that person over there. Go find out if she has a kid." The technique would allow investigators to hone their skills in ferreting out information in inconspicuous ways that they could potentially deploy during future workplace situations.

The type of personality an investigator adopts varies depending upon the individual's skill set and disposition, but styles run the gamut between two poles. One the one hand, investigators might adopt a fly-on-the-wall attitude where you quietly observe situations. Bob Guilfoyle operated in such a fashion. The advantage of it, according to him, was "a lot of people, especially like shitty, insecure people, will just kind of project to that blank slate whatever they want to or whatever they want me to be." As a result, they can reveal a lot more about themselves and the general workplace than he might have initially suspected.

On the other hand, there is the very active investigator who adapts their personality to the situation. Pete adhered to such an approach. "I want to be engaged with the subject," he told me. "And I want to read them and be able to be exactly who they want me to be" in order to encourage subjects to loosen up and reveal vital information.

Most importantly, the training taught investigators to be adaptable to ever-changing situations. According to Pete, "everything about training is going to be real-world hands-on practical." Similarly, Sean Thomas reflects, "The biggest thing with investigators and training people for the field is not about how to use a camera or how to document these different things. The biggest thing is how to be adaptable, how to be constantly evolving in these situations."

Close calls are the nature of the game since investigators are ostensibly drifters briefly wading into small, tightknit communities to work at factory farms, slaughterhouses, hatching facilities, or the like. Suspicion is the norm. However, the severe turnover rate at most of these facilities (up to 95 percent within a year) was a significant advantage.[75] As a result, despite the suspicions foremen and owners might harbor toward their workforce, they have no choice in hiring almost everyone since they never know who might show up the next day for the job.

Most people going through the training, however, never actually become investigators. As Scott David notes, "We do get a lot of people who either like decide against it or ... they go through a part of training and get out into the field, they get like a taste of what it's like ... and it ends up not working out for them."[76] This in part explains why there are so few undercover investigators in the field at any one time.

Animal rights organizations initiate an investigation based on intelligence from a whistleblower or through word of mouth about substandard conditions. Many times, investigators might not even have a clear sense of exactly what they are looking for. Instead, they simply need to stay vigilant. In general, most people within the animal rights community believe that almost all factory farms or agricultural facilities are doing something wrong—particularly in regard to ever-increasing line speeds and a general desire to produce more meat for less money. Astrid recalls: "I have actually hoped that it would be different because a lot of people believe that it isn't all farms, that there are plenty of farms that don't abuse their animals. But every farm I've investigated had some level of abuse occur, whether it was a newborn chick being impaled on a metal nail, cows being dragged by tractors, fish being violently slammed against walls."

Occasionally, an investigation won't pan out at a smaller facility. Bob Guilfoyle recollects having doubts about going after a small animal removal business: "The problem wasn't with them.... They were just following state rules. Do I really want to expose these people?" Likewise, Chrystal Ferber remembers jettisoning working on a small chicken facility: "There was nothing that could have happened with this facility. They were just too small."

As mentioned earlier, investigators cannot lie about their names even though they create false backgrounds. Similarly, they use temporary addresses, usually hotels or motels that lie around a half hour away from where they are working. The distance between residency and workplace creates a certain buffer to protect investigators from haphazardly running into coworkers when off-duty.

The worst thing that can happen to an undercover instigator is having their identity blown as an undercover investigator and their name leaked to the industry. Pete, for example, changed his name three times in order to remain in the field. Taylor Radig had her name revealed when a local prosecutor falsely charged her with animal cruelty in Colorado. Bob Guilfoyle's stint as an undercover investigator was derailed when his identity as an undercover investigator was blown. He was recently hired at a pork farm and returned home to email HSUS that he got the job. "And then I got a strongly worded email from them [the factory farm]" he notes, "to never come back." He knew he was done doing undercover investigations since he didn't want to have to keep officially changing his name.

The length of investigations vary tremendously. "Walk-ons," where one doesn't necessarily work for a facility but has other interactions with it like trying to see if a puppy mill will buy a dog from an unlicensed person, could be as brief as a few hours. Employment-based investigations can last around six months but are usually shorter. On rare occasions, they might last longer.

Undercover investigators work grueling hours. Shifts can run anywhere from six to twelve hours, but this doesn't incorporate all the additional work required for the investigation. Since most investigators reside around a half hour away from their workplace, this means at least an hour drive to and from work each day. It can take another half hour suiting up for work by taping the camera and wires in place on one's body and adequately hiding the equipment behind layers of clothing. One must also test the equipment to make sure it is functioning properly and check that batteries are adequately charged. Bob Guilfoyle outlines a typical day: "I would get up at 4:00 a.m., maybe a little earlier just to get up, get my head right, get my camera on, like, make sure my stuff's good. Maybe like do the header on my report just to get a head start on it."

Many investigations take a rough toll on the investigators' bodies. Astrid recalls having cracked and bleeding skin on her hands from hanging birds while working at a chicken facility. Bob Guilfoyle had a similar experience where at the end of his shift at a chicken facility his hands cramped and "were like mittens." Pete temporarily developed carpal tunnel syndrome hanging turkeys at a slaughterhouse. At a hog slaughterhouse, Bob developed "a really noticeable limp like my entire lower half just felt uneven" after working eleven-hour shifts on uneven flooring with inadequate boots.

Many of my interviewees commented on the awful smells that permeated all the facilities they worked at. Astrid commented on the heavy ammonia smell in chicken factories that "burn your nostrils to the point where you need a gas mask." Dairy facilities smell like spoiled milk and shit. Hog facilities were routinely cited as the worst, where a combination of shit, blood, and urine mingled to produce an intolerable atmosphere. "It smelled like pork chops and bacon but cut with blood, shit, and piss," Bob Guilfoyle recalls. "Like two weeks after I started there, I went to a diner, and someone got bacon next to me, and I almost gagged."

Unmitigated violence defines daily life at the factory farm. Although all the investigators witnessed extreme cruelty from some coworkers, most stressed that the environment transformed workers into their worst selves. "I encountered people who were very generous to me sometimes on these farms," Astrid notes. "But their demeanors would shift when dealing with animals. Otherwise, good people become aggressive when trying to force the animals to cooperate in an unnatural environment."

Some investigators could feel this dehumanization and cruelty seizing hold of themselves in such conditions. Bob Guilfoyle recollects a frightening moment while working in a hog slaughterhouse: "It's an eleven-and-a-half-hour workday, and you're on your feet, and you're exhausted, and you're tired, and you're stressed, and it's one goddamn pig that doesn't want to do what everyone else is doing. And there were times, and I never lashed out or did anything, but there were times during that job where I would get frustrated, and I would get like, holy fucking shit, go to your death, you pig. It's just from the conditions that they set up to kill as many pigs as possible, like breeding an anger and frustration in me."

At factory farms, investigators became familiar with killing on an intimate level. Ferber recalled having to euthanize a chicken with broken legs.[77] She had killed other animals at the facility such as tossing bins of male chicks into a macerator that grinds them up alive. But in that instance, "there was some space between me and the action of killing the animal." Euthanizing the chicken, however, required Ferber to break the bird's neck with her own hands. "When I broke it with just my hands on the bird's neck," she recalls, "That was very difficult to do because the bird was very heavy. And so I kept having to do it over and over and over again until the bird died."

A pervasive sense of fear of being found out coursed through investigators' thoughts and bodies while at work. Pete refers to his nineteen years in the field as "nothing but close calls." We witness one in the 2006 HBO documentary *Dealing Dogs* that features Pete uncovering animal cruelty and the illegal purchasing of dogs at a kennel. The owner's wife, on camera, tells her husband that she believes Pete is an undercover investigator. But the owner's sexism gets the better of him and he dismisses his wife's concerns as paranoid. Astrid would be overcome with such fear, she notes, "I remember on some cases I would feel my heart pumping so hard in my chest that I could barely breathe."

Perhaps least anticipated by investigators was the creeping loneliness and alienation that enveloped them while at their jobs. Scott David recalls "the isolation that you feel out in the field." He expands: "When you become an investigator, they tell you that you can't really tell anyone what you're doing. So basically everyone back home had no idea what I was doing, and they just knew I was gone almost constantly, and they never saw me." Astrid eloquently notes, "It's like you become another person for a month. You're just another worker wondering when your time there is going to end. The days start to bleed together.... It just seemed to break down that person's spirit over time."

The unpredictability of undercover work makes any kind of intimate relationship nearly impossible. Many investigators spoke to me about relationships crashing against the relentless demands that undercover work necessitated. Bob Guilfoyle raised an issue he has encountered when his partner wanted to go on a vacation with him, and wanted to know what month might work best. "I really don't know," he continues. "Because who knows what I will be involved in. You know, there's never any kind of consistency. You have to just kind of say, my life is open to the job."

Female investigators held mixed attitudes regarding whether their gender assisted or hindered their work. Chrystal Ferber felt it assisted her in gaining footage since male coworkers would try to impress her with their knowledge and strength as well as flirt with her. For example, she recalls needing to document the condition of a chick hatching facility. She recalls, "When I was trying to film some birds, I'd say, well, that one has blue eyes. And he'd say, yep, they all have blue eyes. And I would continue to say that one has blue eyes. And we'd just do this weird game where I could stand there filming longer without being told to go away or for him to feel suspicious of me."

Taylor Radig, on the other hand, felt male coworkers would act less abusive around her toward the animals. She reflects, "So men might be more cruel toward animals in front of other men versus in front of women. So that can be difficult for investigators. Men-on-men relations can typically be a lot more macho and domineering."

Astrid believed she was denied employment opportunities because of her gender where bosses didn't consider women well suited for the type of work she was seeking. "There is some degree of managers or workers on factory farming sites," she notes, "assuming that a male worker will perform better than a female worker." This was evident when she did land a job: "I found myself having to work almost twice as hard to prove myself in those situations, afraid that I would be fired or something like that for not being able to perform to their expectations."

Chrystal Ferber and Taylor Radig also mentioned recurring sexual harassment or tense situations of vulnerability. Radig remembers "constant comments about my appearance, and shit like sexual come-ons." Ferber recalls working with a lone male employee at a hatchery and "he was just being very creepy and odd and then telling me he just seemed suspicious of me."

Rides with male coworkers could be particularly fraught. Ferber rode shoulder to shoulder with male colleagues on a golf cart. "I have a tattoo on my top right shoulder," she explains. "And one of them pulled my shirt aside and told the guy, 'Tommy, look she's got a tattoo here.' And I don't think it's hard to imagine that they would not have felt comfortable touching a guy in that type of way." Radig similarly remembers, "I was going to work before the sun was rising with three men I didn't know. And I'm the only female. And so that's a little bit scary."

After finishing their shifts, all investigators returned back to their lodging to upload and document their footage, fill out reports, and often debrief with someone from their animal rights organization. But before that, they first had to shower. Smells from the farm permeated their clothes, car, and hair. "I remember hopping in the shower after work and setting the water to the highest temperature to try to burn the filth and the smell off my skin," Astrid tells me. "And I would blow my nose in the shower and so many fecal particles would come out of my nostrils." Similarly, Guilfoyle recalls, "[When] the water first hits you, and you look down, and it's kind of like all almost red, but not red. Not like *The Shining*, but it's off-white kind of red. Like the stuff in your hair."

Often investigators debriefed with a manager by phone. Ferber checked in with her investigations manager to "talk about what happened that day and then talk about the footage and everything." They would review old footage she had sent in earlier and have "an ongoing conversation about things that would be great to have in the investigation or shots that I could improve on."

Guilfoyle, who had prior private investigator experience, checked in less often, around two or three times a week with his point person and maybe only every two or three weeks with the senior director of investigations. Radig would chat regularly with a team of attorneys who could help inform her of infractions they noticed at her worksite that she might have missed. HSUS attorneys, for example, caught a key detail for what would become one of the biggest meat recalls resulting from an undercover case at a Hallmark/Westland slaughterhouse where "downer" cows, animals unable to walk, were being pushed, dragged, beaten, and violently prodded to slaughter despite such actions being illegal and leading to tainted meat being supplied to the National School Lunch Program. "In the Hallmark case," Mary Beth Sweetland relays to me. "It was a huge catch by somebody in our litigation department. They saw a piece of video that the director of investigations at that time had thought was just not a big deal, but it turned out that that piece of video was the catalyst for a major lawsuit because what we've seen on the video was a downed cow being dragged to slaughter on the plant floor."

It was important that investigators make contemporaneous notes. "They have to be contemporaneous to be any good for the USDA or other law enforcement officials," Mary Beth Sweetland explained. "Because they will ask you, are these contemporaneous log notes? If you don't say yes, they're going to say, well, when did you write them up? You know, you might remember incorrectly."

Different investigators had different methods of documentation. Ferber relied on a spreadsheet: "I would label the video and I'd say, from like four minutes to like five minutes you can see this animal being thrown against the wall." Time stamps were important so that those reviewing the footage at the home organization would not be wasting time watching the vast majority of unusable footage most investigators shoot. Guilfoyle's manager "would put together like weekly compilations of [his] videos, like the best parts or the most impactful parts" that would be forwarded to legal and other managers.

There was always the consideration of how such footage would appear to law enforcement. "We have absolutely everything laid out, you know," Radig told me. "Here's the video. You know, a minute and fifteen seconds you see a calf being kicked in the face by this employee. And just like documenting every aspect of abuse."

There are also miscellaneous tasks that undercover investigators need to do like renewing their rental car or getting a new hotel room "because you don't want to ever book too far in advance" which can reveal your cover, according to Guilfoyle. Getting your clothes washed and other daily tasks also consume whatever downtime investigators have when not working a shift.

Some investigators stay involved with post-investigation procedures by approaching a district attorney with evidence of animal cruelty or working on their video for public distribution. Ferber, for example, narrated and appeared in Animal Outlook's compilation film *Beyond the Lies* (2018). Ferber sat for a two-hour recorded interview which provided snippets for the video. According to "Radish," who assisted in compiling the footage, the editor and Ferber "would go through different drafts together. It was very much team collaboration."[78]

For some videos, Sean Thomas would work intimately with the video editor. "I would sit with him, and we would work on an edit, and then present that edit to the director of investigations and the communications director," Thomas explained. "They would make some suggestions, and we would make changes [based on them]."

Undercover work creates immense trauma for most investigators. Almost all that I spoke with suffered frequent nightmares from their work and had difficulty assimilating back into the rhythms of normal everyday life. Ferber recalled that it was hard interacting with her cats since she learned to shut down her empathy while undercover to such an extent that it was difficult to access it again. Investigators frequently lashed out at their friends who seemed to occupy a different reality from them. Thomas recalls a dinner he had with some friends who were making idle chat, laughing about inconsequential things. "But my brain was just so diverted into this other kind of area, it just felt alienating and disconnected," he notes. "I actually got very angry and annoyed with everyone and ended up leaving and pushing everyone away at that time." Ferber recollects a similar moment: "I drank a little too much, and I just totally had a breakdown. I was crying on the floor and kind of yelling at my two friends, neither of them are vegan or vegetarian. I remember feeling like so enraged at them."

Astrid had nightmares that would startle her awake "because I thought I heard screaming, like pigs screaming or animals screaming in some way." Scott David was haunted by the image of a half-paralyzed pig he recorded during his investigation: "I can see him drag himself towards me on just his front legs since his back legs don't work."

Many investigators wrestled with the accompanying guilt of both the killing they engaged in as undercover investigators and the feeling that they have betrayed other-than-human animals by quitting undercover work. Although many animal rights organizations have more recently provided free therapy for undercover investigators, not one investigator I spoke with ever used it. The reasons for not seeking therapy are varied. Some mentioned that they considered it a liability and were afraid that if they did so their organizations would consider them "soft." Others believed that they needed to sacrifice themselves for the animals, so suffering this trauma was appropriate. Still others didn't believe in the value of therapy. But whatever the reason for avoiding therapy, it is clear that undercover work makes severe psychic demands on those who engage in it. It is thus critical to interrogate the value video footage provides since it enacts such high costs on investigators' psyches and lives.

Undercover Videos and Results

There is no simple way to assess the impact of undercover videos. Some lead to radical changes in animal welfare regulations, some have led to the prosecution of animal abusers, and some have even been the catalyst for shutting down of a factory farm or slaughterhouse. But the impact of most videos is more nebulous. Generally, undercover footage is part of a larger constellation of videos—a growing archive that is constantly being repurposed for different campaigns and remixed into different forms. Most videos will largely be forgotten. Others with particularly captivating footage will have excerpts of that footage endlessly circulated.

For the investigator, however, it can be frustrating to spend many weeks or months on a job with few immediate results. Sean Thomas explains, "You can't really have that sense, that needing to accomplish something good, because there's never a clear-cut victory in investigations. Like the animals that you're filming, that you're studying while you're there, all of those animals will most likely be dead by the time the footage is released." But, he continues, "You might have an impact on animals in the future. Maybe a year from now, five years, ten years from now. But we struggle still just to get acknowledgment that some things that happen on these farms are cruel."

In a more general sense, all the videos challenge the fetishization of meat, the goal of the industry to conceal the brutality and often unsanitary conditions inherent in its production. From its shrink-wrapped packaging to the air-conditioned aisles of local grocery stores, the agricultural industry does everything possible to wash meat clean of the taint of the slaughter-house that might reveal its brutal origins or prompt consumers to make connections between the animals they consume and the pets they love.

Carol J. Adams usefully refers to this process of fetishizing meat as the absent referent. She explains, "Through the function of the absent referent, Western culture constantly renders the material reality of violence into controlled and controllable metaphors."[79] The absent referent renames dead calves as "veal," dead cows as "beef," dead animals in general as "meat." This language strategy provides a dissociative function enabling consumers to overlook the violence and cruelty that they sanction with every purchase and every bite of meat, eggs, and dairy they consume. Undercover videos, therefore, play a vital function in exposing the absent referent by drawing stark attention to the material conditions in the bloody rendering of meat, eggs, and dairy. Although one might question whether video documentation alone is enough, it would be difficult to say that it is not necessary at all.

Perhaps one of the most famous and impactful of all undercover videos was shot by Sean Thomas for the Humane Society US regarding the aforementioned Hallmark/Westland slaughterhouse. Downed cows are not supposed to be used for human consumption, according to California state law, since they are often contaminated. But since USDA inspectors only inspect slaughterhouses once or twice a day, a vast game of hide-and-seek by slaughterhouse managers ensues where they attempt to misdirect and divert inspectors from looking too closely. Timothy Pachirat documents this dance between USDA inspectors and slaughterhouse managers thoroughly in his book, *Every Twelve Seconds: Industrialized Slaughter and the Politics of Sight.* Sean Thomas witnessed similar actions when working undercover at Hallmark/Westland. "As long as we can get them to stand up for the veterinarian, they'll be fine," he was told. "So, people will literally shock them, put cattle prods up the rectum, in their eyes and their mouth, to get them to stand and call over the veterinarian. It's like, okay, they're standing up. And once the veterinarian walks away, they would collapse again after five minutes or so."

Crimes of Hallmark Westland Meat Company (2008) documents these conditions throughout its five minutes. Like Ingrid Newkirk in *Unnecessary Fuss*, Sean Thomas narrates the video in a calm, measured tone. It opens with him saying matter-of-factly: "For several weeks, I documented the treatment of dairy cows at a California slaughterhouse." Grainy black-and-white footage plays under his words, but it is difficult to discern what we are seeing. His mention of dairy cows prods the viewer into identifying the amorphous shape before us as that of a cow lying on the floor. The camera pulls back slightly and we see a man's foot kick a cow out of a holding pen. Many of these images are horrific, but many of them are not clear without explanation.

The images are often blurry or shaky and require contextualization to bring exactly what we are seeing into focus, and Thomas's narration and the video's periodic text help guide us. In one instance, white text on a black background explains that California law requires that cattle unable to stand or walk be either euthanized or removed from the property. The sequence cuts to a long shot of a cow appearing to be sitting halfway out of the door of a truck. At first glance, there might appear to be no issue, but we occasionally hear grunts from the cow. Thomas explains, "This cow was down on the truck before she arrived. Workers are behind her, shocking her, trying to get her up, but she's too weak to stand." We never see the worker behind her except during a brief instance when he leaves the truck with what appears to be a long prod extending from his hand.

FIGURE 1.10: Often within animal rights videos, the image alone is not enough. What might appear to simply be a prostrate cow is revealed by the voice-over as one that has been "down on the truck before she arrived. Workers are behind her, shocking her, trying to get her up, but she's too weak to stand." The image's authority is based on a complex network of cues including voice-over and text.

The need for such commentary is not unique to animal rights under-cover video but serves a central function in most documentaries. As Bill Nichols writes, "commentary guides us towards those aspects of the image that are most important to the argument."[80] The narrative in this video likewise provides vital information that workers off-screen torment the cow and orients the viewer in time, explaining that the downed cow we see had not just suddenly fallen but "was down on the truck before she arrived." The narrative also stitches together scenes to provide transitions between what might appear to be unrelated footage. The earlier downed cow sequence cuts to a forklift that attaches a chain to drag what is presumably the same cow.

At other times, the narrative is used to emphasize what is actually self-evident in the footage. We watch a downed cow being pushed by a forklift, her body being roughly rolled and tumbled as she moans in pain. Thomas emphasizes, "When she's being rolled and pushed along the concrete, you can see it is causing her so much pain." He adds, "When he drives into the pen, he runs over her leg and he runs over her face with the wheels of the forklift." Ominous keyboard music swells as we watch the footage before Thomas states, "I never heard a cow scream like that before," which the viewer also hears. Voice-over, music, and image all converge to relentlessly press the horror we witness into the viewer's consciousness through all audiovisual registers.

The release of the video in 2008 received wide media coverage and led to multiple concrete results. The USDA recalled 143 million pounds of beef, the largest recall in US history.[81] Criminal charges were leveled against two workers and five felony counts against a pen manager. Tellingly, only the criminal charges against workers stuck. A US House of Representatives Energy and Commerce Committee forced Steve Mendell, president of Hallmark/Westland Meat Company, to testify and admit wrongdoing.[82] The US Department of Agriculture vowed to randomize USDA inspections so slaughterhouse workers cannot easily conceal ill animals from their view.[83] The negative coverage, beef recall, and potential for immense fines ultimately closed the slaughterhouse in 2008.[84]

Although one might debate how much impact the closing of one slaughterhouse and the minor changes made to USDA inspection procedures might have on the overall consumption of meat and our speciesist attitudes, it nonetheless had immediate and clear impacts for animal welfare. Matthew Liebman, an animal rights lawyer for the Animal Legal Defense Fund, suggests that such videos play a part in the battle of attrition against animal agriculture. "I am skeptical that regulatory reform is the ultimate solution," he notes. "But if it marginally decreases suffering, it's probably a good thing even if it's not the key to the kingdom. If such videos ultimately shine a light in a way that transforms the public conversation, they can be kind of fundamentally revolutionary [in the long term]."[85] But it ultimately depends on how videos are utilized to determine if they are moving the needle toward a less speciesist world.

Another highly publicized undercover investigation video was produced by Mercy for Animals in 2012 regarding Idaho-based Bettencourt Dairy Farm where cows were ceaselessly beaten by workers with blunt instruments and kicked and stomped. Pete shot this footage.[86] Although the video only runs for three minutes, it delivers a relentless montage of violence. Rare for undercover videos, it provides no narration or text for its first minute and a half. We are assaulted with fast clips of workers breaking cow tails, dragging them by their necks behind tractors, kicking, punching, and jumping on cows trapped in their stalls, and beating cows with blunt objects.

Sustained low keyboard music plays ominously during this footage early on. But primary diegetic sounds of workers grunting and yelling at the cows then take central focus. Midway through the video, text from various veterinarians and scientists condemn the workers' actions. The music swells toward the end of the video where a shot fades on a downed cow and the words appear: "Ditch Cruelty. Ditch Dairy." The URL "BurgerKing. cruelty" follows, forcing the link between the cruelty to these animals and the product served at Burger King.

By not stating upfront that these cows are being readied for slaughter, the video makes the violence seem not as a means to an end but an end in itself, where workers take out their aggressions on the animals they oversee for no other purpose than to do so. The video received over 664,000 views and garnered wide news coverage, with ABC's highly watched *Nightline* news program featuring it.[87] It also led to the firing of five workers with three being charged with misdemeanors of animal cruelty.[88] Mercy for Animals requested that Burger King drop the supplier for its meat, but nothing seems to have resulted from this.

Although the video provides powerful evidence of animal abuse, one might question its relentless focus on workers and the violence they perpetuate. First of all, the video seems to imply that the problem is with the workers and not the industry. By having fired the workers from the dairy, Bettencourt isolates the problem and offers a superficial fix.

Second, as Claire Rasmussen notes, "Because vulnerable laborers— often undocumented workers—are those who have actual contact with animals, they are more likely to be prosecuted for animal cruelty than those who design policies or most directly profit from them."[89] This plays into a deeply problematic carceral logic that defines much of the animal rights movement. As Justin Marceau notes, "Cruelty prosecutions allow for the collective transference or displacement of guilt from mainstream society onto the 'other,' the socially deviant animal abuser."[90] So rather than dealing with the wider disciplinary practices of speciesism that course through all of our lives and make a majority of people indirectly responsible for the torture, pain, and slaughter of other-than-human animals, cruelty charges isolate the violence onto some of the most vulnerable individuals, often targeting undocumented people of color. Furthermore, such visceral videos, according to Rasmussen, fail "to interrogate the processes by which these forms of labor are stigmatized and the effect that has on the ability of workers or animals to be perceived as valued subjects and not as abject objects of derision."[91]

Interestingly enough, rather than reevaluating its dairy facilities and practices, the Idaho legislature doubled-down on them by passing an ag-gag law in 2014 as a response to negative undercover footage. It jailed anyone filming without permission on an agricultural facility for up to a year and fined them up to $5000.[92] This law was quickly ruled unconstitutional by a federal judge in 2015 as violating the First Amendment. But in many ways, the example bluntly illustrates the ways in which the agricultural industry prefers to kill the messenger than address the inhumane and cruel conditions that define many of their facilities.

Death on a Factory Farm (2009), the second HBO production to star Pete, who chronicles abuse on a hog farm, provided some prestige for undercover investigations and also illustrates some of the difficulties undercover investigators face in making their case in the courtroom. Pete had come into contact with HBO while he was working at Last Chance for Animals. HBO originally wanted to produce a documentary about animal lab testing but soon realized that they weren't going to gain any access. As a result, they teamed up with Last Chance for Animals, which was conducting a series of investigations with Pete at the helm. Although HBO's original intent was to document widespread animal abuse in a series of facilities, they ultimately whittled their focus down to a dog kennel for *Dealing Dogs* and a hog facility for *Death on a Factory Farm*.[93]

According to Pete, *Dealing Dogs* and *Death on a Factory Farm* legitimated undercover animal investigation by having the imprimatur of an HBO production upon it. As a result of both documentaries and word of mouth, Pete was in high demand to conduct undercover investigations at a series of animal rights organizations as well as piloting a training program for future undercover investigators by 2009. He also received a flurry of emails, half of which praised his work and the other half of which critiqued it as too reformist and not doing enough for other-than-human animals.

Death on a Factory Farm reveals the tensions undercover investigators must navigate between their filming practices and making their case in court. All undercover investigators oscillate between what Bill Nichols refers to as the interventionist gaze and professional gaze of documentary filmmaking. In the former, an intimate relationship exists between filmmaker, subject, and the threat being documented.[94] The relations can be somewhat permeable and shifting. In most undercover animal rights videos, the investigator serves as an ally for the other-than-human animals being documented. The investigator is there on the behalf of an animal rights organization. The investigator often believes in the abolition or strict regulation of animal agriculture. The footage is shot with the intent of exposing the underbelly of a facility.

Concurrent with the interventionist gaze, the undercover investigator wields a professional gaze, which Nichols describes as "a disciplined one inoculated against displays of personal involvement."[95] The photojournalist would be the embodiment of such a gaze where the goal is not to intervene in a tragedy or assist someone suffering but instead document it. Undercover investigators play a similar role. They witness and often take part in the slaughter of animals. The very strength of their material rests upon allowing cruelty, abuse, and other negligence to take place. So, they must distance themselves from their own impulses to care for other-than-human animals and instead coolly observe some of the worst abuses taking place to produce footage documenting their observations.

In *Death on a Factory Farm*, Pete documents compromising footage of sick hogs being euthanized as they were hung to death from a chain on a forklift. To him and Last Chance for Animals the footage seems like a slam dunk—any jury witnessing his footage of chained hogs kicking and writhing as they are hung from a forklift until dead would agree that it easily qualifies as cruelty. But once he enters the courtroom, he quickly learns otherwise. First, the defense debates the interpretation of what the jury sees in the video. The kicking of the hung hogs that Pete says represents their struggling against abuse is reclassified by the defense attorney as nothing more than "involuntary reflexes." A battle over the indexical, over what the images "really" mean, ensues. Kicking might seem like struggling, according to the defense attorney, to the untrained eye. The attorney stresses Pete's lack of expertise by identifying that he doesn't hold a bachelor's degree in animal science or a related field. According to the defense's scientist, the hog's movements are nothing more than reflexes.

Most interestingly, the defense attorney presses Pete on his nebulous role filming on the farm. Having clearly established that Pete works for an animal rights organization, the attorney then hones in on the apparent contradiction of Pete's animal rights beliefs and his actions as an undercover investigator. For example, Pete said he documented pigs dying from malnutrition. The defense attorney responds, "You could have taken food in and helped them out. But you didn't do that, did you?" When Pete reminds the attorney that management never instructed him to do so, the attorney nonetheless relentlessly persists, "On your own, you could have gone over and helped that animal and you didn't, isn't that right?' The defense draws direct attention to the uneasy position Pete occupies between interventionist and professional gazes. He has a vested interest in animals but isn't willing to save one when he sees it suffering on the farm. Yet the veracity of his documentary footage is "compromised" by being employed at an animal rights organization that opposes animal agriculture in general.

After three hours on the stand, Pete confesses to us: "This is completely different than I thought it would be because I always thought the evidence would speak for itself. And once the evidence speaks for itself, it is very clear what is going on." He pauses and continues, "But it's not. There's all these rules we have to go by . . . like playing a game in there. I thought if I get the video footage of people committing cruelty to animals it would be obvious and that's it. But it's not."

To hammer the point home regarding the unexpected denial of the indexical power of undercover footage, where an image is no longer seen as univocal, a townsperson attending the court hearing notes, "We can't have these type of people come in here and destroy our business." Despite what the footage might show, there is a bigger ideological battle occurring between vegan, animal agriculture abolitionist outsiders and the townspeople who are trying to make a living. No amount of animal cruelty footage is going to dislodge that dynamic. The judge ultimately issued a single count of animal cruelty resulting in a $250 fine, probation, and a mandatory training program for one employee on the humane handling of animals. Tellingly, although the documentary received decent coverage, one reporter for the *New York Times* who comes from an agricultural background, acknowledges the farm owners' point of view, writing, "I can also understand why members of the farm owners' community would be reluctant to send their neighbors to jail. As one sympathetic farmer in the gallery says, "We can't all eat lettuce."[96]

As video has become a central medium in animal rights activism, agricultural industries have responded by advocating for legislation that makes it much more difficult for investigators to film inside agricultural facilities. This produces a feedback loop whereby animal rights organizers assume that video is an effective medium since industry fights so vehemently against it and are inspired to produce even more video. The agricultural industry in turn responds to the flood of undercover recordings with even more legislation. Nevertheless, both sides tend to take for granted that video represents a central medium of struggle.

Ag-Gag Legislation and the Glass Walls Project

Kansas passed the first ag-gag law in 1990, but few others followed through-out the 1990s and the first decade of the twenty-first century. However, during the second decade, with the rise of cheap, portable technology like cell phones with video capabilities and the growing influence of social media that can easily distribute video, ag-gag laws were passed in states like Missouri, North Carolina, Arkansas, Wyoming, Iowa, Idaho, South Carolina, Utah, and Alabama. These laws criminalize one or more of three things: (1) filming on an agricultural facility, (2) gaining access to an agricultural facility under false pretenses, and (3) not reporting animal abuse within a certain period of time.[97]

Idaho was the first state whose ag-gag law was struck down. But Utah's rejection of its ag-gag law in 2017, which was used against investigator Amy Meyer (mentioned at the beginning of this chapter), was particularly important in that the federal judge overseeing the trial articulated a very detailed and in-depth opinion that would serve as precedent for other cases.[98] Keep in mind that all ag-gag cases within the United States have been argued by a rotating team from a central hub of lawyers: Justin Marceau, Matthew Strugar, Matthew Liebman, Alan K. Chen, and David Muraskin, with different attorneys taking the lead in different cases. Therefore, they are collectively establishing precedent against ag-gag laws by building upon the different rulings in their favor and sharing information with one another.

Much ag-gag legislation has been struck down because it violates inves-tigators' First Amendment rights in documenting abuse. The agriculture industry uses all forms of questionable logic to argue against individuals' right to work undercover or videotape facilities. Still, the United States holds some very solid protections that place a difficult burden on industry to explain how such legislation is not abridging investigators' First Amendment rights.

Ag-gag laws remain largely unpopular across the political spectrum. Repeatedly, conservative commentators will suggest that while they do not support the animal rights agenda, they do oppose the censorship that ag-gag laws embody. Professional curmudgeon and reporter John Stossel encapsulates the overarching sentiment of many conservatives: "Whatever you might think of the activists, and I have problems with many of them, government shouldn't pass special laws that prevent people from revealing what's true."[99]

Ag-gag laws, though, are not the only way to punish undercover inves-tigators. An inventive district attorney can contort existing laws to interfere with an undercover investigator as Taylor Radig learned in 2013. She documented abuse at Colorado-based Quanah Cattle Company filming workers' rough handling of dairy calves by pulling their ears, and dragging, pushing, and kicking them off trucks. When she returned home to California after the investigation, Radig received a call from the Colorado DA she had been working with who required her return to clarify some details regarding her case. She recalls the meeting: "The questions at first were pretty fine: tell me about what happened. And then slowly throughout the interview they start asking me like, oh, why didn't you go to the police after your first day?" The DA briefly left her in his office only to return with "a little piece of paper saying that I was being charged with a misdemeanor of animal cruelty." Negative publicity highlighting the hypocrisy of the charge and a high-powered lawyer working on her behalf got the charges dismissed within three months.[100]

The industry also creates its own propaganda videos. An early instance is the 1964 short, *This Is Hormel*, which conveniently skips agriculture industry farms and the slaughterhouse to cut straight to the packaging plant where a male voice-over praises different cuts of meat.[101] This is a fairly common tactic of pro-industry videos: elide the horrors of the factory farm and the slaughterhouse, replacing them with appeals to the consumer about product quality. A more recent video by Smithfield, a repeat offender of animal abuse and constantly under surveillance by animal rights groups, *Hog Production at Smithfield* (2013) shows well-lit, spacious conditions on a hog farm and conveniently ends before the hogs "go to market" (the slaughterhouse). The absent referent looms large in these videos where euphemisms like "market" push off-screen the violent and repellent practices found within slaughterhouses and factory farms.

An interesting exception is the Glass Walls Project, initiated in 2012 by the American Meat Institute to counter the flood of undercover investigator videos found online. These videos actually take us into the slaughterhouse because if they have any hope of countering animal rights undercover footage, they have to engage in a war over the indexicality of the images of slaughterhouse practices. Industry can no longer get away with hiding the slaughterhouse since undercover videos have pushed it to the forefront. This is one way animal rights footage has worked in a positive fashion: it has forced the industry to present the very location it vehemently tried to keep from view—the killing floor—if it wants to seize control of its messaging.

Temple Grandin, a professor of animal science at Colorado State University and agricultural industry apologist, narrates the Glass Wall films.

All the films have lengthy prologues that document Grandin's pedigree in order to legitimate her views. In a video within a cattle slaughterhouse, Grandin gripes: "One of my biggest frustrations is you go out there on the internet, and there's all these terrible undercover videos, and there's not much video of things being done right."

For another ten minutes, Grandin leisurely strolls through the slaughterhouse explaining to us how things might not appear as they seem. For example, much like the defense attorney in *Death on a Factory Farm*, Grandin explains away the kicking we see of recently slaughtered cows hanging from a conveyor belt as "spinal reflexes." She explains: "The circuits for walking are in the spine. And when you destroy the brain, that walking circuit gets all hyperactive. So, it's normal for that free leg to do some kicking." She further wields her expertise, adding: "There's a lot of undercover video where they show that leg kicking and go, oh, it's a live animal. What they need to be looking at is its head." If the head is floppy, she asserts, it is dead. "If, in the rare occurrence," she cautions, "that an animal is found showing a return to sensibility it is immediately reshot with a captive bolt gun."

Interestingly, much of the video is shot from a high angle, these distant shots emphasize the spacious and clean conditions around the cattle. This framing also provides a vital ideological function that keeps us emotionally distant from the other-than-human animals. We do not see any cows in their singularity but only as an indistinguishable mass of bodies, a strategy which Karen Davis rightfully observes elsewhere "renders all of them invisible and unpersonable."[102]

In another video regarding a pork processing plant, Grandin draws particular attention to the importance of cinematic framing in biasing one's understanding of other-than-human animals' living conditions on the factory farm. We see a shot of pigs seemingly crowded on top of one another. Grandin comments, "This shot might show some pigs that appear to be crowded. And activists might say that they are crowded. But, actually, when it's cold, pigs like to bunch together." The shot then zooms back with Grandin commenting: "And when you open up the shot, you can see that the pigs have plenty of room. They have just chosen to lay together."

Again, this sequence marks a battle over the indexical in different ways. Grandin employs her pedigree to refute what might appear to be "crowding" on multiple levels. First, it might be the pigs' choice to huddle together for warmth. So "crowding" might not necessarily be a bad thing but actually desired on the hogs' part. Furthermore, she draws attention to how framing

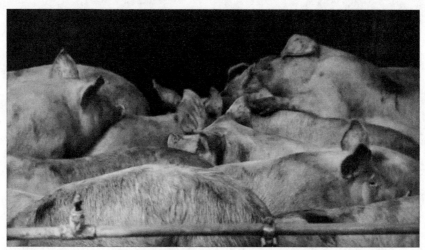

FIGURE 1.11: The Glass Walls Project was funded by the American Meat Institute to counter undercover video footage of factory farm cruelty. Hosted by industry apologist Templin Grandin, its video on pork (2012) shows how framing can be misleading. The video demonstrates how a distant shot from a long angle lens can make it appear that pigs are contained in cramped conditions.

FIGURE 1.12: Yet when the camera pulls back, the video reveals that the pigs have adequate space. The Glass Walls Project attempts to sow doubt regarding animal rights undercover video by having viewers question what they see.

can deceive viewers by making relatively uncrowded spaces appear otherwise by a disingenuous undercover investigator. Unmentioned, however, is whether the hogs want to be in a slaughterhouse in the first place.

The Glass Walls Project is worth discussing because it reveals a more complex dynamic at work regarding the use of video among animal rights groups and the industry. It is not adequate to suggest that animal rights groups simply want to make visible what industry desires to hide. Glass Walls videos show the industry as willing to reveal certain aspects of the slaughterhouse to public view. Jan Dutkiewicz usefully refers to this as the industry engaging in a decontextualized and selective transparency. This represents "the corporate meat industry's new strategy of taking on its critics on their own terms."[103] Activist groups need to more fully grapple with this point: the image itself has become a terrain of struggle over meaning. Not only does this require a more robust strategy in contextualizing such footage, it may also require a fundamental rethinking of how it is employed.

Open Rescue Videos and Virtual Reality

During the raging battles over ag-gag between the government and animal rights activists and the growing timidity of many animal rights organizations in light of the further criminalization of their activism within the United States, an opening emerged for other tactics and groups to take hold. Direct Action Everywhere (DxE), founded in 2013, attempts to push animal rights in new directions by reviving open rescue. As mentioned earlier, groups like Animal Equality and Mercy for Animals engaged in open rescues during the start of the twenty-first century but increasingly regarded them as a fraught tactic as stricter federal laws against animal rights activism appeared.[104] But, for better or worse, DxE made open rescues central to their arsenal.

DxE, embroiled as it is in various controversies, represents one of the most contentious animal rights groups discussed in this chapter, which is saying a lot given that PETA had been the favored enfant terrible of the movement before DxE's arrival. A series of online groups have called out DxE for different offenses like bullying, sexism, and racism.[105] Well-known animal rights feminist Carol J. Adams refuses to participate in any events that host DxE since she considers them a cult.[106] Many of these critiques circulate around DxE cofounder Wayne Hsiung.[107] I have no firsthand experience with Hsiung since he never responded to multiple requests for an interview. Although one might be able to chalk up such critiques as the normal bickering and jealousies that often percolate among activists, the level of ambivalence or outright contempt for DxE among activist groups is notable. Out of my twenty-five interviews with non-DxE people for this chapter, only two openly supported the group, whereas the rest were either highly critical of them or held deeply mixed attitudes. The tenuous position DxE occupies within the ranks of animal rights is worth noting before discussing some of their work.

DxE argues that open rescues "undermine the industry's strongest weapons—ignorance and complacency—and bring the horrendous oppression of animals to the fore." In particular, these rescues "can narrow their focus down to the individual and tell stories of not just horror and violence, but of happiness and liberation," which serves as an important corrective to much undercover animal rights footage that luxuriates in suffering.[108] Almira Tanner, the lead organizer of DxE, eloquently notes: "It's a very pure expression of what we want to see. It's like here is this individual. They are suffering. We are going to help them … and it's also very powerful in terms of creating a dilemma for the opposition."[109] Open rescue confronts industry with two equally bad options: (1) either the industry doesn't punish such actions, thus setting precedent for future similar actions to occur; or (2) industry bring charges against the activists, which makes the industry seem particularly monstrous in punishing those who are saving other-than-human animals from confinement and slaughter.

Furthermore, for a small organization like DxE, open rescues are cost-effective. Lewis Bernier, head of DxE's direct action committee, told me: "The tactic of open rescue largely came out of necessity for DxE because it's extremely expensive to do a lot of these undercover investigations that other organizations are involved in."[110]

In general, DxE has received some positive coverage regarding their open rescues from major news organizations like the *New York Times* and the *Washington Post* and more niche outlets like *Wired* and *The Intercept*.[111] "Stealing Lauri," an article in the *New York Times*, provides overwhelmingly positive coverage of DxE stealing a six-month-old pig from a farm in North Carolina that supplies Smithfield, the nation's largest pork provider. The article not only portrays the activists in a positive light, but more importantly, creates an individual identity for Lauri, the pig. The article chronicles how she "came to life" when examined by the vet school residents at the University of Tennessee, Knoxville; and how "she nibbled on a gloved hand, wiggled her ears and grunted with curiosity." Accompanying the article are pictures of Lauri playing with DxE members and in a sanctuary with other pigs. The article and photo essay balance their focus between the activists and Lauri in ways that exemplify the power of open rescue stories in exposing the industry and highlighting the individuality of other-than-human animals once trapped in factory farms.

FIGURE 1.13: *They Rescued Pigs and Turkeys from Factory Farms* (2018) is an idealized portrait of Direct Action Everywhere (DxE), a media-savvy animal rights group that gained coverage from *The Intercept*, the *New York Times*, and other publications. Leighton Woodhouse, who codirected, coproduced, and coedited this video for *The Intercept* eventually joined DxE.

The Intercept's twenty-one-minute video, *They Rescued Pigs and Turkeys from Factory Farms* (2018), which chronicles various open rescues by DxE along with the multiple felony charges pending against many of its activists, also provides positive coverage that veers into pro-DxE propaganda by its end as the activists stage an open rescue at a Petaluma egg farm. During the video's finale, an angelic-sounding keyboard plays as activists walk in slow motion beneath an overhead drone shot that tracks their path to the farm. A close-up follows of activists' hands held up in defiance before a chain-linked fence. Brief footage follows of Wayne Hsiung confronting the farm's owner, but the video quickly transitions to more slow-motion footage of activists removing chickens from the farm. The entire sequence shows activists looking almost saintly as they line the road holding white flowers in their outstretched hands. Any aggression on the activists' part is smoothed over by tranquil music and slow motion that transforms their removal of animals, and potential theft, into a ballet of activism.

DxE's actions align with the sympathies of the filmmaker, who eventually joins DxE.[112] The choreography between the subjects and the action bluntly illustrates Judith Butler's observation that "we cannot separate the question of who the people are from the technology that establishes which people will count as the people."[113] Throughout the video, we hear from the activists and reporters and scientists sympathetic to them. We never hear from industry figures. We only get a brief sighting of the owner of the egg farm as the final sequence of the video romanticizes the activists and their actions under slow-motion photography and soft lighting.

As Butler notes, "street and media constitute a very contemporary version of the public sphere" where both the physical and the virtual, the action and its future distribution need to be thought of as mutually informing one another.[114] In other words, the action itself is in part choreographed in advance as a media event meant to be distributed online and elsewhere. The media is no longer an afterthought to an action but a part of its constitution.

But choreographing one's direct action for ideal media coverage doesn't mean it will necessarily be covered that way. Let's rewind back to the same event covered in *The Intercept* video—the Petaluma open rescue of May 2018. Vice Media covered the same event to create a hit piece on DxE, which provides an interesting counterpoint to *The Intercept*'s idealization of the action.

It is not even clear why DxE would team up with Vice, which has been riddled with controversy and opposes DxE's purported "intersectional" approach that sees animal rights aligned with and responsive to other movement struggles. Only five months before the DxE action took place, the *New York Times* broke a major story on how sexual harassment plagued the Vice workplace at all levels.[115] In 2019, Vice reached a $1.87 million settlement for paying female staffers less than men.[116] This is not surprising given the fact that one of Vice's founders was Gavin McInnes, the misogynist and xenophobe who founded the Proud Boys and was finally fired by Vice after tweeting himself hanging out with former KKK leader David Duke.[117]

When I asked members of DxE why they would team up with such a media organization, they generally seemed unaware of these controversies. Cassie King, head of communications at DxE, told me, "The people we talked to [at Vice] made the trip to document our Animal Liberation Conference, our big annual gathering. They seemed very personally supportive."[118] Assessing the quality of coverage one will receive based on the brief interactions with its staff seems hopelessly naive. Moreover, the entire endeavor is tone deaf in teaming up with what is generally considered a sensationalistic and superficial media organization that has been mired in sexism for years.

Vice called its video on DxE "Animal Rights Extremists: Terrorism or Protest?," which signals the hyperbolic and reductive way the video covers the group.[119] Goofy techno music plays over shaky footage of activists

FIGURES 1.14 & 1.15: *Vice News*, on the other hand, did a hit piece on DxE that pitted aggressive DxE activists led by an Asian American troublemaker against a white small-town farmer in *Animal Rights Extremists: Terrorism or Protest?* (2019). Miraculously, DxE teamed up with *Vice News* during the pandemic despite their first encounter.

shouting and engaged in a skirmish with factory farm workers to enter its premises. The sequence immediately cuts to a medium close-up of Wayne Hsiung, with a smug expression, being asked by an interviewer, "Has your group been labeled a terrorist organization? Have you been labeled a terrorist?" Before he can answer, the footage cuts back to activists storming the farm with Wayne barreling past the farm owner who pleads, "You have no right to do this." The sequence then briefly cuts to farm owner Mike Weber in medium close-up stating, "We get threatening phone calls. There are people following our trucks." More protest footage follows as he continues, "They are terrorizing our local farmers. They are terrorizing us." The title "Break-In in Petaluma" emblazons itself across the screen.

From this opening alone, one can tell that the video was not a puff piece like *The Intercept*'s aforementioned coverage. The activists are framed as a horde invading the property of this relatively good-natured and understanding farmer. Weber represents a media-savvy farmer who knows how to position himself as the victim. When the interviewer asks him if he could ever have a conversation with Hsiung, he replies, "If you own a house, and an arsonist wants to have a conversation with you, how could you come to an agreement on something? He wants to shut down all animal agriculture."

Wayne Hsiung and Cassie King responded to the Vice piece with a belabored forty-four-minute video with some insightful critiques.[120] One point they stress is that the Vice video allows Weber to give a prearranged walking tour of the farm for Vice that shows the chicken facilities in pristine conditions whereas none of the DxE footage provided to Vice was used. A second issue concerns the underlying racism that guides the Vice video that positions Hsiung as the Asian foreigner against the all-American, white farm boy. This representation of Hsiung is all the more insidious in that, according to Cassie King, Vice shot three hours of interview footage with her, none of which was used.[121]

Throughout the video, though, Hsiung keeps exonerating the Vice reporters whom he considers well-intentioned by displacing blame onto "the corporate overlords" of Vice management that manipulatively arranged the reporters' material. Cassie King explained to me that when DxE followed up with Vice regarding the coverage, they "didn't get a substantive response at all. I don't think they even responded to more than maybe one email." So why then, I asked, would she give the reporters so much benefit of the doubt? She responded, "They were nice people. I don't want to shit all over them. It might not be their fault." Such a response dumbfounded me until I belatedly realized that despite Vice's hit piece, DxE, attempting to capitalize upon the fear of pandemic-based illnesses from COVID-19, teamed up with them again for a raid on a pig farm to collect pig feces to test if any pathogens were in them.[122] No pathogens were found.

What DxE gains in positive coverage of its open rescues from such outlets as the *New York Times*, is undermined by teaming up with sensationalistic media organizations like Vice. Such collaborations throw doubt upon the group's understanding of what it means to ally itself with other movements.

FIGURE 1.16: Wayne Hsiung and Cassie King provide a belabored forty-minute livestream response to the Vice video, *Animal Rights Extremists.* They offer some valid critiques of the video. But with Hsiung doing most of the speaking throughout the livestream with the microphone by his mouth, it is difficult to believe that he has stepped down from control of DxE based on the control he exerts in the video. It also reveals a troubling gender dynamic in that King is not properly miked. Despite DxE's moments of media savviness, it has equally embarrassing missteps in its self-presentation.

Even the video where Hsiung and King respond to Vice holds an air of carelessness in its staging and the type of gender dynamics it presents. Hsiung and King occupy a box in the lower right-hand side of the screen as they review and comment on the Vice footage. Rather than properly miking each of them, the sound person has Hsiung and King share a pair of ear buds. Tellingly, the microphone resides on Hsiung's side, so his voice consistently overpowers hers. Likewise, Hsiung controls what parts of the video they will watch, pause over, and rewind along with largely directing the conversation with King chiming in from time to time. Ostensibly, Hsiung stepped down from any DxE leadership position in 2019 due to the multiple felony charges he faces.[123] Yet the video suggests otherwise: Hsiung at the helm with King as his assistant.

This speaks to a larger organizational failure of DxE's. Purportedly, they want to become "a massive social movement"[124] and "enact revolutionary social and political change for animals in one generation."[125] Their leadership constantly references other social movements like women's suffrage, LGBTQ+ rights, and the civil rights movement, but I never learned of any concrete steps they were taking to extend animal rights into constituencies beyond the usual suspects and forge alliances with other groups. They recently released a strategic road map that envisions the growing momentum of their campaign to 2040 when they project an "end to animal farming in the US."[126] The problem is that this plan offers no concrete actions. Instead, the road map speaks in abstract hyperbole like: "Launch massive mobilizations for animal liberation that capture national press attention for weeks. An individual animal rescued from factory farming has become a household name, and a symbol for why we need to end animal agriculture."

When I spoke with Almira Tanner, DxE's lead organizer, she kept referring to the group's "community building and outreach." I initially assumed this to mean ways in which DxE was working with other communities beyond animal rights to build relationships and future actions. But eventually Almira clarified that she meant "building our own [animal rights] community," which of course isn't outreach at all. This explains why Cassie King in another interview complained that DxE is "trying to break out of that regular 150-person group bubble. That seems to be like where you get stalled [when holding events]."

Located in the Bay Area, a hotbed of activism, including animal rights, DxE has effectively attracted a younger generation to its ranks. But one wonders if it has hit its limits within this geographical area. If DxE wants to extend its ranks further to become a mass movement, it seriously needs to rethink its overall strategy and tactics to move beyond individuals and communities that are already sympathetic to animal rights. It is fairly common for organizers in any social movement to hit a certain threshold limit at which it becomes challenging to engage new participants. This is where the difficult work begins with community outreach, which means rethinking some of your strategies to appeal to other constituencies. As far as I could tell, DxE has not yet engaged in this vital work.

In many ways, the organizing problems that haunt DxE pervade the entire animal rights community. Instead of seriously rethinking their mobilizing strategies, they often revert to the belief that technological innovation might further extend their influence. Enter virtual reality (VR). From 2015 to 2018, some animal rights organizations, including DxE, seemed enamored by the potential that VR held in growing the movement.

Ever since VR's widespread appearance in the 1980s and 1990s, venture capitalists and well-intentioned but naive computer programmers tried to convince a skeptical public about the need for such technology.[127] The hype died down by the late-1990s as the technology reached its limits. But with the arrival of the Oculus Rift in 2012, a new round of hype and overstatement ensued. Ben Delaney, market researcher and creator of the VR industry newsletter, *CyberEdge*, observes, "I've been really, really getting a chuckle out of reading the hype about the Oculus, because it just feels like they're recycling the same old press releases and nonsense that people were talking about 20 years ago."[128] Apparently, animal rights is not immune to such silicon snake oil either.

Groups like Animal Equality and PETA started experimenting with VR around 2014, teaming up with interested filmmakers and tech companies in designing technology and media specifically for use by animal rights groups.[129] By 2015 and 2016, Animal Equality and PETA both toured college campuses with cumbersome VR contraptions that required elaborate assembly and disassembly. But the initial interest by students justified the costs. Kenneth Montville, project manager of PETA's campus mobilization and live events, recalls: "We had people lined up for two hours waiting to try out the VR with *I, Chicken*," one of PETA's first forays into VR filmmaking, which took viewers on a tour of a factory farm and slaughterhouse from a chicken's perspective. This college touring circuit built upon earlier tours by PETA with video vans in the 1990s and portable tablets in the early 2000s.

Repeatedly, animal rights people enthuse about VR's immersive and empathetic capabilities. Amy Meyer, someone who is generally skeptical about technology advancing animal rights, told me how the immersive experience of VR deeply affected her: "But when I put on the virtual reality experience, it sticks with you. . . . Just that one time inside the virtual reality experience is just like seared into your brain in a way that video usually isn't." Jose Valle of Animal Equality comments that the "VR experience was much better and much more immersive" than regular video.

VR has been often referred to by those within the industry as an "empathy machine," which animal rights activists likewise view as its central advantage.[130] Jose Valle, for example, reported that when screening VR footage during the 2015 Animal Rights Conference, "People were shocked by the footage. Many of them were crying" after exiting the video. Kenneth Montville reflects, "We had this idea . . . to do empathy-building virtual reality products."

But various media studies scholars have pointed out that empathy alone is not enough. Effective witnessing and political action, according to Kate Nash, requires both empathy and analysis. Empathy creates an affective response with the experience of the other. Yet "analysis calls for a more distanced relationship that recognizes the distinctiveness of the other."[131] Nash refers to this as "proper distance" established by media that both emotionally connects *and* "contextualizes the suffering of others and recognizes the distance between us."[132]

VR often runs the risk of delving too far into empathy and not providing enough analysis, which can leave viewers with a sense of hopelessness. "Compassion, like other forms of caring," Sara Ahmed cautions, may "reinforce the very patterns of economic and political subordination responsible for such suffering."[133] Ostensibly, animal rights organizations get around this problem by asking follow-up questions of VR viewers after their experience as well as discussing the literature and ideas behind animal rights.

However, this approach still doesn't eliminate the danger of such VR footage reinforcing social hierarchies that many liberal documentaries rely upon, such as bolstering an audience's ego by making them feel they are "compassionate" and "a nice person" when watching the suffering of others. Such a position reinforces unequal power relations whereby audience members serve as active agents to help passive "victims." All of the VR animal rights documentaries I have seen—*I, Chicken* (PETA, 2015); *I, Orca* (PETA, 2015); *iAnimal: Through the Eyes of a Factory Farmed Chicken* (Animal Equality, 2016); *iAnimal: Through the Eyes of a Pig* (Animal Equality, 2016); *I, Calf* (PETA, 2017); and *iAnimal: The Dairy Industry in 360 Degrees* (Animal Equality, 2017)—represent animals as helpless victims on their way to slaughter or imprisonment. The PETA videos place viewers in the position of an other-than-human animal being rounded up for slaughter but fading out before the actual slaughter takes place. The Animal Equality videos, on the other hand, graphically and uncomfortably immerse viewers in the violence and blood of the slaughterhouse. Normally an appeal follows each video—don't eat meat, distribute this video online, and get involved somehow. Despite these recommendations, the videos are not univocally pro-animal since they reinforce a deeply problematic speciesist dynamic that views animals solely as victims, featuring them in extravagant emotional appeals designed to engage viewers.

Many animal rights activists reveal a certain gullible faith in the power of virtual reality. Activists repeatedly told me that VR footage would provide irrefutable evidence. Lewis Bernier explained to me, "One other benefit to virtual reality is the industry doesn't have the opportunity to say this is staged footage." Filmmaker Leighton Woodhouse further explains, "We can't edit VR footage. The technology gives activists a rejoinder to the hackneyed allegation that we selectively edited the videos." Elsewhere, Wayne

Hsiung asserts, "Virtual reality will undermine this corporate spin, as the public will see exactly what activists see in 360 degrees."[134]

All these outlooks imply that new technology and its practices will easily refute skeptics. But as Bill Nichols points out, the belief that photographic images are indexical, meaning that they can capture reality itself, does not reside in the image nor in its technology but is instead asserted in the context that surrounds them. He writes that "Not only is the historical authenticity of the image subject to uncertainty; the meaning it bears as evidence, even if it is authentic, is subject to interpretation. Facts make sense only within systems of meaning."[135] To critics, the context—the system of meaning—within which they interpret any kind of footage from animal activists is that in one way or another, it's faked. Whether VR footage is subject to any kind of manipulation is irrelevant.

As a matter of fact, the digital is itself fraught terrain on which to make any claim about authenticity. Its very existence is premised upon coding that can be manipulated in endless ways. According to Dale Hudson and Patricia Zimmermann, digital media overall represents a paradigm shift away from representation "to one of capturing, processing, manipulating, and repurposing images."[136] The rise of deep fakes where famous personalities can be realistically replicated by digital technology throws doubt upon the veracity of any digital technology in capturing "the truth." And in an age where the basic tenets of reality itself are up for debate—for instance, the false claims that the 2020 US presidential election was "stolen" or that Democrats run a pedophile ring—a faith in VR somehow putting to rest any doubts industry might throw at animal rights activists is wishful thinking.

Despite overhyped claims that "the future of media—and perhaps all communication—lies in virtual reality," VR holds very mixed results in its effectiveness for activism.[137] A few studies suggest that VR might create a higher level of empathy than other 2-D forms of video.[138] Yet other studies reveal no significance difference between 2-D video and virtual reality in affecting viewers.[139] Animal Equality commissioned its own study that similarly found no difference between the two forms of video.[140]

The most nuanced study so far was produced by Donghee Shin and concluded that the impact of VR depends predominantly upon the user's background and motivations. Embodiment or presence "is not an external factor bestowed upon the user [by the technology]; rather, it is a fluid state that is reprocessed and redefined by users."[141] This is a credible explanation of why animal rights viewers find VR such a compelling format—they are already predisposed to empathize with other-than-human animals they see. It might also help explain why the Animal Equality study found activist videos more impactful on the West Coast than East Coast in the United States. Animal rights holds a stronger presence on the West Coast so, therefore, West Coast viewers might be more receptive to such footage. Overall, the Shin study offers a more nuanced account of how empathy and immersive participation don't simply flow from the technology, but instead are at least in part determined by the user's relationship to the material being screened, a point that cultural studies scholars have been making about audiences' understanding of and relationship to media objects for some time.[142]

By 2018, with the decreasing novelty/popularity of VR among college students, its high costs, difficulty in distribution, and mixed results in achieving activists' goals, animal rights group stopped touring with it. Kenneth Montville of PETA reflects on the challenges of using VR, "We moved away from the big rig because obviously there's a lot of logistics involved with traveling with something that size. And then obviously there is the cost factor." With the advent of Google Cardboard VR headsets, distribution of already existent videos could happen more easily among animal rights groups. Sharon Núñez, cofounder and president of Animal Equality, said her organization wanted to share videos "with as many activists as possible to ensure that we reach more people."[143] What impact this switch is having remains unclear.

Conclusion: Limitations and Paths Forward

Although some progress has been made by animal rights groups in establishing better welfare standards for other-than-human animals like the California fur ban in 2019 and the USDA providing more random inspections along with more sympathetic coverage of other-than-human animals in mass media and the growing acceptance of veganism, the animal rights movement has been mired in outdated strategies. Most animal rights organizations claim themselves as "intersectional" and responsive to other social movements, but their tactics and strategies generally do not reflect this.

It is not uncommon for animal rights videos to cater to reactionary gender clichés. For example, quite a few videos employ the tropes of the Hollywood maternal melodrama where a mother's pain over losing or abandoning her child serves as a structuring principle. According to film scholar Linda Williams, the maternal melodrama relies upon "a body caught in

FIGURE 1.17: PETA's 2015 virtual reality film, *I, Orca*, has actress Edie Falco play a distraught mother whale who agonizes over the capture of her baby by SeaWorld. Such videos truck in the conventions of the maternal melodrama where mothers separated from their children provide the emotional leverage for a viewer's sympathy.

the grip of intense sensation or emotion."[144] Furthermore, "the bodies of women figured on the screen have functioned traditionally as the primary *embodiments* of pleasure, fear, and pain."[145] Both of these assertions hold true for the ways in which female bodies function in animal rights videos.

The maternal melodrama explicitly guides PETA's 2015 VR film, *I, Orca*. Narrated by Edie Falco, playing a mother whale, the film shows her panicking outside the enclosed underwater walls of Sea World, fretting about the fate of her captured baby. In trembling voice, she relives her separation from her child: "One minute my little baby was with me. The next he was pulled up out of the water. There was nothing I could do to save him. He was taken away from me. I heard his cries there. I can still hear his cries. Can you?" Viewers occupy the mother's position, a helpless victim. Her suffering serves as a constant motif throughout the video.

Furthermore, the video naturalizes the notion of motherhood, suggesting that it is the default position of women. At one point, the mother whale laments, "I can recognize my own baby's calls. Any mother would." But Western feminists have been bristling against and resisting such assertions of the alleged natural instinct between mother and child, a notion rejected by the appearance of Kate Chopin's brilliant takedown of motherhood in her 1899 book *The Awakening* where main character Edna Pontellier would rather drown than be saddled with her child and husband.[146]

Her mom tried to break her out

FIGURES 1.18 & 1.19: DxE also relies on the maternal melodrama in *Piglet Refuses to Give Up* (2017), in which a mother pig helplessly witnesses the suffering of her baby.

DxE does no better in many of its open rescue videos. Swelling strings and melodramatic music opens *Piglet Refuses to Give Up* (DxE, 2017). Wayne Hsiung, in a medium shot, cradles and kisses the piglet in his arms. Over his image, fairy-tale-like text appears: "This is the story of a piglet who was saved." The video cuts to nighttime footage of Hsiung picking Lily, the piglet, from her cage. The text continues over this image: "and of a man who found her in a cage."

As mournful strings dominate the soundtrack, text tells us of the plight of Lily's mom who "gave birth at a 'crate-free' farm." We see the mom behind

FIGURE 1.20: Wayne Hsiung becomes the piglet's surrogate mom by rescuing her from the factory farm in *Piglet Refuses to Give Up*, which perhaps troubles that notion of the maternal being associated solely with women. However, the mother suffers and is left behind with the promise of her child having a better life elsewhere, a typical plotline of many maternal melodramas.

steel bars as piglets scramble to suckle her. The text stresses, "But the bars stopped her from caring for her babies." When the piglet's foot gets stuck and injured between boards, the text informs us that her mom tried to break out to help her, "but she couldn't escape." Standard eyeline match defines this segment as we watch the piglet struggle with a trapped leg between boards. The video cuts to the mother biting at her bars in a fruitless attempt to break free.

The second half of the video announces, "Then a strange man appeared. He heard Lily's mom crying. He saw Lily couldn't walk, and he knew that she had to be saved. He said goodbye to her mom. He promised to give Lily a better life." The video summons some of the worst gender clichés: the suffering and passive mother is unable to protect her child while Wayne Hsiung plays the prince saving her child. We eventually see Lily frolicking with other piglets, and the final shot of the film shows Lily swaddled in blankets with Hsiung, again, leaning down and kissing her. Here, he occupies the position of surrogate mother. While it troubles the gender binary of men not being maternal, the video reverts to a typical gendered plotline of maternal melodramas, as the mother suffers and is left behind with the promise of her child having a better life elsewhere.[147]

Even in videos where the maternal melodrama does not entirely frame its narrative, a mother's suffering creeps in. In Animal Equality's *With My*

Own Eyes (2019), actor Rooney Mara visits a chicken and pig factory farm under the cover of night. As we watch someone lifting a piglet from a crate, we hear Mara's voice-over become increasingly emotional as she reflects: "I just kept thinking about my sister who just had a baby, and how beautiful that was, and that instant desire to nurture and protect your child. So, I can't imagine how awful it must be to be literally trapped and crushing your own babies and not able to do anything about it." During her voice-over, we watch a mother pig, sequestered in a crate presumably looking helplessly on at her piglets. It is only a brief instance in the video, but it nonetheless reveals a common trope that guides many animal rights videos that use the suffering of helpless mothers to play upon viewers' emotions.

These videos appear particularly tone deaf in light of the #MeToo movement coming to animal rights in 2018 where a series of high-ranking, white male predators were identified in the animal rights movement. Some were fired while others were shuffled around in the movement.[148] The disparity between the cisgendered, white male leadership in animal rights with the women who comprise anywhere from 75 to 80 percent of the rank-and-file has been repeatedly critiqued.[149] Although a shakeup has happened to some extent where much male leadership has been replaced with women, it is still debatable how substantively these issues have been addressed.

Carol J. Adams stressed to me, "We need to deal with sexual exploitation against grassroots activists, and the way that employment at minimum wage often is really low for a lot of activists who work within the movement." This makes "their financial stability, already tenuous," worse and makes it "harder for women of color to be employed in in the movement. They might be responsible for families. They can't live on that amount of money." So taking action against sexual harassers and predators is not enough. Activists must also shine a light on the political economy of animal rights that places female staff and volunteers in vulnerable positions or excludes sustained participation of the most marginalized communities given their needs.

A recent study revealed how issues of sexism and racism have led to significant burnout for women and people color within the movement. Anyone involved in the animal rights movement deals with the stresses related to being retaliated against by law enforcement and/or employers for their activism along with the low pay or free labor that defines much of its work. But for women and people of color, sexism and racism compound these issues. Eight of the thirteen women activists interviewed in the study "attributed their burnout in part to sexism they experienced from men in the AR movement." Additionally, "the activists of color were demoralized by the failure of movement leadership to reflect the racial composition of movement activists."[150]

This turmoil has caused some within the movement to seriously rethink its strategies such as its carceral approach that centers on criminalizing and enacting tougher laws around animal abuse. According to Justin Marceau, a carceral logic "permeates the thinking of activists, organizations, and commentators in the animal protection movement."[151] Yet John Seber of Mercy for Animals notes how this is being rethought, "I think the Animal Rights movements is thankfully taking a good look at the roles that it's played historically. I think that everything going on in this country and in our criminal justice system and that's coming to the forefront, it's sparked a lot of healthy conversation about this."[152]

The founder of Vine Sanctuary, pattrice jones, wonders if the restorative justice model advocated by prison abolitionists might be adapted to animal rights, which poses its own distinct problems. "With regular restorative justice the victim can speak. And the victim's family can be there to speak. And so, the victim is able to say what would feel like restoration to them," mulls jones. "But with animal rights, we would have to be counting on some appointed advocate for the animal."[153]

Alternative models have also long existed within the movement but had not been heeded as much as they should have been. Carol J. Adams, for example, had been conceptualizing how speciesism contorts our language and charts the intimate ways sexism and speciesism mutually reinforce one another. Reflecting on her 1990 book *The Sexual Politics of Meat*, Adams notes, "It was a theoretical innovation that helped contextualize their [animal rights] activism and showed that the oppression of animals cannot be separated from talking about a variety of forms of human oppression."[154]

She also is concerned with establishing alternative modalities to address animal oppression other than undercover video followed by criminal charges and incarceration. "What is it that we're asking people to conceptualize?" she asks me. "Are we asking them to conceptualize that meat comes from this dead animal? And why do we think that documentary is the most profound way to change people?"[155] The reliance upon documentary, according to Adams, can be deeply patriarchal and narrow-sighted by requiring a viewer to endure the violence and suffering of other-than-human animals in order to become angry and engaged. She lists a whole host of other ways people become engaged in animal rights such as reading or "meeting vegans who aren't telling them to become vegan." She mentions innovative younger writers like Aph and Syl Ko who inspire younger activists. She also cites artistic work like David Lynch's "Eat My Fear," where a statue of a cow with a severed head and forks and knives sticking out of its body was supposed to be a part of the New York City "Cow Parade" until being banned by city officials.[156] However, during the last twenty-five years, undercover video has occupied a prioritized position in outreach that tends to occlude these other strategies.

The Food Empowerment Project and VINE Sanctuary provide two alternative models for animal rights activism. Lauren Ornelas founded the Food Empowerment Project in 2007 after consistent frustration with animal rights activists' singular focus on other-than-human animals while ignoring the working and living conditions of workers who are an essential part of the factory farm and slaughterhouse. She highlights, for example, a Eurocentric attitude espoused by many animal rights activists at conferences when they would use the term "America" when referring to the United States as if Latin America didn't exist. Or she would challenge activists on their inherent colonialism in advocating for chapters of their group in the Global South, which replicates an imperial dynamic where power flows from the United States into other countries.[157]

The Food Empowerment Project asks how farmworker interests can be served along with those of other-than-human animals, which requires a more multifaceted approach than most animal rights organizations offer at the moment. For example, the Food Empowerment Project assisted in supplying meals to out-of-work farmworkers as COVID-19 raged.

Miriam Jones and pattrice jones founded the Eastern Shore Chicken Sanctuary in Maryland in 2000 and later moved to Vermont and founded the VINE Sanctuary in 2009. Among animal rights activists, jones is unusual because she had already been involved with LGBTQ+ and antiracist movements in which she developed a skill set that enables her to see the linkages between these struggles and engage diverse communities. For example, when holding campus talks, she asks different groups to collaborate that might not be working together: "It might be an animal rights club. It might be a queer club. . . . I'll say, okay, so can you reach out to someone to cosponsor this with you? And I talked to a room that was about half vegans and half non-vegan, LGBTQ+ folk. And I did a lot of prompting them to think about things they could do together."[158]

Likewise, at home, she holds workshops on vegetable gardening at the local library, understanding that such efforts lead to building community support: "And we may not agree on everything, but I know we all agree that everybody should be eating more fresh fruits and vegetables. And I know we all agree that people should have access to fresh produce." She continues, "This is like the ABCs of coalition work: find something that you can all agree about, work together on that. As you work together on that, you become a more trusted person. And once you're a more trusted person, then you can actually begin to talk about the things that you don't agree about and you'll be listened to and accorded, you know, a fair hearing." Such an outlook, however, has never been a core mission of most other animal rights organizations that remain singularly focused on other-than-human animals to such an extent that they fail to consider how to readjust their messaging and practices to ally themselves with other communities that share related but not necessarily identical interests.

People like Adams, Ornelas, and jones hold a lot of hope for a newer generation of animal rights activists who tend to be women, people of color, or both and hold perspectives that challenge many of the norms and practices that have defined standard operating procedures of animal rights for so long. Adams observes that there are "a lot more people interested in the analysis that frames animal agriculture and anthropocentrism within this larger context of oppression."[159] Ornelas hopes that they will found their own organizations since she considers the current ones too far stuck in regressive ways of thinking.

Breeze Harper, for example, has become one of the leading figures of this new generation. She directly notes that "the tone and delivery of the message [of most animal rights organizations] ... has been offensive to a majority of people of color and working-class people in America."[160] This comes not from ill will but inexperience. Harper reflects that most leaders in animal rights "weren't trained or well-read enough in antiracist and antipoverty praxis to deliver their message to me in a way that connected to my social justice work as a Black working-class female trying to deal with sexism, classism, and racism at Dartmouth."[161]

Some of the central animal rights organizations, as a result, have brought Harper in as a consultant to better educate themselves in antiracist and antipoverty theories that might align with an animal rights mission. For example, John Seber from Mercy for Animals told me how Harper was working with them to assist in conducting programming that is meaningful to a variety of communities as well as establishing adequate salaries for those who work for MFA.

The problem is that many organizations may not even realize how off-putting they might be to communities of color in their framing of issues. For example, repeatedly, leadership of DxE kept emphasizing that veganism is not their group's goal. Cassie King told me, "DxE's theory of change isn't to create more vegans. It isn't to get people to practice consumer choice changes." Similarly, during a virtual training I attended, Almira Tanner stressed, "Personal consumer habits are important moral statements but not enough. We focus on systems, not individuals."[162]

Although it might be true that veganism might not be enough, it actually serves as a vital bridge, especially within Black communities. The NAACP recently advocated for plant-based meals in K–12 schools, hospitals, and prisons.[163] What might seem like only a lifestyle choice to DxE leadership actually constitutes a critical strategy for the decolonization of Black bodies. As Breeze Harper notes, "Black people struggle daily to get access to proper health information, food, and resources to maintain optimal wellness."[164] She continues, "This is why compassionate and environmentally sustainable health and nutritional practice must be part of our antiracist and antipoverty praxis in our own fight against the continued colonization of our Black and brown bodies and the ecosystem."[165] As a result, animal rights groups might want to reconsider the centrality of nutrition and diet in communities where it is not a given. Although from a privileged perspective, regulating one's diet seems like a relatively small matter, within low-wage Black communities often located in food deserts, this proves a significant challenge and goal where heart disease and cancer rank as the top causes of death.[166]

Sunaura Taylor, an outstanding writer who intertwines theory with concrete examples in an engaging writing style, brings disability studies to animal rights activism to mutually illuminate both. She observes how "ableist values are central to animal industries, where the dependency, vulnerability, and presumed lack of emotional awareness or intellectual capacity of animals creates the groundwork for a system that makes billions of dollars in profits off of animal lives."[167]

She also calls out the ableist discourse that pervades much of animal rights. For example, she mentions PETA's "Got Autism" campaign, which riffed off the dairy industry's "Got Milk" advertisements, falsely amplifying the idea that drinking milk leads to autism.[168] Furthermore, even the claim that many animal rights activists make that they are "a voice for the voiceless" is steeped in many problematic assumptions. It is not a simple matter, according to Sunaura, of "identifying who does and who does not have a voice."[169] Animals actually do express themselves in many ways. So maybe instead of considering them voiceless, Sunaura suggests that they are more often "deliberately unheard."[170] And even within human communities, not all are given an equal voice. Usually, the most privileged voices prevail, drowning out others from more marginal positions.

Returning to media, this is not to say that video is no longer needed or that there is no value in exposing the inhuman practices of factory farms, puppy mills, circuses, slaughterhouses, and laboratories to larger audiences. There is always a need to stay updated on the conditions that define these places, so industry cannot claim that documentation is outdated and therefore irrelevant. This footage is also vital in getting a certain new segment of people engaged with animal rights, as many of my interviewees attested to.

However, a significant strategic realignment needs to occur where some of the foundational premises of animal rights activism needs to be reconsidered. Many animal rights organizations genuflect to diversity, inclusion, and equity. However, they remain mired in a single-issue perspective, off-putting rhetoric, and unsustainable, low paying jobs. It is critical that activists must consider how the conditions of employment need to change to support more inclusive voices within the movement. Likewise, they need to seriously reconsider the type of outreach required to ally the animal rights movement with communities that have not necessarily seen animal rights as an important cause, such as the Latinx and Muslim American ones to be discussed later in the book. Anything less will lead to more stasis and seem increasingly out of alignment with other social movements that are taking intersectional concerns seriously.

Additionally, the animal rights movement needs to adopt a more sophisticated understanding of how visual culture operates and the limitations of the politics of visibility that it has long relied upon. The 1999 conference hosted by United Poultry Concerns marked an important moment within the movement, in which the intricacies of framing, aesthetics, and narrative were being discussed along with the videos being screened. More of this analysis needs to occur and engage with the challenges that accompany emerging technologies. What advantages and disadvantages does livestreaming provide? How can video be mobilized in more vital ways than simply distributing it online or arranging a press conference around it? How does social media inhibit and advance the movement?

In many of its practices, animal rights suggests that visibility serves as a main fulcrum for change. But in an age where we are drowning in images and information, such a strategy is no longer adequate, if it ever was. I would repeatedly remind my interviewees that most of my students, friends, and family never heard of their organizations or campaigns in order to point out that what they might consider successful messaging to the public has been largely unheard by most people outside of their circles. So what must they do to change this?

Video and technology are not the sole or even the main solution. Nevertheless, they are vital techniques to be utilized in the struggle. Still, one must remain vigilant against the technological determinism that underlies corporations' messaging—that their technology "will change the world." As this chapter shows, some within the movement are rethinking the carceral logic that defined much of the movement's tactics up until now. And a new generation of animal rights activists from more diverse perspectives are pushing movement thinking and tactics in promising directions beyond simply single-issue concerns around other-than-human animals. Yet questions remain: What new strategies will the animal rights struggle adopt to adequately address the critiques that a new generation of activists are raising? How will video and other forms of technology be employed in achieving this goal?

CHAPTER 2

Here Come the Anarchists

State Repression, Video Activism, and Counter-summit Protesting

U nsteady footage documents protesters marching down crowded streets in Washington, DC, chanting, "Whose streets? Our streets," for twenty long minutes of the forty-five-minute livestream. Around the twenty-one-minute mark, black-clad protesters with matching balaclavas scatter along the sidewalks to smash the windows of a coffee shop. Alexei Wood, the livestreamer, yells off camera, "Whoa, yeah, that was cool." The footage goes from unsteady to turbulent as he is swept along with the crowd fleeing the police and the sound of concussion grenades that trails behind him. After a few blocks, he slows his pace and comments, "It's going to be a long day y'all. Fuck," as his camera focuses upon a couple of police cars lining the street.[1]

Wood became one of the thirty-two journalists who were arrested during the Disrupt J20 protests against Donald Trump's inauguration on January 20, 2017. Tellingly, Wood's livestream footage would play a central role for both the prosecution and the defense. The prosecution argued that Wood's periodic exclamations throughout the video exhibited his conspiracy to riot and encouragement for property destruction. His role as a journalist, according to this account, was nothing more than subterfuge. The defense, on the other hand, noted Wood's long-standing practice as a freelance videographer. It presented his emails to local newspaper editors inquiring to see if they needed coverage of the protests as evidence of his intent to conduct independent journalism. He was facing up to sixty-one years in prison.

Nearly a year later, Wood was found not guilty.[2] The judge cited Wood's video as clear evidence demonstrating that his "personal enthusiasm for destruction...is qualitatively different from urging others to destroy."[3] As we will see throughout this book, video often plays an integral role in courtroom cases where defense and prosecution reframe imagery into narratives that favor their position. These cases illustrate that documentary video alone does not occupy some uncontested space, but marks a central site of struggle between opposing forces.

Ultimately, the meaning of the documentary image does not reside solely in the video alone but must include the surrounding contexts that imbue the video's sounds and images with particular meanings and implications. Although the judge in Wood's case saw the video as self-evident in vindicating his actions, another judge could have just as easily read it in a reactionary direction that supported the prosecution's case. This is not to claim that the documentary image can absorb whatever meaning someone imposes upon it. But it often serves as a point of contestation or cultural struggle between opposing forces, as we will witness in every chapter of this book.

Additionally, not only were more than two hundred people, including journalists, arrested during the J20 protests, but also the Department of Justice demanded the IP addresses of the 1.3 million users who visited the DisruptJ20.org website, which served as an information hub for the protests. Although a judge eventually limited the information the Department of Justice could seize from the site, the government's efforts not only reveal the trail of vulnerable information that organizers and participants leave when mobilizing online but also the extent of governmental efforts in prosecuting it.[4]

These tactics of repression wielded against protesters have longer roots and were given a dress rehearsal nine years earlier during the 2008 Republican National Convention (RNC) in the Twin Cities. Although this chapter will document earlier instances of state repression against independent media and protesters that set the stage for the crackdowns at the 2008 RNC, the state's targeting of both offline and online media activism during the convention marks a moment that anticipates the direction state repression will take during the age of social media. Authorities preemptively detained and harassed media activists before the convention even began and arrested eight youths who created a website where planned protests were announced. Such preemptive actions gain increasing traction as the war on terror rationalizes such actions by law enforcement as being for our own good, even when they clearly are not.

This chapter looks at two major developments regarding activist uses of video during street protests. First, it reveals how video and digital media making have become central activist tactics in exposing state violence through alternative frameworks and distribution networks. Such media making can be used to assist in organizing protests, provide evidence in court to clear protesters of inflated criminal charges, and help to organize support for those charged. Still, as indicated through Wood's example, this same media can be used to provide ways for the state to infiltrate movements and undermine their credibility, as will be demonstrated throughout this book. The second development is that the state has increasingly criminalized dissent by extending the definition of "domestic terrorism" to include many forms of civil disobedience and direct action, which has legitimized police actions like attacking and arresting media makers attending protests. In particular, I focus on the 2003 FTAA (Free Trade Area of the Americas) protests in Miami and the 2008 RNC (Republican National Convention) protests in St. Paul because they represent key moments of state repression against protesters and independent media of the Global North and illustrate some of the innovative strategies video activists have utilized to counter such repression. Nevertheless, as chapter 1 shows, this history builds upon the ways in which largely socioeconomically privileged animal rights and environmental activists were accused of terrorism and sedition against the state two decades earlier.

Neoliberal Influences

Both the escalation of police repression against protesters and the rise of video activism have their origins in the rise of neoliberalism. As various scholars have pointed out, the police need to be understood less as a self-contained institution and more as an organization responsive to a series of internal and external pressures and contexts.[5] The police as an institution are caught in what Michel Foucault has deemed "a technology of power."[6] Such an approach de-emphasizes power originating within a specific institution by instead resituating it more broadly "within the perspective of the constitution of fields, domains, and objects of knowledge"[7] The institution, as a result, is as much a product of these power relations as it is their perpetuator.

A broad body of research has shown how police conduct, tactics, and attitudes result from a host of external pressure from diverse sources placed upon them during specific historical moments. For example, the seemingly contradictory practices of community policing and militarization of the police within the United States arose due to the threat of various urban rebellions throughout the 1960s as well as from the tarnished image the police suffered due to extensive television coverage of their violence against those demonstrating at the 1968 Chicago Democratic National Convention.[8] Recent forms of militarization and the development of Special Weapons and Tactics (SWAT) teams became hardline tactics that police adopted while community policing became the soft line of policing to supposedly win the "hearts and minds" of those communities that they patrolled.[9]

Ronald Reagan's drug war during the 1980s led to the exponential militarization of police. As Petra Bartosiewicz notes, "After Congress relaxed the Posse Comitatus Act [in 1981], which was intended to keep military and domestic policing separate, there was a massive flow of military-grade tanks, helicopters, bomb-sniffing robots, and assault rifles to local police."[10] SWAT teams employing this weaponry led to a rapid increase in the use of deadly force by the mid-1990s.[11] As military researchers and state security officials began to view the police as a new market for their technology and an extension of intelligence gathering, protest activity gradually became evaluated "through the lens of 'threat assessment,' grouping it into a larger category that included terrorism, war, and violent crime."[12]

These changes were accompanied by even larger neoliberal transformations at federal and state levels that redirected funding from welfare and housing to incarceration. Sociologist Loïc Wacquant has demonstrated the complete inversion of money dedicated to public housing in relation to corrections that occurred in the US throughout the 1980s. In 1980, $27.4 billion was allocated to public housing whereas $6.9 billion went toward corrections. By 1990, the numbers inverted with corrections receiving $26.1 billion while public housing was allocated a meager $10.6 billion. He notes, "The construction of prisons has effectively become the country's main public housing program."[13] Wacquant sees the growth of the penal sector as a response to the social upheavals caused by the low-wage, precarious work that increasingly consumed more and more of the population and led to attendant hardships and resistances.[14]

A new neoliberal subjectivity was being ushered in by such macrostructural changes as defunding welfare, privatizing public goods, and precarious and low-wage jobs becoming an increasing percentage of employment. Rather than the state protecting its citizens, the market now dictates the state's practices. Maurizio Lazzarato notes how citizenship is replaced with the figure of the self-made entrepreneur who assumes "the costs as well as the risks of a flexible and financialized economy, costs and risks which are not only—far from it—those of innovation, but also and especially those of precariousness, poverty, unemployment, a failing health system, housing shortages, etc."[15]

As a result of this paradigm shift, the police could not help but alter their views toward protest and protesters in the face of predominating "tough on crime" policies. Meanwhile, structural changes in the global economy were making work ever more precarious and ill-paid and contributing to growing unrest. Intelligence-led policing that promised to save money and increase convictions for local police forces led to partnerships with private corporations that sold the most recent technology. Post-9/11 has led to a tremendous transfer of military technology and logics into the realms of policing, driven largely by the private corporations of the security-industrial complex—though it should be mentioned that the military and police have always had blurred boundaries.[16]

The 2001 USA Patriot Act expanded the definition of terrorism within the US to include any activities intended to "influence the policy of a government by intimidation or coercion."[17] Coupled together with the FBI's dubious claim that terrorism incorporates "violence against property," much direct-action protest and civil disobedience could then be viewed as domestic terrorism. The blurring of criminality, terrorism, and protest increases the likelihood of a militarized response to protest. Police tactics intersecting with militarized outlooks, and economic pressures on the security-industrial complex make it advantageous to market nonlethal crowd dispersal weapons like Tasers, tear gas, and rubber bullets as necessary equipment for police departments.[18] The repressive tactics of the state that were initially aimed against poor communities of color have intensified and expanded into more privileged sectors of the population including those coming from white and/or middle- to upper-class backgrounds who attend counter-summit protests.

Nonetheless, surveillance remains a deeply racialized practice. John Fiske notes, "Surveillance allows different races to be policed differently, and it has an insidious set of 'chilling' effects upon the freedoms of opinion, movement and association that cumulatively produce racially differentiated sense of 'the citizen.'"[19] Surveillance and normalization go hand in hand, as Foucault observed long ago.[20] Whiteness serves as the norm that surveillance wants to protect whereas Blackness often represents the deviation from the norm, particularly in the United States. Tellingly, as will be discussed shortly, when authorities in Minneapolis criminalized the mostly young, white, middle-to-upper class protesters of the RNC 8 in order to defame them, authorities stressed the protesters' hidden and "nefarious" anarchist background, which held certain bestial and racist connotations. Unlike when poor communities of color are targeted by the state and racial signifiers alone can speciously imply their links to criminality, the racial and class privileges of the RNC 8 afforded them a certain protection that most others do not share.

Overall, in a neoliberal, Western world, subjectivity itself provides a key terrain of struggle where capital tries to generate surplus value, such as the free labor and access to personal information that users of social media sites like Facebook and Twitter supply. As a result, video and other forms of digital media production become increasingly important practices for activists, where new collective and resistant forms of subjectivity might form. Media production, distribution, and exhibition/reception are where such critical subjectivities are nurtured and developed.

In the West, many social movements have incorporated video and digital technology into their activism, seeing it not just as a form of documentation but also as an intervention to help build coalitions, bolster support, and directly intervene against corporate and state malfeasance. Media activism builds a counterpublic sphere that challenges the state's narratives and practices by allowing activists the means of producing their own stories and framings along with establishing wider networks of solidarity.[21] With decreasing costs and increasing portability, video became a key form of activism within counter-summit protests by the start of the twenty-first century and afterward. The rise of the internet during the 1990s provided a whole new level of distribution for activist media to blossom, which I explore in the next section.

The Emergence of Indymedia
By the mid-1990s, activists attached with Z Media Institute were conceptualizing how to form an alternative media network to support progressive movements and develop its organizational patterns and practices along ostensibly nonhierarchical lines.[22] During the 1996 Chicago Democratic National Convention, they formed Countermedia, an internet-based news source located in Teamster City, to create an autonomous space for media making open to all. It served as the incipient idea that would blossom

into the Independent Media Center (IMC) during the Seattle 1999 WTO protests.[23]

Unfortunately, convention coverage was plagued with technical and strategic difficulties along with police repression. Evan Henshaw-Plath, one of the central IMC techies, observes, "They didn't have the level of software to make the thing work. It kept crashing. You also didn't have a massively successful protest that gave name to the movement."[24] Additionally, the police actively targeted independent journalists. Participant Jay Sand reported, "Rather than arrest demonstrators, the police seemed to be focusing on the media makers. That surprised us, but in retrospect we realized what that said about both our novelty (kids running around with video cameras making sure the police stayed in line?!) and their appreciation of our effect."[25] This police strategy would be emulated to a certain degree in Seattle and escalated during the 2003 FTAA protests in Miami.

The year 1999 saw the formation of Indymedia at the Seattle WTO, an event that will not be recounted in detail here since it has been well documented elsewhere.[26] During the protests, Indymedia broadcast a half-hour show each day that drew attention to not only the unexpected police violence against demonstrators, but also to the ingenuity of the activists in shutting down the convention. Its website allowed for people to post stories, photographs, and videos in a short time span, a true innovation at the time when social media had not yet been developed. The Indymedia website had over a million hits during the protest and forced commercial media to focus on police repression since the story was being scooped by a bunch of amateurs who made professional journalists look inept.[27]

Although the creation of Indymedia marked a significant development in activists' use of the internet to assist social movements and distribute alternative content, its importance has often been overstated. For example, even though the website provided unprecedented access, one should keep in mind that in 1999 only 50 percent of US households had computers.[28] Furthermore, 70 percent of the households that had access to the internet had a median income of over $75,000 per year. Only 18.8 percent of households making under $15,000 a year had internet capabilities.[29] So access to the website was deeply class dependent.

Also, *Showdown in Seattle*, the IMC's five-day broadcast during the 1999 WTO protest, has often been championed as incorporating hundreds of individuals' video footage into its series. But in reality, most footage was provided by only seven media groups—Pepper Spray Productions, Paper

Tiger Television, Changing America, Whispered Media, Headwaters Action Video Collective, Video Active, and Free Speech TV—who occupied the editing house, which unlike the Indymedia Center, was not open access. As Eric Galatas, one of the initiators of Indymedia, observes about the seven media collectives: "They would shoot what they wanted to shoot. They stayed up all night long and then edited their footage into short segments. I was down in the media center ingesting tapes, making sure they were labeled and filled out the proper forms. But they were rarely using things other than their own footage. Probably because they knew what they wanted to shoot, they had good B-roll films. But in actuality there were maybe five or six cameras telling those stories you saw on *Showdown*."[30] This lack of democratic access produced some hard feelings among other video groups that participated in the protests.[31]

Regardless of these limitations, however, Indymedia represented a threat to government and law enforcement officials who wanted to shield their repressive and violent actions from public view. This footage was used at the time of the protests to offer alternative understandings of events and directly intervene during tense moments between protesters and cops in the hope of de-escalating tensions between them. It was also employed later as evidence used to acquit protesters who had been arrested under false charges and for prosecuting police by documenting their use of unjustifiable force.

Tellingly, the lesson learned by Seattle's police after the protests was not to use less force in the future, but instead to become better prepared by amassing more police and weapons while keeping protesters at a greater distance from official venues. In general, Seattle caused a crisis for police nationwide in the US and led to a reassessment of tactics.[32] The ghost of the WTO hung over all future protests in the Global North and was often used as justification for escalated militarized and intelligence-led strategies.

Repression Builds

The counter-summit protests against the G8 in Genoa, Italy, in 2001 marked a new development in state violence against protesters and independent media. A twenty-three-year-old demonstrator was shot dead by the police. On the night of July 21, the police invaded a school where protesters were sleeping. Over ninety people were relentlessly beaten, dragged outside, and arrested.[33] Across the street, the Indymedia Center was raided. According to one participant, the police "crashed through the front gates of the Indymedia

Center in an armored truck, then smashed up computers, confiscated files and film and broke cameras, terrorizing the journalists inside."[34]

Such actions were not simply representative of a few police officers gone rogue. Instead, it was a deliberate effort by the state to intimidate protesters and quash their use of alternative media. As Silvia Federici and George Caffentzis concluded at the time, "What happened in Genoa reflects a premeditated institutional plan to repress and terrorize the demonstrators, to convince them to never again participate in such protest."[35] Silvio Berlusconi, who was prime minister of Italy during the protests, dismissed such police violence as necessary in countering "the violent anarchists who had wrecked the city."[36]

With the arrival of the FTAA protests in Miami in 2003, a new model of repression, later deemed "the Miami model," became fully apparent. Numerous newspaper articles spread widespread fear of the supposed hordes of anarchists about to invade Miami. The stories written conjured the worst clichés of an unwashed and violent anarchist mass. References were made regarding how the "smell of body odor hung in the humid air."[37] Police Chief John Timoney was routinely quoted warning how protesters were nothing but "outsiders coming in to terrorize and vandalize our city."[38]

This demonization of anarchists by the commercial media and police provides a vast oversimplification of how anarchist practices have been increasingly incorporated into new social movements developing since the 1960s. As scholars like Andrew Cornell, Francesca Polletta, and Barbara Epstein note, anarchist practices like consensus-based decision-making, the use of direct-action techniques, and the desire for nonhierarchical relations define key aspects of many new social movements.[39] Although most participants of new social movements do not primarily identify themselves as anarchists, they nonetheless share anarchist affinities in how their organizations should operate and the protest tactics they utilize.

But the need to stress and demonize protesters' anarchist backgrounds speaks to the racism that underlies state surveillance. According to John Fiske, "Surveillance is a technology of normalization that identifies and discourages the cultural expression and behavior of social formations that differ from those of the dominant."[40] In the West and in the United States in particular, poor communities of color represent deviance from the norm. We see this most visibly demonstrated in the racist tropes of commercial news and in reality television shows like Cops that routinely portray African American men as criminals.[41]

Western counter-summit protesters, however, are not solely from disadvantaged groups. Many of the participants have privileged white and middle-class backgrounds and therefore provide a unique problem for authorities. To criminalize a demographic of the population that normally serves as the norm requires other means, so anarchism becomes the new marker to signify deviant behavior. If Fiske is correct in deeming surveillance "a machine of whiteness," *anarchism* signifies that these white, middle-class protesters are not what they seem.

Demonizing anarchists as black-clad young thugs engaging in property destruction serves another purpose for law enforcement—to justify massive expenditures on personnel, military equipment, and other security devices as well as to rationalize the use of more repressive and violent actions against protesters. Miami represented a massive escalation of repressive tactics: flooding of the streets with police (both undercover and uniformed); preemptive arrests of peaceful protesters; and police surveillance of all kinds before, during, and after the protests such as planting informants in key meetings discussing upcoming protest actions.[42]

The state manufactures and stresses the delinquency of anarchists in order to undermine the validity of certain protest movements. As Foucault observes, the disciplinary apparatus of a punitive society does not attempt to quash delinquency, but instead promotes delinquency in order to profit from it and render more systemic resistances ineffectual. "It is not so much that they [the punitive society and its disciplines] render docile those who are liable to transgress 'the law,'" he notes. "But that they tend to assimilate the transgression of the law in a general tactics of subjection.... In short, penalty does not simply 'check' illegalities; it 'differentiates' them, it provides them with a general 'economy.'"[43] The defense against "anarchist hoodlums" has become one of the most significant alibis of the state in transferring enormous amounts of public money to private companies in order to further militarize police and cast a wider net of surveillance over public spaces.

Taking a cue from our practices in Iraq, most commercial media reporters were embedded with police units in Miami. Independent journalists who remained unattached were routinely arrested and at times beaten as had happened to Ana Nogueira of *Democracy Now!* and Celeste Fraser Delgado, a *New Times* reporter. Naomi Klein suggested that the repression in Miami represented "the official homecoming of the 'war on terror.' The latest techniques honed in Iraq—from a Hollwoodesque military to a militarized media—have now been used on a grand scale in a major US city."[44]

The Miami IMC produced a full-length video, *The Miami Model* (2004), which offered a sophisticated notion of how such repression was coordinated between the police, the commercial news, and local government. The video was shot during the protests by forty to fifty people, mostly from out of town, who were assembled into ten different editing teams based upon their geographic origin. After the footage had been shot, each group covering a specific section of the film returned home to work on collectively editing it. After each individual section had been assembled, the rough cuts were then mailed to the San Francisco IMC for the final cut. There a select group worked on postproduction, color correction, the insertion of graphics, and fine editing that created a more coherent film.[45] In many ways, Indymedia productions like this represent an auteurless cinema where issues of coherence, singular vision, and artistic perfection give way to more immediate concerns like creating a timely release to provide alternative reportage and analysis of an event that could mobilize future actions. It is an opening gambit to imagine what an anarchist type of film production might look like.

The Miami Model addresses the linkages between the city's passing of a reactionary ordinance against the right to protest and the commercial news media's implicit support for such legislation. In one sequence, we witness the implementation of a 2003 protest ordinance that requires groups of eight or more people meeting for over thirty minutes to get a permit. It also outlaws two or more people drawing public attention and disrupting the flow of traffic. Tellingly, before focusing on the November 13 city council meeting where the ordinance is passed, a series of news clips play. A local NBC news anchor introduces her segment claiming, "Tonight we take you inside the anarchists' world for some answers." Sensationalist footage from the 1999 WTO Seattle protests follows showing burning trash dumpsters, youths clad in black returning volleys of exploding tear gas canisters, and a police cruiser with an anarchist symbol spray-painted on it. The newscaster states, "Miami is supposedly the next target." The footage then cuts to the November 13 city council meeting. This news footage reveals how disinformation provided by the commercial news that characterizes counter-summit protesting as nothing more than hordes of black-clad anarchists descending onto the city to destroy property encourages the creation of such reactionary legislation. This sequence in *The Miami Model* weaves together the links between commercial news hype and draconian city legislation that are both premised upon false and reactionary information.[46]

The sequence is followed by handheld footage of the cops harassing protesters. In a faux friendly tone, a burly bike cop tells a group of people that they have to disperse within twenty minutes if they don't have a permit. When asked why twenty minutes, the cop states that other police had already been observing them for ten minutes. The cop peppers his threats with pseudo friendly phrases like, "We'll be here to make sure you guys are safe." But the real message is: If you defy this ordinance, we will crush you.

The video exposes how sensationalistic news reports enable the local city government to enact reactionary legislation that further allows the cops to harass the city's populace. It is not simply the problem of a few renegade cops, but a systemic issue where commercial news, city officials, the police, and corporations ally their interests against human rights and free speech in the name of "public safety." The film later points out that the *Miami Herald* donated $217,000 of advertising in support of the FTAA and $62,500 in cash to subsidize the summit. The notion of unbiased reporting gets jettisoned when a news organization invests in the event that it is covering.

Essentially, this sequence exemplifies Michel Foucault's notion that the state is the product of transversal power relations where power does not originate from a single source but instead courses through institutions and various practices to establish its hold. *The Miami Model* notes how state power seeps into both micro- and macro-relationships that traverse public and private terrains.[47] This is demonstrated during one sequence where poor Black Overtown residents are interviewed about how they were encouraged by the police to beat-up independent journalists and steal their equipment. According to one resident, whose face has been blacked out, "The police told us to rob y'all. The police told us to beat their ass. Rob them. Whatever y'all take from them. Be we said, no. Why should we rob them?" Here we have testimonials that attest to the police encouraging illegal behavior in order to disrupt the functioning of independent media—yet again showing the police manufacturing delinquency in order to undercut a more threatening resistance.

Overall, the sequence traces the lateral ways in which state power operates in its attempt to co-opt historically disenfranchised people into repressing independent media. It also reveals, however, that embedded within the circulation of state power is resistance or what Foucault calls "counter-conduct," explained as "the sense of struggle against the processes implemented for conducting others."[48] The refusal of Overtown residents to engage in such practices against protesters and their understandable mistrust of a police force that has repeatedly harassed them in the past, suggests the dialectical nature of state power and repression that attempts to absorb individuals into a wide network of practices but also makes a space for fissures of resistance within them.

RNC 2008 and the RNC 8

Law enforcement's labeling of some protest actions during the 2008 RNC protests as "domestic terrorism" speaks to a longer history of casting these charges in response to mostly white animal rights and environmental activists two decades earlier as documented in chapter 1. The passage of the 1992 Animal Enterprise Protection Act (AEPA) and the 2006 Animal Enterprise Terrorism Act (AETA) coupled with the Patriot Act's expanded notion of terrorism to include civil disobedience and direct-action protest has led to the imprisonment of a series of activists for criminal property damage, who would have earlier received no more than a misdemeanor.[49]

Fifty million dollars were spent on security for the 2008 RNC.[50] By contrast, security for the FTAA protests in Miami in 2003 cost $8–$12 million.[51] By August 29, 2007, local law enforcement had already begun to surveil protest groups in response to the appearance of the RNC Welcoming Committee Website.[52] The Welcoming Committee consisted of a group of mostly white, middle-to-upper-class college-aged participants who were self-described anarchists, who while not engaged in any protest actions of their own, assisted outside protest groups in coordinating their demonstrations. They did, however, help to establish what became known as the St. Paul principles. The principles supported a variety of protest actions taking place—from moderate ones like marching to more aggressive ones like direct confrontation with the police, denounced any form of state repression, and demanded that criticism of protest actions remain internal.[53]

The police became alarmed by the inflammatory rhetoric appearing on the RNC Welcoming Committee website, such as its insistence: "What we create here will send the convention crashing off course into insignificance."[54] Equally alarming to the police was a short promotional video produced by the RNC Welcoming Committee in 2007 for the upcoming protests, "We're Getting Ready" (2007).[55] The video self-mockingly portrayed the Twin Cities as solely occupied by black-clad and masked anarchists engaged in mundane actions like eating breakfast, going to work, and raising kids. Blondie's "One Way or Another" plays over the soundtrack as we follow one female anarchist to the convention center where the RNC will be

FIGURE 2.1: "We're Getting Ready" (2007), a tongue-in-cheek promotional video created by the RNC Welcoming Committee for upcoming protests against the 2008 Republican National Convention in the Twin Cities, was used by prosecutors to argue that the group was advocating for violence by having a Molotov cocktail within the video.

FIGURE 2.2: Conveniently overlooked by the state was the humorous tone of the video, particularly mocking clichés of bomb throwing anarchists by having the Molotov land in a grill to fire it up.

held. By the video's end, distant framing shows the edifice of the convention center dominating the screen, suggesting the convention's oppressive and outsized presence. The video cuts to black with white words announcing: "We're Getting Ready RNC 2008 St. Paul/ Prernc Aug 31–Sep 3 07." The video directs the viewer to the RNC Welcoming Committee website for more information.

The video inverts some of the derogatory clichés that haunt anarchists. For example, we see a masked woman with bolt cutters moving toward a fence inviting the viewer to conclude that she is about to cut through the fence and invade someone's property. But instead, she hands the cutters to another anarchist who uses them to trim nearby hedges. In another sequence, the same female anarchist is seen lighting a Molotov cocktail and lobbing it over a fence. But when the sequence cuts to over the fence, we see the Molotov land in an open BBQ, helpfully igniting it as a black-clad and masked anarchist in a chef's hat gives a thumbs up for the help. Gus Ganley, who shot the video, highlights its absurdist intentions: "Sarah Palin, she was the most absurd candidate at the time. The economic collapse was just about to erupt. We were living through absurd times. In the face of that widespread absurdity, there was no other way to respond but in kind."[56]

Despite the video's playful tone, it ignited a $300,000 investigation into the Welcoming Committee and led to the infiltration of the group by a series of undercover officers along with recruiting informers from within it.[57] The Ramsey County police department became particularly alarmed at the presence of a Molotov cocktail in the video and used it as evidence to justify a series of raids and "preemptive" arrests the weekend before the convention. The search warrant for the raids notes, "During one scene, an individual (identified as Carrie Feldman by several sources) is seen throwing a Molotov cocktail."[58] Tellingly, the police apply a selective close reading of the video that excludes the sequence of the Molotov landing in a BBQ that follows, which would have revealed the video's humorous intentions. As I will show later, the reference to Molotov cocktails takes on particular importance, since the FBI used an informant to encourage some protesters to manufacture Molotov cocktails in order to justify state repression against them. According to Ganley, "That was the smoking gun. It is lighting a grill. But according to the police, 'They are preparing to light off Molotov cocktails.' They set up the RNC 8 to be terrorist conspirators."

Interestingly, however, the police would offer more detailed analysis of the video when it suited their purposes. The warrant observes: "The video depicts several persons dressed in 'black bloc' attired with their faces covered to disguise their identity. It should be noted that 'black bloc' is not a particular group, but a tactic that typically dresses in black with faces covered and have caused significant property damage and carried out acts of violence towards law enforcement in the past." Although the fact that black bloc is a tactic is irrelevant to the point that people who engage in it might attack cops, labeling it as a tactic adds nuance and a sense of authority to a report that is largely inaccurate.

Elsewhere, the warrant notes: "Also, Feldman also [sic] rolls a bowlilng ball labled [sic] 'RABL' in front of a military recruiting station. It should be noted that RABL is an acronym for an anarchist group known as the Revolutionary Anarchist Bowling League. The RABL was responsible for vandalizing military recruiting stations by throwing bowling balls through the windows." This attention to detail contrasts against purely fabricated readings like "the video depicts an individual throwing rocks at persons dressed as riot police." The video has no such scene.

If anything, the warrant reveals the high stakes that accompany their selective close reading of the video and signals a common tactic used by other federal and state officials in relation to other videos, as we will see throughout this book. In the RNC 8 case, the seeming obliviousness to the video's satirical and humorous intent and its omission from the video's analysis allowed the Ramsey County police to interpret the video as a dire warning rather than a sophomoric prank, a matter of domestic terrorism rather than a tongue-in-cheek, self-mocking portrayal of the anarchist community. And, in this case, because a judge takes the police interpretation of the video at its word, six members from the Welcoming Committee were arrested the weekend before the protests. Two others were arrested on September 1. They were not released until after the convention. The group was soon christened by the local activist community as "the RNC 8."

The commercial press largely endorsed law enforcement's preemptive arrests and raids, explaining that the inhabitants of the five houses that were raided were supposedly hording feces and urine and dismissed them as out-of-control anarchists. Law enforcement claimed to have "had information it [urine] would be thrown at police during the convention."[59] The threat of anarchists lobbing bodily waste at police has been a typical smear campaign used by police since the 1999 Seattle protests even though there has never been any evidence of this threat actually having been carried out.[60] But as Lesley J. Wood has shown, such disinformation is a useful tactic in dehumanizing protesters and depoliticizing their actions, thus making their arrests seem justifiable to the general public.[61] Furthermore, the anarchist association with feces and urine stresses surveillance's racist practices that need to provide additional labels to dehumanize white protesters in ways that had been commonly done to people of color for centuries simply through their skin color and other racially charged symbols like clothing.

These preemptive raids and arrests also mainly targeted independent media personnel. One of the duplexes raided prior to the convention housed I-Witness Video. I-Witness was a New York-based video organization that documented police abuse to serve as evidence later in court for defendants. During the 2004 RNC in New York City I-Witness had four hundred cases dismissed through its video evidence.[62] In addition to the raid before the 2008 convention, law enforcement raided their house a second time during the convention week. Although no one was arrested and no equipment was confiscated, the raids disrupted the group's work preparing to document the protests. Earlier in the week, three members of the Glass Bead Collective, also from Manhattan, had been stopped by the police. Their computers and video equipment were confiscated and not returned until after the convention, thereby rendering their work to document the protests much more difficult.[63]

Unembedded reporters and video crews were also targeted during the convention. Three members of the independent progressive news show *Democracy Now!* were attacked by the police and arrested. When Amy

Goodman, one of those arrested and executive producer of the show, asked Police Chief John Harrington how the press was supposed to operate under such conditions, he replied, "by embedding reporters in our mobile field force."[64] In other words, he suggests that the only way freedom of the press could be exercised was if it were contained to the perspective of the police.

In total, there were over 800 arrests during the four days of the convention. Of these cases, 578 were eventually either dismissed or declined.[65] The great number of arrests demonstrates that they were clearly less about stopping crime than about the wholesale removal of protesters from the streets by any means necessary. Multiple lawsuits were filed and won against the city for unlawful arrest, police brutality, and the curtailment of civil liberties. The three members from *Democracy Now!*, for example, won a $100,000 settlement.[66] But the most pressing issue by the end of the convention week was the arrest of the RNC 8, all of whom were being initially prosecuted under enhanced terrorism charges.

The RNC 8 and the Use of Video as Arrestee Support

Monica Bicking, Garrett Fitzgerald, Erik Oseland, Nathanael Secor, Eryn Trimmer, Luce Guillén-Givins, Rob Czernik, and Max Specktor comprised the RNC 8. They were charged with enhanced terrorism for a "conspiracy to riot" and a "conspiracy to commit criminal damage to property in the first degree" as defined by Minnesota's even more draconian version of the Patriot Act.[67] The Community RNC Arrestee Support Structure (CRASS) and the Committee to Defend the RNC 8 formed to assist the RNC 8 and others arrested on false charges. CRASS provided arrestee support such as sending letters to those jailed, offering travel funds and housing to those from out of state who wanted to fight their charges, providing benefit shows to raise money for prison support, and sending money to prisoners' commissary funds.[68] Most relevant regarding the use of independent media, was the video *Terrorizing Dissent* (2008) produced by Twin Cities IMC and the Glass Bead Collective and used by both groups to raise funds for and support the RNC 8.

Terrorizing Dissent is composed of four sections. Each section had a separate editor. The first three were edited in St. Paul by the Twin Cities Indymedia collective whereas the final section was edited in NYC by Glass Bead. Vlad Teichberg, a former derivatives trader on Wall Street who used the money he earned to go into independent video and form the Glass Bead Collective, served as the director of the project. According to Teichberg,

"The only thing I did was to make sure that each subsection [of the video] connected together."[69] *The Miami Model* provided inspiration and guidance for those involved in the making of *Terrorizing Dissent*.

The infrastructure to provide footage for what would become *Terrorizing Dissent* had long been established. Twin Cities Indymedia, founded in 2000, provided a central group of videographers to film the protests and police. Similarly in 2000, Communities United Against Police Brutality (CUAPB), formed as a response to the killing of Alfred "Abuka" Sanders by the police who had shot him over thirty-three times, enlisted people who could copwatch and videotape protests during the convention as well as supply legal support. After the Glass Bead's house was raided by the police, Michelle Gross, founder of CUAPB, housed them and members from the IMC in the Walker Church where they would edit the film for the next few months.[70]

A full-length film was not initially envisioned, but with the growing mischaracterization of the RNC 8 as domestic terrorists, a longer video became necessary in terms of support and creating a counternarrative to the state's version of events. As Dan Feidt, the director of the third section of *Terrorizing Dissent*, recalls, "We had these piles of videos around. There was a sense that we needed to, yeah, partly pick up the loose ends, partly nail down deceptions that the state did."[71]

Originally, Twin Cities IMC wanted to release short clips before distributing the entire film. But Feidt notes, "We didn't have the time to do that.... The idea was to attract people's interests with short clips and then hit them with the movie. We did one that took nine days to do—managing huge volumes of information in the process. But we were critiqued for taking so long to edit it."

So instead, they focused their energy on producing the film itself. In particular, its third section entitled "And Then They Came for the Anarchists" directly addresses the RNC 8 and serves as a corrective to the misinformation that the commercial media and Ramsey County sheriff's department disseminated. According to Feidt, "We confronted the RNC 8 about how they wanted themselves represented. That quarter of it became their defining thesis explanation." It was this section that was widely screened among activist communities in the St. Paul area and elsewhere for arrestee support.

The third section humanizes the RNC 8 and others caught up in the preemptive raids as scared college students, not devious criminals as the sheriff's office insisted. Their testimonials counter the misinformation regarding the raids propagated by the commercial media. For example, the video presents a sequence from the local news that shows a police officer looking through buckets on the floor of the evidence room explaining, "They've been collecting urine for some time in bottles and buckets." We never see into the bucket to justify his claim, but a voice-over of the female news anchor nevertheless lists, "Five gallons of urine, bricks, baseball bats, and even a slingshot." We see footage of the items followed by two police officers holding ends of a three-person slingshot with another officer demonstrating how it works. He states matter of fact while doing so, "Rocks... for the cops." The seamless dialogue between newscaster and police officer reveals the unquestioning nature of the commercial news and how it serves to bulwark police misinformation.

But a montage of testimonials by those who had been raided follows. Tom Greiling explains in a moderate tone, "My tools were taken [he laughs] because they assumed they were for... I don't know what. A thousand dollars' worth of tools they took... so I was out of business in regards to scraping." A white, male youth follows by stating, "They love to pretend that we are always hording feces and pee. Of course, they did not find any feces or pee." A woman named Carol further explains while speaking at a public event, "In this house it worked like there was this bucket underneath the sink. The pipes were disconnected so that the water from the sink would drain into the bucket. We then take that bucket upstairs to use it to flush the toilets."

The calm demeanor of those who were raided counters the stereotypical image of wild and irrational anarchist protesters. They seemed rational compared to the police who manufactured the most absurd fears about a group of college-aged protesters. By directly challenging the state's demonization of them as anarchists who horde feces and urine, the interviewees implicitly reassert their racial and class privileges through their accounts in their composed manner and measured words by employing standard grammatical English rather than slang or profanity. The testimonials establish "white" cultural signifiers in terms of their style of speech, dress, and demeanor. Their retelling of the raids and arrests allows them to gain control over a situation that overwhelmed them at the time.

The testimonials are juxtaposed with handheld footage of the raids taken by the house's inhabitants. For example, we see the police attempting to deliver a search warrant to one of the duplexes raided. Roughly framed footage shows a cop at the door speaking to one of the house's female inhabitants. A group of uniformed police officers hovers menacingly just outside the doorway. When he shows the woman the warrant, however, she notes,

FIGURE 2.3: Police provide a search warrant for the wrong house in *Terrorizing Dissent* (Twin Cities IMC and Glass Bead Collective, 2008).

"That is not our address." Another woman off-frame says, "They can't do that. It doesn't cover both houses." While we watch the woman step outside and speak to the police, the woman off-frame explains to the camera, "So we're in one half of the house. This is 949. The warrant said 951." This provides an interesting moment that not only reveals the bungling of the police department, but also the attempts by white, middle-class activists to gain control of the situation by challenging the police, filming them, and explaining to future viewers the situation. Video making allows participants to step temporarily outside of the moment of police intimidation by using video and legal knowledge to create a certain critical distance. The police initially back off.

Yet moments later, footage follows looking up the stairs leading to a door connecting both houses. The door flies open as the cops demand, "Come out with your hands up!" The camera backs away into the living room as the cops enter it with guns drawn directly at the camera. As the cops zip-tie the inhabitants, the camera continues to film discretely from the hip until a cop says, "No, you can't hold onto it. You're being detained right now." The scene goes black.

Such moments reveal the porous nature of activist documentary filmmaking where activism and video production merge. Patricia Zimmermann notes that such filming "unsettles the very space of politics and views the space of the film and the space of the political as different registers organized around a site that is jointly shared."[72] The camera's

FIGURE 2.4: Using the camera as a buffer in *Terrorizing Dissent* to carve out a sense of agency during intimidating moments.

presence is not to simply document what is occurring, but also to keep the police on guard, letting them know that their actions can and will be used against them either in court as evidence or in future documentaries like *Terrorizing Dissent*. Video making provides a moment of intervention, particularly for those who hold certain racial and class privileges, which challenges the police's authority and unilateral control of the situation. It allows for a space of agency for those filming in what are often extremely tense and intimidating situations. It is a form of activism that wants to differentiate itself from the activism that it is documenting so that the space of the film can act as a buffer between those filming and the space of the political unfolding before it, perhaps creating new opportunities of resistance in the process.

Additionally, this sequence demonstrates the significant power of activist documentaries to "make struggle visceral" rather than address viewers at a solely intellectual level, as Jane Gaines notes.[73] Such footage can be used later to mobilize future participants. Therefore, in regard to this section of *Terrorizing Dissent*, it was crucial that the video makers capture the confrontation between police and activists to convey the sense of struggle and the contradictory emotions of fear and assertiveness in the moment, to model for future activists both successful and unsuccessful interventions by participants to counter the police, and to generate outrage within viewers at the civil liberties blatantly being violated to motivate them to become further involved in the struggle. Yet as repeatedly stated, filmmakers' ability to do so

FIGURES 2.5, 2.6 & 2.7: Through its editing and use of music, *Terrorizing Dissent* shows anarchism in action as individuals weave a collective account of what occurred without any singular voice predominating.

effectively is partially contingent upon mobilizing certain class and racial privileges in their interactions with the police and before the camera.

The third section of *Terrorizing Dissent* also powerfully stitches together the RNC 8's accounts into one collective story. For example, the video unites the RNC 8's narrative of state repression through montage by making their individual accounts cohere into a singular tale. All of the individuals are filmed in typical talking head shots in different locations, encouraging the viewer to see their accounts as a single narrative by employing the same shot, thus visually uniting them. Monica Bicking starts by stating, "You need an enemy to justify the raids. None of their stories...works without an enemy." Max Specktor continues, "They're charging the eight of us because of the organizing work that we did." Rob Czernik adds, "By labeling us leaders of the Welcoming Committee it shows a complete nonunderstanding of what anarchism means." Erik Oseland explains anarchism as "people actually being in charge of their own lives rather than a president or congress or a police officer." The montage continues with others members of the RNC 8 completing each other's thoughts. Near the end, Luce states, "The point is we want a society where we don't even need to protest in the first place. How to get to that society? That's the question.... We want a different world." Erik concludes, "They don't want protests organized by people who are too radical for them to co-opt." Although the subjects are filmed in different locations like a coffee shop and a park, their words and shared outlook further unites them. Finally, a musical score plays underneath the subjects' accounts, further cementing them into a unified whole.

The stitching together of protesters' anarchist vision to create one seamless narrative demonstrates anarchism in the video's very form so that no one voice trumps any others but instead, voices are mutually complementary. Their collective account of anarchism and the police's fear of anarchist organizing provides a coherent if somewhat naive understanding of their situation and the threat they represent to some. The collective montage of their account dramatically contrasts with the aesthetic form of the commercial news that generally relates the raids and the RNC 8 through the sole account of an authority figure, normally the news anchor, who often misrepresents the events and protesters' motivations. Unlike the unilateral authority presented by the commercial news that positions viewers as submissive and uncritical, *Terrorizing Dissent* uses a collective form to relate alternative understandings of the raids, anarchism, and the protests that encourages viewers to become involved. It creates a pluralized identity, a common element in many activist documentaries.[74] Yet their alternative understanding is deeply dependent upon culturally white, middle-class mores: measured speech where emotions remain subdued with speakers using midwestern grammatical English and refraining from profanity or even emphatic gestures while speaking. Their presentation is denatured, devoid of any behavior that might negatively connote ethnic or racial signifiers or origins.

The video's ability to assist in creating an alternative collective subjectivity and build coalitions was fully realized when it was used for local and national screenings to raise money and other support for the RNC 8. A typical screening in the Twin Cities would consist of a potluck at some public location. According to Gus Ganley, who edited the video's third section, "People would bring some food and jerry-rig a screen at the back of a bookstore and screen either the whole film or a section of it. Q&A would follow with me or another member of the IMC or a member of the RNC 8 answering questions."[75]

Screenings were particularly important, according to Melissa Hill, a member of the Twin Cities IMC, because they "would bring in people who were not necessarily active on the streets like people of the art community or the local community. It was a good way to get people together in a room to talk about the issues and fundraise."[76] Because it took over two years for the RNC 8's legal troubles to conclude, screenings and other events kept their case public and widely discussed, in essence creating a counterpublic sphere that rejected the narratives promoted by law enforcement authorities and mainstream news while capitalizing upon the racial and class privileges belonging to most of the RNC 8.

Hill recalls, "The RNC Defense Committee put together a series of events every Friday. There was a dinner and a different theme each week. This week was on Indymedia. Last week was radical spaces. Another was on COINTELPRO. The RNC 8 was supposed to have a trial in November or December 2010, so we wanted to have a film screening during every Friday to mobilize."[77]

Screenings were done in conjunction with other fundraising events like benefit shows, house parties, as well as the selling of T-shirts at events and meetings.[78] Michelle Gross recalls holding garage sales: "We had more crap than you can think of. People were buying a T-shirt and giving us $20 for a T-shirt when you would normally charge much less. I couldn't believe how generous people were."[79]

Also, there was an organized campaign against Susan Gaertner who was the prosecuting attorney against the RNC 8 and who was running for governor in 2010. For example, during Gaertner's birthday party at the Minneapolis Athletic Club, protesters created a mobile dance rig to throw a protest dance party, reminiscent of a Reclaim the Streets action that had become popular during the mid-1990s. A series of helium balloons held streamers draping down that demanded: "Drop the prosecution of the RNC 8." Gross proudly notes, "Everywhere she went, we showed up. We killed her campaign."

Equally important, while the RNC 8 engaged in its defense, CUAPB requested the footage from the hundreds of street cameras that the city installed for the convention. After much balking, the city provided them with eight hard drives of footage. CUAPB immediately uplinked the footage to a central server and linked it to a webpage where people who were fighting charges could search for the date and location of their arrests to see if there was any accompanying exonerating footage. Many defendants used this footage in court to beat their charges. The footage remained online until 2012 when the church where it was housed burned down under suspicious circumstances.[80]

Although the exact impact of *Terrorizing Dissent* on the RNC 8's cases cannot be known, it nonetheless provided vital support for the accused to continue to fight their felony charges and buy some time. By April 8, 2009, all terrorism charges were dropped, and eventually all conspiracy felony charges were dropped, too. On August 27, 2010, Erik Oseland pled guilty to a gross misdemeanor and served ninety-one days in jail. Bicking, Guillén-Givins, and Trimmer had their charges dropped. The remaining four—Fitzgerald, Secor, Czernik, and Specktor—pled guilty to misdemeanor charges with no time served and between one and two years of probation with some community service. Yet the RNC 8's legal troubles put a considerable strain on their relationships with each other and the larger activist community. In addition, the infiltration of the group by government informers had a significant traumatic impact.

A Brief History of Agents Provocateurs and Informants

Michel Foucault observes, "The penitentiary is in reality a much broader phenomenon than imprisonment, that what is involved is a general dimension of all the social controls that characterize societies like ours. The penitentiary element, of which the prison is only one expression, is a feature of the whole society."[81] In his classic book *Discipline and Punish*, he refers to this as the carceral network that extends in quantity and scope to influence the functioning of hospitals, schools, and public and private enterprises.[82] One core element of the carceral network is surveillance, which comprises "a network of relations from top to bottom, but also to a certain extent from bottom to top and laterally."[83]

Before they were even arrested, the RNC 8 was already enmeshed in this system of surveillance more than they knew. Not only had the police been tracking them since 2007 with the appearance of the Welcoming Committee website, but a vast network of informers that initially focused on eco-activists, and was extended considerably after 9/11 (mainly targeting Muslim Americans, as the final chapter of this book will show), had already infiltrated their ranks. As Foucault notes, the use of informers and agents provocateurs is one of the most insidious ways to establish "a means of perpetual surveillance of the population; an apparatus that makes it possible to supervise, through the delinquents themselves, the whole social field."[84] The use of informers has exploded in numbers since 9/11. Whereas the government only employed around 1,500 informers in 1972, by 2014 there were roughly 15,000 in circulation.[85]

Indymedia, almost from its inception, was plagued with disruptions that might have been caused by agents provocateurs. Most often, however, the infiltration remains unclear. A disruptive person would enter the group, which led to chaos, often capitalizing upon the weaknesses of the specific Indymedia chapter. In 2001, for example, the Twin Cities IMC, which had

an entirely different staff than it had in 2008, was accused of racist practices. The charge had some validity. John Slade, one of its founders, admits,
"The group probably had some white and middle-class privilege going on.
Although there was a political range between the Green Party to anarchists
to communists, there was a lack of self-consciousness towards race."[86] Yet
the one person of color, an African immigrant, addressed the matter in an
extremely hostile manner—less willing to discuss the issue than simply
accuse others and disrupt meetings.

Similarly, at the Miami IMC, one Hispanic participant objected to some
of the procedures in developing the website and running the meetings.
Although some members suspected him of being an agent and attempted
to do a background check on the individual, they could not locate much
information about him to prove or disprove their suspicions. Participants
could not determine if the disruptive person was a plant or simply someone
with interpersonal issues. The members of the IMC could never absolutely
be sure since, as participant Jeff Keating admits, "We were not taking the
time to understand where other people were coming from. There were no
Black people involved in it. The Hispanic people wanted to do their own
site."[87] Since the IMC was in a rush to establish itself before the upcoming
2003 FTAA, its participants never engaged in adequate community outreach
and organizing.

These two cases are revealing in that their inability to identify whether
the person was an agent provocateur at work stems from larger issues like
racial privilege and inexperience at community outreach that plagued both
IMC chapters. In many ways, these two instances signal one of the major
failures of the creation of IMCs and much anarchist organizing in general:
a naive notion that tends to overvalorize individual will at the expense of
never adequately addressing the socioeconomic limits that do not allow
people to participate equally in such projects. Because of the absence of
community outreach and organizing that should inform the development
of an IMC, the project takes precedence over the people. Thus, infiltration
by outside agents is easier because no significant relationships have developed among the participants before the establishment of the IMC.[88] Also,
confirming instances of infiltration was nearly impossible since a network
of trust was restricted to certain privileged actors within the IMC and did
not extend to the general membership. Tellingly, when people of color are
suspected, it complicates the issue even more since IMCs in general did an
inadequate job in incorporating diverse communities into their numbers,

so that the boundary between agent provocateur and rightful indignation at being marginalized uncomfortably blurs.

Usually, the only way IMCs ever confirmed their infiltration was when the commercial news revealed the names of agents or informers. This was particularly true in the case of the Portland IMC, which had the bad luck of having one of the most infamous informers of the recent activist scene infiltrate them: Anna. While enrolled at college in Miami, Anna proposed an extra credit project to her professor to infiltrate some of the organizing meetings for the 2003 FTAA protests in Miami. After presenting her material to the class, a classmate who was in state law enforcement asked if he could present her paper to his superiors. Soon afterward she met with two police officers and an FBI agent who asked her to infiltrate upcoming protests at the G8 in Georgia and the 2004 Republican and Democratic national conventions.[89]

In the summer of 2004 she befriended twenty-six-year-old activist Eric McDavid at the CrimethInc. conference in Iowa. She would eventually manipulate McDavid and two others, Lauren Weiner and Zach Jenson, to make bombs for potential targets in northern California like the Nimbus Dam. By 2007, McDavid received nineteen and one-half years in prison. Weiner and Jenson received reduced sentences for testifying against McDavid.

In January 2015, McDavid was released from prison due to his family's persistence in filing Freedom of Information Act requests regarding the trial. They discovered approximately 2,500 pages of documents the prosecutors withheld at the time of the trial. These documents reveal that McDavid had been entrapped. As Trevor Aaronson and Katie Galloway write, "Anna, at the direction of the FBI, made the entire plot possible—providing transportation, money, and a cabin in the woods that the FBI had wired up with hidden cameras. Anna even provided the recipe for homemade explosives, drawn up by FBI bomb experts. Members of the group suggested, in conversation with her, that they regarded her as their leader."[90] Unfortunately, entrapment by informants is not unusual. Aaronson writes in his book *The Terror Factory*, "Of the more than 150 terrorism sting operation defendants, an FBI informant not only led one of every three terrorist plots, but also provided all the necessary weapons, money, and transportation."[91]

When Brian Bailitz, one of the members of Portland IMC, read an *Elle* exposé on Anna, he realized that she was someone he had been friends with. The psychological effects were devastating on him. He reflects: "This lady was an FBI informant. Everyone knew I was friends with her. She was a cute lady. What if my friends thought I was also an FBI informant? If anyone ever accused you of that in the activist scene, the accusation is as damning as if it was true. I didn't want to deal with it."[92] He withdrew from the activist scene as the FBI ramped up its assault against environmental activists. Bailitz admits, "I don't feel that much conviction [in my activism] to spend time in prison for it."

As mentioned in chapter 1, the FBI launched Operation Backfire in 2004 to target what they deemed "domestic terrorism" by the Earth Liberation Front (ELF). By 2006, thirteen activists had been indicted and given lengthy prison sentences for acts of property destruction. The same year seven members of the Stop Huntington Animal Cruelty campaign were found guilty of inciting attacks against Huntington Life Sciences simply for posting material critical of the organization on their website.[93]

As a result of FBI repression, the Portland IMC became more closed. They stopped having open meetings in coffee shops, holding them instead at clandestine locations. Bailitz recalls, "The only way someone could attend was if you were invited. And even then, people were skeptical of new folks." The personal psychological impact upon Bailitz was devastating: "I went into shell mode. It sort of destroyed me as a person. I trusted this person. I couldn't believe the length the government would go through to destroy the activist movement."

The use of informants and agents provocateurs represents the culmination of what Foucault refers to as "a new optics: an organ of generalized and constant surveillance; everything must be observed, seen, and transmitted"[94] The goal is to move beyond physical structures to infiltrate all of society so actual surveillance is no longer needed since the mere suspicion of it regulates peoples' words and actions. Essentially, pervasive surveillance remolds people into compliant subjects.

This is exactly the impact that informers and agent provocateurs have upon activist communities: they infuse paranoia into the scene to sow distrust and make everyone seem a potential informant, to make everyone surveil their own actions and those of others. As Bailitz mentioned, his mere proximity with Anna made him feel suspect. Accusations of complicity are as damning that it doesn't matter if they're true or not—they're taken as true. Ideally, this is how surveillance operates: guilt is assumed and innocence needs to be proven.

As Gus Ganley observes, "It is psychological warfare. They [informants] are more than gathering information as a spy. They are sowing seeds of deep distrust in activist communities." Not surprisingly, there were at least four known informants and agents provocateurs who infiltrated the RNC Welcoming Committee: Andrew Darst (aka Panda), an FBI informant; Marilyn Hedstrom (aka Norma Jean Johnson), a Ramsey County narcotics officer; Chris Dugger, an undercover cop; and most notoriously, Brandon Darby, an FBI informer who sent shockwaves throughout the activist community once his role was exposed.

Darby's case is the best known since he was well enmeshed in the activist scene. He became well-known as one of the passionate yet egomaniacal founders of Common Ground, an anarchist-inspired New Orleans relief organization during Hurricane Katrina. Sometime between his time at Common Ground and working in the Austin, Texas, activist scene in 2008, Darby flipped, becoming an informant for the FBI. In Austin, Darby met David McKay and Bradley Crowder, two young naive guys starting in the activist scene.[95]

All three drove up to attend RNC 2008 protests. While doing so, Darby instigated McKay and Crowder to make Molotov cocktails despite their misgivings about doing so. This was key since Ramsey County police already stressed Molotov cocktail making being "advertised" in the "We're Getting Ready" video. Ideally, state and federal authorities needed the threat to materialize itself to make its case "stick" against those who would eventually become the RNC 8 as well as those who had the misfortune of being drawn into their wake like McKay and Crowder. Ultimately, the two were convicted of making the cocktails. But there was not enough evidence against them to show an intent to use them. McKay was sentenced to four years in prison (actually serving three). Crowder was sentenced to two years in prison. Both maintain that they had been entrapped by Darby.

Needless to say, the exposure of the other informants who had directly infiltrated the RNC Welcoming Committee traumatized many activists. Gus Ganley had been close with Andrew Darst. He recalls, "He was around for a year. I got to know him fairly well. He came over my house a bunch and we had a lot of conversations, some in-depth conversations with him. He knew a lot of my close friends well and was in a romantic relationship with one of my friends." Ultimately, after he learned about Darst's deceit, Ganley came to view the state as "using human beings as weapons to break psychological trust in communities, turning people into bombs."

Max Specktor, one of the RNC 8, recalls the utter psychological devastation of learning that he had been speaking to an informant: "The realization that I was chatting with an FBI snitch made me feel like I would never again be able to experience a genuine social interaction, or fully trust people that I work beside."[96] He adds, "Fortunately, I am slowly gaining some of that confidence back, but it definitely left an incredible impression."

The psychological warfare on the RNC 8 and those associated with them had already begun with the preemptive arrests, raids, and other harassments. Luce Guillén-Givins recalls, "Many of us noticed being followed by squad cars, and cops would drive by our houses, shining searchlights into our yards and front windows and creeping along at a snail's pace."[97] During her arrest, Monica Bicking recalls Sheriff Fletcher taking her out of her cell and speaking with her in the middle of the block so that everyone could see them speaking together, leading to suspicions that Bicking might be assisting the police. She was then released before the first day of protests under the condition that she would try to de-escalate them, which she never agreed to do. Nonetheless, during her freedom, she observed: "I was in a constant state of fear. I was scared of being rearrested. I was scared that I would do something that would be construed as illegal. I was scared that I would be somewhere that would be raided. I was scared of running into the informants and of being followed."[98]

Michelle Gross recalls the raid on the convergence center, a place where activists would meet, plan, and prepare materials, that happened before the first day of protests. The police actually blocked main roads to prevent many activists from even reaching the center. But for those who did, the police descended upon them, detaining them from hours on end with no proof of any illegal activity occurring. During her temporary detainment after the raid, Gross was unaware that her garage had been broken into by the police searching frantically for any incriminating evidence. Luckily, her young daughter remained asleep in the house while the assault occurred. Nonetheless, Gross recounts, "It pissed me off. I was so freaked out. I took her out of there and got a hotel way the hell out in the suburbs. I was petrified they would do something to her."[99]

All these accounts reveal the intense psychological warfare and coercive use of power that accompanies surveillance. Its purpose is to keep people on guard, afraid, and second-guessing their every move. Informants and undercover officers are the most insidious forms of disciplinary power since their effects burrow into the psyche in order to redefine it in more passive and compliant directions.

Carceral Disciplining and Jail Support

The courts and their processes are also disciplinary mechanisms to break solidarity and undermine community-based organizing. As Foucault has noted, "The control of time is one of the fundamental points of the hyper-power organized by capitalism through the State system."[100] During the seventeenth and eighteenth centuries, individuals had to be made compliant with the new forms of consolidated capitalist production emerging. Cyclical time periods were supplemented with linear notions of time. Time could now be segmented and regularized, and time zones were eventually implemented during the nineteenth century. Labor needed to be conceived as a temporal unit to be exchanged for wages. Foucault writes, "The problem of a capitalist society is not so much to tie individuals down locally, as to capture them in a temporal mesh that ensures that their life is effectively subjected to the time of production and profit."[101] This has intensified in recent years as mobile digital technology has further segmented time by keeping its users on perpetual alert through email, texts, and (more rarely) phone calls as well as immersing them in an endless flood of commercial platforms like social media, gaming, and the like.

Subjecting activists accused of crimes to a lengthy court process and its inconveniencing temporal flow, impedes their ability to fully engage in community building, activism, and collective resistance to the flows of capital and other inequities. But a way to minimize the negative effects of the justice system on organizing is through jail solidarity strategies, which were widely used at the 2000 RNC in Philadelphia. Such tactics include preparatory meetings before the action in which roleplays of being arrested are enacted, noncompliance such as not giving one's name to the police or following directions, hunger strikes, and public displays of solidarity like marches and vigils.[102] These actions help build links among arrestees that can continue long afterward and be utilized in future actions and organizing.

By all accounts, jail solidarity was not widely used during the RNC 2008 protests. This left an immense burden on CRASS "to create relationships among arrestees long after many people had left the area."[103] The absence of such solidarity led many defendants to take a more individualized approach in their defense rather than the collective one that the RNC 8 initially adopted. The Chicago 8 trial in 1968 provided inspiration to the RNC 8 and its supporters. Gus Ganley recalls: "The nature of the charges were similar, with terrorist enhancement and a kind of forebearer that a trial could expose the justice system for what it is, which is a mockery."

The unified front among the RNC 8 was breached when Erik Oseland pled guilty on August 2010, initiating the disintegration of solidarity among the RNC 8 and their support community. As Garrett Fitzgerald recounts, "I had hoped that taking our case to trial could be part of a shift in how radicals handled charges like ours. Much like how I, as part of the RNC-WC, wanted to encourage anarchists to think bigger and more strategically, I wanted our case to demonstrate another way to challenge the system of control we stand opposed to."[104] But with Oseland's plea and the others following soon after, Fitzgerald asserts, "We lost credibility on that issue and demoralized supporters."[105]

Many of the RNC 8 felt an inevitable conflict between their attorneys' goal to get the best possible outcome for their individual cases and their collective desire to present a unified political front to expose the brutality of the police and the stupidity of the court system. This is an inherent tension in many cases that involve activists. Kris Hermes writes, "Criminal defense attorneys are motivated by what's 'best' for their individual clients. Meanwhile, working group members were focused on felony support not just because of the consequences, but also because the cases were politically charged."[106]

After Oseland's plea, the defense committee wrote a piece calling the lawyers sellouts. But some members of the defense committee disagreed. Michelle Gross was outraged at not being properly consulted over the essay since she had a close relationship with many of the attorneys. Although she has since made peace with members of the defense committee, she recalls: "These lawyers do their damnedest within a system stacked against everyone. To put that on them was not fair. The lawyers were extremely upset about it. They felt they were getting shit on."[107]

Yet other members of the RNC 8 like Guillén-Givins felt the lawyers were not simply operating within a deeply flawed legal system but also perpetuating additional inequities like sexist practices. She asserts that the lawyers "barely acknowledged Monica's existence, interrupting her as a matter of course in meetings and rarely bothering to seek her opinion on matters that pertained to her as much as to any of us."[108] Regardless of how much truth lies behind this specific observation, it exposes the generally toxic environment that had infected the relations between the RNC 8 and their lawyers as well as between the defendants. Guillén-Givins reflects, "In the weeks leading up to the end, and in the days afterwards, I felt like I watched the trust and solidarity I'd helped build over two years get torn apart from the inside … [and] I questioned whether I would ever be able to work with them again."[109]

The state employs a whole arsenal of disciplinary procedures against individuals. The courts, legal apparatus, informers, preemptive raids, and the like are not used merely to detain and temporarily incapacitate activists, but to work from within movements to instill fear, doubt, and suspicion that can hollow out the community. Although many of the members of the RNC 8 have continued with their lives, and some continue to engage in activism, their experiences show the subtle ways in which disciplinary powers like surveillance work in people's lives to transform radical activists into disempowered and individualized bystanders.

Disaster Capitalism and Counter-summit Protesting

Because the arrests in St. Paul were so grievous, the city was forced to create a review board to look into police abuse and hold town hall meetings. It released its findings on January 14, 2009. The eighty-two-page report is revealing in how it rationalizes police violence against protesters. Although it found "instances" of police misconduct in the use of force and pepper spray and suggests that the kettling of protesters on September 4 "had the feel and appearance of a mass arrest," overall the police were commended as acting "restrained and professional under the circumstances."[110]

The preemptive raids, use of undercover police and informants to infiltrate activist groups, and intimidation of other activists who were interested in joining the Welcoming Committee were all justified as warding off the impending "anarchist" threat. The term "anarchist" is used 348 times throughout the report. It defines an anarchist as "one who uses violent means to overthrow the established order," a blatantly simplistic understanding.[111] In spite of many people testifying before the board that their understanding of anarchism was inaccurate, the report is intransigent in maintaining that the anarchists were not "unruly or wayward students. They were well organized and sophisticated and tenacious. They had state-of-the-art communication devices, coordinated plans and well-thought-out tactics that included the use of Molotov cocktails, human waste, caltrops and other items to hurt police and citizens and to damage property."[112]

Contrary to some of the RNC 8 claiming that the police and city didn't understand anarchism, the report shows a willful misinterpretation of events rather than a simple misunderstanding. The report's distortion was intended to justify vast expenditures of public money to employ law enforcement during protests and to purchase military-grade equipment and security devices from private corporations in order to surveil the threats that mainly existed in the bureaucratic minds of law enforcement, weapons contractors, and the local and federal government. The report's main conclusion was not to prevent such repressive measures in the future but instead to prejudice the public against protesters in advance. The report recommends that communities holding future summits: "Show the community pictures of anarchists engaged in unlawful conduct and MFF [Mobile Field Force] in riot gear to prepare the community for what they might see," and "prepare residents for the presence of helicopters during the convention."[113]

The report served as a virtual blueprint for repressive measures taken during later counter-summit protests. For example, during the Toronto G8/G20 protests in 2010, city residents were given a four-page booklet beforehand innocuously named, *G20 Summit Resident Guide*. It advised residents to barricade themselves behind their doors for seventy-two hours with enough food and water to survive.[114] It served as a de facto disaster guide for the pandemonium they were predicting would be unleashed by the deluge of anarchists invading the city.

The Toronto summits were the most expensive to date, racking up $1.1 billion in security expenditures. SNC-Lavalin, the largest Canadian private contractor, received a multimillion-dollar contract to establish security and a communication infrastructure in downtown Toronto.[115] Transport Minister John Baird justified such expenditures in an Orwellian tone: "The reality is, in a post-9/11 environment, security will not come cheaply."[116] Wartime measures were enacted that subjected anyone to random searches and arbitrary arrests. The police met with protest groups days before to intimidate them.[117]

Undercover police targeted and infiltrated independent media organizations. Melissa Hill recalls while attending the Toronto protests, "At Toronto they were targeting the media. I could see them targeting media people that the cops knew from other experiences. There were times when they were blocking my camera."[118] Dawn Paley, a member of the Canadian Media Co-Op, reflects on the effects of having her organization infiltrated, "That was hard on a lot of us. I developed a friendship with this person, who had been in my home numerous times and traveled with us to Toronto. That was something that took a few months to set in: how debilitating it is."[119]

Over 1,100 people were arrested, the largest mass arrest in Canadian history. Tellingly, only 330 of them were charged. Out of those, 201 cases were dismissed with only 32 pleading guilty.[120] Again, the arrests had less to do with criminal behavior than the wholesale removal of demonstrators from the streets. André Marin, the ombudsman of Ontario, later declared such unilateral actions illegal and a distinct blow against civil liberties.[121]

If anything, these massive expenditures reveal how counter-summit protesting has partially been incorporated into the logic of disaster capitalism. As Naomi Klein writes, "Wars and disaster responses are so fully privatized that they are themselves the new market; there is no need to wait until after the war for the doom—the medium is the message."[122] By decontextualizing protesters' actions and highlighting some of the incendiary rhetoric that they employ, the state manufactures a dire risk assessment to justify vast expenditures of public money for employing law enforcement during protests and purchasing military-grade equipment and security devices from private corporations for the police. The rhetoric of "preparedness" that guides such actions aligns itself with a post-9/11 mindset where surveillance and readiness have become central tropes to justify government action/encroachment and the pilfering of public money by the security-industrial complex.[123]

By the time of the Tampa 2012 RNC, the threat no longer needed to be real to justify such expenditures. The local press repeatedly suggested that fifteen thousand protesters were expected to invade the city. News stories routinely trotted out familiar anarchist clichés like suggesting that they "resort to violence against the police and vandalize property belonging to the establishment," once again preparing the way to arrest a series of relatively privileged people.[124]

The Tampa police and city government were actively speaking with St. Paul authorities about how to best prepare for 2012. Tampa mayor Bob Buckhorn admitted, "I prefer going in with overwhelming force to prevent that [the disruptions in St. Paul] from happening."[125] Neither Tampa police chief Jane Castor nor local city authorities showed any concern about repeating the gross misconduct that the St. Paul police leveled against demonstrators, unembedded videographers, and other independent media people.

Tampa spent fifty million dollars on security. Half of the money was spent on personnel and law enforcement. Two million dollars went to riot gear and another two million for sixty new surveillance cameras.[126] The city council established a temporary "event zone" near the convention that prevented demonstrators from carrying water pistols, rope, gas masks, or any other object remotely seen as a threat.[127]

Yet after all the expenditures and preparation, only around three hundred protesters showed up. Three people were arrested during the convention. Rather than asking for accountability from the city for the obscene expenses incurred against a nonexistent threat, the press instead praised the restrained manner of the police. After realizing that the anarchist threat would not manifest, police chief Jane Castor switched rhetorical gears by spouting New Age-ish aphorisms during her multiple interviews regarding her interaction with protesters—"I don't know in the past if anybody's gone in and really talked to the demonstrators. 'Exactly what is your goal?'"—and her philosophy on law enforcement—"The greatest tool that any of our officers have is their discretion."[128]

Castor's words efface the heavily fortified and militarized presence that I and others witnessed while walking in downtown Tampa toward the convention center. At one moment, police forced me to cross the street and walk on the other side for no apparent reason. I passed clusters of cops with truncheons, Tasers, and camel bags they occasionally drank from. A security officer warned, "Careful, sir, the streets are dangerous." I couldn't help but ask myself: "From whom?"

By the time I reached the intersection of North Ashley and East Whiting Streets, where a protest was supposed to occur, sixty cops guarded the street's four corners. The police were visibly bored. One officer from Orlando said he had nothing to complain about: "We get a lot of goodies." "And overtime," I asked. "And overtime," he smiled.

I asked about where they stored the riot gear. He said it was on reserve at a nearby location. He then further commented, "We're in a more conservative state, but we're laid back. Out there in Chicago [during the NATO summit protests of summer 2012], they're more liberal, but also more brutal." Little did I know that this was to become the general line of the Tampa police force: a kinder and gentler police state. Their presence constantly reminded you that they could smash you like a fist at any moment, but that they instead humored your actions as insignificant enough to not warrant much reaction on their part. In other words, we weren't worth fighting. As a result of the low attendance by demonstrators, independent media was left largely unmolested by the police to cover the small protest actions occurring across the city.

Politicians and law enforcement similarly conjured up hordes of protesters invading Trump's 2017 inauguration in order to rationalize state repression and wasting taxpayer money on surveillance equipment and personnel. Roy Blount, chair of the congressional committee planning the inaugural ceremony, claimed that the intelligence community predicted "more threats from more directions than ever before."[129] Security costs exceeded $100 million.

Reality proved otherwise. The inauguration had lackluster attendance, anywhere between 300,000 and 600,000—far beneath the planning committee's estimate of 800,000–900,000 and the Trump administration's inflated figures of 1–2 million.[130] Nonetheless, over two hundred protesters were arrested; most either had their charges dismissed or were acquitted at trial.[131] Furthermore, Washington, DC, eventually paid out $1.6 million in settlements to the protesters who were denied access to food, water, and restrooms while having their right to freedom of assembly trampled upon.[132] But as this chapter makes abundantly clear, such crackdowns have little to do with actual threats and more to do with criminalizing dissent.

We have gotten to the point where the threat of counter-summit protesting has been incorporated into a bureaucratic and capitalist logic that rationalizes vast expenditures for militarization and law enforcement as necessary to deter "anarchist" violence from erupting, as the St. Paul RNC report reveals. Contrary to viewing the state as some external threat to activism, we need to reconceptualize how the state is dependent on utilizing micro and macro forces that attempt to coopt resistant elements like counter-summit protesting. Although protesters might have caused a general disruption during the 1999 Seattle WTO protests, these kind of protest tactics have become normalized to such an extent that their predictability and stereotyped imagery has been harnessed by the state and capital to justify channeling large amounts of taxpayer money into private coffers under the guise of "security" and "preparedness." The state employs a post-9/11 mindset where surveillance and readiness have become central tropes to justify government action/encroachment and the pilfering of public money by the security-industrial complex.[133]

This is not to say that counter-summit protesting doesn't still have some advantages like drawing together various groups and organizations that would have never met elsewhere and developing new affiliations and ideas. Also, as many anthropologists have shown, this type of protesting creates new affective bonds between people and reminds them that they are not alone in their struggles. It also provides for a network of resources that activists can tap into.[134] But until they understand the ways in which their strategies and some of the imagery provided by their black bloc tactics have been co-opted to establish a new form of disaster capitalism, they overlook a major weakness in their movement—how their presentation of self and rhetorical strategies are used to rationalize violence, hierarchy, and capitalism—the very things that such protests ostensibly oppose.

Conclusion

Overall, video- and internet-based activism plays an important role in counter-summit protesting, along with other forms of activism that this book documents. This kind of activism exposes and challenges the unwarranted ways in which the label of domestic terrorism has been applied to condemn everyday forms of civil disobedience and used to hamper and silence independent media. More generally, it both counters the commercial media's portrayal of events, often exploiting the racial and class privileges such protesters possess, and provides support for protesters and arrestees at the local level. The production, distribution, and exhibition/reception practices behind such media-based activism remain as important as what is finally seen on the screen. As media technology increasingly encompasses our lives and neoliberal practices attempt to interpellate us, video and digital media making will have an expanding importance as an oppositional activist practice for generating collective action and fostering a resistant outlook that views the streets as our own and a prime location where new possibilities may be forged. We can already see this occurring as copwatch groups in poor communities of color proliferate across the country in places like Brooklyn, Harlem, Ferguson, and Baltimore while Black Lives Matter activists seize the airwaves to force those in power to finally hear their message. We turn to such copwatching in the following chapter.

CHAPTER 3

Documenting the Little Abuses

Copwatching, Countersurveillance, and Community Organizing

The video of Derek Chauvin kneeling on George Floyd's back for nine minutes and twenty-nine seconds continuously played over the news throughout the summer of 2020, a ceaseless reminder of the unapologetic nature of police brutality, a police force that can kill someone in plain sight with seeming impunity. It was not simply the video's brutality but also its duration that forced viewers to experience a Black man's life being extinguished with painful precision. The inhumanity of Chauvin's relentless action in contrast with the pleas of help from Floyd's prone body starkly illustrates the vast distance that separated their lives and understanding of the world. The video provided powerful evidence, for those who still needed it, not of an out-of-control police force but of one that methodically and in full view disregards the lives of people of color and implicitly consents to Chauvin's actions. This specific instance of police brutality crystalized into a metaphor for the problems regarding policing in general and helped spark the largest Black Lives Matter protests the United States has ever seen.

But one must recall that the video of Floyd's death follows an earlier time, roughly between 2014 and 2016, when a stream of images of young working-class Black men being killed by the police flooded commercial and social media: Mike Brown, Laquan McDonald, Eric Garner, Freddie Gray, Samuel DuBose, Philando Castile, and Alton Sterling.[1] A cycle of brutal footage dominated commercial news coverage where Black bodies were sacrificed twice, a second time over the airwaves in the search for ratings. Surveillance and spectacle suddenly converged, a logical outgrowth of a postindustrial capitalist society, as Susan Sontag once mused in her 1977 book *On Photography*.[2]

Yet at a more local level many working-class communities of color are integrating digital technology in dynamic ways within their community, organizing to not only resist police violence, but also to link it in more structural ways to neoliberal practices of gentrification and structural disinvestment in public resources. El Grito de Sunset Park and Copwatch Patrol Unit (CPU) in New York City stand at the forefront of this work and represent a growing trend of the central role in grassroots activism occupied by digital technology regarding policing, gentrification, and self-determination.[3] The study of community media can provide concrete, on-the-ground examples of historically disenfranchised groups incorporating media-making into their activism, enabling them to both symbolically and literally reclaim their neighborhoods and generate an overall sense of collective empowerment against the reactionary tendencies of neoliberalism.[4]

Kevin Howley stresses how the study of community media can lead to a more systemic understanding of media activism since "locally oriented, participatory media organizations are at once a *response* to the encroachment of the global upon the local as well as an *assertion* of local cultural identities and socio-political autonomy in the light of these global forces."[5] Sunset Park, Brooklyn, and East Harlem, where El Grito and CPU often patrol, represent points where these global forces converge. As Peter Moskowitz and Jeremiah Moss have shown, New York City was ground zero for the implementation of neoliberal practices in the 1970s when the city suffered a debt of $24 million. Mayor Abraham Beame implemented austerity measures that laid off workers, cut salaries, privatized public services, and withdrew city resources from poor nonwhite neighborhoods to force residents to flee in order to make room for luxury apartments, finance-centered institutions, and other amenities that appealed to the rich and tourists.[6] Mayor Michael Bloomberg's twelve years in office unabashedly promoted the city as a luxury product as he rezoned neighborhoods and employed heavy-handed policing, use of eminent domain, and other strategies to clear working-class neighborhoods for gentrification.[7] El Grito de Sunset Park and CPU, therefore, occupy key positions illustrating how local communities can employ digital technology to foster resistance against state repression, whether through policing and the prison-industrial complex, gentrification, or state disinvestment, all defining elements of recent neoliberal practices.[8] Furthermore, El Grito connects its community organizing and video work with past and present domestic and international struggles of resistance against dispossession and state violence within the United States, Latin America, and the Caribbean, thereby punctuating a diasporic mode of cultural resistance that occupies, as scholars like Paul Gilroy and Stuart Hall have suggested, an important position in fights for liberation.[9]

Groups like El Grito, CPU, and others discussed in this chapter, like the Police Reform Organizing Project (PROP), the Malcolm X Grassroots Movement, and the Coalition to End Broken Windows Policing, also draw attention to how policing, gentrification, and the political disenfranchisement of working-class communities of color interlock to mutually support one another. This chapter on the copwatching and community organizing currently being undertaken in Brooklyn, Harlem, Queens, and other boroughs offers a case study of how community organizations integrate their video countersurveillance into wider practices of community organizing and systemic analysis of police abuse and racism, which are intimately tied to issues of gentrification, unemployment, and the gutting of social services.

Policing and Gentrification in the Age of Neoliberalism

As this book argues, policing assists capitalism by attempting to produce a compliant and predictable workforce. Furthermore, it punishes those who either challenge such practices or whose precarious existence poses a potential threat to the state and the economy. As neoliberal practices have eviscerated welfare programs and other forms of federal and state support for those in most dire need, caused wages to stagnate, and rendered much employment unsteady, repression against those most impacted by such changes has escalated. A brief examination makes it clear that the prison-industrial complex's growth directly correlates with the onset of neoliberalism. For example, in 1980 the United States spent $6.9 billion on corrections and $27.4 billion on public housing. By 1990, $26.1 billion was spent on corrections while public housing only received $10.6 billion, and conditions only grew worse when Bill Clinton drastically cut welfare and simultaneously increased harsh prison sentencing.[10] The prison-industrial complex became a new form of public housing. Poverty itself was criminalized rather than being something that should be eliminated.

Nothing represents the criminalization of poverty better than the broken windows policing that police commissioner William Bratton enacted in New York City during the mid-1990s. In essence, the broken windows theory suggests that major crimes and felonies can be curbed if the police start punishing minor infractions.[11] Little to no evidence suggested then or now that broken windows policing was effective. For example, during the 1990s, states where broken windows was not applied had a reduction in crime similar to states where it was enforced.[12]

Although long denied by the NYPD, a quota system prevails that requires police to summons and ticket a certain number of individuals each month regardless of the charges' validity. The most vulnerable become regular targets of broken windows policing since they have the fewest resources for their defense, often do not know their rights, and most likely lack any powerful connections. For example, in 2011, during the height of stop-and-frisk, the number of stops of young Black men exceeded their entire population in the city: 168,000 stops out of a population of 158,406. Even after the supposed end of racial profiling and stop-and-frisk policing, in 2014, out of the 222,851 misdemeanor arrests made by the NYPD, 86 percent involved people of color.[13]

Broken windows policing is intimately linked with gentrification in New York City, as many copwatchers and community organizers emphasize. Josmar Trujillo, a member of Copwatch Patrol Unit and founder of the Coalition to End Broken Windows Policing, reports that the Police Foundation, a nonprofit that serves the NYPD, regularly invites real estate developers to its functions. At one of them, the correlation between policing and gentrification was emphasized: "an audience was shown a map of geographical drops in crime alongside a map showcasing an accompanying rise in property value in the same neighborhood."[14]

Mayor Bill de Blasio is well-known for having deep ties to real estate developers. His supposed affordable housing initiative, Mandatory Inclusionary Housing (MIH), which proposes to build 80,000 units of below–market rate housing is plagued by a free market outlook that refuses to pay union wages to building contractors, offers massive tax breaks to developers for building such units, and proposes an unrealistically high median income for locations where wages have stagnated for decades, thus placing "affordable housing" out of reach for a vast majority of people.

Gentrifiers often employ pioneer imagery to justify their exploitation. For example, during a Brooklyn Real Estate Summit held at the Brooklyn Museum in 2015, Jordan Sachs of Bold New York, a Brooklyn real estate firm, enthused, "There's this new class of people that want to be first adopters, and I think there's a demand for being the first group out there [the Bronx]."

When someone corrected him that people were already living in the Bronx, he recalibrated, "I should have phrased it differently, you know, there's a different type of consumer that wants to be a pioneer there."[15]

According to Neil Smith, pioneer metaphors indicate a much broader revanchist outlook employed by middle- and ruling-class whites to capitalize upon poor communities of color, further disenfranchising them in order to bulwark their own white privilege, jeopardized due to a lack of steady employment, lower wages, and decimated social services.[16] New York City mayors Rudy Giuliani and Michael Bloomberg illustrated this outlook in action as they decimated social services for the poor, structurally disinvested from working-class communities of color to pave the way for gentrification, and emphasized the needs of tourists and the financial sector over that of residents.[17] Broken windows policing serves a central role in gentrification.[18] Although William Bratton quickly ran afoul with Giuliani as police commissioner and was dismissed in 1996, broken windows policing continued and intensified in New York City until Bratton was reinstated as police commissioner by Mayor Bill de Blasio in 2013. Current mayor and ex-cop Eric Adams seems to be following suit by ramping up the policing again of quality-of-life infractions that defined a broken windows policing outlook.[19]

The intensified policing and repression against the poor by the state has been conceptualized by some sociologists and historians as nothing less than a return to Marxian primitive accumulation. Just as Marx theorized that the introduction of capitalism was premised on violence in forcibly removing people from the land, destroying communities and older forms of mutual aid, privatizing the commons, and enacting a sharply gendered division of labor, neoliberalism has led a return to violence against the poor, the homeless, and working-class communities of color to extract profits from their labor and the places they occupy.[20]

Needless to say, Bratton is favored by the wealthy. Trujillo succinctly summarizes the way in which such policing and gentrification enfold one another:

> Bratton represents the coming together of two types of interests. One: militarized policing with the use of surveillance, informed by military computer algorithms to predict where future attacks would occur. Bratton's Deputy Commissioner is John Miller [who had worked for the FBI]. Two: Bratton was a choice of the superrich. What makes everything move here is real estate. He was favored by all real estate

developers....In order to have business and shopping and gluten-free salads and other shit, you need people who can afford it, and that is the connection between policing and gentrification. The changes that we see in terms of housing and gentrification are inextricable from crushing of poor people and the crushing of a specific class and raced group.[21]

George Lipsitz points out that the attack against poor communities of color is the reduction of a location to nothing but profit margins by developers. "Its potential as a site for new development and investment is all that counts from a perspective that sees all space as only market space," according to Lipsitz.[22] The location's use value—as a space for the local community, its networks of friendship, and the accumulated histories that imprint a neighborhood's very being—are rendered irrelevant.

Many copwatch groups and community organizers, as we will soon see, resist estimating a neighborhood's worth solely in terms of its marketability. They further strengthen community ties and traditions and claim its spaces as their own. Lipsitz's observation about Los Angeles activists holds equally true for those in New York City: "[They] seek to elevate use value over exchange value, to discover hidden value in undervalued places and undervalued people, to create new democratic opportunities, to share responsibility for common problems, and to promote mutuality, accountability, stewardship, and respectful interactions across social divides in order to generate new practices, new perceptions, new polities, and new politics."[23] Community organizers' and activists' goal in part is to illuminate the local histories of their neighborhood, to reject developers' translation of land into more profits and the police's reduction of people into statistics by drawing the community to the forefront to occupy both the streets and the imaginary terrain that define a space.

Various local community organizations in New York City stress the links between policing and gentrification. Queens Neighborhoods United's 2015 end of year report states: "As the Anti–Police Brutality movement built momentum, QNU was able to analyze how increased policing is often used as a tool for displacement.... The current style of policing, also known as Broken Windows Policing, does not function to protect immigrant communities of color like ours. In fact, increased reactionary policing will only work to make our community more vulnerable and susceptible to higher incarceration rates."[24]

There has been an increasing push for business improvement districts (BID) in Queens and Brooklyn. BIDs ostensibly can beautify a community and make it safer by forcing local businesses to pay additional taxes for such services. But its long-term goals allow developers and multinationals to get a toehold in communities, which eventually drives up rents, pushes local vendors out, and escalates broken windows policing upon "undesirable" residents (namely, poor people of color). In a word, BIDs are the gateway to gentrification.

As Yul-San Liem, director of development and operations for the nonprofit group Justice Committee, observes, the city is attempting gentrification through the use of intensified broken windows policing: "Because the new business improvement districts weren't able to take hold due to community resistance, the city is trying to achieve it by other means such as the local precincts putting extra cops on the street. They created the Roosevelt Ave Task Force. They target people coming out of the bars at night and people who live in the neighborhood for open container, public drunkenness. They are cracking down on small businesses for nuisance offenses like playing music too loudly and selling alcohol to underage folk."[25]

According to a *New York Times* article, because of the increased police presence and enforcement, "many residents felt they were being stopped and searched by the police without cause." The statistics bear this out. In 2012, for example, over 90 percent of stops resulted in no summons issued or arrest made.[26]

Copwatching Histories and Diasporic Influences

Copwatching has a long history in the United States. The earliest filmed instance of copwatching that I could locate occurs in the 1926 film, *The Textile Strike*, made in support of raising funds for and popularizing the strike in Passaic, New Jersey. The film states through intertitle at the fifty minute mark: "To hide their crimes, the police drove out the newspaper men and smashed the movie cameras. But they didn't see us get this one from the roof." Overhead footage follows as police officers lunge through the crowd, encircling, beating, and carting off demonstrators.[27] The Black Panthers and Young Lords are two of the most well-recognized community-based groups that integrated copwatching into other grassroots efforts concerning education, health, and political action.[28] AIDS video activists also employed video in the late 1980s and early 1990s to deter police violence against direct action protesters and to serve as evidence

FIGURE 3.1: Influenced by the Black Panthers, the Young Lords were a community organization for the self-determination of Latinx communities that created their own free breakfast programs, health care, sanitation, and other needed social services. This image is from the Newsreel film, *El Pueblo Se Levanta* (1971), which features the Young Lords.

in court.[29] But the first officially named copwatch group began in Berkeley, California, in 1990 by Andrea Pritchett in response to the police harassing homeless people.[30] Jacob Crawford, who joined the group in 2000, has been one of the main figures in creating WeCopwatch, which travels across the country to assist various grassroots groups with copwatch efforts in often small, isolated communities that might lack the infrastructure to initiate such a project. For example, with the killing of Michael Brown in Ferguson in 2014, Crawford flew out to meet and assist David Whitt, who helped found copwatch group Canfield Watchmen. Through donations and a GoFundMe campaign they purchased two hundred body cameras to arm local residents for copwatching.[31] Brown's death became a transformational moment regarding the need to film the police. The lack of video evidence and police accountability regarding it caused waves of outrage from various communities and served as fodder for robust discussions regarding policing over the airwaves.[32]

Although this general history is important in contextualizing copwatching overall, El Grito de Sunset Park has been more directly influenced by specific domestic and international resistance movements, according to its cofounders Dennis Flores and Jason Del Aguilla, due to the unique opportunities New York City offers for diasporic and activist cultures to converge and be sustained. The group is located in Sunset Park, Brooklyn, a quickly gentrifying neighborhood located just downstream of Park Slope, a hipster haven that crouches along its northern border. El Grito is a Puerto Rican-based group, which has evolved a more general Latinx orientation, with deep ties to the Young Lords, a Puerto Rican radical organization that emerged in the late 1960s in part modeled on the Black Panthers. The Lords organized against police violence and advocated for self-determination by running free breakfast programs for kids and an educational center. They also helped organize health care workers and conduct prison support.

Although the Young Lords were only a strong presence until 1972 in New York City, some of their core organizers like Richie Perez and Vicente "Panama" Alba became founders of many other organizations during the 1980s and 1990s such as the National Congress for Puerto Rican Rights in 1981 and the Malcolm X Grassroots Movement in 1995. In 1994 and 1995, Alba reached out to the leadership of various NYC Latino gangs to organize against police violence. Dennis Flores, a founding member of El Grito de Sunset Park, was one of those members. As he recalls, "Richie Perez and Panama brought people together, you know, and basically got all the leadership to meet and create a truce. He pointed out that it's the system's fault that has us pitted against each other. Instead, let's organize against police abuse, which we did."[33] Monifa Bandele of the Malcolm X Grassroots Movement similarly reflects, "Richie took young organizers all night long in an office and talked about strategies, speaking about history. One of the things that would happen at mobilizations was that former gang members would work with community organizers."[34]

Flores was also influenced by international resistance struggles such as the teacher protests during 2006–7 in Oaxaca, Mexico, where he spent some time. He notes, "The stuff we were seeing was how they were working collectively, a bunch of organizations working collectively using the media. They were citizen journalists documenting stuff, exposing the violence and repression. It felt like an extension of copwatch."[35]

Similarly, Jason Del Aguila, a cofounder of El Grito, also did organizing work in Guatemala, home of his parents, and El Salvador. He worked with h.i.j.o.s, a group fighting against the forgetting and silencing of those who have been disappeared in both nations. He reflects, "Guatemala already has a history of social movements and resistance and organizing. And now they're adding these new artistic cultural elements to it [like hip hop and punk rock]. And I could identify with all of it, and that's where I got my organizing/activism boot camp."[36]

El Grito's very name refers to earlier anticolonial revolts like El Grito de Lares, an 1868 uprising on the island of Puerto Rico by poor people to abolish slavery and cast off Spanish colonialism. As Claudio Gaete-Tapia, another core member of El Grito, observes, "During colonial times for the past five hundred years there has always been a shout, an outcry. So even if you're outnumbered and outgunned and outspent, there are some things you don't put up with. The indignity is non-negotiable. It is a really human thing. So that's the people—the scream. It is a communal scream."[37]

These transnational influences on El Grito emphasize the importance diasporic cultures have within social movement organizing. As Paul Gilroy notes, the historical experiences of various diasporic populations "have created a unique body of reflections on modernity and its discontents, which is an enduring presence in the cultural and political struggles of their descendants today."[38] The convergence of the multiple influences of the Young Lords, striking Oaxacan teachers, and Caribbean and Latin American resistances against colonialism and state repression upon El Grito illustrates Stuart Hall's observation that diasporic cultures engage in a "symbolic 'detour' to the present that moves through the past, marking the site of collective investment in stakes made on the future."[39] Gilroy and Hall felt that the syncretism and hybridity of diasporic cultures held much potential for social struggles to move beyond nationalistic identities to embody a transcultural and transnational resistance. El Grito marks a recent iteration of this diasporic resistance, which is enfolding digital technology into older forms of organizing and culture.

The original impetus for copwatching in Sunset Park emerged much earlier from a need to keep the police from harassing celebrants of the Puerto Rican Day Parade that overflowed from Manhattan into Brooklyn. Copwatching was initially a yearly event. But as Flores and Del Aguila began to speak more in-depth with their neighbors, they realized more routine copwatching was needed as well as more substantive community organizing like they had encountered in Latin America.

Using a $270,000 court settlement Flores won in 2006 through a lawsuit he filed after the police beat him up in 2002 for attempting to stop them from harassing one of his students, Flores and Del Aguila founded El Grito de Sunset Park. As a result of their efforts, they began to understand community issues in a more systemic way. As Del Aguila observes, "We ended up catching more injustices in the neighborhood whether it be slumlords or police or people targeted by jobs for documentation issues. We saw these things build up. They are landing in our lap, and we can do something about it." They became a more permanent organization in 2013 and only in 2015 achieved a 501(c)(3), nonprofit status.

Sunset Park and Gentrification

Sunset Park is a little more than half a square mile, located on the southwest side of Brooklyn and is most readily accessible by the D train from lower Manhattan. In the 1980s and 1990s it was consumed by the crack epidemic like many working-class communities of color in the city at the time. Gang activity was rife. When I was walking home one night with someone who grew up in the area, he pointed down a side street to mark the location where he was shot as a teenager in the eighties. The police generally avoided the area.

However, with rising gentrification, as upscale white residents have gradually infiltrated the area, police presence has increased. The price for an average townhouse has shot up from $746,000 in 2013 to $948,000 in 2015.[40] Yet wages have stagnated, with the median income in the area remaining $48,000 from 2000 to 2014. Although average rent has only increased $300 in the same time frame, incomes remain stagnant and depressed. As a result, the rent burden—where families pay more than 30 percent of their income—has increased from 27.5 percent to 38.2 percent.[41]

El Grito's video activism is part of a long line of media activist efforts that labored on the front lines against exploitation, racial stereotyping, and state violence. Film historian and activist Chon A. Noriega has chronicled the extensive media activism that emerged out of the Chicano/a movement during the 1960s and 1970s.[42] A vibrant Chicano/a public community television and experimental and documentary cinema resulted. For example, the public television show *Realidades* first aired in 1972 when members of the Puerto Rican Education and Action Media Council occupied the studios of WNET during a pledge drive.[43] *Realidades*, along with shows like *Acción Chicano* and *Ahora!*, presented issues important to Chicano/a communities like immigration, fair wages, and housing and brought broader Latinx cultural traditions that included poetry, theater, music, and film in a weekly format into people's homes.

Additionally, Third Cinema, an anticolonial cinema movement from Latin America, the Caribbean, and Africa throughout the 1960s and 1970s, played a vital role in revitalizing radical film traditions in the United States. New York Newsreel aligned itself with Third Cinema's perspective and served as the major distributer of their anticolonial films throughout the 1960s and 1970s.[44] Newsreel also teamed up with residents of various Puerto Rican communities in New York to produce an outstanding documentary on the Young Lords, *El Pueblo se Levanta* (1971), and another film about the struggle over affordable housing, *Rompiendo Puertas* (1970).[45] Chicano filmmakers were openly supported by New Latin American Cinema directors in a declaration they made in Havana, Cuba, in 1978,[46] and in turn, various Chicano filmmakers openly championed Third Cinema aesthetics and practices in their manifestos during the 1970s.[47]

Although groups like El Grito might not be fully aware of these traditions, earlier practices and attitudes nonetheless filter down into their media making. For example, documentary has consistently served an important role among Latinx filmmakers due to its relatively affordable nature and ability to relate pressing political concerns to viewers in a timely manner. Additionally, El Grito's media activism is similarly influenced by the Chicano/a Arts Movement that valued resistance against oppression, maintenance and affirmation of community values and cultural traditions as well as negotiating complex interactions with the dominant culture.[48] These elements can be seen throughout the diversity of El Grito's videos that resist dispossession by gentrifiers, politicians, and the police, celebrate various Hispanic musical and spoken word cultural traditions, and employ commercially produced digital technology to counter the commodification of their neighborhood by developers, and offer alternative visions of Puerto Rican life that normally remain off screen or stereotyped by commercial media.

For example, one of El Grito's videos addresses their support for the Sunset Park Rent Strikers. El Grito teamed up with Occupy Sunset Park to assist the rent strikers in 2012. Three buildings on 46th Street in Sunset Park had been in extreme states of disrepair, contaminated with asbestos, rats, and mold, lacking heat in the winter, and with basements overflowing with garbage. The tenants went on rent strike in response. El Grito assisted by strategizing and producing a multimedia campaign. Claudio Gaete-Tapia recalls, "We brought some cameras in and pushed the envelope and got people engaged in their own fight. You know, Dennis started filming and bringing attention, and then they reacted, and we drew attention to who was behind it." Because Flores and Del Aguila had vast experience with organizing, they assisted the rent strikers in strategizing. Gaete-Tapia, who is an urban planner, helped the tenants navigate the city bureaucracy.

El Grito helped publicize the strike by engaging with the local news, creating an art exhibit featuring photos of the neglected buildings and rundown apartments, and establishing a Facebook page. The art exhibit provides a particularly interesting example of how media making served as a nexus that fused art and politics for coalition building and community engagement. Bedford-Stuyvesant photographer Noelle Théard purchased fifty disposable cameras through a grant he received. After a brief training in image composition, Théard and Flores distributed the cameras to the tenants to document their deplorable living conditions.

The visual testimony played an important part in tenants reclaiming a sense of agency. Although some of the tenants were reluctant to display their decrepit living conditions to all, they ultimately saw value in the project. Alex Beatrice, a thirty-eight-year-old resident asserted, "This makes me feel like I'm being heard."[49]

The photos were then displayed in an art exhibit during a neighborhood festival that drew together artists, musicians, and various community organizing groups. The festival emerged because its organizers were tired of seeing the art and music of communities of color exploited by corporations while those very communities that produced such works continued to be marginalized. In between DJs and dancing, groups like the Bronx Defenders held a "know your rights training," the Committee Against Anti-Asian Violence (or CAAV: Organizing Asian Communities) provided information regarding tenants' rights, and the rent strikers discussed the living conditions that prompted their art exhibit.[50]

Because of its location within a festival, the art exhibit represented a dynamic intervention that not only validated tenants' concerns but also brought them into dialogue with a cross section of other organizations where their struggles against policing, delinquent landlords, and racism converged and complemented one another. Furthermore, the festival became a reclamation of space by the community against those who only saw it as something to be bought and sold. The festival celebrated the community's vibrant use of its neighborhood to display its diverse interests and talents where art and politics intertwined and flourished.

The Facebook page created a space where videos, pictures, news coverage, and activist events converged.[51] For example, an October 31, 2014, entry presented nine photos that document the substandard living conditions of the buildings and apartments. The caption beneath them reads: "What if you didn't have to leave home to find a scary house on Halloween? Tenants have been living in a house of horrors caused by devilish landlords, ghostly speculators, evil spells cast by unscrupulous lenders and hobgoblins looking to gobble up their homes." Afterward, it lists the organizations forming a coalition around the strike. Finally, it announces a protest occurring the same day at the buildings at 3:30 p.m.

As Tina Askanius has shown, social media can extend struggles from the street into cyberspace. Although it is possible to overestimate the potential of social media, these platforms can nevertheless serve as forums where information can be found, solidarity can be expressed, and actions declared that build on community organizing. As the Sunset Park Rent Strikers' Facebook pages illustrates, organizing over social media does not just chronicle ills occurring in the past and present, but also points toward future mobilizations.[52]

Additionally, as Paolo Gerbaudo observes, social media provides "crucial *emotional conduits* through which organizers have condensed individual sentiments or indignation, anger, pride, and a sense of shared victimhood and transformed them into political passions driving the process of mobilizations."[53] The Sunset Park Rent Strikers mobilize on the notion of shame, exposing through photography and video the substandard living conditions that their slumlord imposes upon them.

For example, El Grito produced a rent strike video for their Facebook page.[54] Although only three minutes in length, it quickly establishes Flores's expertise as a filmmaker not only by its high production quality, but also by its succinct editing and careful framing. It begins with a piercing noise evocative of tinnitus as the camera tilts down from the top of the building and descends down cement stairs into the basement like a voyage into rental hell. The discordant noise is soon matched with a visual cacophony of a mountain of trash and crumbling basement walls. A low guttural noise follows on the soundtrack as the sequence cuts to a discarded, broken porcelain sink on the floor.

Immediately contrasting this dark imagery are close-ups of a goldfish in a tank, a religious saint figurine, and some dolls on a table as the camera pulls back to show the inside of a tenant's apartment directly across from the rubble in the basement. A female voice-over in Spanish says: "Here lives a family. This is part of the basement. A family with kids and a woman

FIGURE 3.2: "Sunset Park Rent Strikers" (2012), a video produced by El Grito de Sunset Park to document uninhabitable living conditions.

A family with kids and a pregnant woman soon to give birth.

FIGURE 3.3: Such imagery from "Sunset Park Rent Strikers" (2012) asserts the dignity and humanity of those living in squalid conditions who nonetheless make art a part of their daily life.

soon to give birth. In front of this door, there is a basement full of garbage infested with rats and insects. This is an injustice."

In a quick sequence of shots, the video establishes the poor living conditions of the building, and the humanity of the residents through its close-ups of their belongings, while one of the tenants describes the landlord's neglect. The video documents other tenants speaking to reporters as shots of deteriorating and cramped apartments with deteriorating walls, moldy ceilings, and crumbling asbestos insulation follow.

Testimony is an important device in much activist documentary since, as Patricia Zimmermann notes, it provides "a way of opening up the repressed trauma to enter history again."[55] Testimony is the first step of allowing people to seize back a sense of agency. Although when the video was shot, the tenants had only just begun to organize themselves, the video's use of editing connects various tenants' voices together to assert a collectivity that had not yet been fully formed. Testimonies allow individual traumas to coalesce into collective understanding and political action.

Alongside documenting the condition of the buildings and establishing the humanity of the residents, the video is intended to publicly shame the landlord. The importance of affect should not be underestimated since it is one of the strengths of using art for activism. As Sara Ahmed points out, emotions and affects can be both social and individual and serve as markers where hierarchies are established and boundaries are defined.[56] Art plays a central role in mobilizing emotions in either a progressive or regressive fashion. Activist video, for example, is often employed to relay a sense of collectivity and the shared emotion its participants feel.

In the case of the rent strikers' video, the primary emotion is outrage with the intent of shaming the landlord into action. According to Ahmed, shame is a powerful emotion that implicitly suggests the failure to approximate an ideal by the person who is the object of that shame.[57] The video documents the deplorable conditions of the apartments and buildings. The art exhibit, the video, and the rent strikers' direct actions all drew wide attention from local news agencies since the ideal of minimally adequate housing was clearly not being met by the owner.

The strike was picked up by a host of local news outlets. All of the coverage was supportive of the rent strikers and documented the unsanitary living conditions they had to endure. It also frequently mentioned notorious slumlord Orazio Petito as one of the worst in the city with even Mayor Bill De Blasio criticizing him.

The shame campaign initiated by the tenants and El Grito's video and art exhibit was amplified by local commercial news media that provided sustained coverage of the strike for months. It reveals how grassroots media campaigns can catalyze commercial media into action given the right tactics and historical conditions. One must remember that Occupy Wall Street was in full bloom at this moment and had shifted the national discourse toward addressing economic inequality.[58] The rent strikers became a living embodiment of these issues, showing poor people living in subpar conditions while a wealthy landlord ignored their concerns. The historical moment allowed for their story to gain traction over local commercial media.

Although the shame-based campaign helped mobilize tenants and alerted the local news to these appalling conditions, it had limited effectiveness in improving the tenants' living conditions since the particular object of shame remained elusive as the building passed between multiple owners. The three buildings' original owner, Orazio Petito, is sadly not unique in his neglect. As we will see, divestment is a structural principle used by many landlords in their quest to gentrify neighborhoods. As geographer Neil Smith points out, landlords "pocket the money that should have gone to repairs and upkeep" to establish a rent gap between the worth of the building and the value of the land it resides upon.[59]

Divestment becomes a multipronged tactic by landlords, not only to take money that should have gone into repairs, but also to make their property more attractive to developers. Insufferable living conditions would clear their buildings of pesky working-class tenants to make room for upscale clientele who can afford higher rents once the buildings are renovated. The buildings in Sunset Park have been in receivership for many years with rotating owners who briefly purchase the buildings to flip them for a profit rather than improve their conditions. Although the building was eventually renovated, increased rents priced out most of the original tenants.

Copwatching, Community Organizing, and Culture

As noted earlier, the copwatching that El Grito conducts is integrated with other community actions against gentrification. Copwatching is only one aspect of local resistance against a neoliberal outlook that eviscerates wages and welfare benefits, privatizes public space, enforces discriminatory broken windows policing, and gentrifies neighborhoods of working-class communities of color. A fairly representative type of copwatching is found on Dennis Flores's YouTube page: "7–19–2012 COPWATCH Films NYPD Transit Cop Assaulting."[60] The video has been viewed over 284,000 times. "Theft of service" or fare beating accounts for the largest amounts of arrests and summonses made by the NYPD. In 2015, for example, NYPD made 29,000 arrests and 124,000 summonses related to it. Of those cited and arrested, 92 percent were people of color.[61] Transit cops typically target subway stops in working-class neighborhoods of color in Brooklyn, Queens, Harlem, and the Bronx since this kind of harassment remains largely unchallenged by busy commuters with limited resources.

Like much copwatching, the video is captured on a cell phone by a bystander waiting for the train. The unsteady footage tracks down the stop's platform showing a transit officer who approaches a short Hispanic male in his late teens or early twenties. Two other young Hispanic males sit on a bench in the foreground watching the action take place. The camera zooms in on the white officer spreading the young man's arms against the wall. Some indecipherable words are exchanged between the cop and the man apprehended. The Hispanic male jumps, and the cop grabs him by the shoulders and slams him to the ground. The man attempts to stand. The police officer lifts him off the ground and slams him back down again.

As they struggle, a second young Hispanic male nears the incident, directly filming the cop from his phone. His presence serves two purposes. First, it is fairly typical of copwatchers to have two cameras filming. One films the incident while another films the camera filming the incident. This is to record any police harassment of the person who is doing the filming. Furthermore, if the cops decide to arrest the person filming (and destroy the footage in the process), the second camera can document it and flee with additional coverage.[62] Also, the second person filming nearby is using his camera's presence to mediate the cop's actions. Although originally the cop might not have been aware of a camera filming him, he is now on notice. The use of the camera to partially intervene during a political action or arrest is common in activist video making. Film theorist Patricia Zimmermann notes how the camera in such instances operates as "a permeable surface through which relations between and alongside maker and subject pass and commingle."[63]

We witness this multilayered negotiation through the reactions of the police officer and Hispanic youth being apprehended. As soon as the officer becomes aware of the camera, he begins to articulate his words more clearly, yelling toward the camera, "Stop resisting." The man, also aware of the camera, replies, "But I am not resisting." As the officer becomes more assertive, the young Hispanic man yells, "You got that on video, right?" In essence, both the officer and detainee perform for the camera, recognizing that the recording can serve as future evidence to either condemn or exonerate their actions.

As the officer passes by those filming, the nearest camera person asks for the officer's name since under NYPD regulations an officer has to provide his name and badge number when asked. The young man being apprehended responds, "Yo, ask him his name," causing the filmmaker to request

FIGURE 3.4: Image from a June 19, 2012, copwatch video that shows those being recorded alter their actions to create a more camera-friendly presence, realizing that such video can ultimately serve as evidence.

the officer's name again along with what command he is with. This is an interesting moment of intervention, something that El Grito attempts to avoid. Dennis Flores notes, "I am looking to de-escalate and document now. When I started doing this twenty years ago, I was a lot more confrontational. I wanted to film the cops and kind of like push back; and I still want to push back, that hasn't changed. But I want to be smarter about it. We need to document them being what they are, not interjecting."[64] Yet the video clearly exhibits how the moment dictates some minimal interaction by the cameraperson.

The handheld roughly shot nature of the video provides the recording with a sense of urgency, immediacy, and authenticity as if it happened to catch an unmediated moment. As Susan Sontag notes, "People want the weight of witnessing without the taint of artistry, which is equated with insincerity or mere contrivance."[65] Yet, as documentary film scholar Bill Nichols also points out, the image's authenticity is contingent upon a whole host of additional factors that legitimate its accuracy and alignment with reality, as I will soon discuss.[66]

As the situation winds down, the cameraperson asks the young man, "Se habla Español?" He replies affirmatively. In response, the cameraman directs him: "No diga mas nada. Dile que 'quiero un abogado.'" (Don't say anything more. Tell him 'I want a lawyer.') The officer remains silent during this exchange and walks off with the kid as the second camera follows him.

Once again, we witness the permeable membrane of the camera that wants to document the event but also intervene on the man's behalf so he knows his rights and doesn't offer any self-incriminating evidence. Just as the camera provides a sense of empowerment and protection, the use of Spanish functions in a similar way, assuming that the police officer doesn't understand it. Both verbal and visual acuity converge to create a sense of solidarity between the copwatcher and the one being apprehended. Tellingly, as the video progresses, the cop's actions become more subdued, and he speaks less. We are witnessing the balance of power shift at least to some degree.

The YouTube page where the video is posted has hundreds of comments, mostly supportive. Although there are a couple of posts that defend the police, many of the comments express solidarity, sharing similar tales of harassment. They also provide telling close readings of the video. For example, in response to a post that claims that the officer did nothing wrong, one user responds: "at 0:40 the cop has his hands between the boys legs and the boy reacts to his private parts being fondled. notice people that the young man has his hands still against the wall. the young man is reacting to an illegal indecent search. and he gets abused for refusing to be searched in this manner. hate the cops." Yet another user questions the partial nature of the video: "yea because the video only shows an officer using some force on someone. Nothing existed before this video. These two just appeared out of thin air with the officer chasing him for no reason what so ever."

The debate between the two postings reveals the contested nature of documentary footage and its slippery relation to the events it documents. Bill Nichols asserts, "The image and the text—its conventions and techniques—combine to provide the basis for our inference or assumption that the photographic image's stickiness has within it the stuff of history."[67] The second commentator undercuts this relation by highlighting the partial nature of the video and its isolation from the moment that led up to it. The warring comments reveal the assumptions that viewers mobilize to either legitimate or question the footage's authenticity. They reveal how one's reading of an image is contingent upon a host of other factors and assumptions.

The website attempts to establish a sense of solidarity among the many members who have experienced police harassment, but it relies more upon a logic of aggregation than collective networking. Jeffrey Juris explains the difference between the two: "Whereas networking logic entails a process of communication and coordination on the part of collective actors that are already constituted . . . logics of aggregation involve the coming together of actors qua individuals."[68] Unlike long-sustained networking that often occurs face-to-face in physical spaces, logics of aggregation suggest a budding collective vision that needs to be further integrated off-screen or risk fragmenting back into its individual parts. As Claudio Gaete-Tapia cautions, "Your electrical device is only as important as the networks that it creates. If it is connected, but you aren't connected to anyone, what good is it? If you are connected to someone who already has an established relationship, it is that much stronger. It's not an either/or. It is what machines are supposed to be for: to help out."

Because of the limitations of online organizing, YouTube is only one of many ways in which El Grito distributes its videos. For example, they have projected videos on buildings in Sunset Park to organize Know Your Rights and copwatch trainings around them. Del Aguila reflects on part of the reason for using the projector: "When you're handing out a flyer, people will take it but toss it. With projection, they come to us. Those people who would have taken a half an hour to convince to get interested are now standing before us. The first time we did it, the crowd was so big, the police drove by and were wondering what was going on. The police were shocked, intimidated, and impressed."[69] Still, such projections were effective because El Grito had already established deep ties within the community. They weren't some outsiders invading Sunset Park but were already considered well-respected community members, organizers, and media makers.

Furthermore, the projection of copwatching images on buildings is an important reclamation of public space. It demonstrates in its very action the type of self-determination and autonomy that copwatching hopes the local community will practice. Similar to the Black Panthers and Young Lords, "[It provides a model] to the community that, if it exercised its power and stood on its rights, and prepared to defend itself 'by all means necessary,' the immediate forms of oppression could be held at bay. In this way, a powerless community, schooled to the mentality of colonial subordination, could be transformed into an organized, self-conscious, active social force."[70] The fact that the police did not intervene and try to shut the screening down demonstrates the power of reclaiming one's space.

The control of public space should not be underestimated. As Murray Bookchin emphasizes, "Ultimately, it is in the streets that power must be dissolved: for the streets, where daily life is endured, suffered and eroded, and where power is confronted and fought, must be turned into the domain where daily life is enjoyed, created and nourished."[71] The streets are where abstract issues are made concrete. Through El Grito's public screenings, spectators witness self-determination and autonomy in action by reclaiming buildings and the streets to project videos and engage in copwatch skills sharing. Video making and exhibition serve as central conduits in reasserting community control without fear of police reprisals.

Along similar lines, El Grito sees their actions around the Puerto Rican Day Parade as equally important and symbolically charged. Their YouTube video "Copwatch June 8th 2014" chronicles the battle over the streets with the police.[72] The video begins with handheld footage documenting a highly heated discussion between a police officer and Enrique Del Rosario, a seventeen-year-old resident. The camera swivels to a white cop putting his hand before the camera, complaining, "Put that down outta' my face. It's illegal to photograph." The cameraperson yells back, "No, it's not illegal. No, it's not illegal" while the camera tilts backwards toward the sky to avoid his grasp.

The video marks the struggle with the police over both physical and symbolic terrain. Like their attempt to intimidate partygoers on the street, the police are also trying to wrest control over video documentation by falsely claiming that photography is a crime. The terrain between the political and the filmic temporarily collapses as the police redirect their gaze and actions away from boisterous celebrants of the festival to the videographer. Any sense of agency on the locals' part—whether it be dancing in the streets or filming the cops—is being contested by the police. Video making reveals itself as one way to negotiate one's space and challenge the police's authoritarian actions.

Perhaps most remarkably, the video would eventually serve as important evidence regarding how the police attempted to frame Del Rosario on charges of assaulting a police officer, resisting arrest, and larceny. The footage suddenly cuts to the police swarming around Del Rosario, who was copwatching until they attacked him. The video documents in slow motion that the officer supposedly assaulted by Del Rosario was actually accidentally struck by another police officer's baton. Although the initial footage is nothing more than a blur of bodies, slow-motion suddenly opens up the space by revealing the officer swinging his truncheon into another officer. Postproduction allows the videographers to command space after the fact in the editing suite; this emphasizes not only the immediate power

FIGURE 3.5: "Copwatch June 8, 2014," through its use of slow motion, reveals how an officer who claims to have been assaulted by Enrique Del Rosario was actually accidentally struck but a fellow cop.

of videotaping in the streets to challenge police intimidation and abuse, but also video's retroactive ability to manipulate footage to gain control over the events it documents. Walter Benjamin's observations regarding the political potential of film applies here: it "extends our comprehension of the necessities which rule our lives"[73] In this case, it discovers abuse and mendacity hidden within a blur of movement.

The footage circulated widely over social media and gained significant traction among the progressive and commercial press like *Huffington Post* and *ThinkProgress*.[74] Both articles link to the video and emphasize police abuse. Furthermore, the press kept the story visible until its resolution when a grand jury decided not to indict Del Rosario for assault and the district attorney dropped all remaining charges against him. Rebecca Heinegg, Del Rosario's lawyer, suggested that the DA's office offered a deal to avoid a trial where the video evidence could be used. Del Rosario wanted to bring the case to trial specifically to use the video to expose the police's lie.[75]

One suspects that it was not simply the footage of Del Rosario being assaulted by the police that made the DA reluctant to go to trial, but also the further evidence the video provided of an out-of-control police force terrorizing a community. As one commentator for Russia Today states, "I would encourage people to watch the video, which is posted online. . . . [The police] are shouting; they're macing people who are standing by; they're yelling at people using the f-word as they're pushing people while the crowd

FIGURE 3.6: "Copwatch June 8, 2014," exposes the NYPD as an out-of-control force harassing residents (El Grito de Sunset Park, 2014).

does not seem to be acting violently to police."[76] The footage, in other words, justifies the need for copwatching and community organizing as it exposes the police as an aggressive occupying force.

The second half of the video reveals a wall of officers lunging at locals who have their hands raised. The camera scrambles to document the multiple instances of abuse, such as when a gang of cops descends upon one person to tackle and ambush him in a hail of blows. The cops keep yelling "back up" with random profanity sprinkled in like "get the fuck off of there" as they push violently into the nighttime crowd. The camera focuses on the officers' chests to document badge numbers as the crowd chants, "We're moving. We're moving. We're moving." The camera jostles among the bodies, translating the crowd's resistance into its uneven framing and shaky footage while random officers attack individuals. It is less reminiscent of a parade than battle footage where the streets are being struggled over inch by inch, foot by foot. The representatives of law and order are being unmasked as a gang of thugs unleashing chaos and violence into the streets.

In addition to this footage that exonerates Del Rosario and unveils police violence, El Grito had footage from eight other cameras that document the incident. Furthermore, NYPD had footage from twelve surveillance cameras that surrounded the area, but they would not release it claiming that they had lost the footage. Heinegg subpoenaed the police department while El Grito filed a public records request for the footage.[77] One can therefore better understand why the DA dropped all charges since not only was the video incriminating to the police, it would also usher in a whole host of other issues like police accountability and the public's access to surveillance footage and by implication, bodycam video.

As Bill Nichols stresses, the authenticity of the image is always subject to uncertainty. It is the systems of meaning that can marshal it with a certain power and authority. He notes that "the photographic image in legal proceedings is far from cut and dried," as anyone familiar with the footage of Rodney King being beaten could observe as the police used it in court to exonerate their actions.[78] But in Del Rosario's case the footage was bolstered by wide critical news coverage of the police, a heavy social media presence, footage from eight additional cameras, and the NYPD's refusal to release their own surveillance footage. It would be difficult, if not impossible, for the DA to undermine the authority of the video in the courtroom since its authenticity would be supported by a wider constellation of evidence that pointed toward police malfeasance.

Other El Grito videos, however, celebrate Puerto Rican culture where people reclaim the streets absent of police abuse, which generate a large number of hits on social media. Once again, the Puerto Rican Day Parade serves as a privileged moment where community celebration occurs. The video "El Grito de Sunset Park June 9th 2013," which has over six thousand views, begins with a close up of a conga.[79] In contrast to the abrupt and jostling handheld imagery of the prior video, this footage is steady and in control. The camera drifts from the drum to a woman singing along with it. She is dressed in a Boricua T-shirt, a white visor with the Puerto Rican flag on it, and has the Puerto Rican flag draped over her shoulders. The camera focuses on her dancing as locals photograph her from the opposite side and we hear shouts of encouragement like "go on, mami, go on, mami."

The camera smoothly traverses between the dancer and the elderly drummer, eventually showing a man from the crowd dancing with the woman. The camera then steps back to offer a high angle shot and pan smoothly over the crowd of both young and old dressed in colorful outfits enjoying themselves. In the background, we catch a glimpse of the diversity of shops that line the streets: Chinese food, a bagel shop, a jewelry store. Tellingly, no brand name stores are to be seen, signaling the ways in which the neighborhood has still resisted gentrification.

The camera pans back to the right to see Dennis Flores standing in the middle of the sidewalk with a few police officers at a distance behind him. He makes a couple of hand gestures to temporarily silence the music and

FIGURE 3.7: This image from the 2013 Puerto Rican Day Parade shows self-determination in action as celebrants and musicians take over the streets without fear of police reprisals. (El Grito de Sunset Park, 2013.)

calmly states: "We want to avoid a confrontation with the police. This is about know your rights. This is our community." People express approval at his words. He continues: "So we want to open up a pathway here so folks could walk by. As long as we are not blocking pedestrian traffic, we're not breaking the law. We can do this."

People take heed and start making a space as the music continues while the camera documents the crowd. As the music restarts, some locals start chanting in rhythm, "Let the people walk. Let the people walk," and dancing to it. Unlike the earlier footage of the police inciting chaos and violence during the 2014 Puerto Rican Day Parade, this footage shows people in control of their own lives being respectful and happy. The video relays a sense of joy and celebration. Politics and culture intertwine not only by Dennis Flores integrating "know your rights" within the celebration, but also through the music, dancing, and chanting.

Bomba music emerged four hundred years ago from colonial plantations where West Africans and their descendants toiled. It has deep connections with anticolonial, diasporic politics in both its sounds and lyrical content that address maroon histories and other forms of slave rebellions. Many bomba musicians in New York City are also community activists fighting against police abuse, gentrification, and other forms of oppression.[80] Therefore, the seamless way the music realigns and fuses with Flores's directive in the video to clear a pathway suggests how the work of El Grito and the Puerto Rican Day Parade in general aligns with older diasporic traditions of cultural resistance.[81]

The video exemplifies why El Grito de Sunset Park finds it equally important to document the local culture in order to fight the criminalization of its community. Jason Del Aguila stresses, "Broken windows turns innocuous violations into full-level crimes. Our goal is to show the music and the art [of our community]. That's part of why I wanted to record our local people, the characters of our community. We wanted to show who our community is. We are the artists, musicians, thinkers." This is particularly important because of the ways in which people of color are still largely underrepresented in commercial media. According to one study, "No [media] platform presents a profile of race/ethnicity that matches proportional representation in the US."[82] Communication scholar Leo R. Chavez has clearly documented the long tradition of commercial media portraying Latinx communities as a constant threat.[83] Even media franchises like Fast and Furious that are courting Latinx groups still privilege whiteness and have Latino/as serve as spectacle for a superficial multicultural aesthetic rather than as fully developed characters embedded in their own distinct cultural traditions.[84] El Grito's video serves as an important representational corrective not only by validating more nuanced representations of Latinx life than commercial media provides, but also celebrating communal pride in this work being done by and for their community.

A sense of control and self-determination is suggested by the video's aesthetics. Unlike the jarring editing of the earlier video of the 2014 Puerto Rican Day Parade, this video comprises one smooth shot. The self-possession of the crowd becomes embodied in the precise framing and the fluid camera movement. The videographer demonstrates his/her intimate knowledge of not only the locale, but also the festivities as the footage effortlessly weaves itself between music, dance, a sense of place, and political action. The feeling of autonomy and self-worth is reinforced by the video's content as the chanting of "Let the people walk" integrates itself with the music, showing how the realms of the cultural and political mutually inform one another.

Not coincidentally, El Grito de Sunset Park began organizing its own Puerto Rican Day Parade since 2015, and the police have been largely absent. Claudio Gaete-Tapia stresses its political importance: "We aren't taking no more shit. It may seem a small victory, but, fuck it, we'll take it: Puerto Rican Day Parade without the cops. That sends a message that people can organize themselves in the community by and for ourselves." Although the pandemic derailed the parade from occurring in 2020 and 2021, El Grito organized it again for 2022 and are in the process of planning it for 2023.[85]

Copwatch Patrol Unit

Copwatch Patrol Unit (CPU) was founded by Jose LaSalle in 2012 in part as a response to the Ramarley Graham shooting. Graham was an unarmed Black teenager from the Bronx who the police shot to death after invading his apartment for his possession of a small bag of marijuana in February 2012. During the same year, LaSalle's stepson Alvin made a phone recording of being harassed by the cops as they called him "a fucking mutt." The recording went viral and created a minor sensation in the progressive press.[86]

LaSalle recalls the spontaneous and intuitive way he began copwatching:

> I needed to go out to the community and start documenting things and see where that takes me. For the whole year, I started by myself.... I got a phone that can record. I didn't know my rights. I didn't know nothing. I was just out there recording and seeing what would happen. Many times when police officers would tell me to put away the camera or get the *f* out of our faces, I would put the camera away and left. After two months of doing it and marching with the Ramarley Graham family, I started learning my rights, started learning that the constitution protects me to video record anyone out in public view and started using that against the police.[87]

As of 2020, CPU has patrol units in Brooklyn, the Bronx, Queens, Staten Island, Harlem, and Connecticut. Unlike El Grito de Sunset Park, CPU does not have 501(c)(3) status. It is funded mainly through donations. CPU members are outfitted with a Sony Handycam, cell phone, and black uniform. They often wear a black baseball hat with the letters "CPU" in white on the front. An iron-on badge on the front of their shirts states: "Copwatch Patrol Unit: Silence Is Consent," and "COPWATCH" in white letters runs along the back of the shirt. Cargo pants pockets hold their equipment: cell phone, notebook, cameras, and the like. LaSalle notes, "People see us, then they know we are copwatchers. It's similar to the Black Panthers. They had black, wear black, the beret; that was how people could tell the difference between them and the cops. It also lets NYPD know that we are out there to document the police and make sure that we are creating breathing room for the people."

FIGURE 3.8: Copwatch Patrol Unit was founded in 2012 as a response to the Ramarley Graham shooting as well as the daily harassment working-class communities of color suffer from the police. The group wears uniforms that assert their presence within their communities and to the police officers who surveil those communities. (Image by CPU.)

Prior to the pandemic, CPU provided weekly trainings wherever they were needed. Kim Ortiz, a member of CPU, states, "We do one in each borough each month. We go to a community center, often in communities of color that are brutalized by the police. A lot of times people contact us. We train people so they can train others so we are no longer needed, so people will have a sense of empowerment. We discuss certain things about how close you should stand to an incident, what to do if you are stopped."[88]

All of the footage recorded by CPU is uploaded to the cloud by the ACLU stop-and-frisk app CPU members use. All too often, when copwatchers are detained or arrested by the police, their footage is erased or damaged. By uploading it to the cloud immediately, no matter what the police might do to their equipment, their footage is protected.

LaSalle relates the strategy by which CPU uses NYPD's own data gathering against them:

CPU patrols all the precincts, particularly where the majority of Civilian Complaint Review Board complaints occur. We also look at the NYPD crime map and their posts. In the areas where crimes are being committed, we know they are going to put bigger amount of

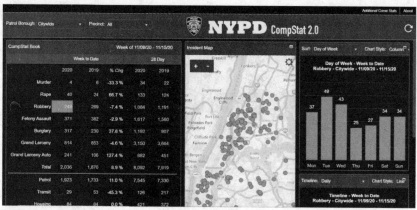

FIGURE 3.9: Copwatch Patrol Unit uses NYPD's own data against them. Jose LaSalle, the group's founder, notes: "In the areas where crimes are being committed, we know they [the police] are going to put bigger amount of officers in that area and be aggressive. In other words, the NYPD is helping us pinpoint the locations of where we need to be with the CompStat website and the crime map." As one can see, the CompStat website is easy to navigate and utilize.

officers in that area and be aggressive. In other words, the NYPD is helping us pinpoint the locations of where we need to be with the CompStat website and the crime map. We use all these things to pinpoint their location where there will be aggressive policing based upon complaints or crimes in the area.

CompStat is rather user-friendly.[89] Various categories like rape, robbery, grand larceny, and burglary are listed on the left side of the display. Statistics indicate if infractions are up or down compared to the numbers occurring a year prior. When one clicks on one of the categories, a series of blue dots appear on a map of New York City at the bottom of the screen to indicate where the incidents occurred.

Like the Black Panthers, CPU establishes itself as a parallel but alternative institution to the police. T.V. Reed observes how the Panthers used law books and civil codes "to symbolize that the police were engaged in uncivil disobedience to law, and that the Panthers were there to enforce the letter of the law."[90] The Panthers reversed the gaze of surveillance back onto the police. CPU heightens such countersurveillance by catching the police engaging in minor infractions according to their own codebook. LaSalle notes: "We use the NYPD patrol guide so if they are smoking in uniform, they can't do that. If they are on the phone in uniform, they can't do that. A lot of times, we'll write them up, you know, a fake ticket and the violation that they did, and we'll bring it to their commanding officer."

FIGURE 3.10: The Copwatch Patrol Unit YouTube page aggregates all the police abuse the group has documented from the minor harassments against vendors to physical violence. Such aggregation has become increasingly used by media activist groups. The videos, according to LaSalle, are important because they "give you a picture of broken windows policing beyond the facts."

Although there will often be no action on the commanding officer's part, the police are nevertheless being called out for their hypocrisy. If the police can harass communities of color through broken windows policing, then the cops can likewise be called out by copwatchers for similar petty infractions.

Unlike many copwatch groups that post their videos more selectively, CPU uploads all of their videos so that one is overwhelmed by the sheer number of videos found on their YouTube page.[91] CPU's latest activity is documented on their YouTube and Facebook pages. One goal of posting all of their videos is to add substance to the statistics, to illustrate the brute reality of the numbers the Office of the NYPD Inspector General, an oversight division of the NYPD, documents and often undercounts. La Salle notes, "We are documenting so other people can see it. They only have a report of police on paper: this officer brutalized me, he harassed me, he used foul language. This is all that they get on paper. The videos give you a picture of broken windows policing beyond the facts."

Josmar Trujillo observes: "Showing the human face to those types of policies is also important when we want to change policies or want policies eradicated. It's not just about catching the bad cop doing the bad thing, which lends itself to a bad apple kind of narrative. We do want to do that. But we also want to go deeper and impact the fundamental policies and ideas that fuel what the police do every day." The sheer mass of videos proves violations by the police occur regularly.

The aggregation of such videos challenges the belief that only a "few bad apples" ruin the integrity of NYPD. Instead, we witness the daily harassment by NYPD upon communities of color that naturalizes this treatment and sets the conditions for travesties like the murder of Eric Garner. As Sasha Costanza-Chock observes, movement activists have increasingly relied upon aggregation, curation, and amplification functions to propel their digital media activism.[92] For copwatchers like CPU, this aggregation has been a core tactic in revealing NYPD's standardized and consistent harassment of working-class communities of color.

As Trujillo notes, these videos are "not even at a fraction of a fraction of what policing does to our communities. That can only happen when we have multiple, multiple people filming every single day the little abuses that the police do." He sees two types of copwatching cultures: the more professionalized units like that of El Grito and CPU and the casual observer recording a police stop. "What Jose and Dennis do," Trujillo stresses, "and what a lot of other copwatch groups do is inspire people." LaSalle agrees, "We want people to feel empowered with the right to pull out their phone and document when the police are doing something wrong. The more we expose these officers, the more they realize that they need to do the things right. There is no way they are going to get away [with their actions]. If not an official copwatcher, then someone else will be watching."

Still, CPU's high visibility also leads to their greater surveillance by the police. LaSalle admits that the police readily followed CPU's YouTube channel: "They were becoming my bigger fans. They started asking me, 'This isn't what really happened. You edited this. You took this out.'" He claims that the number of police viewing his channel made him feel that the videos were "reaching the chiefs and captains and inspectors and all the way to Bill Bratton," commissioner of police during the time of my interview with LaSalle. But there is no way to prove this claim.

However, LaSalle's online visibility and physical presence in the streets led undercover police to regularly spy on him. Documents obtained by *The Intercept* showed that LaSalle was mentioned numerous times in undercover reports as he participated in Black Lives Matter protests. Under the Handschu agreement, NYPD's monitoring of political groups is regulated. According to Nusrat Choudhury, an attorney for the ACLU, "They [the police] cannot identify someone and have their photo in their files unless they have evidence supporting reasonable suspicion that he was about to commit criminal activity or had engaged in criminal conduct."[93] In 2019, LaSalle won

$925,000 in two settlements with NYPD for false arrest, imprisonment, and conspiracy related to his work as a copwatcher. He secretly taped officers incriminating themselves while celebrating his arrest.[94]

I witnessed such police intimidation firsthand when I interviewed LaSalle on a sweltering July afternoon in 2016 in a Starbucks in West Harlem just north of the iconic Apollo Theater. He wore an all-black outfit with white letters of CPU emblazoned across his baseball cap and the back of his T-shirt. He apologized for being slightly late as he lowered the static of the police scanner he had attached to his hip. As he did so, two police officers trailed in behind him, staring distinctly in our direction. Sensing their presence, LaSalle looked behind him to catch their sight line and turned back to me with a raised eyebrow. "See what I mean?" he commented as he shuffled in line to order a coffee. The cops eventually ordered their coffees and left the building all the while staring us down at our table.

Later that day while reviewing my hour-long interview with LaSalle, an inexplicable high-pitched sound periodically pierced through the recording making it nearly inaudible. I had been using the same digital recorder for hundreds of other interviews in equally public and noisy spaces and have never encountered any similar issues. When I brought this up with another copwatch member, he noted matter-of-factly, "Oh, yeah, the police jammed your recording. What do you expect?"

These are just some of the daily issues that copwatchers have to contend with. A digital media arms race escalates between grassroots organizers and state forces that want to contain their organizing. During another phone interview with a Brooklyn copwatcher, I repeatedly heard clicking noises over the line when the call itself didn't drop out (which happened several times). Again, I was told by my interviewee, "That's just NYPD." The problem, of course, is that my experience cannot be concretely documented as police interference, which is part of the police's goal that leads to paranoia and the stifling of movement growth. But given the wealth of evidence of NYPD's track record in infiltrating social movements, I consider it safe to assume I experienced some of this as well.[95]

This also raises bigger questions that many activists have addressed regarding the soundness of using commercial social media for activist purposes. Although LaSalle states that he only uses Facebook for activist information, a chronology of activist actions can be mapped out by the police and federal agents, activist networks can be traced through Facebook "friends," and locations can be documented using ISP addresses. As Christian

Fuchs observes, user data is an intimate part of the surveillance-industrial complex. It is privatized by social media companies to data mine users and profit from this information, and finally, it is used by "secret services who bring massive amounts of data under their control that is made accessible and analyzed worldwide with the help of profit-making security companies."[96] Yet, at the same time, social media has been incredibly productive in organizing protests and publicizing issues to a wider audience. The question becomes: how much should activists disclose online, and at what point do the costs outweigh the benefits?

Copwatch Patrol Unit Videos

Similar to El Grito, CPU also has video documenting the way in which various street vendors are being harassed by the police. As mentioned earlier, vendors were on the front lines of attack when Giuliani began enforcing broken windows policing in the early 1990s. In "TD 20-No CPR, These Officers Should be Fired (The Case of the Churros)," a bystander documents from the side as two transit officers force an older female churro vendor to haul her churro cart up steep stairs in the subway.[97] The footage is badly framed with poor sound, clearly the work of an amateur. The officer yells, "Get the hell out of my station." The person behind the camera comments, "Get out of *your* station? He owns this station?" Although they never touch the woman, the two white officers' physical presence is intimidating. The footage then focuses on the woman struggling to haul her churro cart up the stairs as one of the white, husky transit cops menacingly stands at the bottom of the stairs, making no attempt to assist her. The footage roughly cuts out after twenty-five seconds.

The video's YouTube page offers the following description: "These officer [sic] should be fire [sic] for treating and [sic] elderly woman like that. These are the kind of animals hired to protect us. That could of [sic] been my mother or their mother. Commissioner O'NEAL is going to allow this kind of abuse to continue." It is worth noting that the video takes place on October 27, 2016, under a new police commissioner, James O'Neil, who was appointed by de Blasio in September 2016. Although Bratton had left his post, the video clearly shows that broken windows policing continues.

The caption under the video continues: "CPU is going to assign Copwatchers to the station where the incident took place for the next few week. The train station belongs to the people, not to the police." Furthermore, it states, "CPU wants to thank the young lady that documented this incident.

FIGURE 3.11: A bystander catches a burly police officer harassing a churro woman in the subway, forcing her to climb steep steps with her dolly of goods. The video was posted on Copwatch Patrol Unit's YouTube page with the heading: "These Officers Should Be Fired." Incidents such a this reveal the constant harassment by NYPD upon working-class people that leads to more serious incidents like the murder of Eric Garner for selling cigarettes.

If you see something, record it!" This final sentence is a riff off the New York Metropolitan Transit Authority's campaign, "If You See Something, Say Something," that was plastered all over the interior of subway cars immediately after 9/11. Yet, in this case, the expression targets the police rather than seeing the police as the body one should report such information to.

The churro incident is exactly the type of little abuses that CPU wants to document. As Bob Gangi, founder of the Police Reform Organizing Project, states, "We need to focus on the day-to-day abuse, the day-to-day intimidation. It is not just the egregious incidents that happen, but this daily intimidation creates the context that lead the police to engage in the use of excessive force. It's the day-to-day practice of targeting Black and brown people that gets inside the minds and psyches of many police officers even if they are good people when they join the force."[98] Although documenting a relatively minor incident, the churro video reveals the hostility and oppositional attitude of the police toward the people they are supposed to protect and serve.

The harassment of vendors, even those with licenses, is pervasive across the city. I have heard numerous accounts and witnessed many incidents as well. For example, when I was interviewing Jose LaSalle in West

Harlem at Starbucks, a vendor entered and began speaking Spanish to Jose, clearly relating his thanks for something Jose had done. After the vendor left, LaSalle explained the situation to me:

> He was being harassed by the local precinct. He sells icies. I was going on their behalf to the precinct. They were being harassed about not being the proper distance from the curb. These people are working hard. They have licenses. Why are you harassing them? Then the cops started backing up and leaving them alone. This is what we experience. In the community we have their back. He has two kids. It's a struggle for him. Since the police have nothing to do, they harass them, pick on them, those who are less able to fight back. But now when they have somebody to fight back, it changes the game.[99]

Many of CPU's videos document such little abuses and intimidation. In "NYPD Shuts Down Music Video at the Wagner House" we watch rows of uniformed police officers stand guard in the courtyard of a housing project. Police presence had been intensified in the area for over a year since the death of a police officer who had been shot in the vicinity. Documented in the video is the police arrival while people in the community were shooting a music video memorializing Juwan "Chico" Tavarez, who had been killed a few days before.

The video, recorded by Josmar Trujillo, a member of CPU, shows handheld footage panning across the courtyard as mostly Black male residents express their frustration with the police. The sound is muddy, but the residents gesticulate in frustration at the police while the cops stand guard against the building's entrance. One Black male gets especially animated by clapping his hands to emphasize what he is saying until a woman sympathetically reaches over his shoulder and draws him back for his own safety.

A written piece accompanies the video stating, "To not allow residents to congregate in front of the building, which has benches and playgrounds there specifically for the purposes of people being able to hang out in the front, makes little sense—especially if they're mourning the loss of one of their friends. That sort of frustration, in fact, could easily escalate a situation that many think will undoubtedly lead to a violent retaliation against residents of the Jefferson Houses."[100] The police presence signifies a threat, visually suggesting how the housing project is nothing more than an occupied territory. Rather than subduing tensions, we can see how their presence escalates them as residents are refused freedom of movement.

As one resident expresses in frustration, "You can't make us leave our own home. We have to go inside because you say so? We live here."

CPU also takes a much more aggressive stance in its copwatching than El Grito. Their strategy represents another dominant strain of copwatching where copwatchers taunt the police. The video "46 Pct v. Copwatch Patrol Unit (Harassing the Community & Interfering with Recording)" announces its confrontational stance from its opening freeze frame where we see an officer baring his teeth at LaSalle standing before him.[101] A white title appears detailing the Bronx location, date, and time of the incident to provide critical evidence in court if needed. Someone explains off-screen that the police arrived because of a noise complaint due to a nearby house party. He states, "What they [the police] did was they agitated the group that was only trying to get home, and two people wind up getting arrested."

As he speaks, the camera surveys the block, showing the police congregating just before them. The footage then flashes back to an earlier incident where Jose LaSalle confronts a police officer. The officer stands inches from his face as LaSalle yells back, "Don't touch me. Don't touch me." An officer from the side films the incident on his cell phone. The handheld CPU footage strays to watch another copwatcher being confronted by a police officer before returning back to LaSalle.

As tensions escalate, a group of officers stand between LaSalle and a particularly agitated officer. The person filming says off screen: "Get your asses back to your fucking precinct. Get out of my fucking community and get back to your precinct." The officers start to retreat, pretending to ignore the copwatchers as LaSalle yells, "Do watch'ya gotta do. I'm not backing down."

The footage dissolves to some copwatchers demanding that an officer give his name and badge number. Although the officer keeps pointing to his badge before a Black male copwatcher, the copwatcher holding the camera taunts, "You have to cite it, officer." Interestingly, when the police officer finally responds citing his number, the Black copwatcher taunts, "Good, good puppy," leaving the officer clearly agitated.

This sequence reveals once again, as Patricia Zimmermann has stressed, the permeable membrane that exists between filming and the event being recorded. Although there primarily to document the incident, the videographer will occasionally interject in support of those directly engaging with the police officers. The video conflates the actions of various copwatchers and those being filmed to create a sense of collective identification through

FIGURE 3.12: In "46 Pct v. Copwatch Patrol Unit (Harassing the Community & Interfering with Recording)," Jose LaSalle (right) takes a confrontational stance with the police. Such tactics remain questionable in their effectiveness, but they represent how some male copwatchers perform a certain masculine bravado in standing off against the police.

the event occurring. As Bill Nichols notes, documentary can at times "convey the feel or texture of an event or experience."[102] Furthermore, it "can reclaim a dimension of human experience... that runs the risk of being dismissed as fiction," which might happen to such dramatic confrontations between the police and copwatchers were they not recorded.[103] The police officers' aggression is shocking to those who did not grow up accustomed to such confrontations. As many copwatchers that I have spoken with noted, in the past without video evidence they had to convince people they spoke with about the police's bad behavior. Nowadays, however, with the onslaught of copwatch videos documenting the cops' aggressive behavior, people's attitudes are changing in response to the vast amount of video evidence that exposes the systemic problems with policing in the United States. Rather than the cops' bad behavior being dismissed as fiction, the sheer volume of copwatch videos released have transformed a supposed fiction into an undeniable reality.

Just as important is how such videos model copwatchers' resistance to the police, causing the cops to stand down. The video demonstrates how anger might be channeled in productive directions rather than landing one in jail. As Sara Ahmed notes, "Anger is not simply defined in relationship to a past, but as an opening up the future."[104] A productive use of anger channels it away from a specific object toward more systemic issues.[105]

Although CPU video alone does not provide such analysis, the group's alliances with other organizations allow for it. LaSalle notes this connection between CPU and the Police Reform Organizing Project: "The videos give you a picture of broken windows while PROP is gathering the facts." PROP engages in citywide events such as holding panels where current and former NYPD officers document the existence of a quota system, conduct mock summonses in privileged neighborhoods like Park Slope and Williamsburg to expose the selective nature in which broken windows is applied, and speak with the local news regarding the implicit racial and economic biases of broken windows policing. The anger witnessed in the videos works with the analysis of groups that have allied themselves with the copwatchers to provide a fuller and more productive picture of how such anger can be channeled.

An analysis of copwatching must also account for the gendered nature of these videos as men of color utilize anger in certain machismo ways, stretching back to the Young Lords if not further. The Lords, it should be recalled, initially championed "revolutionary machismo," as part of their thirteen-point program. Although the program acknowledges that "the doctrine of machismo has been used by our men to take out their frustrations against their wives, sisters, mothers, and children," the men of the Lords suggested that machismo could redeployed in productive directions.[106] Needless to say, the women disagreed. Iris Morales reflects, "The women felt like, 'revolutionary machismo,' hmmm, is there such [a thing] as 'revolutionary racism?'" suggesting that despite whatever adjective one might attach to it, the concept still remains reactionary at its core.[107]

Still, this machismo persists to a degree in much copwatching. The men involved in copwatching often spoke about it in specifically aggressive masculine terms such as using metaphors of war and sports. Dennis Flores observes, "We are engaging in a war that we have not created and our people have suffered." Jose LaSalle analogizes copwatching to boxing: "We always say when we are out there with the police, it's like a boxing match. We're going to shake hands, but we're going to go for whatever rounds we need to go, for whatever hours we need to go. They are going to be aggressive. We are going to be aggressive. We have to show that we are not going to be backing down."

In many ways, copwatchers referring to their work as a form of guerrilla warfare stretches back to similar analogies that Third Cinema directors made about their work in the 1960s. For example, directors Fernando

Solanas and Octavio Getino state in "Towards a Third Cinema": "In this long war, with our camera as our rifle, we do in fact move into a guerrilla activity."[108] There is some truth in this description. The conditions within which both copwatchers and many Third Cinema directors act are clearly hostile. These parties often face a standing army or police occupation, so such analogies are accurate, at least to some extent.

Furthermore, if one considers the ways in which Black and Latino men have been placed in conditions where their masculinity and sense of agency have been routinely threatened and compromised by poverty, racism, a police presence, unemployment, and other related factors, one can see copwatching as a form of masculine reclamation. The question arises, however, whether copwatching is an appropriate venue to work out one's psychic issues. Andrea Pritchett warns: "We have to be careful about this masculine performance of resistance. If I stand on a corner and talk shit about a cop, and I feel bold about this, and its four o'clock in the morning, who is going to back it up? I get nervous when copwatchers do this. We don't want to make it personal. The issues are very much systemic. With this masculine performance, it is tempting to be all about that moment of conflict. Your emotions are rising, and we can choose to indulge those emotions or take a step back and deescalate." It's important to remember, however, that this sense of emotional distance comes more easily to those who are not directly under police surveillance and feeling the psychic impact of constant oppression.

Like most forms of video activism, a gendered division of labor can plague copwatching. Men are often the ones before the cameras, who speak to the news media, and who engage in the higher testosterone activities, usually leaving the women behind the scenes to do the more monotonous and underappreciated work like balancing the books, cleaning, and stuffing envelopes. Andrea Pritchett notes: "There's a whole follow through of traditional office work where you have to do some writing, you have to do some phone calling, and you have to do the less glamorous stuff than just being the one who bagged the big footage; that work is sometimes gendered oddly enough. There can be a sexiness behind going out and getting the footage versus coming into the office and filing and doing all the infrastructure work that keeps Copwatch in existence."[109]

The number of women involved in copwatching in NYC is difficult to determine. CPU in 2016 reported that four women were involved, though I only spoke to one. No women are at the forefront of El Grito. Nico Fonseca from the Audre Lorde Project told me that women would be involved with copwatching during the LGBT parade in New York City—though I was never able to speak with any of them. The very inaccessibility and invisibility of female copwatchers in NYC speaks to the way in which the activity is thoroughly gendered and fits into larger practices of a gendered division of labor that haunts much media activism.

Despite the gendered division of labor behind the scenes, some of CPU's videos document the presence of strong women in the community confronting the police. In "30 Pct. – Police Try to Arrest 2 Young Girls and the Community Did Not Allow It," we see unsteady cellphone footage shot from a distance observing a teenage Latinx girl apprehended by her wrist by a burly police officer.[110] The videographer speaks off frame citing the location where the incident is taking place and occasionally advises the girl, "Tell them you want your parents."

Around halfway into the video, a Black woman approaches the cop yelling: "They have no business touching you." As the woman speaks, the videographer demands the name of the officer, which leads the woman and other community members to demand it also. Here, we are witnessing a collective resistance building as the community discovers its singular voice in confronting the police.

As community momentum escalates, the Black woman encourages the girl to approach the cop car and get the officer's name and badge number. The woman advises her: "You make sure you get it to your mother." The girl tentatively approaches the patrol car's open window asking for the information. As she gets the information, the girl berates the cop until he threateningly gets out of the car and chases her down. As he approaches her, the community gets more involved by blocking the cop's path as the cameraman asserts, "She's expressing her first amendment rights." This is an interesting moment when the filmic and political world nearly converge as the community defends the teenager's rights. The community pulls the girl back away from the policeman. This goes on for a remarkable two minutes of cat and mouse where the cop attempts to apprehend the girl with the community defending her until the cop finally slinks back to his car and leaves.

This footage shows how copwatching empowers communities. The comments on the video's YouTube page further stress this. One states: "Each person has the right to resist an unlawful arrest. In such a case, the person attempting the arrest stands in the position of a wrongdoer and may be

FIGURE 3.13: A remarkable video shot by Copwatch Patrol Unit that shows women in a community intervening to stop an undercover police officer from arresting a teenage girl, forcing him to retreat to his car. (Copwatch Patrol Unit, 2015.)

resisted by the use-of-force, as in self-defense. (State v. Mobley, 240 N.C. 476, 83 S. E. 2d 100)." Another comments: "One may come to the aid of another being unlawfully arrested, just as he may where one is being assaulted, molested, raped or kidnapped. Thus, it is not an offense to liberate one from the unlawful custody of an officer, even though he may have submitted to such custody, without resistance. (Adams v. State, 121 Ga. 16, 48 S. E. 910)." Case law complements the jarring footage of resistance showing that the community's spontaneous resistance is justified in a court of law, reminiscent of the way that the Black Panthers and Young Lords used state laws to support their self-defense.

Tellingly, however, only a few comments remark about the Black women's strength in resisting the police. One person writes: "The women are doing the fighting while the men film and run their mouths." Similarly, someone comments: "I notice that it's Black women who protected those girls while Black men idly stood by." It is interesting that the focus on the women's strength is always mentioned in conjunction with the suggestion that the men failed in their gendered role as protectors. The comments in part reinforce the gendered assumptions illustrated within the "46 Pct CPU

Confront" video where the male copwatchers aggressively confront the police. The absence of such posturing in the "30 pct." video, on the other hand, is read as masculine failure rather than simply as another form of copwatching. Clearly, the psychic dimensions regarding masculine posturing and copwatching are far more complicated than I can address here. But such moments at least draw attention to how gender issues permeate copwatching.

The Risks of Copwatching: Ramsey Orta

Although the footage of "30 Pct. – Police Try to Arrest 2 Young Girls and the Community Did Not Allow It" suggests a seamless way in which the community can perform their own forms of copwatching and self-defense, there is considerable danger involved in individuals copwatching on their own without the proper resources or knowing their rights. The case of Ramsey Orta illustrates a troubling instance.

Orta became a sensation when his footage of the murder of Eric Garner by Daniel Pantaleo went viral. Orta had no familiarity with copwatching. He came from a rough background and had accrued many arrests by his early twenties. But after filming Eric Garner's murder, he became a hero to many copwatchers. Kim Ortiz states in so many words, "He is New York's hero." Josmar Trujillo observes, "His instinct [to film] represents the natural ability of people on the streets; they know most about what cops are capable of doing. When he filmed Garner, he did it not because the video would go viral. He was trying to protect his friend." Just a week prior to Garner's murder, Orta filmed another Black man being beaten by a cop with a baton in the same location on Staten Island.

Yet Jason Del Aguila relates Orta's vulnerable position: "Here is the case of a real hood kid with minimal resources, with a criminal record, really being taken [for] a ride by a powerful gang: the NYPD. He did something to make this system accountable. But it is concerning to me that here is a kid who is not aware of the historical background. He didn't even understand Black Lives Matter. He said, 'All lives matter.' This kid had no idea what was to unravel around him."

After his footage went viral, Orta was targeted by the police. He was arrested three times by September 2015, a little over a year after Garner's death. He received some financial support through a GoFundMe webpage that allowed him to be released on bail. Some members of El Grito provided advice and legal support. But because El Grito and other copwatch groups are poorly funded and most don't even possess 501(c)(3) status, they cannot offer adequate support. As Monifa Bandele of the Malcolm X Grassroots Movement notes, "At the end of the day, we are not a resource organization. We are all volunteers. People work during the day. People give an hour or two on the weekends. We don't have any full-time staff people. When they support Ramsey or go to the [2013] Floyd hearings [regarding stop-and-frisk policing], they are using vacation days. People can barely build infrastructure for their own groups. Beyond that, it is going to take resources that we don't have."

Orta was vulnerable in two respects. First, he didn't have a clean record and continued to engage in suspect activity even when targeted by the police. Second, he was a working-class man of color who lacked resources, powerful connections, and cultural capital. Orta had none of the advantages of the RNC 8, who could marshal more resources as well as perform within a prescribed middle-class and white norm on television cameras and in the courtroom. Orta's case starkly reveals how racial and class privileges led to very different outcomes regarding his activism. On July 13, 2016, Orta pled guilty to various charges and received a four-year sentence in Rikers Island starting October 2016.

Orta is not unique in being targeted by the police for his copwatch footage. Taisha Allen also filmed officer Daniel Pantaleo who killed Eric Garner. In March 2015, Allen was arrested for being in a park after closing time. The officer allegedly said, "You're that little girl from the Eric Garner case."[111] Chris LeDay, who posted the video of Alton Sterling being shot to death by the police, was detained the next day by the police for dubious reasons. Abdullah Muflahi, who uploaded the second video of Sterling's death, was also detained by the police for four hours as they searched his convenience store. Diamond Reynolds, who streamed Philando Castile's murder, was held for eight hours in custody. Kevin Moore, who filmed the police tackling Freddie Gray and shoving him into a van, was arrested and then released without charges.

In response to police abuse against copwatchers, a group of more than forty documentary filmmakers including Laura Poitras, Alex Gibney, Barbara Kopple, and Joshua Oppenheimer wrote a statement in 2016 supporting the right of people to record the police.[112] Encouraging as this gesture was, it does not change the fact that an organizational infrastructure needs to be created to support an ethically responsible form of copwatching culture that anyone can participate in.

Copwatching Support: The Police Reform Organizing Project

The Police Reform Organizing Project (PROP) was founded by Robert Gangi in 2011 with the goal of ending the abuse of discriminatory policing. Gangi had been an activist and community organizer in New York City for over forty years and served as executive director of the Correctional Association for twenty-nine years. PROP regularly conducts studies regarding broken windows policing's discriminatory results and the problems of the NYPD quota system. In the years since its origins, PROP has become more critical of NYPD practices. As Gangi explained to me, "We are getting more blunt and simplistic in our message: end broken windows policing and abolish the quota system. Don't come to us about better training or police diversity or body-worn cameras or the like. Just stop it. The racism in policing in New York City is so deep and endemic you can't fix it."

PROP has teamed up with other organizations to highlight the dysfunction of broken windows policing. For example, PROP, Bronxites for NYPD Accountability, and the Coalition to End Broken Windows engaged in the "Swipe It Forward" campaign that provided free rides at subway terminals in low-income districts that police frequently targeted.[113] The campaign also draws attention to the fact that the majority of arrests and summonses in New York City revolve around "theft of services" such as fare evasion or turnstile hopping. The idea originated with a local union organizer who would rather remain anonymous. Trujillo connected her with PROP to fund the action.

Over the course of three days, PROP conducted actions at five high traffic subway stop locations in poor communities of color. According to Gangi, "NYPD assigns police officers to subway stations in primarily Black and brown communities. It is targeting. It is harassment. It is a waste of resources. If they wanted to stop it (fare evasion), they should post security people at a turnstile. Instead, cops hide in the shadows and wait for someone to jump a turnstile and then arrest them." Even though people may have unlimited Metrocards, for example, they cannot use it twice withing a period of eighteen minutes— an arbitrary time limit. So, a parent can get arrested or summonsed for using one Metrocard to allow their child through the turnstile with them.

Because of such targeting and tactics, people of color accounted for 92 percent of the arrests for fare evasion in 2015.[114] Even the passing of the Criminal Justice Reform Act of 2016 that decriminalized many quality-of-life arrests like open container, littering, public urination, and noise complaints did not help, because theft of services was not included.[115]

FIGURE 3.14: The Police Reform Organizing Project, Bronxites for NYPD Accountability, and the Coalition to End Broken Windows teamed up for a "Swipe It Forward" campaign in 2016 to swipe subway commuters through turnstiles for free while drawing attention to the way NYPD targets low-income communities of color for such violations. In "Fare Beating" (2016), we watch a female community organizer shame the police from their stations in the subway.

A video, "Fare Beating," done in connection with Elite Daily, a millennial website, contextualizes and shows the "Swipe It Forward" action in process.[116] This is the most professional looking of all the videos discussed earlier, suggesting that significant resources were dedicated to it. The video's extensive editing, well-framed sequences, and crisp sound suggest a group of well-trained video makers who had access to decent postproduction equipment. The video addresses an audience unfamiliar with these issues. It dramatically opens in medias res with a low-angle shot of a Black woman holding a sign in a subway terminal yelling at two police officers who scamper off screen: "like he's ready to hurt somebody. Shame on you! Shame on you!" The footage cuts to the officers rapidly ascending stairs out of the terminal. The camera cuts back to a close-up of the woman, "We are fighting back, New York." In a few economic moves, the video establishes how activists have seized collective control of the terminal.

Superimposed over the footage of activists swiping people through turnstiles are a series of statistics like the following: 29,000 people were arrested in 2015 for fare beating—92 percent of whom were people of color. The video relies heavily on montage to create a sense of collective organizing. A young woman of color explains to a bystander outside the terminal as the sun creates a halo around her: "People get arrested and ticketed every single day for being swiped into the subway. And if you think about it, that's not a crime at all." A Black woman speaks as we watch people swiping through turnstiles, "We've had enough of NYPD putting a financial strain on our communities through transit summonses, fines, arrests, warrants, harassment, etcetera." Josmar Trujillo, in black cap and jacket then adds, "It's always been the subway system. It is the heart blood of New York, and it's been the heart blood of the policing of New York for at least the last twenty years."

The activists' articulate accounts of the problems with enforcing fare beating not only humanizes them as being respectful, organized, and intelligent, but also shows how their activism draws a diverse constituency of people together since theft of services policing effects a wide range of people of color. Furthermore, by interspersing activists' accounts with footage of them interacting with people such as a woman hugging one activist or someone swiping strangers forward and seeing their gratitude, the videographers show how collective organizing grows through these actions.

Through editing and framing, the video relates a moment where public space is at the command of the people, where those engaged in resistance are articulate and in control. If, as cultural studies scholar John Fiske suggests, surveillance is about dehumanizing those who do not fit into the norm of whiteness, then countersurveillance activities such as the video documents are about reclaiming both a sense of individual and collective humanity and action.[117] This is punctuated in a sequence where a Black male eloquently states, "The beauty of this action is that the cops can't do anything about it. It's still resistance, but it's within the law so they're just stuck." While he speaks, we watch activists swiping people through turnstiles. In one shot, a cop is framed from a distance between two metal turnstiles, contained, trapped, and marginalized, unable to do anything about the activists' actions.

The man continues, "unless they do something stupid. And we got cameras for that." Quickly edited together are a sea of extended hands holding phones filming from multiple directions. The anonymity of those holding the phones further stresses that people aside from the activists might be filming the event, too—not simply to ward off the police, but also to chronicle the surprising moment of collective agency and goodwill as strangers swipe forward other strangers in solidarity.

Typical of much activist video, "Fare Beating" creates a sense of collective identification. As Patricia Zimmermann notes, many activist videos "form new battalions across identities within new spaces."[118] "Fare Beating"

but it's within the
law. So they just stuck,

FIGURE 3.15: "Fare Beating" (2016) frames a police officer in the distance cramped between two subway turnstiles to suggest his lack of authority and irrelevancy as the community action takes place.

reconfigures the subway terminal from a site of individual commuters with separate interests into a collective moment of resistance where mutual aid and well-informed discussion ensues. The action challenges and marginalizes the police, which the video emphasizes through its distant and cramped framing of police officers. The video offers viewers an alternative to simply opposing the police by proposing its own initial solutions whereby strangers might be able to help one another in previously unforeseen ways.

Body-worn Cameras and Anticopwatch

In May 2015, Barack Obama said the Department of Justice would fund $75 million over three years for the introduction of body-worn cameras (BWC) into various police forces.[119] Although BWC have been championed by some as a significant intervention into making police officers more accountable for their actions, the data around such results is mixed. Most support for BWC is based on one study conducted between the years of 2012 and 2013 in Rialto, California. When officers wore BWC, use of force—when officers used excessive force against people—dropped by 59 percent and complaints against the police dropped by a whopping 88 percent. The two authors of the study cautioned that the use of BWC alone cannot account for the significant change, which did not stop Axon, a division of Taser and one of the main manufacturers of BWC, to champion the statistics to promote their devices.[120]

Another study published in May 2016 offers very different results. It analyzed over 2.2 million officer hours of eight small and large police departments in the United States and Britain. It found that use of force only decreased 37 percent when officers recorded every interaction with their BWC. More troubling, use of force increased by 71 percent when officers could switch their cameras on and off at will.[121] Most recently, a January 2023 report by the National Institute of Justice concluded that "research does not necessarily support the effectiveness of body-worn cameras" after comprehensively reviewing over seventy studies of their effectiveness."[122]

Nonetheless, BWC have become a cash cow for companies like Axon and VIEVU, the two main manufacturers of the devices. In 2015, the Cleveland Police Department invested $2.4 million in them. A year later, the Los Angeles Police Department purchased 7,000 cameras at a cost of $42 million. In December 2015, the NYPD started a pilot program to outfit officers with cameras in poor communities of color that were targeted by stop-and-frisk policies.[123] By August 2019, NYPD had deployed 24,000 cameras.[124]

Most activists and organizers within New York City remain skeptical toward BWC programs since they feel that the discussion detracts from more systemic issues regarding policing and how BWC enact more surveillance upon poor communities of color. Andrew Padilla, a copwatcher and filmmaker, states, "All this energy toward accountability ... can be flipped into increased surveillance in communities of color and increased budgets to police."[125] Josmar Trujillo similarly observes, "In terms of surveillance, I don't want more cameras in the world that are going to help incriminate people and put more people in the criminal justice system." If surveillance is a "technology of whiteness," as John Fiske observes, then the deployment of BWC by police into poor Black and brown neighborhoods signals a further extension of this racist regime.[126]

Andrew Padilla notes, "Body-worn cameras on police [are] fundamentally the opposite of cop watch. BWC on police ... record civilians. In cop watch, you record police."[127] Body-worn cameras further disenfranchise communities of color by implying that police-shot video footage is enough. Josmar Trujillo explains, "The police camera idea takes away the idea of the public to really rely on itself to be the source of police brutality videos and evidence of what has happened. We are supposed to believe that the police somehow after all these years will objectively report on themselves?" Recent data suggests otherwise. Increasingly, NYPD redacts BWC footage claiming privacy concerns. For example, roughly two-thirds of footage turned over to the Civilian Complaint Review Board (CCRB), which independently reviews police misconduct incidents, is redacted. This doesn't include the additional footage where officers intentionally obstruct the camera.[128]

Further issues arise about the inherent bias of BWC footage and access to it. Certain defense lawyers are coming to the realization long understood by cinema and media studies scholars: the placement of the camera holds an inherent bias in its relationship to the subject being filmed. Multiple studies suggest the biases of interrogation videos. One study showed that when someone is being interrogated after being arrested, if the officer doing the interrogation was not shown in the frame, the interrogation seems less coercive to viewers even when evidence suggested the contrary.[129] Like the practice of embedded journalism during the Iraq and Afghanistan wars where reporters accompanying US troops would lead to more sympathetic stories, BWC adhere to the police's point of view and never bother to embody any other perspective.[130]

As mentioned earlier, the public has been repeatedly denied access to BWC footage. This was most dramatically illustrated by the Laquan McDonald case in Chicago where it took more than a year to release the footage that showed officers gunning down a Black man who was running from them.[131] The same issue occurring within NYPD is well documented. A 2021 report from the Center for Constitutional Rights highlights that the NYPD's BWC policy remains limited in scope in making such footage accessible to the CCRB and the public at large.[132]

Jose LaSalle notes the difficulty of getting police footage: "The police will have possession of these body-worn cameras and possession of the image that they record. That is not going to help. Some people have to wait for years to get the footage of that material." For example, El Grito filed a Freedom of Information Act request for police camera and surveillance footage of officers beating Enrique Del Rosario. Dennis Flores has footage of multiple police officers filming the event. The NYPD claims that it still cannot locate the footage. Dennis Flores sued NYPD for the footage to no avail.[133]

A new tactic by police departments is to charge exorbitant fees to access police camera footage. In April 2015, a New York City television station filed an open-records request for five weeks of unedited video from a NYPD BWC program. The NYPD insisted that they pay a $36,000 copying fee. The station sued NYPD for the footage, which was finally released three years later in 2018.[134] The state of Texas is forcing all its police departments to charge a $10 fee for each police BWC recording made available with an additional charge of a dollar a minute if an identical copy has not been released. Strangely, the same fees do not apply for police dash cam footage.[135] Most shockingly, a new North Carolina law classifies police camera footage as outside the scope of public records requests, making all of it unavailable to the general public.[136] So rather than making this footage easily accessible, various police departments enact a series of obstructions to obtain it.

Despite most states having laws restricting BWC footage, the murder of George Floyd in 2020 caused a few states like Minnesota, Connecticut, and Colorado to provide more access to their footage. Even legislators in North Carolina are discussing legislation to release BWC footage forty-eight hours following an incident due to the police killing of Andrew Brown Jr. in April 2021.[137] Increasingly, the use of BWC is being questioned by police departments and government officials for a whole host of reasons such as its mixed impact and the high costs in both purchasing and maintaining the equipment and the vast amount of storage space needed for its footage.[138]

Conclusion

A wave of community organizations against gentrification and broken windows policing in New York City has surged to the forefront since 2014 with the killings of Eric Garner and Mike Brown and the rise of Black Lives Matter. According to Yul-San Liem of the Justice Committee: "When Communities United for Police Reform launched in 2012, there was a core team of seven or eight groups organizing around it.... Now there is a lot of newer groups that have come up in the last two-year period. Twenty sixteen is significantly different than 2011 and 2012. We are developing relationships with the new groups and nationally."

By 2018, copwatching became such a hot topic that the Copwatch Patrol Unit agreed to partner with Black Entertainment Television (BET) to produce *Copwatch America,* a program that documents the copwatching done by select groups in New York City and Atlanta. According to LaSalle, one of the show's producers claimed the series would involve copwatchers across the United States. "But in reality," LaSalle notes, "Copwatch Patrol Unit is the only group that really has a lot of evidence of the work they do."[139]

The show aired in fall 2019. Initially, some CPU members held reservations about the show, particularly in the way in which it highlighted infighting between CPU and Black Lives Matter Greater New York in early

FIGURES 3.16 & 3.17: Copwatch Patrol Unit teamed up with Black Entertainment Television in 2019 to produce the show *Copwatch America*. The show provided slick production values and wide distribution. But some of CPU's members felt that producers were trying to focus on intragroup fighting rather than on police abuse.

episodes. Kim Ortiz states, "I had my concern, you know, about maybe it being a little bit too much like a reality show and maybe a little too much infighting and drama and not enough focusing on the work being done even though these little dramas and beefs, you know, are real."[140] As a result, Ortiz stopped giving producers details about the infighting between groups, which forced the show to focus more on copwatching in its later episodes.

The show yielded some concrete results, like the firing of Atlanta police officer Sung Kim who shot and killed an unarmed twenty-one-year-old Jimmy Atchison in January 2019.[141] According to news stories, Kim was given two options: resign or be terminated. The show provided valuable traction for needed media attention that the attorney for the Atchison family had been seeking ever since the killing.

Originally slated for ten episodes, all of which had been shot and edited, the show was suddenly pulled off the air by episode seven in December 2019. Episode eight was supposed to air on December 8, but BET announced shortly beforehand that the show would be going on hiatus for the holidays, which was not an uncommon move. Other BET shows like *Sisters* and *The Oval* also paused over the winter break.

But when *Sisters* and *The Oval* announced their return dates while *Copwatch America* did not, CPU members became alarmed. Ortiz recounts, "We were texting our people that we've been able to reach out to [individuals from BET] and who've always been responsive up until this point who are now not responding to messages, not getting back to us. You know, sending us straight to voicemail." Similarly, Jose LaSalle recalls, "[A producer from the show] gave us a thing about that his lawyer was looking into it, and he'll get back to us, and never got back to us."

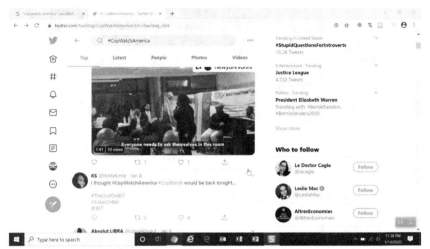

FIGURE 3.18: *Copwatch America* ran for seven episodes before mysteriously being taken off the air for unknown reasons. Such a partnership reveals the difficulties any activist group has working with commercial media where most of the decisions are made by executives at distant locations often without the consultation of the groups participating with them. Twitter followers were disturbed to realize the show had been suddenly cancelled.

CPU members speculate that the show "pissed off political people" in Atlanta and New York City for its critical portrayals of the police. But neither Ortiz nor LaSalle could confirm this. Even worse, CPU signed a binding contract with BET to not allow any other network access to their material.[142] So while the show is in limbo, CPU is stuck without a mainstream distribution outlet.[143]

CPU's experience with BET reveals the nebulous shared terrain between grassroots digital media activism and the interests of commercial media. CPU wanted to get its coverage out to a wider audience whereas BET wanted to capitalize upon the increasing popularity of copwatching. Although tensions existed from the beginning, CPU and BET established a delicate balance between their respective interests for social justice and viewer ratings. But as the show produced concrete results and/or ruffled political feathers, BET quickly withdrew, leaving CPU in the lurch. Kim Ortiz humorously reflects on the experience, "We went with Black Entertainment Television thinking they were about *black entertainment television,* our dumb asses."

Nonetheless, LaSalle ultimately imagines CPU creating its own YouTube series intertwined with livestreaming. He contemplates, "We will document from the moment we start the livestream to the end. We will push

FIGURE 3.19: Some fans of *Copwatch America* created a petition in support of the show. The petition received little traction and made no impact. CPU members at the time of writing still have never received a response from BET as to why the show was cancelled. Cast members suspect the show's cancellation arose because of police pushback in Atlanta for the show getting an officer fired and/or complaints from representatives of the New York Police Department.

it out there because people want to see that, people are very interested in seeing that."[144] Whether or not this will become a reality remains to be seen since the internet is littered with abandoned alternative media projects that sounded good in theory but revealed themselves as requiring more resources than initially anticipated. Furthermore, commercial platforms can remove content for any given reason. So, reliance upon such unpredictable capitalist platforms seems deeply problematic for activists to create long term, sustained media projects. But CPU, like many social movements that use digital media in their activism and community organizing, continue to copwatch in their local communities despite their troubles with BET and other outlets.

El Grito de Sunset Park continues copwatching and community organizing, but with the devastating impact of hurricanes Irma and Maria upon Puerto Rico, they started organizing relief efforts in 2017 for the island. Dennis Flores dedicated his full-time attention to hurricane relief while Jason Del Aguila ran the copwatching aspect of the organization.[145] Flores took three months off from his job at the Metropolitan Transportation Authority to oversee volunteers collecting supplies and travel to Puerto Rico to ensure that the supplies reached their intended destinations.

While engaged in relief efforts, Flores befriended Nelson W. Canals, a former professor and journalist who had been involved in the Puerto

Rican Independence movement. When Canals learned about Flores's shared outlook in terms of community organizing and self-determination, he donated twenty-nine acres of land in Puerto Rico to El Grito.[146] The land will be used to establish an activist retreat space, a media lab, and a recording studio along with supplying low-cost produce for those in need. According to Flores, "We have been meeting with farms across the island to form a cooperative with them to export coffee and use the profits to go back to the farms and our space."[147]

In the meantime in 2017, WITNESS, a Brooklyn-based nonprofit that uses video and digital technology to document human rights abuses, teamed up with Berkeley Copwatch and El Grito to establish online databases on copwatching.[148] In 2020, El Grito received a small grant to organize and update the database with hundreds of hours of footage. The database helps identify and analyze larger patterns of police abuse and provides a toolkit for other organizations to engage in copwatching and set up their own database.

In addition to all this, El Grito launched Copwatch Media in 2021.[149] The site supports community journalism by people of color that focuses on law enforcement's multiple impacts on local neighborhoods within the tri-state region (New York, New Jersey, and Connecticut). Josmar Trujillo along with other journalists like Raven Rakia who have been covering policing for a significant amount of time, comprise part of Copwatch Media's staff. All of this work represents a logical extension of copwatching becoming part of a larger grassroots media ecosystem and community-based movements. El Grito's recent digital forays with WITNESS and creating Copwatch Media deepens its analysis of and connection with various communities pushing back against policing, gentrification, and political disenfranchisement. El Grito's acquisition of twenty-nine acres of land provides the needed infrastructure to expand their efforts both digitally and on the ground. It serves as a reminder that such digital work always has a physical element to it and requires concrete resources to make it possible.

As one might imagine, the deaths of Breonna Taylor and George Floyd in 2020 inspired a new generation of activists who took to the streets. Youthful enthusiasm and improvisation defined much of the protests that occurred in NYC by these new groups of people who had little to no connection with any of the organizations discussed in this chapter. By July 2020, mobilizations reached a crescendo when it was discovered that Najieb Isaac, a central organizer with the group Why Accountability, was a parole officer, a representative of the very criminal justice system that such groups were protesting against. The fallout grew ugly as infighting and some physical altercations among activists resulted from a sense of a betrayal of trust and the growing fatigue and burnout that often accompanies months of ceaseless activism.[150]

Groups splintered and some momentum was lost, but, as often happens behind the scenes after the visible wave of protests recede, new contacts flourish as reassessments of tactics, strategies, and partnerships ensue. Isaac Ortega, one of the organizers of a series of Black Lives Matter protests that took place over the summer of 2020 in Washington Square Park, eventually met Dennis Flores. Dennis showed Ortega his short documentary on Ramsey Orta and his ordeal with NYPD after filming Eric Garner's death. According to Ortega, "the footage convinced me of the usefulness of recording the police and generally showing cop misconduct."[151]

That Ortega only became familiar with copwatching in 2020 was surprising. After all, the highly publicized killings of Black men that this chapter started off with had occurred a mere six years before Taylor's and Floyd's murders. But, as Ortega reminded me, "I was only fifteen at the time." It is not that those murders didn't register with Ortega, but the intricacies of copwatching and activism had not come into full focus for him yet.

Ortega now works part-time with El Grito in building up its copwatch database. "I basically comb through protest footage—some of the ones I organized, which is a little trippy," he notes. "I input the cops' names, the incidents, the date and time. I screenshot faces and badge numbers of the police who were in the footage." It is a laborious and time-consuming process, but Ortega considers it important since it is "one way of holding cops accountable, or otherwise those incidents would fade out of collective memory."

Fostering a collective memory is particularly salient in maintaining the progress of movements by providing connective links between different generations of activists. Footage that an older generation takes for granted becomes inspiring to a new one. Copwatching is not only about making the police accountable or even establishing practices of collective organizing for self-determination by historically disenfranchised communities, though they are both important elements. It is also about founding a vernacular archive of sound and images of everyday peoples' actions and ideas that serve as the mortar for collective memories of communities that mainstream historical accounts have largely ignored. Preserving these videos remains an important task since recordings of the past can inspire the actions of future generations. These videos not only assist in collective organizing and self-determination for the present-day communities but also future ones. The Young Lords and earlier anticolonial struggles inspired the founders of El Grito de Sunset Park. The actions of Ramsey Orta, documented by Dennis Flores, inspire Isaac Ortega. But videos alone are not enough. It is the network of social relations and connections that provide the conduits between generations that resurrect such videos and make them relevant.

As this chapter has demonstrated, digital technology has played an increasingly important role in community organizing, holding the police accountable, and analyzing the links between how policing, gentrification, and the withdrawal of needed state resources all interlock to target working-class communities of color. But the technology is only a part of the story and can only maintain relevancy as long as different generations of activists build off of one another's struggles and inheritances.

This newer generation of activists need not necessarily follow in the wake of their elders. While updating El Grito's database, Ortega continues to work with a younger generation of activists and community organizers. He belongs to a newly established collective, For Our Liberation. When I asked him if they have any connections with any older groups, he replies that the collective did not. When I asked him why, Ortega paused in reflection before stating: "I think the older groups are pretty established. They have their own way of doing things. Younger folks like being on the streets. I mean, we're younger, and I think we have the kind of energy and want to be on the street and confronting the state directly."

As I spoke with Ortega, I could not help but feel a sense of hope. He splits his time between doing archival work with El Grito to preserve those vital collective memories of community resistance against state repression and strategizing new directions with For Our Liberation. Ortega looks both forward and backward simultaneously, coming to grips with older activist histories and practices while also forging into the future as his generation discovers new paths and creates new collective memories while looking forward to the day that copwatching will no longer be necessary at all.

CHAPTER 4

Somali American Narratives and Suspect Communities

Visibility, Representation, and Media Making in the Age of Islamophobia

O minous music plays across the sound track as an avalanche of rapid-fire, grainy scenes of homemade footage quickly edited together showing suicide bombers self-detonating, turbaned men declaring the end of America, terrorist beheadings, and trails of strewn and dismembered bodies overload the screen. Wayne Simmons, narrator of the video and a self-styled expert on terrorism, stands before an American flag and states in stark terms, "The Islamo-fascists who are attacking the world want to impose their beliefs on the world." Eight years later, Simmons was exposed as a charlatan, having falsely claimed to be a CIA operative while serving as a regular host on *Fox News*. He received thirty-three months behind bars.[1]

This sequence comes from *The Third Jihad: Radical Islam's Vision for America* (2008), financed by the Clarion Fund, a nonprofit group that the Southern Poverty Law Center has labeled an anti-Muslim hate group.[2] During the same year, Clarion made twenty million copies of its 2006 film, *Obsession: Radical Islam's War Against the West*, to distribute to homes in swing states during the 2008 presidential election.[3]

The Third Jihad could easily be dismissed as far right conspiracy propaganda until the *Village Voice* in January 2011 revealed that the film had been incorporated into the New York Police Department's counterterrorism training.[4] After initial denials by then police commissioner Ray Kelly, who actually is interviewed in the film, a freedom of information request revealed that the film had been played on an endless loop and viewed by 68 lieutenants, 159 sergeants, 31 detectives, and 1,231 patrol officers—although the exact role the film played during training never became clear.[5]

The film contributed to a culture of Islamophobia that defined the NYPD. Its notorious Demographics Unit targeted Muslim groups during 2002–14 by infiltrating mosques, community centers, and local colleges with informants, essentially treating the entire Muslim American community as suspicious.[6] In 2007, the NYPD published a controversial study entitled "Radicalization in the West: The Homegrown Threat" that claimed to identify "jihadist ideology" through four identifiable stages an individual passes through, a theory that has since been discredited.[7] If anything, the screening of The Third Jihad as part of NYPD training reveals the disturbing prevalence of how right-wing paranoia has penetrated state institutions like the police.

Although The Third Jihad emerged in 2008, the conspiracies that it promotes continue to metastasize. A sequence in The Third Jihad zooms in on a "Welcome to Islamberg" wooden town sign as eerie music plays. The narrator explains, "In upstate New York there is a small community that on the face of it appears to be a faithful group of devotional Muslims, but when you look into it, you will find a lot of very concerning activities going on there." In a series of interviews, white people purportedly from surrounding communities, wonder aloud if Islamberg has "two faces" and whether there are sinister reasons behind the gun shots they claim to hear. These accounts contribute to the Islamophobic conspiracy theory that Islamberg is one of a cluster of covert radical Muslim communities serving as breeding and training grounds for terrorists. As a result, self-appointed white male saviors occasionally attempt to storm the town. In 2017, Robert Doggart received a twenty-year prison sentence for his plans to recruit militia and attack the town. In January 2019, three young men were arrested for similarly planning to infiltrate Islamberg. They were apprehended after discussing their scheme on Discord, the anonymous group chat site that has been favored by white supremacists and was used by the organizers of the Unite the Right hate rally in Charlottesville, Virginia.[8]

These instances emphasize the fact that representation matters and has very concrete consequences, and as a result, groups that have been underrepresented in commercial media strive for visibility. In each limited appearance on the screen, a single character serves as a synecdoche, standing in for the community as a whole because its richness and diversity is not represented. African Americans, Asian Americans, LGBTQ communities, Native Americans, and many other groups constantly confront the ramifications of this limited exposure.

Muslim American and Arab American communities have long been subject to a very narrow representational range within US popular culture; these communities have typically been shown as exotic sheiks and seductresses, villains and victims, and most recently—terrorists. Black American Muslims remain largely absent from commercial screens except for the recurrent figures of Malcolm X, Louis Farrakhan, and Muhammad Ali. A long history of Orientalism and Islamophobia emerge in representations of Muslim and Arab Americans in Western popular culture.[9]

The situation has grown more dire since September 11 as Arab American-looking communities and individuals have been drawn into the crosshairs of US national security concerns, which have always been imbued with white supremacy and the Othering of nonwhite groups. The ramifications of this are increasingly dire. The Council on American-Islamic Relations noted a 44 percent increase of anti-Muslim hate crimes throughout 2015 alone.[10] The election of Donald Trump has further emboldened white nationalists and garden variety racists with his administration's desire to impose a Muslim ban, separate children from families detained at the Mexican border, and his repeated failure to condemn racist groups and actions.[11] Conservative media plays a vital role in amplifying such Islamophobia in order to unite and mobilize a wide array of supporters.[12]

As Ella Shohat and Robert Stam argue, the use of stereotypes serves as a form of social control and reveals disequilibriums of power.[13] The desire by communities of color to improve and broaden their representational images is nothing less than the desire to claim full cultural citizenship.[14] The question of visibility is one of the core elements of contemporary disciplinary regimes. Michel Foucault writes in *Discipline and Punish*: "Disciplinary power ... is exercised through its invisibility; at the same time it imposes on those whom it subjects a principle of compulsory visibility. In discipline, it is the subjects who have to be seen. Their visibility assures the hold of the power that is exercised over them."[15] Although Foucault mostly wrote about prison in *Discipline and Punish*, he acknowledged that apparatuses of visibility form a carceral continuum that extends outward through "hospitals, schools, public administration and private enterprises," and one can add media organizations, social media platforms, and digital technologies as other disciplinary matrices where visibility functions. This chapter will address Muslim American communities in general and more specifically hone in on Somali Americans in Minneapolis and their resistance against governmental and commercial regimes of power that attempt to surveil them and contain their actions while limiting their representational visibility.

This chapter explores how communication in the form of films, social media, print journalism, commercial television, and cell phone videos bolsters and/or challenges the accumulation and centralization of knowledge about Muslim American communities. Surveillance and state repression serve as a part of a much wider disciplinary apparatus where media platforms are simultaneously a nexus of existing power relations and efforts to short-circuit these relations with counterrepresentations that challenge the prevailing regime. Media making must be read relationally to the prison-industrial complex, federal, state, and local law enforcement, and other governmental apparatuses like schools and social services since regimes of visibility and surveillance course through all of them.[16] Aware of this, community organizers view a struggle over representation and visibility as foundational in challenging oppression and marginalization.

This chapter particularly focuses on the resistance fostered by various Muslim American communities across the United States as community members have been drawn into the cross-hairs of not only the federal government but also commercial media as potential terrorists. As Sohail Daulatzai has stressed, the rhetoric of terrorism has "become a proxy for race, generating tremendous political and ideological capital. As the embodiment of the 'terrorist,' the Muslim haunts the geographic and imaginative spaces of US empire, a specter and menace not only to US national identity but also to the global community the United States claims to defend."[17] Surveillance provides a way of managing and disciplining Muslim and Arab American populations together with those who appear to be in that population whether they are or not.

The chapter begins broadly by focusing on the wide coalition of newly emergent and reinvigorated Muslim American organizations fighting over various terrains of visibility including physical spaces, commercial media representations, and countermedia practices that challenge the practices and regimes of representation that reinforce Islamophobic outlooks. The chapter then focuses upon Minneapolis as a case study where Muslim American youth have taken the lead in fighting against assumptions by the federal, state, and local government, as well as much commercial media that their communities are a hotbed of Islamic extremism. Minnesota's centrality as a media hub in the Midwest provides a rich terrain to investigate media activism that protests against Islamophobic representations and provides counterrepresentations through independent filmmaking and alternative media collectives. Grassroots media activism by members of the Somali American community reveals a multilayered and sophisticated approach, which can help lend insight into the upsurge in Muslim American media activism happening across the country.

Muslim American Grassroots Organizing against Countering Violent Extremism

Multiple factors contribute to the rise of grassroots Muslim American activism and the reinvigoration of older Muslim American organizations like the Council on American-Islamic Relations (CAIR). First, all levels of law enforcement have significantly targeted Muslim American populations after 9/11. The Department of Justice and the FBI rounded up at least 1,200 Muslims immediately after September 11.[18] The FBI has been increasingly pressuring Muslim Americans to become informants.[19] Undercover agents swarm and trawl the internet for potential Muslim terrorists.[20] The FBI, Department of Energy, and the New York Police Department have all been exposed secretly monitoring mosques.[21] Furthermore, police departments in Boston, Fresno, Denver, and elsewhere had been employing third-party services like Geofeedia, LifeRaft, and Sonar to conduct online surveillance targeting Muslim American and other activist communities.[22]

Second, as this book emphasizes, US legislation has increasingly expanded the definition of terrorism and enabled law enforcement to increasingly surveil communities and punish individuals with harsh sentences. In 1996 Congress passed the Antiterrorism and Effective Death Penalty Act that broadened the notion of material support funding terrorist activities to include and criminalize charitable or expressive activities, regardless whether those donating to such charities are aware of their terrorist links.[23] The 2001 USA Patriot Act broadened the definition of terrorism and conflated it with legitimate protest activity; it also eased FBI agents' ability to obtain personal records without warrants and subpoenas.[24] As mentioned in chapter 1, this legislation was initially employed against environmental and animal rights activists during the mid-to-late 1990s and into the early twenty-first century. But once 9/11 occurred, such legislation redirected itself primarily against Muslim American communities.

Third, anti-Muslim and anti-Arab hate crimes and Islamophobia rose precipitously by 1,700 percent in the first six months after 9/11.[25] According to FBI statistics, anti-Muslim hate crimes increased by 67 percent in 2015 and 19 percent in 2016.[26] Although these numbers have dropped more recently, the Council on American-Islamic Relations suggests consistent issues with anti-Muslim hate crimes.[27] Such statistics are often underreported to federal and state authorities for a variety of reasons like fear of retaliation and distrust of law enforcement.

Finally, Muslim American community organizing constitutes a part of global youth activism occurring after the Great Recession. During 2011–12 uprisings erupted in Egypt, Tunisia, Syria, Spain, England, and the United States. The highly publicized rise of Black Lives Matter in 2013, along with a surge in copwatching groups nationally, further mobilized youth in working-class communities of color. The rise of Trump has further spurred on Muslim American activism with his explicit Islamophobic and anti-immigrant policies. Islamophobes like Frank Gaffney who dismiss Islam as a religion held Trump's ear to influence policy decisions.[28] During the first eight months of his presidency, ICE increased arrests by 42 percent.[29]

As a result, many new Muslim American organizations have arisen while older ones have been revitalized. Some of the new ones that play a central role in this chapter are: Stop LAPD Spying Coalition (2011), Muslim Justice League (2014), MPower Change (2015), Vigilant Love (2015), Young Muslim Collective (2016), Justice for Muslims Collective (2016), and Poligon (2017).

Both MPower Change and Poligon are predominantly digital efforts to provide platforms to connect with grassroots communities and lobby in Congress.[30] Linda Sarsour, one of the founders of MPower Change, reflected, "I realized eventually a lot of marginalized groups had an online voice that reached back to grassroots organizing. Why is it that every other community has this place to insert their voices in larger national discourse but not Muslims?"[31] Sarsour had organizing roots with the Arab American Association of New York and thus saw online organizing as complementary to grassroots mobilizing. The organization hired Ishraq Ali in 2018 as organizing director. Ali is responsible for the creation of "a network of organizers that has the accountability and the professional environment and infrastructure to organize."[32]

CAIR chapters in Minneapolis and San Francisco brought on inspiring, young executive directors like Jaylani Hussein (2015) and Zahra Billoo (2009) who engaged with local communities more actively and visibly. The Electronic Frontier Foundation, typically assumed to be solely an online advocacy organization with a libertarian bent, hired Shahid Buttar in 2014 as director of grassroots advocacy.[33] In an interview Buttar noted that the foundation recognized how "a strictly online focus leaves a lot of cards on the table. We realize how local activism can impact national questions."[34] For example, NSA surveillance is a national issue, but it impacts specific communities differently. Not surprisingly, a lot of surveillance work is directed toward working-class communities of color and Muslim American neighborhoods. As a result, the foundation can integrate its focus on policy regarding digital surveillance with grassroots organizing efforts representing these targeted communities.

These groups focus on a wide array of issues like workplace discrimination; hate speech; anti-Muslim policies of federal, state, and local governments; discriminatory policing; white nationalism; gentrification; the prison-industrial complex; and many more. A particular issue that has galvanized and focused the energies of these groups is their opposition to the federal government's implementation of the Countering Violent Extremism program (CVE), which has impacted specific Muslim American communities very directly and severely but remains relatively unknown to the general public.

The idea for CVE had been kicking around since the days of the Bush presidency after the 9/11 attacks. The idea behind the program had origins in Britain with its own community policing of its Muslim population through such efforts as the Preventing Violent Extremism Program (2006) and the Channel Project (2007). Law enforcement would create partnerships between the community, schools, and local authorities to keep tabs on Muslim communities and identify any would-be radicalized individuals.[35] Many people, however, were critical of these social programs due to their top-down approach and their visualizing Muslims as a whole as a suspect community.[36]

The British programs had their own problematic precursors in the Prevention of Terrorism Act of 1974 used to surveil Irish communities living in Great Britain who might harbor sympathy for the Irish Republican Army or any other Irish sovereignty movement. Both the Terrorism Act and the Preventing Violent Extremism Program had roots in response to bombings and respectively viewed the Irish and Muslims as threats to Anglo society.[37] According to Paddy Hillyard, who studied the impact of the Prevention of Terrorism Act upon Irish communities, the act was less about locating criminals and more about criminalizing the community as a whole. Not only "certain *types of behavior* are designated prohibited acts by either statute or case law," but also "certain *categories of people* are drawn into the criminal justice system simply because of their status and irrespective of behavior."[38] As we will soon see, these are exactly the same concerns many Muslim Americans have over CVE's implementation.

CVE policy became codified under Obama in December 2011. Interestingly, its foundational document, "Strategic Implementation Plan for Empowering Local Partners to Prevent Violent Extremism in the United States," identifies some of the potential issues that many Muslim Americans had with the implementation of the program: that it could "do more harm than good" and "narrow our relationship with communities to any single issue, including national security."[39]

Of course, because the program emerged from the Department of Homeland Security (DHS) it gave the impression that Muslim Americans were primarily viewed through a threat lens despite the rhetoric of "local engagement" and "partnerships" that DHS officials employed. As one academic study on CVE concluded: "There is an inherent tension in attempting to build community partnerships and trust while at the same time executing the DOJ's primary criminal justice mandate.... It created an enduring perception that the CVE pilots were actually an intelligence gathering effort intended to cultivate community informants."[40]

The Obama administration announced three primary pilot cities for CVE in 2014: Boston, Los Angeles, and Minneapolis. In 2015, DHS asked Congress to fund CVE grant money. The idea would be that CVE would distribute grant money to law enforcement, community organizations, schools, and other local government entities with the vague hopes of countering violent extremism. But as soon as word went out regarding CVE, letters were sent to Congress by Muslim American, civil rights, and other community organizations concerned about CVE's underlying premises. A July 10, 2015, letter sent by twenty-nine organizations addressed to the House of Representatives, raised concerns about the stigmatizing and alienating of Muslim communities, the threats to freedom of speech and religion, and the program's lack of oversight and ability to determine its effectiveness.[41]

Despite the seemingly neutral language of many CVE documents, the fear of targeting Muslim communities proved accurate. Statistically speaking, far right and white nationalist groups have given rise to most domestic terrorist attacks. Between 2008 and 2017, for example, these groups produced 71 percent of extremist fatalities.[42] Yet 80–85 percent of CVE grants were dedicated to Muslim American community organizations or law enforcement efforts directed toward Muslim America communities.[43]

Emmanuel Mauleón succinctly lists all the problems Muslim Americans had with CVE: "CVE programs have been criticized for the lack of evidence supporting radicalization theory; for the lack of meaningful community input into community-centered programs; for the chilling effect they have on Muslim political expression and behavior; for further blurring the lines between social services, civil rights, policing, and intelligence gathering; for the lack of a clear and cohesive directive; and for alienating the very communities that they claim to assist."[44]

Surveillance and racial profiling of Muslim communities became a tremendous concern. DHS and other organizations relied on threat "indicators" that encompassed entire areas of everyday actions. DHS's booklet, *Homegrown Violent Extremism: Mobilizing Indicators*, which was released in 2015 and updated in 2019, suggests that "indicators are modestly diagnostic on their own and require one or more other indicators to gain diagnostically."[45] Such indicators include: "inquiring about jobs that provide sensitive access" like transportation, law enforcement, and the military; "outbursts of behavior, including violent behavior, or advocacy that results in exclusion or rejection by family or community"; and "deleting or manipulating social media or other online accounts to misrepresent location."[46]

People involved in CVE often emphasize how such indicators need to be contextualized and not simply taken on their own. But when CVE grants are being funneled toward primarily Muslim communities of color, the entire community cannot help but come under suspicion since the very existence of the program is targeted at communities of color where Islamic radicalization has occurred. Additionally, the appeal to contextualization conveniently overlooks the bias in applying CVE in a culture that is largely Islamophobic and cannot help but replicate these biases in community policing and the use of the grants.

We can observe this bias in the ways in which CVE grants have been applied. In 2016, DHS ran a "Peer to Peer: Challenging Extremism" competition. A student project at the Rochester Institute of Technology won a $149,000 grant for its #Exout Extremism social media campaign. An assistant professor of marketing, with no background in Muslim or Arabic culture, assigned her class the challenge. According to RIT publicity, the class "created a public relations and strategy agency, with a logo, website, social media, video platforms, and events to raise public awareness both on campus and in the community."[47]

Despite working with the Muslim community in Rochester, the website and campaign the students created focused exclusively on Muslim Americans. As one student notes in a promotional video: "ISIL uses fear to motivate. And we just thought if we put a counternarrative online to what ISIL is putting out, we could at least provide that platform for individuals to come seek out different aspects of the education." Furthermore, part of the project encouraged high school students "to report online promotion of violent extremism."[48] Such a focus ultimately ends up replicating the surveillance of Muslim American communities and failing to acknowledge much more prevalent forms of extremism perpetuated by the far right and white nationalists.

One Somali refugee student at RIT worried, "I was like oh no, they're only going to target people that are Muslims or people that are from a certain group. You know if you read any newspaper, they just think that refugees are ones that are more susceptible to becoming terrorists, or you know, Muslim refugees especially." When this was brought to the attention of those who helped create the campaign, a participant assured reporters that the project would expand to other forms of extremism.[49] But, like many web-based endeavors, the project quickly fizzled out and never expanded beyond Muslims.

My purpose here is not to harshly critique well-meaning but ill-informed students and faculty about how they reinforce an Islamophobic framework, but instead to illustrate how CVE grant money propagates such narratives. According to Shannon Al-Wakeel of the Muslim Justice League: "Peer-to-peer, sort of broadly speaking, is an example that regardless of generation people can be lured into getting involved in some pretty bad projects if they don't know better and if there is professional advancement and funding opportunities attached."[50]

CVE Enters Minneapolis: Rising Resistance

Minneapolis provides a unique location to examine grassroots organizing by Muslim American youth within a relatively small city of 422,000 people. Furthermore, it is also a central hub for a wide array of media making from independent and Hollywood films, local news, and grassroots alternative media organizations where much Muslim American activism directs its focus. The city has a strong industrial media base for corporate television and video for companies like Ameriprise, Best Buy, General Mills, and 3M, all of which have corporate headquarters in the state. Furthermore, the city and state have frequently served as locations for Hollywood productions like *The Mighty Ducks* (1992), *Fargo* (1996), *North Country* (2005), and *Wilson* (2017). It also hosts both the Minneapolis-St. Paul Film Festival and the Twin Cities Film Fest. According to Lucinda Winter, former executive director of the Minnesota Film and Television Board, the state's GDP for film and television production varies between 350 and 400 million dollars a year.[51]

As the final section of this chapter will reveal, Minneapolis provides an interesting case study of how Muslim American activism intersects with various kinds of media productions stretching from the grassroots to commercial sectors. But before doing so, we must first gain a better understanding of the Minnesotan Somali American population and the contours of the Muslim American community and grassroots organizations within Minneapolis.

Nearly 48,000 Somali Americans live in Minnesota, making it the largest Somali population in the United States. Most arrived after 1991 due to the Somalian Civil War. Fifty-nine percent of this population is foreign born with 41 percent born in the United States. Around 80 percent of Somali Americans in Minneapolis live in poverty with a median age of twenty-two.[52]

The Mississippi River cleaves through Minneapolis, dividing the city's Black Muslim neighborhoods from its white ones. The University of Minnesota with its red bricked buildings is mostly on the East Bank, with a bustling student population that is 67 percent white and roughly less than 8 percent Black.[53] On the West Bank sits Cedar-Riverside, a neighborhood that has always housed the city's various immigrant and refugee populations. During the nineteenth century, Scandinavians populated the neighborhood. Korean and Vietnamese refugees predominated during the mid-twentieth century. By the early 1990s, East Africans from Kenya, Ethiopia, and Somalia migrated in. Forty-nine percent of the neighborhood is Black with a 31 percent white population. To put this in perspective, Minneapolis in general is 64 percent white and 19 percent Black. The community is relatively young, with nearly 36 percent of its population between eighteen and twenty-four years old, and whose youthful energy might help explain the significant activism the neighborhood fosters.[54]

Cedar-Riverside is a relatively impoverished community. The average median income here has decreased from $21,137 in 2000 to $20,126 in 2017. (The average median income in Minneapolis is $55,720.) Forty-four percent of those in the neighborhood hold incomes below the poverty level. (Minneapolis as a whole has a poverty rate of 20 percent.)

Light rail glides north–south throughout Minneapolis. The ride from Stadium Village Station, which marks the heart of the south side of the University of Minnesota, to the northern West Bank Station, which crouches beneath a cement overpass in the Cedar-Riverside neighborhood, takes approximately ten minutes. But as the train shuttles over the Mississippi, the two worlds' minimal geographical distance stretches to near astronomic psychic proportions, fortifying an extremely segregated city.[55]

I sit at a concrete bench beneath the towering Riverside Plaza, a thirty-nine story Brutalist apartment complex that houses a large portion of the city's Black and East African population. The building is a defining feature of Cedar-Riverside that one can see from a distance while driving along Highway 35 into the city. A mural stands behind me displaying various flags of Africa—Ethiopian, Somalian, Kenyan, and others— with the US flag tucked quietly in the lower right corner. From the mural's center, a fist rises up ascending to the colorful blue and red patterned Riverside Plaza apartments that loom in the background. Visitors commonly pose before the mural to take pictures. Two Hispanic boys and a white friend, all in their early teens, dressed in baggy pants and oversized T-shirts, tease one another before taking selfies. Later, a group of four young Black women, in their early twenties, dressed in tight skirts and tops, clearly ready for a night out, joke and celebrate themselves while taking multiple pictures. Eventually, four young white men stroll into the neighborhood, two wearing University of Minnesota paraphernalia—a cap and T-shirt. They suddenly gain their bearings and quickly retreat toward Riverside Avenue.

Cedar-Riverside announces its East African presence. The neighborhood is densely packed with restaurants and markets specializing in African food. Numerous coffee shops line Cedar Avenue; inside them bustle mostly East African men in an assortment of white thobes or button-down shirts and slacks talking loudly in Somali over a television often blaring CNN in the background. The near-ubiquitous presence of CNN playing throughout numerous restaurants and coffee houses in Cedar-Riverside suggests how the community is mainlined into world news and hyperaware of broad political events, always on the alert for any catastrophe that might unleash a swarm of reporters onto the community to hear "the Muslim" perspective.

Middle-aged and older women in hijabs traverse the street carrying grocery bags in both hands, shuttling back and forth between their apartments and the shops. Sometimes they will briefly pause in passing,

FIGURE 4.1: The heart of the Cedar-Riverside neighborhood in Minneapolis, Minnesota, site of the largest Somali American community. An international perspective prevails, as the mural suggests with its flags of various East African nations along with that of the United States. (Photo by Chris Robé.)

exchanging snippets of information with one another. Younger women often wear colorful headscarves but are dressed in jeans and stylish shirts, waiting for the bus for work or on their way to classes at Augsburg University, University of Minnesota, or one of the other numerous colleges that populate the city.

Yet if one walks east on Cedar Avenue and then turns down Riverside Avenue, a different world unfolds. Walking south on Riverside, Muslim restaurants give way to a crusty punk scene with the Hard Times Café squatting on the right. A Bratmobile song from the early 1990s plays over the café's speakers as one chooses from an assortment of herbal tea and sandwiches. Disenfranchised white punks and old socialists reside upstairs in the rooms for rent. The University of Minnesota has a few buildings sprinkled along the east side of Riverside Avenue, and the occasional wayward student ventures into the café or wanders up to Cedar Avenue. About a five-minute walk from the intersection of Cedar and Riverside Avenues sits Augsburg University. It's a small campus whose student population reflects the diversity of its neighborhood with a 58 percent nonwhite student body.[56] Many Muslim American activist events are held on campus.

The Twin Cities had already been the site of multiple community policing programs prior to the arrival of CVE. Between 2007 and 2013 twenty-three people from Minneapolis left to join al-Shabaab, an al-Qaeda affiliate that was initially assumed to be an Islamic nationalistic movement fighting against Ethiopia's invasion of Mogadishu. As the organization grew increasingly violent (launching suicide attacks) the United States declared it a terrorist organization in March 2008.[57]

As a result of al-Shabaab's recruitment, Dennis Jensen, police chief of St. Paul, created the African Immigrant Muslim Coordinated Outreach Program, which was funded by a $670,000 Department of Justice grant in 2009 to help identify gang members and potential terrorists. The program met twice a month with a police liaison. One of the members of the program was asked to keep track of those who attended the meetings, which he refused to do.[58] Roughly around the same time, the FBI established what they referred to as "Specialized Community Outreach Teams" in the Somali community in Minneapolis and elsewhere where intelligence and outreach missions blurred. "Operation Rhino," the largest terrorism investigation since 9/11, was part of this effort. A flurry of FBI activity descended upon Somali American communities. Arun Kundnani writes that al-Shabaab's recruitment of young community members had consequences for Somali Americans. "Federal agents claimed a wide-ranging pretext to place themselves everywhere that young Somalis gathered—on college campuses and in high schools, shopping malls, and libraries—to question them about those who had disappeared."[59]

By 2014, Minneapolis experienced an increase in young people traveling to join ISIS, which had built upon the al-Shabaab network already established in the Twin Cities. There were eight known departures alone in 2014, plus some attempts that failed, and still others that eluded federal and local law enforcement.[60] One should keep in mind, however, the relatively small number of Americans traveling overseas to join the Islamic State, which was 250–300, compared to the 5,000–6,000 attempting to do so in Europe. A disproportionate amount of media attention has been drawn to Muslim American recruits as opposed to the many homegrown white nationalists and far right terrorists who have inflicted more damage domestically, which finally began to receive coverage after the 2017 Unite the Right rally in Charlottesville and the January 6, 2021, insurrection at the US Capitol.

Furthermore, a recent RAND study reports a dramatic demographic shift in those likely to join ISIS. Counter to the image of the foreign-born Arab terrorist, the report suggests that recruits are more likely to be US born and African American, Caucasian, or Latino than Middle Eastern. Furthermore, recruits are more likely to convert to Islam as part of being radicalized than being born to it.[61] In a significant understatement, the report notes that actual recruits "may not match the mental image held by law enforcement, policymakers and the general public."[62]

In February 2015, the FBI arrested Hamza Ahmed along with others who were planning to travel to Syria to join ISIS. By April 2015, the US Attorney for the District of Minnesota, Andrew Luger, charged six more Somali Americans with conspiracy and providing material support for ISIS.[63] The trial that ensued was highly controversial since many members in the community thought that the youths being prosecuted had been entrapped by law enforcement.[64] Prosecutors made their case mainly based on the recordings provided by Abdirahman Bashir, a Somali American youth who became an informant by December 2014 and taped his friends discussing radicalization and leaving the United States in mosques, homes, and elsewhere. The FBI paid Bashir $100,000 over the summer of 2015 while Bashir led a sting operation claiming that he had a contact in San Diego who could get him and a couple of other friends fake passports to help them leave the country. The person supplying these passports was an FBI agent.[65]

The trial represents an increasing reliance on informants by the FBI. Only 1,500 informants existed in the United States in 1975. By 2010 the number swelled to 15,000.[66] Human Rights Watch notes: "According to multiple studies, nearly 50 percent of the more than 500 federal counterterrorism convictions resulted from informant-based cases; almost 30 percent of those cases were sting operations in which the informant played an active role in the underlying plot."[67] The Minnesota ISIS trial firmly illustrates this trend.

Because of the centrality of the informant in advocating terrorist activity, the question arises: How many of these cases are actually rooting out terrorism or are instead fostering it to justify further counterterrorism funding?[68] As Stuart Hall and others have shown, "the selectivity of police reaction to selected crimes almost certainly serves to *increase* their number" since resources, manpower, and media attention are being drawn to them and in many instances manufacturing them.[69] Many of those studying the FBI's domestic terrorism cases have suggested that the organization "has put a number of Americans in prison for plotting crimes they would likely never have become involved in had they not had the misfortune of encountering an informant on the FBI's payroll."[70]

One has to keep in mind that the ISIS trial loomed over the city from 2015 all the way until the final convictions in June 2016 of three of the accused men who were sentenced to thirty to thirty-five years.[71] The trial's devastation of the local Somali community and its exposure of the ways in which federal law enforcement employs informants to manipulate situations hung heavily over Cedar-Riverside even before the arrival of CVE. Given the community's long and troubled history with law enforcement, it is not surprising that CVE would be viewed with skepticism.

In a September 9, 2015, press release, the Department of Justice announced that Youthprise, a local nonprofit Somali American organization, would act as the main distributor of CVE grants to other organizations in the Twin Cities. The title of the press release is revealing: "Twin Cities Somali Community Leaders, Government Officials, and Private Partners Present Plan to Build Community Resilience."[72] Only two purported community leaders are quoted: Hodan Hassan, cochair of the Somali American Task Force, and Wokie Weah, president of Youthprise. But both Youthprise and the Somali American Task Force were deeply challenged by activists for not being representative of the Somali American community. The Young Muslim Collective (YMC), for example, called out Youthprise for taking CVE money and for its problematic use of counterterrorism rhetoric such as claiming that poverty and unemployment "can open them [new immigrants] to recruitment by extremist groups."[73] Ramla Bile, one of the behind-the-scenes people who researched and wrote about CVE in Minneapolis, explained to me the problem: "You can't do social services with law enforcement. I mean it needed to happen very much independent of that. And people were not getting it."[74]

Central to this issue is the contested nature of who gets to define "the community." As Paul Gilroy states, "Community cannot be viewed as either static or given by some essential characteristics of the class or class fractions which come to constitute it."[75] Who should define "the community" was a constant point of contention in Cedar-Riverside in almost all of the interviews I conducted there. Organizations like CAIR, Young Muslim Collective, and the West Bank Community Coalition saw themselves as opposed to what they considered more government created or approved organizations like the Somali American Task Force and Youthprise.

To obscure its connections with law enforcement, CVE was renamed "Building Community Resilience" even before it started fully functioning on the ground; this anticipated the troubles it was to experience upon

FIGURE 4.2: The Brian Coyle Community Center squats behind the Riverside Towers, which house around 9,600 residents. The center provides numerous community services geared toward refugees and immigrants like skills classes in reading, writing, and speaking in English; information for navigating city bureaucracy and the transit system; and community discussions regarding pressing issues like the Countering Violence Extremism program. (Photo by Chris Robé.)

its arrival. Muslim youth organizers were wary of such name changes. Ayaan Dahir, one of the founders of the Young Muslim Collective, explains, "With CVE, a lot of it centered around language. 'Building Community Resilience.' That sounds beautiful. They had different names in different cities. Beautiful names. Very empowering names. But not an empowering program."[76] Providing a superficial fix by renaming the program while not recognizing its structural problems severely annoyed the Muslim youth organizers I spoke with since it treated them as gullible and easily fooled by these disingenuous tactics.

The government's unveiling of the program at the Brian Coyle Community Center on November 7, 2015, proved equally ill-staged. This one-story brick community center squats behind the Riverside Plaza towers with the Mississippi River flowing nearby. The building serves as the heartbeat of a community of roughly 9,600 people, with a constant pulse of activity in its slightly worn halls with peeling paint.[77] According to its director, Amano Dube, the center provides job training, youth engagement programs, and classes and workshops on running small businesses and navigating housing.[78] Mohamed, an elderly man who works behind the

FIGURE 4.3: The thirty-nine story Brutalist, colorfully designed apartments that house a significant number of Somali American families. They tower above the skyline and can be seen from the distance while driving toward Minneapolis. (Photo by Chris Robé.)

counter, knows nearly everyone who enters its doors. With a broad smile he greets and directs them to where they need to go.

Using Brian Coyle as a site for initiating CVE served an important symbolic function for the federal government because of the importance of this institution in the community and the trust the population has in it. Jeh Johnson, then secretary of Homeland Security, held a meeting along with assorted local and state law enforcement representatives and some members of the Somali American Task Force. The media was barred from attendance to no avail; the event remained problematic for many in the community. Burhan Israfael Isaaq, an important Somali youth and community organizer from Cedar-Riverside observed: "I remember Jeh Johnson and his secret service had a whole block, like shutdown."[79] Filsan Ibrahim, another community organizer involved with a host of organizations, reflects: "The federal folks and all the bigwigs came to the community. It was their attempt to explain the program and justify why they were doing what they were doing. And a lot of us, a majority of us in the room were not with it. It felt like they were coercing the community to feel like this is for your own good."[80] Isaaq similarly observed that there was "nothing but law enforcement in the room: federal, local, national. Everybody was there talking about community. I was like, I don't see no community members here. This the law enforcement community. Are we getting ready to arrest somebody?" Amano Dube, who attended the forums recalled, "They were very tension-filled forums. We even had to stop hosting those kinds of forums here at some point because the community tended to fight."

The need for funding social services in the face of such a strong presence of law enforcement sent mixed messages. The community was systematically deprived of resources. Between 2004 and 2014 annual philanthropic support sharply declined from $948,500 to $127,800.[81] Meanwhile, the population of Cedar-Riverside increased by 2,000 people during roughly the same time period.[82] Congress allocated $10 million for CVE nationally during 2016, yet estimates suggest that the Twin Cities alone needed at least $5 million for social programs.[83] Youthprise received a paltry $216,000 to distribute to multiple organizations in 2016.[84] Yet as Ramla Bile notes, it is questionable how much of this money actually went to youth and not administrative costs. Furthermore, she adds, "Some of them [the organizations given CVE money] served Somalis but weren't Somali-led necessarily. So, at the end of the day in terms of resources trickling into the community, it was so minimal."[85]

Amano Dube articulated the dilemma the community faced:

> It is very complicated in a sense there are aspects of why we need this resource. There is so many thousands of youth that are not being served and have no meaningful engagement or meaningful programming to really change their life in the future. They need to be resourced. But the dangerous aspect of this is, okay if kids are going to be involved, they need to be tracked: who they are; where they live; basic demographics. Not to say like every kid who comes through this is a terrorist. But like any social service, we track people we serve. We report those basic numbers.[86]

The question then became: what organizations gained access to such sensitive information after CVE money had been distributed and "partnerships" between the police, the federal government, and community organizations had been established? CVE grants and program-building tapped into some social services that already tracked those who used them. But by maintaining connections with DHS, such partnerships cast the legitimacy of their social services in doubt.

As mentioned earlier, the presence of CVE grant money fomented division within the community. Isaaq, for example, saw the Coyle Center's role in the CVE forums as problematic: "Brian Coyle played a huge role in allowing it to creep in. They pretty much put together that show, which again legitimized it, you know, because Jeh Johnson is connected to CVE obviously."[87] This assessment is not entirely fair to Brian Coyle Center's mission, which is meant to be a nonpartisan service to the community. The center has a mandate to host forums in order to assess the community's interests and position. To decide beforehand would be undemocratic and equally problematic. The CVE forum placed the organization in a precarious position. If it didn't host the forum, the center would be neglecting one of its main functions of vetting the issue before the community. But also, by holding the forum at all, some in the community saw the organization implicitly legitimizing CVE.

Ultimately, the Brian Coyle Center never took any CVE money. Amano Dube explains the organization's position: "If the community feels as if this is not helping us, we should not dump on them or force them to involve their kids in it. The way we work with the community, it is based on relationship and trust. So, we don't want our families of the communities we serve to distrust us as if we are a government agent or FBI or anything like that. That's not our role." Nevertheless, the seeds of discord had already been sown beginning with the initial forum's appearance.

Due to the appearance of CVE, the spate of highly visible police killings of young Black men and women, the election of Donald Trump and rising white nationalism, and a global financial meltdown, Muslim-based community organizations along with many other groups in various communities of color sprang into existence across the country. Minneapolis was no different, but it was unique to have such a high density of Muslim-led organizations that worked as coalitions, equitably sharing the labor among them, leading to less chance of organizer burnout and feelings of being overwhelmed and isolated by the enormity of the situation.

The West Bank Community Coalition was founded in 2010, but younger community organizers like Burhan Israfael Isaaq and Mohammed Mohaud became more involved leading it toward a more activist bent. Filsan Ibrahim recalls, "They did a lot of organizing. They got a lot of people together. They had a discussion with the community and know what is going on." In regard to CVE, "They did a lot of paper distribution of what it is, who is putting it on, and why it matters, and what we should do about it."[88] No matter who

FIGURE 4.4: The West Bank Restaurant and Grill in the Cedar-Riverside neighborhood serves as a central meeting place for the Somali community. Community organizer Burhan Israfael Isaaq suggested we meet at the West Bank Restaurant and Grill for our interview. (Photo by Chris Robé.)

I spoke with regarding Cedar-Riverside, Isaaq's name repeatedly came up as a highly respected community organizer. He is affiliated with numerous organizations besides the West Bank Community Coalition, such as People Powered Progress, a social justice coalition in the Twin Cities fighting Islamophobia, gentrification, and policing, and more recently the Young Muslim Collective.

It is worth noting that many of the organizers I spoke with held multiple affiliations with different organizations that ebbed and flowed throughout their lives. Some they would tell me about, others they would not, either out of caution or simply overlooking the fact. So I can only approximate the affiliations here and offer a very rough sketch of what was a much more nuanced dance between individuals and long- and short-term organizations.

I met with Isaaq on a snowy night in April 2019 at the West Bank Restaurant and Grill. It had been snowing for several hours, the last blizzard of the season. The diner had seen better days. Some of its booths remained in a state of semidisrepair with benches tilted off and lying on tables. The vinyl of the seats was worn smooth from countless customers. A large television hung over the entrance with CNN blasting its news like a greeting.

When Isaaq arrived, he fist-bumped and greeted many of those sitting at tables before sliding comfortably across from me and slouching into position. He wore a black baseball cap with the Detroit Tigers logo and thick black-rimmed glasses.

Throughout our conversation, many people strolled up to our table to speak with him, often in a mixture of Somali and English, to either thank him for work he was doing on their behalf or fishing for information about some community issue he was involved in. Isaaq would explain my presence as an interviewer to them thus explaining why I was the sole white person in the diner.

The Young Muslim Collective (YMC) received a lot of media attention during its emergence in 2016 for its activist work. YMC arose out of a vigil held for three Sudanese young men killed in Indiana. Ayaan Dahir said, "We were wondering why we were getting radio silence from the Muslim community. Something we expected from the larger community, but because these two of the three Sudanese boys were Muslim, we were wondering why there was so much silence and no attention being paid to their murders."[89] "[Afterward,] we held a discussion, a community discussion about Islamophobia and anti-Blackness. A lot of us are Black Muslim. I myself am. And this is something we wanted to address." The moment started serving as a healing space to finally talk about these issues. One thing that kept arising during the discussion was CVE. As a result, the Young Muslim Collective was born to combat CVE and other manifestations of the intersection of anti-Blackness and Islamophobia.

The formation of YMC illustrates Su'ad Abdul Khabeer's assertion that "Blackness shapes the individual Muslim experience in the United States and interethnic relationships as well as the terms of U.S. Muslim engagement with the state."[90] Many organizations like YMC take an intersectional approach to Islamophobia, understanding it as the convergence of racial, class, and religious oppressions. As Ayaan Dahir stresses about CVE, "We are being targeted because we are Somali, we are Black, we are Muslim, and we are also low-income so we don't have the financial means to litigate away and defend ourselves in that way. We are seen as a very easy target."[91]

YMC's vigil for the deaths of the three Sudanese men drew attention to what Judith Butler has referred to as a "differential allocation of grievability."[92] She explains that "certain forms of grief become nationally recognized and amplified, whereas other losses become unthinkable and ungrievable."[93] What marked this moment as unique was that even Muslim organizations remained quiet about the Sudanese men's deaths, signaling to the future members of YMC the need for a more progressive and visible form of grassroots activism that they were not witnessing from older, Muslim-run organizations.

Many of the collective's members attended the University of Minnesota and Augsburg University. Jaylani Hussein, executive director of CAIR who offered assistance in the creation of YMC, suggested that YMC also arose because "the current student groups that typically should have taken on CVE and other issues similar to it [did not]. Since they didn't, this collective came together to address some of these social justice efforts."[94] Yet Filsan Ibrahim cautions against blaming student groups for more a timid approach: "The University of Minnesota is a good chunk of white students, and the Muslim community isn't that large. They want to be very welcoming and a good Muslim representative on campus and not have sharp political views." She adds: "Maybe it shouldn't be the role for some student groups to be in charge of too blatantly declaring CVE is not a good program."

Dahir met Isaaq when he was at West Bank Community Coalition to discuss CVE. He recalls, "Ayaan was the person that really was like, 'what's this about? I want to know more about this.' She got a little bit of information [and] she just took off." But YMC had help from a series of other partners both visible and behind the scenes that helped effectively organize against CVE and around other issues.

CAIR Minnesota, as mentioned earlier, helped draw attention to CVE and supported the efforts of YMC as well. Hussein recalls: "I don't take credit for the work that they do, but I was one of their advisors when they got launched—and I still play a big role in supporting them any way I can."[95]

Minnesota has one of the most visible and active of the chapters of CAIR. All of the chapters are run autonomously and self-funded.[96] The Minneapolis chapter's offices are on East Franklin Street, sharing the second floor of a building attached to a Lutheran church. A large conference room sits on the left as you walk up the stairs. Beside a long conference table and working kitchen, a large CAIR backdrop decorates the front of the room. Three lights stand before it at the ready for a sudden press conference. Every time I visited, the hallways were bustling with people seeking advice and needing assistance. According to Hussein, CAIR provides legal services and advocacy for the Minnesota Muslim community and takes on between 300 and 360 cases a year.

FIGURE 4.5: The Minneapolis chapter of the Council on American-Islamic Relations is one of the most active. Its offices are located on the second floor of a Lutheran church. (Photo by Chris Robé.)

Communities United Against Police Brutality, discussed in chapter 2, assisted YMC and CAIR with conducting Know Your Rights trainings. Michelle Gross, one of its lead organizers, states, "And now they go off to do their own trainings or we'll bring them along and they are active interpreters in the various communities we are addressing."[97] But even more interesting was the assistance YMC and other groups received from a group of behind-the-scenes people who comprised a powerful research arm that

FIGURE 4.6: Within the Minnesota CAIR office, a backdrop is always in place for media conferences on short notice. (Photo by Chris Robé.)

assisted with gathering information and distributing it in a digestible form to different communities.

I only learned of this crew of researchers while visiting Minneapolis in April 2019. I was trying to set up a series of individual interviews with Kadra Abdi, Ramla Bile, and a few others who had written some pieces about CVE and other issues regarding Islamophobia. While corresponding with Bile, she suggested that I meet with her, Abdi, and one other who preferred to remain anonymous at a local co-op. Bile and Abdi dressed rather similarly in black hijabs and stylish black glasses. Abdi stands slightly taller than Bile. Tellingly, throughout the interview Bile, Abdi, and the third unnamed person would complete each other's thoughts—though Bile took the lead of much of the conversation. Bile brought her six-year-old girl, who played at the table where we sat and occasionally drifted off to engage with one of the other members of the group at another table. All three had a very deliberative way of speaking as if they had considered the matters at hand for a long time and didn't want to rush their thoughts. They referred to themselves as "quiet allies" of the movement.[98]

For example, they worked with West Bank Community Coalition. "We helped provide strategies that the young people could use," Bile notes. "And they ran with it." Abdi continues, "Not taking up spaces was important for us but providing research, providing the material. Again, this issue we saw like it impacts the entire community, but specifically it impacted the Somali youth. So, them as the leaders of this movement, I think, it made sense to all of us. And we were happy having our own thing."

But much of the attention of this group was dedicated to educating philanthropists since their earlier work addressed the problematic ways in which philanthropy operates in a paternalistic fashion that doesn't address core needs. Specifically in terms of CVE, philanthropists used a threat lens, which framed the Muslim American community mainly as a hotbed for potential terrorism, to administer money for social services. As Bile emphasized, "If you're interested in funding us through this threat lens, then you're seeking to minimize terrorism primarily."

One of the central problems raised by this group and every other youth activist I spoke with was the way that CVE was being overseen by Andrew Luger, United States Attorney for Minnesota. While administering CVE, he was simultaneously prosecuting six local Somali kids for conspiracy and material support for ISIS. His dual roles as prosecutor of Somali youth yet advocate of social services for the same population sent mixed messages that further conflated the functions of law enforcement and social services. To make matters even worse, Luger's wife, Ellen Goldberg Luger, became senior vice president of philanthropic services at the Minneapolis Foundation, one of the largest local private granting institutions. The Minneapolis Foundation is highly influential in decisions to assist or deprive community organizations of needed resources. So the motives of the individuals who worked with Andrew Luger and CVE could always be questioned, since the need to be perceived as a "good" Muslim could have concrete benefits from the state's attorney general and one of Minneapolis's major philanthropists.

Other groups allied themselves with YMC and other Muslim youth activists and organizers but did not play a central role. Predominantly white leftist groups like the Freedom Road Socialist Organization, the Antiwar Committee, and Veterans for Peace were considered valuable and well-intentioned allies but were not fully equipped to address the Muslim community's needs. Bile noted, "We shared a lot of the same values, particularly around US foreign policy and being able to call out like this modern imperialism." But, she continued, "when you're facing a massive surveillance program that touches on so many elements of government ... you need a resistance that's strong and that is broad and powerful."

Interestingly, the local Black Lives Matter chapter had mixed reviews from the activists I spoke with. Although some saw BLM as valuable allies in addressing affordable housing and Islamophobia in general, others saw them as primarily an extension of the local Democratic Party that was more connected to the political machine than any grassroots movements. Quite a few stories revolved around BLM actually undermining collective organizing like protests around CVE and the killing of Jamar Clark. Regardless of the reality of BLM's roles in organizing, by most accounts it did not play a central role in challenging CVE's presence in Minneapolis—though one could argue that the broad national movement of BLM chapters helped inspire a younger generation of Muslim organizers to form their own organizations.[99]

Media Activism: Producing Counternarratives

Reframing Countering Violent Extremism

Changing the narrative frame around CVE was a key concern for many of the Muslim-led organizations both within and outside of Minneapolis. Many of them participated every two weeks on a conference call initiated by the Muslim Justice League with roughly twenty-five to thirty people on average, though it could grow up to fifty at moments of peak activity.[100] Shannon Al-Wakeel explains, "Those calls were an attempt to share information and build strategy together, learn what was most effective to build our resources, really."

Similarly, the Minneapolis research team investigating CVE prioritized translating their concerns to a broader public. Bile notes, "We wanted more user-friendly language. We wanted to make connections that were real for people." She continues, "And then you know there's this storytelling piece to it like young people talking about how it's even impacted them and their friends. The ways they found themselves censoring themselves, and the ways they felt their own activism was diminished because of the climate of fear that CVE created locally."

Ultimately, all the Muslim grassroots organizations realized the importance of reframing CVE to challenge its benevolent image (giving out grant money for needed social services) by highlighting its links to criminal justice, white supremacy, and a long tradition of government surveillance perpetuated against communities of color. As Judith Butler notes, such reframings might not be able to prevent atrocities on their own, but "they nevertheless do provide the conditions for breaking out of the quotidian acceptance [of them] . . . and for a more generalized horror and outrage that will support and impel calls for justice and an end to violence."[101]

Much local commercial news media and print journalism proved inconsistent in framing CVE. Ayaan Dahir mentions the problematic nature of the monthly op-eds that the *Star Tribune* produced: "It wasn't necessarily pro-CVE, but what they would do is highlight members of the Somali community and show the good that they are doing. But they would specifically pick people who had received money from the program, and they would say in order to continue their work, there needs to be more funding allocated to them."[102]

A good example of this is an April 23, 2016, editorial board piece from the *Star Tribune*.[103] It leads off by mentioning the underfunding of the West Bank Athletic Club that has over 140 youths on a waiting list to join. The editors continue, "Research shows that social programs are critical in preventing radicalization, yet the federal and state governments are failing to adequately fund basic steps to build community resilience." What exactly this research is remains unmentioned. Notice also how the sentence smuggles in the rebranded name change to CVE: "building community resilience." The *Star Tribune* further asserts that a "paltry $10 million" was allocated by Congress to CVE nationally. According to the paper, Minneapolis-St. Paul alone could use $5 million for social services.

The editorial then briefly pays lip service to Jaylani Hussein, who is "alarmed" at "the funding's dual purpose: countering extremism and improving social services," but argues that Hussein's criticism "overlooks Minnesota's long history of welcoming refugees and the comparatively generous support by both the public and private sectors. It's true that the terror recruitment has highlighted the need for improved support, but Hussein badly underestimates his home state if he thinks that this is the only reason Minnesotans want to help the Somali community here succeed." The argument deflects from the main question of why social services are being coupled with the DHS by instead making it about the character of Minnesotans. The editorial board's response embodies the problems with commercial media that Stuart Hall and others identified operating in the 1970s during the mugging "crisis" in Britain, which resonates with the present "crisis" over terrorism within the United States. News media, although somewhat autonomous from those in power, nonetheless relies on them for information and quotes. A symbiotic relationship exists between the commercial news and those in power. The latter need to publicize their actions and programs while the news media need reliable, accessible, and attributable sources. As a result, those in power frame the issues in an advantageous way (for them) that the news replicates (in no small part because it's easier than finding new ways to talk about issues). As Stuart Hall and others note: "The important point about the structured relationship between the media and the primary institutional definers is that it permits the institutional definers to establish the initial definition or *primary inter-pretation* of the topic in question."[104] Any argument must operate within these parameters. If not, "counter-definers run the risk of being defined out of the debate... labelled as 'extremists' or 'irrational' or acting illegally or unconstitutionally."[105]

This gatekeeping mechanism is precisely what the *Star Tribune* does to Hussein: it dismisses his objections as unwarranted and uncharitable. As Edward Said has observed, part of the problem with the news media in covering Muslims is that its reportage is "determined either by crisis or by unconditional ethnocentrism."[106] The *Star Tribune* editorial does both by unproblematically wedding the crisis of underresourced social programs with that of terror recruitment. Its ethnocentrism is exhibited in the way it appeals to Minnesota's long history of welcoming refugees while refusing to acknowledge an equally long history of the federal government surveillance of communities of color in programs like COINTELPRO and police actions like the Palmer Raids during the late 1910s or more recently the detaining of 1,200 Muslim Americans after 9/11. Islamophobia and racism remain outside the frame as the editorial board makes it a matter of character rather than one of the structural inequities and institutionalized racism that undergird many present-day government programs and efforts.

As a result, many Muslim-run organizations focusing on CVE held forums in their towns, across the country, and online to challenge their framing of the issue. First, they saw these forums as providing a chance for people to engage with the implications of CVE and have a discussion unfettered by the coercive presence of law enforcement. Fatema Ahmad recounts how one forum in Montgomery, Maryland, had pro-CVE people attend. "But that was kind of effective," she recalls. "Because people who didn't know about CVE who came there to learn through seeing that debate did understand that this is really not okay that this is coming into our community. Community members were standing up and pushing back on these people who had gotten a CVE grant before."[107] Similarly, Ayaan Dahir recalls how after a screening of the film *(T)error* (2015), a discussion ensued about informants, CVE, and surveillance of Muslim communities. During it, a young man mentioned that while returning to Minneapolis he was approached by an FBI agent at the airport to be an informant. Dahir continues, "And other people would tell their stories. And some people would disagree. That's fine. But the point of it is that we're having a conversation about it. It's not just some state propaganda being thrown at you. Like, we're an actual grassroots movement. We're not manufactured to look like a grassroots movement."[108]

Perhaps most importantly, the counter-CVE forums overcome secrecy with community and visibility. Shannon Al-Wakeel observes, "CVE thrives on secrecy and it's a very confusingly messaged, multiheaded hydra." The Muslim Justice League emphasized forums that involved "some of the directly impacted grassroots activists who don't have the time and don't have that kind of day job that allows them to join a monthly call to strategize with folks, but who are seeing impacts locally and talking about what works."[109] Furthermore, they decided to initiate these forums in locations where CVE programs were prominent, such as Minneapolis, Los Angeles, and Montgomery County, Maryland. They also invited groups like the Young Muslim Collective to their own forum in Boston, which proved inspirational to local youth. "For them [the Boston youth] to see Young Muslim Collective, especially because they are also Somali youth, to see them really organized," explains Al-Wakeel, "to see . . . how they are holding adults and 'leaders' accountable was really inspiring for the youth here because they felt like: we can do this."

Ahmad also built a website, "Resisting Surveillance," that provided links to each nationally held counter-CVE forum and some recordings of the livestreams.[110] This allowed people who were being impacted by CVE, but who could not attend the forums, to view them and access relevant materials about CVE. Ahmad had ambitious goals for the website. She explains, "I am hoping to add to the website like if CVE is happening in your city, here are the basics of how to do this." But this never happened. At the date of this writing, the website has stalled with no new updates since April 9, 2018. This is not to fault the Muslim Justice League for failing to follow up on their promise, but instead to highlight the resources needed to have a genuine web presence and the difficulty of even basic upkeep.

This is a fairly typical issue for many grassroots movements that recognize the importance of having an online presence yet lack the resources to do so consistently. As a result, the internet is littered with countless deferred dreams—inactive activist webpages announcing events long past and featuring dead links.

Independent Media: Unicorn Riot

YMC, however, was able to avoid the problems that Ahmad and the Muslim Justice League encountered and build a more sustained web presence because they were lucky enough to have the alternative media institution Unicorn Riot in their midst, which could dedicate resources to assisting them. The group was founded in March 2015, but it had origins from discussions beginning in November 2014, where many of its future members were making videos in Ferguson that they could not properly distribute over commercial platforms like YouTube. Niko Georgiades, one of the founding members of Unicorn Riot, recalls: "We couldn't get the editor to approve it. We couldn't get it published. We made thirteen videos. They put up around seven. Why did they pick and choose those seven and not put up the other six?"[111] The group quickly realized that they needed to establish an alternative internet platform where they could exercise full editorial control and produce material that better aligned with their politics.

Unicorn Riot operates by anarchist principles of consensus-based decision-making and the nonhierarchical structure that have been defining features of many video collectives since their origins in the late 1960s and early 1970s.[112] The group started off with around twenty-three to twenty-four people but dwindled down to around twelve in 2019. Five or six members reside in the Twin Cities. The sprinkling of the remaining members are in Denver, the Bay Area, Boston, and Philadelphia. The group is volunteer-based though it pays nominal fees to its contributors when they post an article or video. Most of their internal communication is through texts. This can create moments of miscommunication since inflection is lost and ideas might not be fully expressed in a medium that prioritizes brevity and speed over precision. To overcome the alienation that often accompanies online internal communication, the group held its first retreat in January 2018 where everyone met in one space. Like many video collectives, it is overwhelmingly white, which troubles some of its members who believe a diverse collective is essential in relaying a range of voices and outlooks.

Many of the collective's members have roots in longer video activist histories. Georgiades relates, "Half of our crew was at Occupy Wall Street doing livestreaming and being a part of Global Revolution." Global Revolution had roots in the alterglobalization movement of the late 1990s and early 2000s. One of Global Revolution's founders is Vlad Teichberg, a former derivatives trader who went rogue and founded the video-oriented Glass Bead Collective in 2001.[113] Another member of Global Revolution was Flux Rostrum, a pseudonym assumed when he became a videographer in 2001 as part of the resistance against what he saw as commercial media's acceptance of war.[114]

Another group of Unicorn Riot founders had been a part of the RNC 8 protests discussed in chapter 2. Some had belonged to Twin Cities Indymedia. The Glass Bead Collective traveled to Minneapolis and ultimately coproduced the 2008 video *Terrorizing Dissent* with Twin Cities IMC. For Georgiades, the RNC 8 "was such an eye-opening experience: they're raiding journalists' houses before it happened; they're raiding people's apartments before it happened. They're being called a terrorist. Like what the fuck man. There was a lot of shit that really from *that* more so radicalized me into a media maker, and half of Unicorn Riot was there."

Unicorn Riot initially became best known for its coverage of the Unite the Right rally in Charlottesville since they gained access to alt-right organizers' planning sessions on the Discord platform favored by gamers, internet trolls, and the far right.[115] They also received coverage for releasing top-secret ICE handbooks that revealed some of the troubling ways the organization intimidates immigrants and relies upon problematic procedures.[116] More recently, they produced some of the most detailed coverage of protests against police brutality that arose over the murders of George Floyd and Breonna Taylor. Georgiades serves as the main point person for the organization in their coverage of Minnesota Somali youth. Georgiades personally knew someone whose brother joined ISIS. He states about the surveillance of the local Muslim community, "This is very close to a lot of people, and very near and dear to me, too." Georgiades is a very low-key and sympathetic person with a warm disposition who genuinely listens when others speak. We met for an interview in a bar in Cedar-Riverside. While we talked, he recognized and greeted quite a few of the customers who circulated inside. He emphasized the overall community-oriented perspective that Unicorn Riot embodies: "The best thing about it is the way we are able to work with the trust of the people who we are serving. We develop

FIGURES 4.7 & 4.8: Unicorn Riot's web design is geared to accessing a younger demographic by posting short clips and pithy summaries of events that link to longer articles if a reader chooses to follow them.

more relationships than corporate entities or than other media makers who would just swoop in and swoop out. We know that is the important part."

Unicorn Riot has been covering YMC since its origins at the February 29, 2016, vigil it held for the Sudanese men. The group posted an article on YMC on their website on March 2, 2016.[117] Their webpage represents Unicorn Riot's generally media-savvy approach to all its topics. The article leads with: "Minneapolis, MN— On February 29th, 2016 a group of youth, the newly organized Young Muslim Collective (YMC), held an #OurThreeBoys / #OurThreeBrothers remembrance event at Coffman Union on the University of Minnesota Twin Cities campus." Hyperlinks connect #OurThreeBrothers to its Facebook campaign, and throughout the written piece videos and hyperlinks are posted. Direct short videos of Javaris Bradford, president of the UM Black Student Union, and Jaylani Hussein are embedded. A hyperlink is provided to the archived roughly shot livestream of the vigil. Unicorn Riot understands that most readers will not go to the lengthy livestream but will instead view snippets of the embedded videos. All the hyperlinks open onto separate windows allowing the viewer to navigate multiple pages at once.

The webpage contextualizes all the embedded videos and summarizes their content to draw viewers in. Additionally, boldface pull quotes from the video interviews grace the page just before the video to interest readers. Again, hyperlinks run throughout the text. For example, when speaking about Jaylani Hussein, hyperlinks connect to CAIR's main webpage as well as to an article about the shooting of a Somali teen in Salt Lake City, Utah, that broadens our understanding of the killing of the three Sudanese men as part of wider violence against Muslims.

The webpage is a savvy combination of print journalism, new media, and video documentation. It keeps text to a relative minimum by hyperlinking to lengthier articles. The embedded videos run roughly around five minutes with longer footage often relegated to a hyperlink. Although the turnaround time for Unicorn Riot's posting on the vigil was rather quick, it can sometimes lag due to a backlog of material and the time it takes to produce professional quality news releases.

In addition to protest events, Unicorn Riot also covers general events occurring in the Muslim American communities when it can. For example, on January 15, 2019, it covered the Black Storytellers Alliance (BSA).[118] Georgiades relates how event coverage resulted from his direct connection with the alliance: "I have been working with youth at place called, We Win Institute, a nonprofit organization that has been around for twenty-two years now. We do culturally specific programming. We have been bringing our youth to the BSA every year for a long time." He and another member of Unicorn Riot filmed the event and conducted interviews with both its founders and participants, many of whom can be seen on the website. A short promotional video leads off the webpage providing brief snippets from the multiple interviews they conducted along with glimpses of the performances of the event. The video provides a succinct three-and-a-half-minute summary of the event, professionally shot and quickly consumable for the viewing public with a short attention span. Such coverage celebrates Black and immigrant culture, providing concrete examples of images that counter the demonization of the Somali American community as would-be terrorists or welfare cheats—not unlike what we saw El Grito de Sunset Park doing for the Puerto Rican community.

Because of the infrastructure of Unicorn Riot, YMC and the local Somali community have a unique web presence that many activist groups and local communities rarely achieve. The interests of YMC and Unicorn Riot converge such that Dahir and many other organizers mentioned that Unicorn Riot is always the first media organization that they call when having an event. Isaaq praises them: "Man, they have been doing great. They do a great job of reaching out to the community. They're number one for me, man." This is important praise from an organizer who is highly regarded by his community.

Judith Butler notes how a photograph doesn't simply represent an event, but also builds on and augments it. The photograph "becomes crucial to its [the event's] production, its legibility, its illegibility, and its very status as reality."[119] This can similarly be said about a web presence like YMC on Unicorn Riot. It provides, first of all, a valuable archive of past activist moments and snippets from Black culture that defy a criminalized framework. The various events presented provide a counternarrative to what is commonly promoted by commercial media and news organizations. Although Unicorn Riot's distribution is decidedly much smaller than a commercial organization, it provides nuanced representations and reveals a connection to the communities it covers in a unique fashion. Moreover, the bonds between YMC and Unicorn Riot have grown through coverage of events, thus mutually bolstering both independent media and grassroots activism.

Viral Videos

Three days before he was about to cohost a counter-CVE forum on July 22, 2016, Burhan Israfael Isaaq found two FBI agents knocking on his door. Not only was he a well-known community organizer and opponent of CVE, but he had also defiantly supported some of the young men being prosecuted during the ISIS trial that dominated headlines throughout the late spring. The *New York Times* quoted Isaaq dismissing the trials as "purely political" and commenting: "I didn't think they had enough evidence to convict them on that. I think that was an overreach."[120] So he had a highly visible reputation not only in Minneapolis but nationally at this time.

When the Feds knocked on his door, Isaaq instinctively pulled out his cell phone to film the interaction as he spoke to the agents from behind his closed door. As he explained to me, he filmed the interaction less because of fear of misconduct on the agents' part and more so to prove to the community that he was not a snitch by documenting his resistance of speaking to them. He added: "Just to prove if they ever try to play some games. Here is evidence of me . . . this is the extent of our interaction here. That was it. I was more afraid of the community."[121]

The video provides a glimpse into the badgering and deceit of a random FBI encounter.[122] With the phone pressed to the door, the entire video remains black. You only hear the voices of the two agents and Isaaq. After the agents announce their presence at the door, Isaaq calmly states: "Love to speak with you guys, but I need my attorney." They continue to badger him to open the door, which he refuses. When Isaaq finally asks them to disclose their identities, they only offer first names: Steve and Terry. He asks what they want to discuss. They vaguely reply: "some matters concerning the community, and we heard you are a good guy to follow up with." Isaaq asks for details about the "matters," and they tell him that it is "concerning radicalism." Isaaq firmly states: "I know nothing about that. You got the wrong person."

The encounter only lasts for three minutes, but it is fairly typical of FBI fishing expeditions of the Somali American community since 2009.[123] They are what the FBI refers to as "assessments," which "were the opening salvo to the informant-recruitment process. It was a delicate art of manipulation, persuading a person to work for the federal government against his or her own community."[124] They often targeted highly prominent community members or people occupying a vulnerable status to see what information they can shake out of them and potentially make them into an informant. As Isaaq relayed, "They never know the person until they engage with them."

Isaaq then recounted how another community organizer he knew had the FBI show up at his door but miscalculated his reaction. He let them in and spoke to them for around forty minutes. Isaaq only learned of this belatedly since the young man contacted him to ask for advice as the FBI had been texting him every day for more information after the encounter. As Isaaq knew, the line between cooperating with the FBI and becoming an informant remains blurry. And if one wants to maintain the trust of the community, any interaction with the FBI is too much, since once someone shows a receptiveness to their questions, they press for more information.

Interestingly, such interactions were so commonplace that after the encounter Isaaq never thought about distributing the video. He told me, "I thought it was normal. I didn't think it was a big deal." But an independent journalist he knew eventually persuaded him to send it to certain media outlets. This explains the lag between when the event transpired and the August 28, 2016, AlterNet article on it.[125] The article not only embeds the video within it, but also provides a rare lengthy history of CVE and an in-depth account of the counter-CVE forum that followed after Isaaq was visited by the FBI. The video was also picked up by *The Grayzone*, an investigative journalist website as well as a couple other lesser-known independent publications. The video received around three thousand views on YouTube.

Events took an even stranger turn as the "Terry" at Isaaq's door turned out to be Terry Albury who received a four-year prison sentence for whistleblowing regarding institutionalized racism within the FBI. He was the only African American field agent assigned to counterterrorism in Minneapolis. He said that he had become disillusioned when he encountered racist and xenophobic statements by fellow agents specifically directed against the Somali community he was supposed to investigate.[126] According to one article, "Albury had never heard the sort of unabashed hatred for any group of people as he did for the Somalis, whom agents denigrated for their poverty, or their food, or the habit some Somali immigrant women had of tucking their cellphones inside their hijabs while shopping at Walmart or driving a car."[127] Albury also became uncomfortable regarding the weak evidence used as a justification to surveil Somali Americans, but when he raised concerns, they were summarily dismissed by his colleagues.[128] This led Albury to ultimately conclude, "I helped destroy people for 17 years."[129] Although Albury's account vindicated Isaaq and other community organizers, supporting what they have been saying for years, Isaaq held no sympathy for him: "He's still an imperialist pig. He thinks this is just a part of the department rather than what the department is."

It's Not Just Television: #SayNOtoHBO Campaign

During all this—the FBI swooping down on the community, the contentious forums over CVE, and the state's attorney general charging six men with material support of ISIS—HBO came to town to produce a television series on Somali American life and terrorism in Cedar-Riverside initially called *The Recruiters* but soon rebranded *Mogadishu, Minnesota* after swift criticism resulted from the show's original name. As has been mentioned earlier, Cedar-Riverside had become a focal point for local and international media coverage of terrorism, with the community serving as a stand-in for international terror. Many accounts attest to this. After the 2013 mall attack in Nairobi, which many people mistakenly connected to Somalis in Minneapolis, journalist Jamal Abdulahi recounts: "The Brian Coyle Center in Cedar-Riverside became ground zero for reporters who wanted to break a terror story that never existed. The situation became so intense that it brought operation of the center to a standstill."[130] In a blog, a local teacher relates how her classes had been besieged by reporters, excited by seeing "a sea of headscarves, hijabs, clustered around a table. Exotics. Inscrutable foreigners. Stock footage for the next time a boy far, far away commits violence against another."[131] Abdirizak Bihi, who had been on the Somali American Task Force and had a nephew recruited by al-Shabaab, told me:

"People used to be open to the media, very open to the media. But it has gotten to the point where people avoid the media now."[132] Ifrah Mansour, a local Somali performance artist who had received some acclaim for her one-woman multimedia show, *How to Have Fun in a Civil War*, suggests that the fear of media "is coming from a place of hurt." She frequently does outreach to youth and local schools. She notes, "I can definitely tell and notice that kids feel ashamed for being Muslim and Somali now." She relates the paradox that many Somalis encounter from commercial media representations of being "visible for all the wrong things and invisible for the right things."[133]

Interestingly, due to the media's frequent presence, some members of the local Somali community have become self-appointed ambassadors for it and act as liaisons between the community and the media. The Starbucks on 25th and Riverside Avenue serves as their unofficial news depot where reporters descend. Many of the community's male elders congregate there. At all hours, the place bustles with activity. Although customers of various racial backgrounds quickly circulate through the store to get their coffee, Somali American men occupy the space, sitting around the lengthy tables discussing and arguing over politics, culture, and world events. In the background, Somali women, who are largely absent in person, are portrayed in wall art cooking and smiling. In warm weather, the men flood onto the cement patio in front that lies adjacent to a gas station next door. A parking lot attendant patrols the spaces before the building keeping tabs on cars that have overstayed their welcome. He would periodically enter the building and shout: "Who owns the black Ford? You got to get going, brother. You have been here since ten in the morning."

I am as guilty as any journalist or researcher of frequenting the space. I befriended Osman D. who acted as a liaison between media organizations and film crews and media savvy elders like Abdirizak Bihi. When I arrived, he greeted me with a wide smile, asking how I was before dashing away from our high-top table in search of some of the elders who would like to speak to me. During a quiet moment, I asked Osman what he thought about the constant barrage of reporters in the community who linked it with terrorism. He smiled and enigmatically stated: "You have to give them what they want," a disturbing proposition given the very real ramifications that resulted from such representations.

Starbucks is where I first met Bihi, who stands on the opposite side of the political spectrum from the younger activists I had been speaking with.

Bihi's very appearance speaks to his media-ready personality: gelled hair, a tailored light gray suit, purple button-down shirt, and polished shoes. When I initially told him I was at a no-name university, I could see him visibly wilt at the prospect of having to speak with someone far beneath the caliber he was accustomed to. Bihi runs a weekly Somali American radio program on the local community station, KFAI. When I met him later for an interview at his offices in the Somali Education and Social Advocacy Center in Cedar-Riverside where he is director, we walked to a glass-encased, soundproof room, specifically designed for interactions with the media, a testament to how the frequent swarm of reporters, academics, and filmmakers mandated that a small nonprofit build a media facility to accommodate them.

The film industry has left an indelible imprint on the community as well. *Captain Phillips* (2013) held casting calls at the Brian Coyle Center for Somali American men to play the part of the pirates in the film. Ultimately, they hired four men from Cedar-Riverside: Barkhad Abdi, Faysal Ahmed, Barkhad Abdirahman, and Mahat Ali. During my interview with Bihi, he pointed to individual buildings near Riverside Plaza to indicate where each actor lived. People often told me about the film after they discovered I was a media professor visiting town. At the Starbucks, I sat outside across from an elderly gentleman who was unemployed due to a disability. During our discussion, he mentioned how "John Hanks" had come to town about "that pirate movie."

Interestingly, unlike the HBO show that would become a lightning rod for criticism by many in the Somali community, *Captain Phillips* came and left town relatively unscathed. There were a few reasons for this. First of all, many gave the film a pass since it was based on actual events that limited its ramifications in the community's mind. Bihi stated: "It was an international issue. But they were talking about the specific target and what happened in there. So, they did not call the whole country pirates." Similarly, Barkhad Abdirahman explained to me: "The way they played it was a true story. Yeah, and so most of the people were familiar with the story. So, they were like: what else could they do?"[134]

Second, the script held a certain ambiguity about its relationship to the pirates and the amount of US firepower dedicated to stopping them. In a review of the film, Eric Kohn points out that the lead pirate, Muse (Barkhad Abdi), is not given the same dimensionality as Phillips, who we see outside of his job with his family. Yet the movie "by virtue of its objective, vérité-style readings, opens itself up to multiple interpretations" that appeal to both the right and left political outlooks.[135] The right can celebrate the supremacy of the American military at stopping the pirates. Yet "one could easily see the finale as a cynical representation of America's killer, imperialistic instinct" as well.[136]

This ambiguous reception manifested itself in reader responses to a highly critical review of the film in the *Minnesota Post*. The reviewer dismisses the film as "little more than a vile race-baiting vehicle and recruitment tool for the U.S. Navy."[137] Many readers took issue with the review. Jack Jones writes, "To say that the pirates were depicted as 'bad' makes me feel that the writer did not watch the movie. I found them to be sympathetic characters, caught between poverty and clan bosses who also took advantage of them."[138] Rosalind Kohls objects: "The Muse character was under just as much pressure as Captain Phillips was to 'do his job.' If he was to go back home with only the $30,000 he would have been killed. Even though this is never stated in the movie, the pressure can be seen on Muse's face."[139]

Third, the representation of Somali pirates felt empowering to many Somali viewers. Bihi eloquently stated: "Somalis like one thing about it, because for fifteen years they were powerless due to the civil war. So, they liked, 'Look at me!'" He briefly points to his eyes, replicating Muse's gesture in the film when first confronting Phillips after capturing the ship. He continues: "That made it popular. So that phrase is now part of my culture." This was confirmed by my experience walking around Cedar-Riverside. I had actually heard this phrase once or twice, accompanied by the same gesture.

Finally, *Captain Phillips* came to town during a less highly charged moment and was not directly about Cedar-Riverside as the planned HBO series would be. Given the relative absence of Black Muslim images on commercial screens other than the well-known ones of Malcolm X and Muhammad Ali, any series purporting to represent Somali Americans held a great weight. Initially, the series might have had a promising start since its pilot was written and directed by K'naan, a famous Somali Canadian rapper, who many of the activists and artists I spoke with idealized during their youth.

But HBO significantly blundered during its initial press releases by suggesting that the series would be more of the same representations Cedar-Riverside had become accustomed to. Press releases in both *Rolling Stone* and the *Hollywood Reporter* announced that K'naan would be teaming up with executive producer Kathryn Bigelow to produce a series named

The Recruiters. Sensationalistic and Islamophobic language in both press releases defined the show. According to *Rolling Stone,* it "will draw open an iron curtain behind which viewers will see the highly impenetrable world of Jihadi recruitment."[140] The *Hollywood Reporter* stated, "[The drama] looks to unveil what is considered a world that's hidden in plain sight."[141] The conjuring of veils and enigmatic Muslims plays into the worst stereotypes about Muslim communities. Before HBO even came to town, it had deeply fucked itself through such thoughtless early publicity.

Social media had already been buzzing about the series before it drew the attention and ire of many from the Cedar-Riverside community. There are many forums for the diasporic Somali community like Somali Net and Somali Spot where social media plays an important role in maintaining contact among friends and family and staying current with Somali news. Somali websites have grown exponentially over the years. In 1998 there were roughly around twenty, but by 2006, there were over five hundred. Idil Osman observes, "Somali media based in the diaspora has become pivotal, dominating the Somali media environment in Somalia as well as outside since it costs very little to set up, owners and producers have access to credit cards, and the technical infrastructure in the West is at their disposal as well as having a stable and secure environment surrounding them."[142] Ifrah Mansour explains her own similar use of social media: "There's Somalis all around the world. The way we literally connect is through social media. So, I was like: best believe it if you say anything with the words— 'Somali,' 'Somalis,' 'Somalians.'—I have alerts. OK? And it will get to my mailbox."

Although there was general curiosity about the series online, many people already started critiquing its conception. On a SomaliNet thread "Adali" stated: "Yes let's now turn more negative attention towards Somali diaspora. As long as he [K'naan] can make a quick buck."[143] "Cherine" responded, "All doom & gloom for us Somalis. First it was Black hawk down [saving third worlder], then Desert flower [giudniin], Captain Phillips [Pirates] & now terrorists."[144] It also didn't help that the name of the thread was: "K'naan making MN Jihadi recruitment show for HBO."

The initial press releases for *The Recruiters* played into long-standing stereotypes of Muslim Americans as dangerous. As Sara Ahmed stresses, there is "nothing more dangerous to a body than the social agreement that *that* body is dangerous."[145] As we have seen, Somali Americans had become a suspect and dangerous community due to the endless repetition of news broadcasts associating the Cedar-Riverside community with Muslim terrorism, government practices that wed social welfare with terrorism prevention, and government officials like Trump and others casting the community as a hotbed of terrorism. A former US senator from Minnesota, Norm Coleman, castigated the state as "the land of 10,000 terrorists."[146] Trump crowed, "Here in Minnesota, you've seen first-hand the problems caused with faulty refugee vetting, with very large numbers of Somali refugees coming into your state without your knowledge, without your support or approval."[147]

To have HBO produce a show initially called *The Recruiters* felt nothing less than a complete affront to many in the community. It was perceived as the cheap peddling of an Islamophobic trope that had become a hot topic in the news due to announcements by the FBI and the state's attorney general's office earlier in the year that they intended to prosecute several men for conspiring to join and provide material support to ISIS. It seemed callous to many that HBO would consider filming in Cedar-Riverside where the community was directly affected by these trials, the impact of CVE, and FBI surveillance. HBO quickly scrambled to rebrand the series as *Mogadishu, Minnesota* by upper brass after they realized how badly they had blundered. But the damage was already done.

Resistance against the series centered around four fronts: (1) publicity about the show, (2) the pilot script, (3) the interactions of HBO and its personnel with the community, and (4) the economic impact the show would have on the local community. It is important to understand how all of these issues related to one another and that the script was only one element of activists' attention.

One of the most disastrous aspects of the show's initial publicity was having Kathryn Bigelow's name attached to it. The *Hollywood Reporter*'s article, for example, was titled: "Kathryn Bigelow Prepping Jihadi Recruitment Drama for HBO." This seemed to reinforce all the worst opinions critics in the community held of Bigelow, who they saw as making a living off directing Islamophobic films like *The Hurt Locker* (2008) and *Zero Dark Thirty* (2012). Although one might rightfully argue that these films also critique the military, they still remain fully couched in an imperialist outlook that never moves beyond an American perspective.

Every person I spoke to had issues regarding Bigelow's role. Barkhad Abdirahman claimed he wouldn't even read the pilot's script since it was attached to "some big Islamophobic director."[148] Isaaq exclaimed: "Are we some idiots? Do you know the films she's been involved in? And that was

...like everything K'naan did, that was the most disrespectful thing he did to us."[149]

Similar sentiments were expressed online. "InaSamaale" on SomaliNet said that people rejected the show because of "Kathryn Bigelow's previous problematic work of Muslims."[150] A local activist Iqbal Abdi tweeted her YouTube video, "Is K'naan selling out the Somali Community?," which received over fourteen thousand views.[151] Abdi speaks in a single shot for nearly seven minutes addressing multiple issues with the show, but she makes an early point about how all Bigelow's "viewers are basically Islamophobic," a comment that should be read less as a descriptive statement than a rhetorical device to emphasize a point. She claims if the show doesn't subscribe to Bigelow's outlook, "why the hell would she put her name on your show?"

Isaaq provided a political economic analysis of Bigelow's influence. In an online interview, he explains: "The funders always control what's put out there. You might have the creative genius to put something together. But at the end of the day, the ones who fund it are the ones who have the last say."[152] Early publicity seemed to reinforce this view by constantly mentioning Bigelow and asserting that she is "prepping" for a "jihadi recruitment drama."

Nevertheless, when I spoke with Lucinda Winter, a former director of the Minnesota Film and TV Board who was directly engaged with HBO at this time, she asserted that Bigelow's input was minimal at best. She explained to me: "Bigelow saw talent and a story with this guy K'naan. She made a meeting with HBO and said, 'I think you should meet with this guy and see what he's got cooking.' By then she got a little fee....And that was all her involvement."[153] But the publicity suggested otherwise and took on a life of its own. As Winter belatedly realized: "I think it was derailed from the very beginning and we were always trying to make up for it....Her name was forever fucking tied to it."[154]

A huge amount of ire was also directed at the series' script. Although a pilot was ultimately shot, other than Lucinda Winter, neither I nor anyone I spoke with has seen it. A script of the pilot, however, had been drifting around the activist community despite HBO's explicit instructions to keep it confidential. Winter recalls: "If I wanted to give the script out to somebody for the bigger locations, I got permission and I numbered the scripts and I never sent them electronically. I only would give them a copy of the script and it said all over it: punishable by death if you make copies of this shit." This did not deter community organizers, who had taken pics of the script that circulated through the community to some extent and eventually made it to me.

Distribution of the script in the community was uneven, and many people who had not seen it were basing their knowledge on hearsay. The script might best be understood as an "encapsulated text," which Greg M. Smith defines as "partial versions of the text which circulate popular discussion in place of the text itself."[155] Even when the text itself was literally in circulation among people, they focused on select areas of it. Moreover, in many cases of media activism, the film or television show being battled over becomes less central than other factors, such as, in this case, the discussions and ramifications of the CVE program, FBI surveillance, media encounters with the *community*, economic deprivation, withered social services, and wider Islamophobic discourses. So any discussion of the script should keep this in mind.

Despite HBO's marketing claim that "It's not TV, it's HBO," Avi Santo and others have shown how much HBO's content and practices depended upon the formulas of network television. Santo writes, "Most of the content appearing on HBO draws upon existing television forms, narratives, aesthetics, themes, and economic and institutional practices."[156] *Mogadishu, Minnesota* is no different. The script reads as an amalgam of genres and conventions that have proved appealing to audiences: the gangster genre, the buddy cop film, the interracial romance, and, most disturbing to many members of Cedar-Riverside, Muslim radicalization and terrorism.

Everyone I spoke to opposing the series brought up its terrorism plot and its negative repercussions. Ayaan Dahir highlights her concerns regarding the image of the Muslim terrorist circulating among non-Muslim viewers:

> It's very powerful because when people are constantly being told that there are jihadi sleeper cells or that you know people are coming to rape your women and pillage you, and they have no connection to Muslims. They've never met a Muslim or they've never seen one. If the media is telling you this, and you see the government is doing a program specifically to counter the terrorism in the Muslim community, you're going to start creating an image in your head about who Muslims are. When in actuality, you've been fed an image about who Muslims are.[157]

This, according to Dahir, and many other members in the community, leads to dehumanization and interpersonal violence against Muslims and communities of color that are evidenced by numerous news articles documenting whites attacking Muslims.[158] Overall, the terrorism plot that *Mogadishu, Minnesota* was selling was seen as inextricably intertwined with the antiterrorism rhetoric being perpetuated by law enforcement and commercial media. The community did not have the luxury of seeing the show as only entertainment since they had been living with the fallout of increased surveillance, hate crimes, public vilification, and imprisonment that such terrorism narratives fostered.

The script of the pilot handles the terrorism subplot as a present absence. The pilot centers on two Muslim American teens, Sameer and Ali, and their families. Ali's brother, Mohamed, goes missing at the start of the episode. Suggestions are peppered throughout the script that he might have been radicalized. Ali's uncle focuses viewers' suspicions as he asks early on: "Was he getting mixed up with those Jihadi kids?" Mohamed's absence is remarked on every so often throughout the episode until the final reveal at its end: Mohamed appears at an airport with a white friend. The scene is described as: "It's tropical, and looks like Africa, but the common attire is Islamic." They are greeted by a "BEARDED MAN" who says 'Asalaum Aleikum.'" Burhan Israfael Isaaq questioned the way the pilot concluded with this scene: "We ended up to find that part about the kid who mysteriously disappears. The kid that everybody's worried about. Why would you add this part?"[159]

The script falls in line with a lot of HBO programming around Muslim American stories that frequently involve a terrorist plot even if the shows are challenging it like *The Night Of* (2016) and *The Case against Adnan Syeed* (2019). *Mogadishu, Minnesota* plays with this trope as well. After the uncle suggests Mohamed might be involved with jihadi kids, his sister and Mohamed's mother retorts: "You're brainwashed by the TV, talking like white people now." This meta moment of the show attempts to deflect criticism of it by acknowledging the racist ways in which terrorism is employed by "white people," yet the series trucks in it as well. Ultimately, the show attempts to play it both ways, by perpetuating a stereotypical terrorist subplot while also attempting to critique it in a minor way.

HBO shouldn't necessarily be singled out here since a reliance on Islamophobic conventions pervades much commercial television and Hollywood films. In a revealing 2016 group interview with Aasif Mandvi, actor from *The Daily Show*, and Zarqa Nawaz, creator of the hit Canadian TV show *Little Mosque on the Prairie*, along with showrunners for *24* and *Quantico* where terrorism plots predominate, the interviewees offer testimonies of how terrorism is often required to be a part of plot lines featuring Muslim characters. Cherien Dabis, a Palestinian American actress, director, and producer recounts: "I wanted to create this authentic family drama. When I took it into the marketplace, every suggestion was that I needed to have some kind of terrorist component,"[160] She then obliged.

Community activists also complained about the show's reliance upon a gangster narrative that governed the portrayal of many of its characters. Again, the gangster formula serves as a reliable go-to for HBO given the fact that one of its most popular shows *The Sopranos* (1999–2007) and one of its most critically acclaimed yet generally unwatched shows *The Wire* (2002–8) were deeply steeped in the genre. Straight from the script's opening, we are introduced to "BIG MAN," described as a "killer in the making" and "smoking a spliff." A series of criminal clichés litter the script such as representing the uncle as an old, highly regarded career criminal of the neighborhood who puts a cigarette out on this tongue "out of mindless habit" and beats a travel agent with a lamp to find out Mohamed's location. Isaaq quickly latched on to the problematic nature of such roles: "It had that typical gangsta character, you know what I mean. Somali Thug One. Somali Thug Two. Come on, man." Dahir told me, "So we're either gangstas or terrorists, but not people. Who does that serve? Certainly not us."[161]

Even those who had not seen the script were troubled when *Variety* announced the cast for the show on September 29, 2016, an announcement that used equally problematic criminal descriptions to define the series' characters.[162] Mahmoud Mire wrote an article for the *Huffington Post* critiquing the release: "It seems the show will portray Minnesota Somalis as primarily violent, particularly Somali men. 'Petty thug,' 'renowned gangster,' 'mysterious,' 'street-wise' are words used to describe the male characters in the series, further perpetuating stereotypes the overwhelming majority of Somali Americans prove misleading daily."[163]

Ayaan Dahir released a series of articles across various independent online publications like *Twin Cities Daily Planet* throughout September and October 2016 regarding the ramifications that such stereotypes will have on the community. In one article she argues: "It is not simply that a glossy new TV show about Somalis being portrayed as future terrorists will hurt our feelings. It has been shown that time and time again, these stereotypes of Somali people fuel a climate in which safety is a major concern. Public perception also influences law and legislation that supports CVE could very well be commonplace and acceptable thanks to one-dimensional narratives."[164] In another article she quotes a local activist: "In this particular story, HBO and the CVE policy are in line with the dominant narrative. We are to be seen and received in a certain way, and it's a threat."[165]

One thing that activists did not critique the script for was its reliance on pairing white characters with Black ones in order to provide a racial safety blanket for uncomfortable white viewers being immersed in a predominantly Black Muslim world. This is a part of the encapsulated text that was set aside for whatever reason. But it exposes an equally problematic racial dynamic at work within the script. The lead character, Sameer, has a white girlfriend, Lacy. The pilot shows Sameer struggling to navigate white ways like when he is invited to her house for dinner by her parents. Although such interracial romances can be considered progressive by some, they have also come under fire by holding white women as idealized objects of brown, heterosexual men's desire.[166] These white characters are also there to soothe the anxieties of segregated white audiences whose sense of diversity extends as far as their dinner plate and "exotic" cuisine. Not only is Sameer paired with a white girlfriend, but the script also has a Somali and white cop, and Mohamed is accompanied by a white character to Africa. In other words, the script reveals HBO's anxiety about alienating potential white viewers, their main demographic, by incorporating many white pairings throughout.

Although K'naan was celebrated publicly as the author of the pilot, other people's concerns were being articulated within the script as well. For example, the script explains certain Muslim terms like *edo, haram*, and *hooyo* to non-Muslim readers. Although written by K'naan, the script reveals that it is written for people unfamiliar with the world it is describing.

K'naan also came under fire from local activists for being an unresponsive interloper. As mentioned earlier, many of the local activists and artists I spoke with had been fans of K'naan when they were younger. So he had a lot going for him and potentially could have made amends for HBO's missteps. But by all accounts, K'naan's interactions with the community made things decidedly worse.[167]

K'naan agreed to meet with various Cedar-Riverside groups and grassroots organizers so he could address their concerns. The most important of these—what bothered the community most—was the terrorist plot. Filsan Ibrahim, Isaaq, and Mire met with K'naan to discuss it. Ibrahim recalls: "He was just justifying it. This is a good plot line. It is going to tell a Somali kid from Cedar-Riverside their regular life and how they live and operate."[168] In another meeting with Ramla Bile and others, he allegedly denied that the original title of the show was *The Recruiters*. Bile states: "He said that was never an option. I was like, so where did *Variety* get it? He literally denied that ever happened. And I'm just like they wouldn't just make things up."[169]

The activists asked repeatedly that K'naan remove the terrorism plot from the script, but he would not budge, despite emphasizing his autonomy as writer and director of the series. Ibrahim relates her frustration: "It was just bullshit for us. He wouldn't make any changes to the script. And if he was so gung-ho about really changing the narrative of Somali youth and Somalis in America or in the West, why didn't he focus on elsewhere or in Canada where he is from?" The control that K'naan suggested he possessed was clearly more limited than he was willing to admit. It is hard to believe a first-time director and writer would hold such autonomy. When I asked Lucinda Winter about this, she replied, "He was surrounded by people who had done this many, many times before. They wanted honestly this to be his vision of the story so they weren't climbing all over that, but, after all, this is their investment, so they were making sure that he had really good people around him. Now if he wants to call that autonomy, I guess you could."[170] But as the script reveals, other eyes were impacting the series' overall contours.

K'naan's entitlement and tendency to generalize about the Somali experience also frustrated local organizers since this reinforced a typical top-down dynamic of outsiders infiltrating their community, superimposing their narratives, and claiming it as "community-oriented," much as CVE and law enforcement had done. Bile recalls: "He had this entitlement around this community and saying well, I'm just as much a part of it.... You know, like we live with the stigma of like the fallout of all that."[171] Isaaq recalls somewhat tongue-in-cheek that his response was: "We're all Somalis. He was basically like all lives matter, the Somali version."[172] He thought K'naan looked "at himself as a savior. I'm providing this opportunity. Why would you say no to this? My own people are pushing me out, and I'm sure he'll probably live and die believing that even though we had plenty of conversations with him personally and explained to him our issues."

This overgeneralizing of Somali life manifested itself in the script, which seemed distant from the realities and rhythms of Cedar-Riverside in its rather formulaic approach to the material. Barkhad Abdirahman observed: "The way Somali Minnesotans would do stuff and Somalis in

Canada is totally different. So, when you read the script, you can feel the vibe [being off]." Nevertheless, the script identifies itself as happening in Cedar-Riverside. It mentions "RIVERSIDE TOWERS" described as "a 39-story 'Brutalist' designed BUILDING," an exact description of Riverside Plaza. Part of the problem with the series was that it clearly identifies its setting as occurring in Cedar-Riverside without taking into account the rhythms of life and specificity of the community that lives there.

Although I had not attended any of the meetings with K'naan and can only offer partial reconstructions of them through selective accounts, the fracas was covered by Integration TV, a Canadian English-language television network addressing the Somali diaspora. In "HBO: Who Controls the Somali Narrative?," the debate was partially reconstructed.[173] Isaaq, Ibrahim, and Iqbal Abdi are interviewed as a group. K'naan represents himself. Tellingly, the activists and K'naan never occupy the same space to discuss their issues. They are simply intercut with one another, the filmic strategy suggesting the deterioration of relations between them.

As can be expected, K'naan speaks in generalizations and abstractions. He calls the show "a family drama" occurring in a "fictional Minneapolis neighborhood." He contends that the show is about "themes of identity, which is a very human thing." He speaks about artistic principles apart from worldly concerns: "I work from a place of expression rather than desired outcome. . . . I don't busy myself with what something should yield. Art is best made when you put out the work that you think is true."

K'naan's lofty ambitions held no sway with the activists and revealed his complete disconnection from their reality. Isaaq, Ibrahim, and Iqbal Abdi speak about the distinct outcomes that they would have to confront daily if a show like *Mogadishu, Minnesota* is allowed to perpetuate images of criminality and terrorism associated with the Cedar-Riverside community. Forcing a community to live with such negative repercussions without having sought any significant engagement with that community in conceptualizing the series is egregious in the extreme. Ibrahim states, "It's problematic because we live here. Our brothers and sisters live here. Our parents live here. Our babies live here. And it's a very tense time to be Muslim and Black in America." The way in which K'naan implemented the pilot with its reliance upon a terrorism plot and gangster life seemed oblivious to the community's reality.

Lucinda Winter assured me that HBO did everything possible to address the community after the initial bad publicity: "As much as a large organization like that can address and really take their time in trying to make sure that they were respectful of the complexities of this community, I really do think they tried hard because they wanted to make it (the series) in the US." This is most likely true though it conveniently overlooks HBO's bungling of the initial publicity, its failure to consult the community while the show was being conceived, and its refusal to make any changes after hearing community concerns. Also, the amount of time HBO could dedicate to conducting outreach to a highly traumatized, under-resourced community and produce a production in a timely fashion was at odds with the community's own understanding of outreach and engagement. Winter relates the pressure of the production: "When you are a big production company…and in HBO everybody has a boss, everybody has someone you have to answer to and you can only spend so many fucking weeks trying to get everybody to love you. You know, you have a schedule."

Tensions came to a head during an ill-fated block party in September 2016. The block party was a yearly event organized by the West Bank Community Coalition. K'naan agreed to perform at the one in September, but protesters planned on attending as well. Since I wasn't at the event, it is difficult to reconstruct. A widely circulated video exists of the protest, but it is shot in such a rough style that it doesn't help clarify what occurred other than showing police confronting protesters physically before using pepper spray.[174] What can be safely stated is that K'naan came on stage. Protesters yelled at a distance. The police eventually ended up pepper spraying protesters and slamming a small Somali woman down on the stage when she tried to seize K'naan's microphone. Protesters say the police attacked them without provocation. Others claim rocks were thrown by some protesters. Either way, the event was an unmitigated disaster and put K'naan in a bad light. Perhaps the most neutral response I heard about the protest was from Ifrah Mansour, who had not been involved in the protest but attended the event. She relates her disappointment with K'naan as he insulted a protester over the mic: "I felt like he insulted [her] both in Somali and English, and I'm just thinking, that day I felt like I lost a Somali icon."[175]

HBO's interactions with the community were also problematic at many different levels. One of the locations HBO wanted to shoot at was the Cedar Heights Apartments. Community organizers, who had already made inroads with the community regarding CVE and other related issues, helped residents demand a vote whether to permit HBO to film. Residents voted 51–0 against HBO.[176] In addition to concerns about the stereotypes that the show perpetuates, the residents, many of whom were elderly and disabled, were concerned about the ways that shooting might simply inconvenience their lives. According to Dahir, "So even just filming and shooting there were certain places they were going to close off and then it would be a major, major, major inconvenience to them. These are the concerns they [residents] brought up."[177]

Subsequent to the negative vote, HBO appealed directly to the Minnesota Public Housing Authority for permission to film at a different complex, which they received.[178] This action signaled to the community that their input would be considered by HBO, but not necessarily heeded. This was much like the message they received from Somali American representatives who supported the project. Mohamud Noor, a member of the Somali American Task Force and aspiring politician, dismissively observed: "The youth have every right to be angry about something they know nothing about. But it should not have escalated to this level."[179]

A negative interaction between the production crew and protestors was caught on video.[180] Dahir recalls how the moment occurred: "We had a community forum about CVE, and we got news that they were shooting outside the [Cedar] theater not far away. We got in our cars and showed up."[181] HBO does not come out well as they smugly film and taunt the protesters during the two minute and forty second uncut video. The camera pivots between protesters, mostly young Black women dressed in hijabs, and the HBO crew—many of whom were white. Protesters chanted, "Hey hey, ho ho, HBO has got to go!" Some of the crew danced in mockery and clapped back at the protesters. Overall, the video makes HBO look callous in the face of community concerns.

Finally, community organizers were skeptical of HBO's claims that their production would help the community benefit financially. First of all, a certain arrogance was assumed by some of the crew since they viewed themselves as community benefactors. According to one anonymous source who worked with HBO, some of the crew were like "What's the problem? We are going to drop all this money into the community and do all these great things." But the upper brass supposedly informed some of the crew about community issues arising and the need for sensitivity, so the crew presumably responded by being more diplomatic.

Various community organizers recall the way HBO dangled the promise of money flowing into the community. Bile recounts: "There would be all these investments in the community, and it would support the local economy. They actually used language around that so that it was positive for us and we would cater to local businesses. But they also couldn't quantify that. So, we were like: who is it going to benefit?"[182] Bile's question is a good one since many dubious claims were made about how the series could pump "tens of millions into the local economy."[183] But this begs the question of who exactly reaps those millions.

One of the ways Minnesota attempts to lure runaway productions to the state is through a film tax credit program called Snowbate. Film tax credits have become increasingly common since Canada introduced them in the mid-1990s. Currently thirty-four states implement them. As Vicki Mayer points out, film tax credits are part of an overall shift toward supply-side economics thar provide "welfare for the wealthy" since they promise "a break for corporations and their richest beneficiaries by minimizing their fiduciary responsibilities to states."[184] Snowbate offers 20 percent back on productions shot in the seven county metro area or 25 percent within the state outside of the area on productions with a budget over $1 million.[185] The film tax credit only benefits large-scale productions.

The benefits of film tax credits remain murky based on obtuse bookkeeping and a certain amount of wishful thinking. Mayer, who has offered one of the most in-depth studies regarding film tax credits in New Orleans, points out the disparity that often exists between those who benefit from a public subsidy through the film economy and the working-class communities it encroaches upon.[186] Furthermore, one has to keep in mind that because most states "have a balanced budget requirement, states offering film subsidies must therefore cut public services or increase taxes elsewhere to make ends meet."[187] In other words, for a place like Cedar-Riverside that has high unemployment and low incomes, the money going to Hollywood in the form of tax credits could have instead been invested in needed social services. Rather than directly investing in the community, a "trickle down" economics prevails, claiming that money pumped into Hollywood will flow back into the community.

The promise of jobs in the community resulting from the series proved fairly hollow even though a couple of locals were hired. Repeated press accounts hyped how K'naan made every department hire a Somali assistant. In "Hanging Out with K'naan at the HBO TV Set," K'naan trumpets: "I mandated that every head of department . . . hire a Somali so that we can train the next generation of filmmakers out of Minnesota who are Somali.

When I leave here, they can make their own films."[188] Exactly how many Somalis were hired out of Cedar-Riverside remains unclear. Furthermore, in the same episode, K'naan goads one of the female costumers to emphasize how she is buying the wardrobe from local Somali malls.

The gestures made by HBO felt like window dressing, since a mere fraction of the overall budget went back into the local community. Even if we took these claims at face value, they seemed more symbolic than substantial, alms being tossed at the community to let the production roll on unimpeded. As Dahir notes, "A lot of the people were being hired to act were [from] out of state, and the roles were also going to—surprise, surprise—not Somalis. There were a handful of Somalis, and, from what I saw, the crew was white. So, the little they offered, they couldn't even give that."[189]

What was happening in Cedar-Riverside with HBO correlates in general with most of the literature on the very limited benefits that film tax credits have. As Robert Tennewald observes, "A large portion of the jobs they create, especially with the highest pay—are filled by nonresidents."[190] Due to the highly portable nature of the industry, moviemakers tend to ship in above-the-line talent rather than rely on the local industry. Although some reliance on local below-the-line workers occurs, the greatest expenses occur with above-the-line talent.

A 2017 study of all English-language films produced and distributed in the US from 1998 to 2010 revealed film tax credits as negligible. Results show that "the status quo remains largely intact, despite billions in incentives aimed at disrupting it."[191] In other words, film tax credits made little to no difference at all.

A host of other studies bulwark skepticism about the benefits of the film tax credit to local communities.[192] An independent study on film tax credits in Minneapolis shows negligible results. The authors write: "The data clearly show that while the amount of Snowbate reimbursements remain relatively level, the amount of Minnesota production spending fluctuates quite wildly, showing as much as a $10 million difference between various years."[193] As a result, there is no direct correlation between the incentives offered and the film production activity that it generates. So community members who remained doubtful of the economic benefits of *Mogadishu, Minnesota* were right, since despite the glamour of bringing in runaway productions to the local community, their impact is economically negligible at the local level and dubious for the entire state after film tax credits have been assessed.

The Mixed Results of Social Media Resistance

While the on-the-ground organizing against HBO continued, Bile, Kadra Abdi, and a few others initiated an online campaign. They created the hashtag #SayNOtoHBO on Twitter and wrote an online petition against the show on Change.org, which received 589 signatures.[194] The petition revisited many of the aforementioned grievances: Bigelow's role in the series, the terrorism theme, and the questionable claims that the show would produce an "economic boom" for the community. The petition declares near its end: "K'naan knows nothing of this community, what we have endured and what we encounter on a daily basis, given the focus for the series, the way he approached this community, and the manner with which he has interacted with us since his arrival." It then appeals for people to sign the petition, share the letter critiquing HBO attached to it, and support "existing Somali community initiatives that push back against criminalization and state-sanctioned violence."

Overall, the online campaign revealed mixed results. Most of the traction occurred on YouTube where some videos were posted critical of *Mogadishu, Minnesota* and on message boards like Somali Spot and SomaliNet. Respondents were deeply divided regarding the protesters' actions. The video of the block party protest in September 2016 received over eighty thousand views. User "Keep scrolling" states: "K'naan should have gone to the community and explained to them before cuz by not he seems like another Somali sellout."[195] But many more comments critiqued the protesters in the video. "Wais_45" writes: "Somalis just showing their petty side. K'naan is doing a show about Somalis and of course the vultures come out and try to tear down his name." "Pyro" comments: "Somalia people just disappoint God damn it's just a show that tells things that do really happen and he's also doing great things by bringing in new actors in."

The same holds true for the comments found on SomaliNet and Somali Spot. They alternate between those urging people to give K'naan a chance and others who viewed K'naan as opportunistic and thought the show should be stopped due to the harm it could inflict on the local community. Ibrahim reflects upon the online campaign: "There was a lot of back-and-forth. I don't know why they didn't go for it. It was mixed particularly with people not from Minneapolis and particularly from Canada or Australia. They just see things at a distance."[196] This difficulty of translating local struggles online has been called "context collapse" by Henry Jenkins. The use of electronic online media allows for "expanded communication capacity [that] can also result in expanding conditions of exposure and vulnerability" as "assumptions and norms inside a group are made public to those outside" it, "both potential supporters and potential haters."[197] This "context collapse" plagues many activist campaigns as they extend their work into the online world.

In regard to the #SayNOtoHBO campaign, less credible reasons were posited online as the causes behind the youth's rebellion against K'naan. One was that the youth and K'naan came from different Somali clans, so the conflict was dismissed as a tribal rivalry. "Kubab Sitaak" wrote on YouTube that the protestors were "the same stupid people who destroyed our country with their shitty tribalism ideology."[198] "Mahadalla" wrote on SomaliNet: "We all know Jebertis where [sic] jealous of K'naan, a HG. It was pretty much clan motivated and everyone who hate HG participated."[199] The clan issue often gets played up by older Somalis or outsiders. Although it is true that clan affiliation is still strong among the elders in the Somali community in Cedar-Riverside, the younger generation, who comprised the main protesters against HBO, do not view their identity mainly through clans but much more intersectionally through race, gender, and class.

Another explanation of the context collapse for the #SayNOtoHBO campaign was that much of it occurred in September and October 2016, shortly before the presidential election. As Trump's base became more ignited, the Trump trolls infiltrated the internet and wreaked havoc, galvanized by the Islamophobia being pushed by conservative media like *Breitbart, Daily Caller*, and *Fox News*.[200] Many of their comments appeared on YouTube, which makes sense since they most likely were completely unaware that Somalis have their own message boards. "Damian INSANE-O2" writes: "They don't belong in this country. America rejects Islam and all of its tenets. Shariah is oppressive."[201] "Ann Haris" posts: "Somali Muslims are the most bloodthirsty of Muslims....All they know is fighting and rabble rousing.... VOTE TRUMP or more of this."[202] Such comments were typical of the vitriol not only against the Somali community but all immigrant communities.

Ibrahim's question of why the online community "didn't go for it" speaks to a certain disillusionment with the internet and what Nick Couldry has called its "myth of 'us.'" Social media likes to brand itself as a unified community where people can come together, but such an outlook overlooks how "social resources and power relations are being reproduced and which networks have significant social consequences in so-called network societies."[203] Once protesters at Cedar-Riverside went online they were quickly reminded of the different social resources and power relations beyond their own community. Many from the diasporic community saw K'naan as an exemplary Somali Muslim. Trump trolls who scoured the net looking for fodder to dump their xenophobic and racist views upon, cast Somali Americans as ungrateful immigrants. Moreover, according to Idil Osman, fractures among Somali diasporic online communities are not atypical where "the perpetuation of clan attitudes" and other differences escalate.[204] So the #SayNOtoHBO social media campaign serves as an important reminder of the limits of taking activism online. Although activists were relatively successful at moving their agenda forward and galvanizing community members within Cedar-Riverside, online their momentum was lost as different groups argued over their interpretation of events.

On September 1, 2017, HBO announced that it was not greenlighting the series.[205] Why exactly they didn't go forward with the series is not clear. Protests certainly might have been a factor, but there were other reasons as well. One related to the instability of the Snowbate program. The state only provides two-year allocations of money, so planning beyond that was an unknown.[206] For a series that was expected to run four to five seasons, this was a big concern. Furthermore, Minnesota had unevenly funded Snowbate. Funding varied from as much as $5 million a year to as little as $500,000.[207] The state even cut off funding entirely from 2002 until 2006.[208] Lucinda Winter also noted how Trump's campaign against immigration and accepting visas might have had an impact: "Trump's stuff around immigration was very scary for an industry that is nothing if not global. All this political unrest can have impacts on lots of money and lots of people's lives." So, although community activism most likely played some part in HBO not greenlighting the project, we shouldn't assume that it was the only deciding factor. The activism combined with the unsteadiness of the Snowbate program and the general political opposition to immigration by the Trump administration were likely all contributing factors.[209]

An Independent Production: *A Stray* (2016) and the Contours of Muslim Life

It probably didn't help HBO's cause that about a year prior to its arrival, the community had a mostly positive experience in collaborating with Musa Syeed on an independent film called *A Stray* (2016). One needs to keep in mind that the two different productions were on two completely different economies of scale, which dictates the practices and relationships that emerge from them. As David James stresses, "cinema is never just the occasion of an object or a text, never simply the location of a message or of an aesthetic event, but always the site of manifold relationships among people and classes."[210] Syeed's low-budget production, his experience in documentary filmmaking, and his Muslim background all afforded *A Stray* a totally different relationship with the community. This allowed for a markedly different type of production in terms of both form and content than the one that was in the works with HBO's *Mogadishu, Minnesota*. This section's focus on the production and exhibition history of *A Stray* along with a close analysis of the film serves as an interesting example of how a particular filmmaking practice aligned with the interests of the community members of Cedar-Riverside despite the film having a subplot in which the lead character served as a reluctant informer to the FBI. The rhythms of low-budget filmmaking allowed Syeed to foster relationships with the community much more substantively than HBO's relatively short deadline afforded. This is not to idealize the relationship between Syeed and the Somalis of the Cedar-Riverside community, because there were certainly some differences of opinions and resulting tensions between them. Nevertheless, it is important to examine how a different type of low-budget production style allowed for deeper connections between filmmaker and community, which led to a film that felt truer to the textures of daily life in Cedar-Riverside.

Syeed, a Muslim of Kashmiri descent, grew up in Indiana and attended film school at New York University.[211] One of his earlier films, *Valley of the Saints*, won the Audience Award and the Sloan Film Prize at Sundance in 2012.[212] He began to shoot *A Stray* in summer 2015, but he started visiting Cedar-Riverside nearly a year prior. He was in part drawn to Minneapolis as a location because of his midwestern background. During an interview with me, he said: "I had done films before in NYC about immigrant communities, but it's easy to forget immigrants are not just on the coasts. There are major centers of immigrant life in the heartland of America, and I wanted to tell a story that affirms a world like that exists"[213]

By all accounts of people I spoke with from Cedar-Riverside, Syeed, who was not much older than the Somali youth he hoped to work with, integrated himself fully into the community by teaching a youth filmmaking class, attending other people's events, and just generally being present. Furthermore, he didn't bring a script when first arriving in town. In fact, he did not begin writing it until April after he had interacted with and befriended many Somali youth. Syeed reflects: "I met the actor, Barkhad Abdirahman [who acted in *Captain Phillips*], around that same time and tried to shape the script around him and sharing the script with the community to get their feedback." Abdirahman, who plays the film's lead character, was rather taken aback by Syeed's open approach to reshape the character according to his suggestions. Abdirahman noted, "The way the character was supposed to be was more like Westernized, but if you see the film, I didn't play it that way. The script originally was more like a kid born in the US."[214] This helped ground the film in the Cedar-Riverside community that comprises a majority refugee population and better emulates the nuances of their lives.

Still, similar to the HBO series, Syeed initially experienced a lot of resistance from the community. He recalls how people assumed he might be FBI or have somehow accepted CVE money to make the film. The ubiquitous presence of both CVE and the FBI in the community at the time would understandably lead locals to question the presence of a stranger who interacts with the community with the ultimate goal of filming them.

Additionally, Syeed picked certain plot elements to raise questions of cultural assimilation to US culture that would challenge some within the Muslim community. First of all, his lead character, Adan, befriends a dog, which some in the community felt was troublesome due to their belief that physical contact with a dog can leave one ritually unclean. Ifrah Mansour, who also played a part in the film, recalled: "And I just felt like he packaged it in a story that felt a little, I don't know, a little foreign to us. We don't mess with dogs."

Even more troubling was the film's informer subplot. Throughout much of the film, Adan serves as a reluctant FBI informant. Burhan Israfael Isaaq, who was a core advisor on the film, remembers saying: "I don't feel right about that whole deal. You know, have him see it differently. I said, 'Can you show in the film that he doesn't want this? He doesn't want this relationship with the FBI?'" Syeed rewrote the part accordingly. The first few times Adan engages with the female FBI agent, it is begrudgingly. Initially, he sits in the backseat of a car with her in the driver's seat. For most of the shot, we see only a partial view of her face, occupying Adan's position. His position reveals his reluctance to be close to her. She also complains like a jilted lover: "You never write. You never call." He responds: "I've been busy." This could be dialogue taken from a dysfunctional romantic couple, but it

FIGURES 4.9 & 4.10: The image of an American flag and a chained dog reveal the threat Adan feels of being assimilated into US culture in *A Stray* (2016).

is transplanted to their relationship suggesting a torrent of not-so-hidden resentful emotions between them.

When the agent tries to pump Adnan for information about members of the community, he dismisses her requests by suggesting the person she is going after is "nobody." In the process, he is always trying to negotiate a better deal with her. At one point he asks, "Didn't you say you were going to get me a new phone?" She replies, "You help me make a couple of cases, and we can do something really nice for your mom." He reacts deadpan, stating, "Let's see how you do with the phone first." Their relationship is represented as a matter of mutual convenience without any warm emotions between them as they both jockey against one another for the upper hand.

Near the film's end, Adan finally decides to abandon the relationship. We watch him casually drop the phone she gave him off a bridge into the Mississippi River. This act is precipitated by an earlier scene where the FBI agent gets Adan a house in what seems to be the Powderhorn district in Minneapolis. A series of shots follow from Adan's point of view: an American flag, a white picket fence, a leashed dog in a backyard. Adan then looks to the FBI agent speaking on the phone in her car at some distance. He glances back to the dog who is pulling against his leash. The film cuts back to the agent on her phone, underscoring the connection between the dog's confinement and Adan's own. Not only is he gradually being ensnared by the FBI's maneuvers, he physically moves from the Cedar-Riverside apartment where he started to a white suburb that isolates him from his upbringing and culture.

Syeed relates the importance of Isaaq's influence on creating the main character of the film: "He was the closest to the character I wanted. Seeing the community through Burhan's eyes was very important because he is someone who grew up there." Isaaq also helped Syeed navigate the community. Syeed notes: "If I did something wrong and it got back to him, he would tell me how to fix it or resolve it."

Syeed 's connection with the local community encouraged him to reconsider the bad advice he initially received from industry insiders about the plot. "When I would show the script to people in the film world," he explains, "they would be like 'this needs more tension. This guy at the beginning needs to start off in a worse situation. He needs to be a worse person. Maybe he can commit some crime or something like that,' those types of…those are the kind of tropes of mainstream film." As I have already shown, this is not a unique occurrence. *Mogadishu, Minnesota* employed such tropes and conventions in its pilot to make it palatable to wider audiences, but it was at the expense of a good relations with members of the community.

But in Syeed's case he actually befriended the very people who would lead the charge against HBO. He recalls, "The people I was mostly associating with ended up forming the Young Muslim Collective, the younger generation of people who were more outspoken." And Syeed's near ubiquitous presence in Minneapolis for almost a year before filming endeared him to the youth. Abdirahman remembers: "By the time I met Musa he properly was more community than me. He was volunteering at Brian Coyle, teaching kids how to do their homework and stuff like that." Syeed also attended an

FIGURE 4.11: *A Stray* (2016) employs close-ups of Somali American faces to emphasize the individuality and distinctness of each character, contrasting the ways in which US popular culture often casts Muslim Americans as a uniform threat.

early short performance of Ifrah Mansour's *How to Have Fun in a Civil War* at the Bedlam Theatre. "There was Musa sitting way back in the theater," Mansour fondly reminisces. "There's half naked people around him [from an earlier performance]. I told him, 'I can't believe you came. Do you need a burka for your face?' After that, I was extremely impressed."

Syeed was open to suggestions for the script in order to anchor the story more firmly within the local Somali community. For example, Isaaq suggested opening the film in the apartment where Adan lives in order to provide a more nuanced portrayal of him and place the viewer firmly within the context of Cedar-Riverside. Per Isaaq's suggestion, the film opens on tight shots of Adan lining a parakeet's cage with newspaper, taking out pills for a bed-ridden elderly male relative, conducting daily activities as we hear a male voice singing in Somali in the background. The scene then cuts to a television softly playing a Tony Robbins inspirational speech as a group of young Somali men sit around a coffee table in a living room bantering with each other. One states: "No one is going to hire you because you're Somali." Another adds, "And you're a Muslim." Another character jokes: "All you have to do is make those white people feel sorry for you: [in dramatic voice] 'My mother died. My father died.'" The viewer hears snippets of overheard conversation as each character is shot in close-up. The camera carefully takes in the distinct contours of each individual face, stressing their individuality and uniqueness, implicitly countering the stereotypes that lump all Muslims as the same, a nondescript and suspect community.

The opening sequence of *A Stray* sets the tone of the film; it is observational and proceeding at a leisurely pace without much of a plot. It envelops viewers in a slice of life rarely seen on screen, where Muslims neither represent terrorists nor reinforce some generic positive image. *A Stray* engages with the type of complex storytelling being produced by a younger generation of Muslim Americans. Sangita Shresthova observes, "Many youth-driven storytelling efforts we observed moved away from the 'good' versus 'bad' Muslim binary to express more complex, diverse, and morally ambiguous (yet still nonthreatening) American Muslim experiences."[215] Similarly, Adan is a complex character. After tending to the parakeet, lovingly stroking and feeding it, he then suddenly kills it by throwing it at one of his friends who yells in response to his actions. This all occurs in the films' first two and a half minutes.

There is an inherent politics in this type of filming a Muslim community. In an interview in the *Harvard Crimson,* Syeed recounts a time when as a teen an elder took him to a protest outside of a theater against an Arnold Schwarzenegger film that demonized Muslims as villains. Syeed says that he didn't find such protesting effective. Instead, he reflects, "I could create work that could tell a different story or tell a better story. So, that was part of the initial motivation [to make films]."[216] This provides a clue to interpreting *A Stray.* Although not an explicitly political film, it has political implications, especially in a post-9/11 world where much of what American Muslims creatively produce "could potentially be interpreted as having political meaning."[217]

The film's title, *A Stray,* can as much describe the film's overall relation to Hollywood filmmaking regarding Muslims as it can the film's content. The film defies the tropes and stereotypes of Muslims that have come to define commercial filmmaking and news by burrowing into the singularity of a young Muslim American man's life. One can view *A Stray* as part of a long legacy of what Stuart Hall has defined as Black cultural politics. Even though Syeed is of South Asian descent, his film deals with immigrant Black Muslims, who remain largely absent from commercial screens with the exception of famous individuals like Malcolm X and Muhammad Ali. Black cultural politics, according to Hall, "challenge, resist, and, where possible, transform the dominant regimes of representation."[218] The film provides an unusual depiction of a fully humanized representation of Black Muslim

FIGURE 4.12: In *A Stray*, Adan connects with his Somali past in the Somali Museum located in Minneapolis.

life in a commercial mediascape bolstered by an Islamophobic framework that either squeezes Black Muslim characters from its frame entirely or reduces them to criminals and terrorists.

Ifrah Mansour didn't think that the original script showed much about Somali culture, so she suggested that they film a sequence in the Somali Museum, which is buried in the basement of a three-story building located on East Lake Street. Syeed reflects on the sequence: "I put the scene of the museum in there just so that visually we could get some cues of a past or a place. The character has probably never been to Somalia. So, the museum symbolized an imagined past or connection that he was trying to create."

The scene relays a sense of intimacy and longing. Mansour's character teaches a dance class by the museum's entrance. She claps and laughs with participants as they sing a Somali tune. Even in this brief snippet, the film captures the vibrancy and joy that Mansour relays and that I witnessed first-hand during a long conversation in a local bakery close to where she lives.[219]

In the film, Adan walks into the museum, past the dance class toward its various exhibits. He looks at various wooden artifacts, pottery, and colorful rugs. The sound from the dance class fades as Adan becomes engrossed with what is before him. He moves close to a diorama of camels in a desert. He crouches before it and picks up some sand to let it sift through his fingers. We see a momentary, poignant connection to the past as the sound drifts out to a quiet meditative moment and Adan affectionately touches the camel and a miniature well next to it.

FIGURE 4.13: *A Stray* uses a neorealist style that emphasizes context to locate its characters within its Cedar-Riverside neighborhood and the Twin Cities at large.

Syeed stresses the importance of place throughout the film: "A film should be an immersive experience and so having all these places and people to really create a world was important for me as a filmmaker to approach the story." This is relayed in the film just before the Somali Museum scene. Between scenes, the film lovingly presents brief images of Cedar-Riverside and Minneapolis, not unlike the way that Adan lovingly touches the objects before him in the museum. We see a low-angle shot of Riverside Plaza stretching into a dusky sky. A neon light of the "Gold Medal Flour" factory flashes and reflects off the Mississippi River. A halal deli sign hangs at a local market on Lake Street. We watch passersby going about their day, carrying groceries and bustling home from work. Electrified Somali oud music plays over the images, suggesting a diasporic moment where cultures intersect, and old and new traditions converge in a beautiful segue. Barkhad Abdirahman jokingly observes that the film "picks the most golden places to go to in Minnesota. It should be promoted by Minnesota tourism." But what keeps the film from descending into crass tourism are the sequences' careful pacing that locate Adan and the other characters in a specific place and culture. It juxtaposes the iconic images of Riverside Plaza with the mundane sign from a local halal shop. Ultimately, such sequences immerse the viewer in the rhythm of daily life and normalizes it. It is a rare moment in US cinema in stark contrast to the way that Muslims are usually mainly incorporated into films to stress a particular argument or agenda. They are not there simply to exist, normalized in

FIGURE 4.14: Images such as the halal meat sign in *A Stray* signal the presence of a large Somali American population in Minneapolis.

the rhythms of daily life, but this is exactly what *A Stray* does: it reshapes the film's tempo to the quotidian life of Cedar-Riverside instead of forcing Muslim representations into tightly prepackaged generic conventions and terrorist tropes.

If anything, the filmmaking style is indebted to a documentary aesthetic found in much Italian neorealism and Third Cinema. It provides a collaborative approach between a community and filmmaker rarely found in mainstream cinema but illustrated in such films as Luchino Visconti's *La Terra Trema* (1948) and Herbert Biberman's *Salt of the Earth* (1954). Just as Visconti allowed his fisherman to speak in an obscure Italian dialect for his film, Syeed allowed his actors to translate his script into Somali when needed, thus immersing viewers in the pacing of the language of what is essentially an oral culture.

Illustrated in *A Stray* is the type of collaborative approach that Third Cinema directors envisioned revolutionary cinema embodying. In "For an Imperfect Cinema," Julio García Espinosa writes: "The new outlook for artistic culture is no longer that everyone must share the tastes of the few, but that all can be creators of that culture."[220] Given the expenses attached to filmmaking and the inaccessibility of equipment for most people, this vision was very difficult to achieve in the past. Digital technology makes it slightly more achievable—though other factors like the lack of time, money, and training also prevents most people from engaging in film production. *A Stray* is located on that continuum of documentary-like approaches that both Third Cinema and Italian neorealism embodied in order to relate the stories and lives of marginalized people more accurately to the screen.

Syeed's engagement with the community eventually led to the training of Somali youth in filmmaking. While assisting at the Brian Coyle Center, Abdirahman Mukhtar questioned Syeed about how he might benefit the community while shooting the film. Syeed had already started a running project of training Muslim youth across the country in videomaking. Syeed further explained me, "I could bring this workshop here that I already have funding for," which eventually became known as *Muslim Youth Voices* and was distributed over PBS online.[221]

The project was funded by the Doris Duke Foundation for Islamic Art and the Corporation for Public Broadcasting. *Muslim Youth Voices* provided a mosaic of perspectives from Muslim American youth across the United States. From 2015 until 2018, a series of weeklong workshops were held in Freemont, California; New York City; Portland, Oregon; Plano, Texas; Philadelphia; and Minneapolis with six to twelve students in each location. Syeed developed the curriculum and oversaw the workshops. He explains, "The first two days were scripting, development, and storyboarding. And then the next three days were shooting. I would give them a crew to shoot with since we didn't have time to teach them to operate the cameras. So, they would direct the crew to shoot stuff."

The series was created with and produced by the Center for Asian American Media (CAAM) and emerges from a longer history of youth media making. Two years prior to its production, CAAM teamed up with the Asian Pacific American Center at the Smithsonian Institution to mount a small-scale exhibition at the Museum of Natural History produced by Asian American youth. Stephen Gong, the executive director of CAAM, explains, "That is where it was similar in design, where in three to four cities we found young Asian Americans just to do their own intensive workshop, to do portraits of their community and their identity, their experience."[222]

In the light of the heightened xenophobia since 9/11, CAAM teamed up with Syeed to organize workshops around Muslim youth, producing short videos that showed a diversity of Muslim perspectives. The mosaic approach was important since, as Syeed notes in a promotional video for the project, "No one person should be the representative of the Muslim community." Stephen Gong adds: "You cannot say that there is just one Muslim American experience." The mosaic form challenges any notion of Muslim American homogeneity by providing a broad cross section of youth across a wide geographical terrain, who employ a variety of styles and subject matter in their shorts.

Syeed notes that during the workshop in Minneapolis "every student project was about media representation in some way." For instance, both *Screened* (Iqbal Maxamed) and *Imagination* (Roodo Abdikadir) reflect these concerns. In *Screened* a young Muslim woman forces her personified television to follow her around during her day to counter the Islamic stereotypes it perpetuates. In the film, we watch young Muslim women playing basketball and working at a clothing shelter, but at the end, the television states, in a white-sounding voice, "I don't get paid to tell the truth. I'm just here to make money." The girl ultimately decides to abandon her television as a result.[223]

Imagination starts off similarly with a young woman entranced before the television watching *Fox News* with the muffled voice of Bill O'Reilly dominating the soundtrack.[224] Her mother berates her to stop watching such garbage. Ignoring her mother's advice, the girl passes out, dreaming of a *Saw*-like (2004) scene: a close up of dimly lit hands picking up and sharpening knives as the girl struggles tied up in the corner. A dark clad figure approaches demanding in a growl: "Give me your brain."

The girl awakens and shuts off the television. She sits at a table scribbling on a piece of paper a breathtaking poem she then recites:

> If I were a Black man, what or who should I be? Will I be the next Muhammed Ali, dance like a butterfly, sting like a bee? Will I become the next President Obama with a Harvard degree or will I be hung like strange fruit off a tree?

A series of still images flash across the screen: Ali standing triumphant over an opponent, protesters holding a banner stating "murdered by police," and riot police drawing weapons on a Ferguson protester. The imagery cuts between various close-ups of the girl speaking: "how much Blackness must I shed to equally to be loved, to be praised?" As she speaks, the sequence shifts to her standing before an audience reciting her work, ending with: "If I were a Black man" before applause and her smiling face.[225]

Imagination relays her poetic vision that shows solidarity across genders while also hinting at the ways in which Black women have been erased from the discussion. The power and confidence of her words shows a strong young Black woman both supporting Black men and inserting herself into the narrative, revealing how Black women provide the backbone behind these Black male figures. It is worth stressing here the predominant

FIGURE 4.15: Roodo Abdikadir wrote and directed *Imagination* (2018), which shows a young Black Muslim girl negotiating how to break from racist televised stereotypes. She was one of many Muslim American youth across the United States trained by Musa Syeed to produce their own short videos about their experiences that PBS distributed as *Muslim Youth Voices*.

presence of women involved in the protests against CVE and #SayNOtoHBO as well.

The workshops were conducted in the summer, but before appearing on PBS, the films from each year's workshop were presented at a film festival hosted in the spring by CAAM. Stephen Gong explains the rest of the process: "Musa would work to have them completed in the fall. We could take a look at them and then in the following early spring our film festival was in March. We would bring those previous summer's films and a group of four to six filmmakers out to the film festival. We would pay their travel and lodging and provide a chaperone. They got the full film festival experience." The screenings allowed the young filmmakers to take pride in their achievement with family members and discuss their films before audiences.

The screenings of *A Stray* had a similar community-oriented approach. At the Minneapolis/St. Paul Film Festival where it had its theatrical release, Syeed recounts the words of a white man in the audience reflecting about the informant subplot during a Q&A after the screening. The man said, "I was expecting that something was going to be revealed, and then I realized that was my own prejudice that this guy had to be connected to something nefarious." Syeed comments, "The youth who collaborated on the film felt the film did its job in some way or did something positive; it exposed this person's prejudice to himself."

Syeed arranged a special free screening at the Brian Coyle Center for the Cedar-Riverside community. He had his trepidations about them watching an art film: "I was like people are going to be walking around or people are going to be leaving, but they sat for the most part quietly throughout the whole thing and were reacting to what was going on. They seemed they were engaged because they never seen these very familiar places to them in that kind of way and so that just felt good."

Mansour, however, also relates how certain members of the community were policing the film during the screening. "The people that gave him the hardest time were all in the audience," she remembers. "They were properly policing the movie. They're like: I'm here to watch where he does our story wrong. So, at the end, he [Adan] touched the dog. 'That's it,' they said. 'I knew he was up to no good.' But they watched the whole movie until the last one minute."

Syeed joked about the audience's reaction at Brian Coyle regarding the dog: "Sometimes when the dog would show up you would hear like moms scream. We had a joke like it was a horror movie." The lead character's interaction with the dog did not simply represent the breaking of some Islamic religious taboos. Syeed stresses a deeper symbolism of the dog in Adan's life: "People might see the dog initially as something 'white people do and not something we do,' because physical contact with a dog can, in some opinions, leave one ritually unclean. Having a dog then can be a marker of allegiance or a marker of identity, where it moves beyond just considerations around cleanliness. But I wanted the film to push a little further to ask: How do you love something you can't touch?" The film stresses this symbolism in the scene mentioned earlier that precedes Adan throwing away his cell phone: a chained dog in the white suburbs where Adan finds himself stranded.

A majority of the community, though, had never seen *A Stray*. Nevertheless, according to Bihi, most had positive reactions to it. He states, "They're like, 'Yeah, I heard about the movie, but it's not bad.'" Overall, *A Stray* fostered stronger bonds between Syeed and the community and ultimately produced a unique film that respects Syeed's attempt to capture the life of its protagonist in his community by adjusting both its filmmaking practices, aesthetic forms, and film content around the community's rhythms and desires.

The film had additional screenings outside of Minnesota, among them a showing at South by Southwest Festival and one in New York City, and

Syeed invited Isaaq, Mansour, and Abdirahman to accompany him. During one screening in New York, Syeed asked Mike German, a former FBI special agent who works at the Brennan Center for Justice, to discuss CVE with Isaaq at the end of one screening. At another screening, Syeed tried to encourage Mansour to promote her show *How to Have Fun in a Civil War*. She recalls, "We were on a panel at Film North and Musa is like elbowing to say, Ifrah, talk about your show. And I'm really shy at this point." Abdirahman had such a positive experience that as a result, he moved to New York City for a while. He remembers, "They more, like, got the film. Outside of New York audiences they ask you more about Islam than about the movie. Or ask did the dog die? Stuff like that. In New York they're asking you more about the film itself."

Despite all the film had going for it, *A Stray* never received commercial distribution. Much of this can be attributed to the film's neorealist style and content that refused to adhere to well-worn clichés of Muslim American life. Syeed reflected, "It didn't travel super widely partially because it didn't directly engage the issues that people expected it to engage."

This difficulty over distribution returns us to Stuart Hall's notion of Black cultural politics. He writes that "the struggle to come into representation was predicated on a critique of the degree of fetishization, objectification, and negative figuration which are so much a feature of the representation of the black subject."[226] But this leads to the question: if cultural representation doesn't play into any of the fetishization and objectification, does it always risk lacking wide distribution? And should such distribution be the ultimate goal?

Mogadishu, Minnesota, for example, can be seen as a modulated Black cultural politics. K'naan asserted that he wanted to "put the audience in the point of view of a Somali family," which represents, to him, "a total shift of point of view" from normally white characters.[227] This shows a political awareness on K'naan's part that his music has at times also exemplified. But what this account overlooks is the way the pilot fetishized Black representations through its terrorism subplot and gangster genre, pandering to HBO, which assumes that popularity is at least partially based on these Islamophobic and racist tropes. Syeed reflects on the pervasive way the commercial film industry perpetuates such fetishization: "My Black filmmaker friends who have a Black cast and are not crime films, they just don't play well to the international film festival circuit."

Such aforementioned accounts lead one to question if mass distribution depends on racist and Islamophobic representations since these permeate the entire culture. It in many ways adds nuance to the HBO debacle by juxtaposing two very different cinematic systems: (1) mass distribution by HBO that can only offer small revisions against dominant representations of Blackness within an overall problematic narrative framework and production practices; and (2) independent filmmaking that relies on other traditions like documentary, neorealism, and Third Cinema that distributors will assume audiences will find incomprehensible. Whether this is the case in actuality is another question—depending on how we define the audience. For instance, *A Stray* respected the pacing and concerns of the community by adjusting its filmmaking production and exhibition practices, form, and content to accommodate them. But once it sought wider distribution to the commercial film festival circuit, distributors, who assumed an audience that was mostly white and Islamophobic, saw its singularity as a liability.

Politicized Screenings: *The Feeling of Being Watched* (2018)

Despite the problems of achieving commercial distribution, films like *A Stray* and other low-budget documentaries are getting nontheatrical exhibitions through various Muslim American groups like CAIR, Young Muslim Collective, and others outside of Minneapolis like Muslim Justice League. For example, CAIR Minnesota teamed up with the Justice Coalition, which includes YMC within it, to start the #UnMasking Surveillance Film Series in 2019 where they bring in films about surveillance and host mobilizations around them. Once more, this approach harkens back to the practices of Third Cinema. Fernando Solanas and Octavio Getino suggest in their famous manifesto, "Towards a Third Cinema," that film screenings must be transformed into "the film act."[228] They write, "This means that the result of each projection act will depend on those who organize it, on those who participate in it, and on the time and place."[229] A film could be much more effective if it "took on the task of subordinating its own form, structure, language, and presuppositions to that act and to those actors."[230]

The first screening of the series took place at the University of Minnesota on February 1, 2019, with the film *(T)error* (2015), which never received theatrical distribution but has played on PBS and streamed over Netflix for a brief time. The film concerns a former Black Panther who has become an informant for the FBI and is asked to spy on a white Muslim convert in Detroit. The film chronicles the informant's growing doubts and self-loathing in working for the very institution he once fought against as a Panther and the realization that his target doesn't represent a credible threat.

FIGURE 4.16: The #UnMasking Surveillance Film Series was hosted by CAIR-Minnesota and the Justice Coalition in Minneapolis. It provided a community event for locals to discuss concerns such as CVE, Islamophobia, and policing. (Photo by Chris Robé.)

A panel followed the film with Burhan Israfael Isaaq; a professor at Minneapolis Community and Technical College who spoke sympathetically of two former students arrested and charged with terrorism for providing material support for ISIS; and the two mothers of the young men now serving time. Niko Georgiades, who was filming the event for Unicorn Riot, states: "The shit was like super deep. The moms were crying and talking about their sons' experience" of being set up by an informer when they tried to buy passports in San Diego. A translator was in the audience to ensure the discussion was accessible to Somali-speaking attendants. The discussion elicited a response from a young man in the audience who had recently flown back from Saudi Arabia and been approached by the FBI to become an informant.[231] Such tactics by the FBI have been widely covered by *The Intercept*.[232]

I attended a June 13, 2019, screening and discussion of *The Feeling of Being Watched* (2018), a compelling documentary where Algerian American journalist Assia Assia Boundaoui, who attended the screening, investigates the FBI's surveillance of friends and family members in her Chicago neighborhood. The film becomes an interrogation not only of the FBI's practices, but also the psychic impact such surveillance has on the community and on Boundaoui herself.

The screening was held in the Norman and Evangeline Hagfors Center for Science, Business, and Religion, a modern building of glass and steel located on the Augsburg University campus. According to Dahir, the prior screening of *(T)error* was not fully satisfactory since expensive parking on the University of Minnesota's campus discouraged some people from attending.[233] Augsburg University sits in the heart of Cedar-Riverside and is about a ten-minute walk from a nearby light rail.

Almost everyone I had interviewed over the past year and a half attended either as a participant of the event or an audience member. Filsan Ibrahim conducted interviews in front of the CAIR backdrop that I had once seen in its conference room as she asked what brought attendees to the event. Ayaan Dahir scrambled around, involved in multiple activities that included speaking before the event, arranging transportation for Boundaoui from the airport, and handling whatever else arose. Niko Georgiades filmed the event for Unicorn Riot. A young woman who was a part of the Muslim Student Association at University of Minnesota, who I had interviewed, and many others who I had spoken with greeted me and caught up throughout the night. Isaaq sat in the audience. The hall eventually filled up with around 150 people with a good mix between Muslim Americans of color, some white converts, and other progressive-oriented white people.

A short, young Black woman from YMC wearing a hijab greeted the audience. She encouraged viewers to think about "what and how surveillance looks like. What people are talking about it?" She then introduced Ayaan Dahir who provided a bit of a longer introduction than normal since she was partially killing time since Boundaoui's plane was delayed and Dahir wanted her to arrive at the screening before the film ended in time for Q&A. Dahir thanked a series of groups and promoted the Muslim Organizer Action Network that CAIR organized. She also mentioned the Muslim Youth Leader Program that would be convening over the summer and encouraged members of the audience to become involved. She ended with mentioning that after the screening there would be breakout discussions among the audience to address some of the issues the film raised followed by a Q&A with the filmmaker.

Much of the audience stuck around afterward to engage in the breakout sessions, which took about fifteen minutes. People congregated around one of the multiple questions posted on the walls around the hall on large

Post-it easel paper. Questions ranged from: "What ways do you think that fear and paranoia that results from surveillance impacts the mental health of Muslim people?" to "What are your takeaways from the film?" Some of the responses were: "Power is threatened when communities support one another" and "I'm being watched." Another question asked: "In what ways could you relate to this film?" Responses were: "Incarcerated family members" and "generation gap (youth takes charge)." Eventually these responses were discussed with everyone. One young Black woman in a hijab had a moment of insight as she troublingly revealed: "I just realized: being Muslim is criminalized."

As Q&A ensued, Boundaoui stood in front, an energetic figure who commanded attention with her passion and eloquence as she spoke about the film, her experiences of being surveilled, and the research and filming processes. Dahir facilitated the discussion and stacked questioners to speak while she intermittently interwove issues of CVE and other local concerns into the discussion. One young Black woman comments: "It's amazing you're here, Assia. Your film relates a feeling for movements." Another Black woman asks, after commenting on how strong Boundaoui's mother was in the film in supporting her work: "As a parent, how can we support young people in this work?"

Boundaoui fielded questions and spoke about the gendered way in which people responded to her making of the film. Men, she relayed, kept asking, "Why are you focusing so negative?" She continues, "The women were the first to talk to me.... Big up to women who are organizers in the community. That support was everything." This is an important point worth stressing: the prevalence of Muslim women in community organizing. Contrary to stereotypes about Muslim women being servile or oppressed by Islam, time and time again Muslim women were at the forefront of the struggles I witnessed both in Minneapolis and across the United States. This is not to say that there are not important male organizers, but in terms of infrastructure and mobilizing on the ground, women predominantly organized events and actions. This was represented by Linda Sarsour pressing for the creation of MPower Change, Shannon Al-Wakeel of the Muslim Justice League organizing a biweekly national conference call, Ayaan Dahir setting up the UnMasking Surveillance Film Series, Filsan Ibrahim conducting interviews, Kadra Abdi and Ramla Bile providing research support for the local groups, and the scores of other Muslim women I spoke with who established their own organizations across the United States.

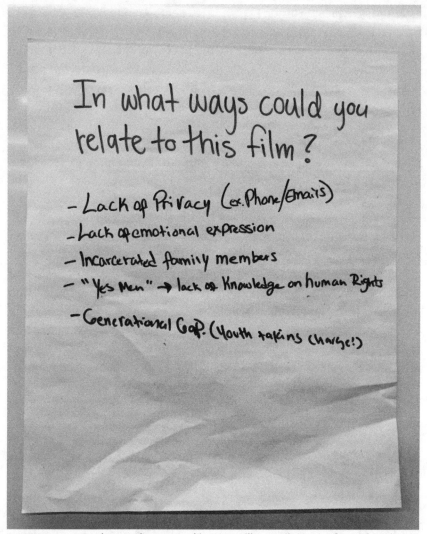

FIGURE 4.17: Attendees at the #Unmasking Surveillance Film Series formed into groups where they wrote notes during a break-out session for the film *The Feeling of Being Watched* (2018). (Photo by Chris Robé.)

Boundaoui mentions the importance of a Chicago screening of the film in October 2018. She acknowledges that "this is triggering to watch" for many who have suffered under such surveillance. So she had arranged ten different Muslim healers to facilitate the conversation after the screening. She comments, "We rarely talk about trauma and healing." She wants to continue the presence of healers at future screenings that are closed, for Muslims only—one she planned to schedule in Minneapolis in October 2019.

After the Q&A, a large group of people clustered around Boundaoui to ask further questions and thank her.

At the end of the event, audience members were given a questionnaire that asks questions like: "Please indicate your level of satisfaction in the following aspects of the event: a) Venue; b) Date/Time; c) Speakers; d) Film; e) Multi-lingual accessibility." The response option is a five-point Likert scale. Another question asks: "Did you gain a better sense of understanding of the following subjects? A) Islamophobia; b) Surveillance; c) Countering Violent Extremism?" There is also a comment section for attendees to fill in their own thoughts.

After the chairs had been stacked and the equipment broken down a small dinner was held afterward in a back room. Somali takeout of chicken, rice, bananas, and salad along with bottles of orange soda and coke sat on two long tables at the back of the room. Twelve women and three men attended the dinner with Dahir, Isaaq, Ibrahim, members of YMC, and other organizations. Near the dinner's end Boundaoui mentioned that she wants different cities on board conducting Freedom of Information (FOIA) requests from the FBI about surveillance of themselves and their community. She said she plans on hosting FOIA workshops the day before screenings. She then asked who locally would like to get involved in organizing FOIA requests, which could take anywhere between one and two years to process. The request was generally positively received, though Isaaq mentioned that during her talk Boundaoui reported that 70 percent of the materials she received were ultimately redacted. She said that even redacted, the 30 percent remaining was useful in telling who and what organizations they were tracking. She also mentioned that it shows law enforcement that the community is active and engaged.

The 30 percent of material remaining after redaction may be useful, but I took Isaaq's question to suggest that the immense amount of labor to conduct FOIA requests may not be worth the time and resources when many other pressing needs and issues need to be attended to. Whether making FOIA requests is a good use of time for organizers who are already engaged in long-term struggles merits consideration and discussion, because Boundaoui's suggestion may come from her work as a journalist rather than her knowledge of what is most fruitful for community organizers. Although the desire to do FOIA requests makes sense for particular purposes and when the resources to do so are available, it seems problematic to do them for their own sake. Still, thinking about her earlier statement that men were the ones who tried to dissuade her from making her film led me to wonder if my own and Isaaq's doubts stemmed from a similarly problematic gendered place.[234]

Dahir concluded the dinner by reminding everyone about the Justice Coalition's conference call happening the following week. The dinner had a lot of energy from these young Muslim organizers who spoke excitedly about the work that they are doing. Their intelligence and courage cannot help but be inspiring. Their generosity was also fully on display; they invited me, a white, male, middle-class outsider, one of endless other outsiders who have descended upon, infiltrated, questioned, surveilled, and undermined the community, into their discussions and to their dinner gatherings. It speaks to their continuing desire to connect to people outside their community.

Conclusion (Sort Of)

This chapter emphasizes the multifaceted ways that grassroots organizing intersects with multiple forms of media making. Muslim American youth used a variety of venues and mediums to organize their community for self-determination and against Islamophobic representations and practices. They held public forums on CVE across the United States that Unicorn Riot livestreamed and were then archived on the web. They created alternative forms of media production practices that gave rise to films and videos like *A Stray* and *Muslim Youth Voices* that offered nuanced representations of Muslim American life that are largely absent from commercial screens. They incorporated Q&A and breakout sessions into film screenings thereby transforming them into film acts where community engagement could take root and future activists be inspired. What might appear as a disorganized and indifferently successful campaign over social media nonetheless revealed a very well-organized localized campaign against CVE and HBO, which organizers saw as both perpetuating Islamophobic narratives and stereotypes about Black Muslims.

Here, we see a complex Black cultural politics at work where countering negative stereotypes in one instance of *Mogadishu, Minnesota* does not foreclose more complex representations of Muslim American life as we have seen in *A Stray*. Muslim American youth activists employ different techniques in different situations, a point that can often get lost in the abstract theorizing of media activism from distant academic worlds. It is nothing less than the struggle over popular culture, which, according to Stuart Hall, "is the ground on which the transformations are worked."[235]

What Muslim American media activism stresses are the enormous stakes of battles over Islamophobic narratives perpetuated by popular culture and adopted within government policies, the allocation of resources, and the ways in which outside communities interact with Muslim American communities. Ultimately, media activism strives for empowerment, according to Ayaan Dahir: "This is about a community who is fed up with being mischaracterized and targeted by those who claim to have good intentions. This is about kids who are afraid to go back to school because they have been bullied for being Muslim and Black. This is about *hooyoyin* [mothers] who live in fear when their children leave for school. This is about *dugsi* [religion] teachers who are afraid to do their calling. This is about young girls who are afraid to wear hijab. This is about young boys who are afraid to practice their religion. This is about a community who is not afraid to speak up even when they have every reason to be afraid."[236]

Coda

As I was completing research for this book, a global pandemic ignited, abruptly altering our day-to-day interactions to pull the online world sharply into focus. Much schooling transferred to online platforms, negatively impacting the most socioeconomically disadvantaged students.[1] A select group of privileged workers were able to work remotely with some inconvenience but nonetheless mostly evading daily interaction with the pandemic while on the job.

Low-wage workers, on the other hand, suffered most brutally from the pandemic. Massive job losses devastated the retail and food service/hospitality industries.[2] Those lucky few who managed to keep their jobs nonetheless occupied the frontlines of confronting COVID-19 daily through their face-to-face interactions with customers and coworkers. Unsurprisingly, some of the worst outbreaks occurred in factory farms where unsanitary and cramped working conditions served as an ideal incubator for the virus to spread among this largely undocumented workforce. During the first year of the pandemic, 59,000 meatpacking workers contracted COVID-19 with at least 269 dying from it.[3] Despite this, Trump invoked the Defense Production Act to force such facilities to stay open in order to prevent a shortage of meat production, prioritizing customers' appetites above the lives of factory farm workers.[4]

Even for the most technologically reluctant of people, the online world positioned itself front and center as many bunkered down in their homes. This forced online engagement led to a windfall of profits for the tech sector beyond its CEOs' wildest dreams. Amazon's profits swelled to over 220 percent as the pandemic forced people to shop online.[5] Facebook's profits rose 101 percent during the pandemic to an overall profit of $10.4 billion.[6] Similar astronomical figures define the revenue gained by other popular online platforms like TikTok and Twitter. As our lives ground to a halt, "social" media entangled itself more thoroughly into our daily routines. Although "social" media's impact upon our mental health and sense of self is still open to debate, many agree that it functions as "a technology of addiction," jacking into our consciousness to hold our attention hostage through algorithmic anticipation that ceaselessly pushes content and suggested "friends" for another hit of dopamine.[7] As Shoshana Zuboff notes, we are the raw material that social media and surveillance capitalism as a whole mines for data and labor, adapting us more to the system than the other way around.[8]

The pandemic extended surveillance further into our lives. At various colleges and workplaces, students and employees were deployed with wearable technology that could track their movements for contact tracing of COVID-19.[9] Many police departments, already experimenting with facial recognition technology, have been ordering fleets of drones to track communities by unmooring surveillance from officers' bodies into the limitless horizon.[10] This is all a part of what Naomi Klein has referred to as the "Screen New Deal," a pandemic shock doctrine that promotes the "seamless integration of government with a handful of Silicon Valley giants—with public schools, hospitals, doctor offices, police, and military all outsourcing (at a high cost) many of their core functions to private tech companies."[11]

At the same time, many community organizers and activists shifted their activities online, which have seen a significant rise in interest. Groups like Berkeley Copwatch and Justice Committee saw a spike in Know Your Rights trainings for potential copwatchers.[12] DxE, mentioned in chapter 1, held multiple online trainings. I attended one on April 24, 2021, that had around twenty-one participants who were mostly women and mostly white. Almira Tanner and Matthew McKeefry led the session. They weaved connections between DxE and other social movements while trying their best to relay their enthusiasm over the anodyne silicon channels of Zoom. During a breakout session, I met two other women both in their twenties. One hailed from Seattle and was trying to resurrect a DxE chapter that had burned out in 2018. The other woman wanted to start a new chapter in North Carolina despite not having much organizing experience. In general, the overall vibe of the training held a nervous but promising energy of mostly newly activated people in animal rights.

How such online activism translates offline remains to be seen. On one level, it has activated more people than ever in social movements. The Black Lives Matter protests that erupted from the murders of George Floyd and Breonna Taylor might be the largest social movement in US history with half a million people participating in nearly 550 locations.[13] Yet a year later, the results are mixed regarding the protests' long-term impact. According to one sociological study, support for #BLM remains high among Black communities. Within Hispanic communities, support remains slightly higher than prior to the protests. Most interesting, however, is that among whites, support for #BLM remains demonstrably lower than before the protests.[14] Although this data is cursory and many unique historical factors play into such mixed reactions such as Trump's whipping up of racial animosity to mobilize his base for the 2020 presidential elections, it raises important questions regarding the lasting impact such flashpoint online protests that migrate to the streets might overall engender. But the pandemic, nonetheless, has forced many organizers and activists to reckon with the importance of the digital terrain in order to keep movement building and members active.

Yet the pandemic has also further plagued activists mired in the criminal justice system into an extended and indefinite purgatory. Many members of DxE, for example, are facing numerous criminal charges for their open rescues or other confrontational actions. As of 2020, Wayne Hsiung faced seventeen felony charges alone. Almira Tanner had seven felony charges weighing on her when I spoke with her in July 2020. Cassie King similarly had eight felony charges at the time of our interview. Their court dates kept getting pushed back and provided a further distraction from focusing their energy against factory farming and mobilizing both online and on the ground. King admitted, "It's actually a huge hindrance to doing more things when you have so many looming felony charges. So we would really like to be able to get to our court date…and increase public awareness about what's happening in these facilities."[15] As discussed in chapter 2 in regards to the RNC 8, the carceral system attempts to crush movements by expending organizers' and activists' energy upon legal minutiae regarding their cases and sows division by pitting movement solidarity against the activists' interest in staying out of prison. The pandemic further extended the onerous criminal justice processes that grind down activists awaiting trial.

In 2022, Hsiung and Paul Darwin Picklesimer were acquitted of all charges for rescuing two sick piglets from Circle Four Farms in 2017.[16] More recently, Alexandra Paul, a former *Baywatch* actress, and Alicia Santurio were found not guilty of theft for rescuing two chickens from a Foster Farms truck in 2021.[17] Both trials received modest media coverage. But many charges still loom over many other DxE activists.

Although one should be encouraged by juries finding these activists innocent, it remains unclear if such trials ultimately push animal rights into the public consciousness in any substantive direction. Furthermore, using trials to expose animal cruelty on factory farms seems mired in a carceral logic that plagues much of animal rights activism. Although DxE does not advocate for the prosecution of low-wage factory farm workers, it nonetheless assumes that the courtroom can be a useful staging ground to amplify their message. This remains a highly debatable strategy both in terms of the relatively minimal coverage it receives and in that it channels limited resources towards court defenses that could otherwise be used in exploring new strategies and tactics that might connect with communities outside of those strictly focused upon animal rights as mentioned at the end of chapter 1.

Perhaps most disturbingly, the pandemic saw the rise of far right activism online, which had already taken root in 2014 during Gamergate as various women were harassed by online trolls for addressing sexism both within the workspaces of the gaming industry and the representations of the games themselves.[18] YouTube algorithms churned out an ever-increasing vitriolic array of racist, misogynistic, transphobic, and other reactionary videos to alienated users who expressed the slightest interest in such content.[19] When Trump was banned from Twitter and Facebook and subsequently lost the 2020 election, hordes of angry MAGA supporters fled to obscure social media platforms like Trovo, Parler, and Epik and infiltrated gaming platforms like Twitch to fuel #StopTheSteal to promote the deluded belief that the election was stolen from Trump. This all would have seemed a ridiculous sideshow except it reached a crescendo on January 6, 2021, with a horde of MAGA supporters invading the Capitol to halt the electoral college vote, beat police, and punish legislators who they viewed as the enemy.[20] Elon Musk's purchase of Twitter threatens to optimize the weaponization of the platform again for far right reactionaries.

This paranoia, racism, homophobia, transphobia, sexism, and other reactionary tendencies of the far right online have helped power in-person reactionary political campaigns recently. In my home state of Florida, Donald Trump and Ron DeSantis slug it out between each other over who can stoke the most paranoia to whip up their base of voters to turn out for them during the 2024 primary season.[21] They both leverage "Stop Woke" campaigns that seek to censor Black history, eliminate gender and LGBTQ+ studies, and ban books, essentially shrink history into a retrograde viewpoint that eliminates all other perspectives and communities that don't align with that of powerful, rich, and straight, white men. They weave their campaigns and policies around the utmost sentimental narratives that Joan Didion critiqued, as mentioned in the introduction to this book. The racialized, gendered, and sexualized Other looms large in their narratives in order to ignite fears and resentment, mobilize voters, and consolidate their power in authoritarian directions.

While Trump stoked the discontent of far right groups and others who got caught in the eddies of conspiracy theories and blinding rage throughout his presidency, he shifted attention to "antifa," various antifascist groups often associated with anarchist communities, as the allegedly true threat to democracy despite the Department of Homeland Security and other federal law enforcement organizations rejecting such views.[22] Yet, as this book shows, the specter of "antifa" and anarchism is not unique to Trump, but instead a tried-and-true tactic used by law enforcement, state politicians, and other reactionaries to justify state repression against groups they consider a threat and to stifle dissent. Although Trump used such rhetoric more bluntly, it falls in line with a long history of conjuring the Other to justify increased surveillance and repression against any movement that remotely threatens the functioning of the state.

The Biden administration has updated the national strategy for countering domestic terrorism in a June 2021 document by focusing more on the far right. The document suggests that "racially or ethnically motivated violent extremists and networks" often target "persons of color, immigrants, Jews, Muslims, other religious minorities, women and girls, LGBTQ+."[23] Yet the document suggests that white supremacy is the exception rather than the rule in how the United States operates. As Andrea Miller and Lisa Bhungalia argue, the document operationalizes whiteness by deploying it to differentiate between good and bad whiteness. But it fails to interrogate the history of genocide, enslavement, and other white supremacist actions and laws that constitute the very fabric of the United States.[24]

Yet all of the federal domestic terrorism practices (critiqued within chapter 4) deployed on Muslim American communities still remain intact, though deployed on a wider range of targets. Government will continue to surveil social media for potential suspects. It will partner with local groups that can legitimize law enforcement's presence and cast certain groups as suspect communities. It equally targets "anarchist violent extremists." Overall, it rationalizes greater funding for deeply fraught practices that criminalize dissent, stifle freedom of speech, and disproportionately impact working-class communities of color. Although the federal government might currently have its sights on the far right, if history reveals anything, the left and communities of color will eventually bear the brunt of the impact regarding such policies.

Much remains to be seen regarding how community organizing and digital media activism might change as a result of the pandemic. At the time of writing this in March 2023, a battle rages in the forests surrounding Atlanta. Forest defenders, the Mvskoke people, and other community activists fight to preserve the land from the police creating a tactical training ground on 300 acres of forest and Shadowbox Studios from clear-cutting 170 acres of forest to build the largest movie soundstage in the US. It seems somehow fitting that the police and Hollywood represent the main threats to the forest and local communities. This book repeatedly illustrates the deep connections through which commercial media and state repression feed upon each other. The framing provided by commercial media outlets serves as the justification for increasing state repression against marginalized communities, protesters, and other-than-human animals. Intensifying state repression, likewise, becomes the fodder the fuels the plots and narratives of popular film and television shows and becomes the topic broadcast over the news.

Digital media plays an important role in the struggle over the forests as well. The forest defenders have created their own barebones website that allows for immediate press releases and updates.[25] Unicorn Riot has been covering the protests and inquiring about the killing of one of its activists, Manuel "Tortuguita" Esteban Paez Terán, by the police. A recent autopsy suggests that Terán "was most probably in a seated position, cross-legged when killed."[26] Yet all this digital work is premised upon on-the-ground actions where community building and collective organizing take place. Many of the trends identified within this book will remain key coordinates in understanding both how activists and organizers are employing digital media to build movements for self-determination on the ground and the ways in which law enforcement and corporations continue to exploit the digital terrain to extend their surveillance and data mining of select vulnerable communities. The struggle over the Atlanta forests is only the most recent instance of this struggle between local communities and the state. But it most certainly will not be the last.

Notes

Introduction

1 Joan Didion, *The White Album* (New York: Farrar, Straus and Giroux, 1979), 11.

2 Richard Slotkin, *Gunfighter Nation: The Myth of the Frontier in Twentieth-Century America* (New York: Harper Perennial, 1992), 11.

3 Adam Hochschild, "When America Tried to Deport Its Radicals," *New Yorker*, November 4, 2019, https://www.newyorker.com/magazine/2019/11/11/when-america-tried-to-deport-its-radicals.

4 *BU Today* staff, "How 9/11 Changed the World," *BU Today*, September 8, 2021, https://www.bu.edu/articles/2021/how-9-11-changed-the-world.

5 Kristian Williams, *Our Enemies in Blue: Police and Power in America* (Oakland, CA: AK Press, 2015), 56.

6 Mark Neocleous, *A Critical Theory of Police Power* (New York: Verso, 2021), 4.

7 Michel Foucault, *The Punitive Society, Lectures at the College de France, 1972–1973*, trans. Graham Burchell (Picador: New York, 2015), 104.

8 Foucault, *Punitive Society*, 260.

9 Neocleous, *Police Power*, 15.

10 Ax excellent overview of the global resistances of the 1960s is George Katsiaficas, *The Global Imagination of 1968: Revolution and Counterrevolution* (Oakland, CA: PM Press, 2018).

11 Jordan T. Camp, *Incarcerating the Crisis: Freedom Struggles and the Rise of the Neoliberal State* (Berkeley: University of California Press, 2016), 15.

12 Elizabeth Hinton, *From the War on Poverty to the War on Crime: The Making of Mass Incarceration in America* (Cambridge, MA: Harvard University Press, 2016), 61.

13 For two excellent sources, see Loïc Wacquant, *Punishing the Poor: The Neoliberal Government of Social Insecurity* (Durham, NC: Duke University Press, 2009); and Brendan McQuade, *Pacifying the Homeland: Intelligence Fusion and Mass Supervision* (Berkeley: University of California Press, 2019).

14 Jake Horton, "Does Trump Have the Right to Send in Federal Forces?" *BBC News*, September 2, 2020, https://www.bbc.com/news/world-us-canada-52893540.

15 Neocleous, *Police Power*, 35.

16   For a good overview of these movements and the state repression against them, see Will Potter, *Green Is the New Red: An Insider's Account of a Social Movement Under Siege* (San Francisco: City Lights Books, 2011).

17   Neocleous, *Police Power*, 4; Simone Browne, *Dark Matters: On The Surveillance of Blackness* (Durham, NC: Duke University Press, 2015).

18   Williams, *Enemies in Blue*, 75.

19   Elizabeth Hinton, *America on Fire: The Untold History of Police Violence and Black Rebellion Since the 1960s* (New York: Liveright, 2021), 16.

20   John Fiske, "Surveilling the City: Whiteness, the Black Man and Democratic Totalitarianism," *Theory, Culture & Society* 15, no. 2 (1998): 84–86.

21   Browne, *Dark Matters*, 79.

22   Fiske, "Surveilling," 69.

23   Nicole R. Fleetwood, *On Racial Icons: Blackness and the Public Imagination* (New Brunswick, NJ: Rutgers University Press, 2015): 30–31.

24   Cedric J. Robinson, *Cedric J. Robinson: On Racial Capitalism, Black Internationalism, and Cultures of Resistance*, ed. H.L.T. Quan (London: Pluto Press, 2019), 79.

25   Stuart Hall, Charles Critcher, Tony Jefferson, John Clarke, and Brian Roberts, *Policing the Crisis: Mugging, the State, and Law and Order* (London: Macmillan, 1978), 38–42.

26   Marjorie Spiegel, *The Dreaded Comparison: Human and Animal Slavery* (New York: Mirror Books, 1996), 28.

27   Claire Jean Kim, "Abolition," in *Critical Terms for Animal Studies*, ed. Lori Gruen (Chicago: University of Chicago Press, 2018), 29.

28   Aph Ko and Syl Ko, *Aphro-ism: Essays on Pop Culture and Black Veganism from Two Sisters* (New York: Lantern Books, 2017), 72.

29   Ko and Ko, *Aphro-ism*, 121.

30   Michel Foucault, *Discipline and Punish: The Birth of the Prison*, trans. Alan Sheridan (New York: Vintage Books, 1977), 187.

31   See Jean-Gabriel Ganascia, "The Generalized Sousveillance Society," *Social Science Information* 49, no. 3 (2010): 480–507.

32   Ring TV can be viewed here: https://tv.ring.com/; Citizen Virtual Patrol can be viewed here: https://cvp.newarkpublicsafety.org/login?redirect=%2F. For more on the latter, see Maya Kosoff, "New Jersey Welcomes a New Surveillance State," *Vanity Fair*, June 11, 2018, https://www.vanityfair.com/news/2018/06/new-jersey-welcomes-a-new-surveillance-state.

33   Michel Foucault, *Security, Territory, Population, Lectures at the College de France, 1977–1978*, trans. Graham Burchell (New York: Picador, 2007), 358.

34   Brendan McQuade, *Pacifying the Homeland: Intelligence Fusion and Mass Supervision* (Berkeley: University of California Press, 2019), 49.

35   Foucault, *Punitive Society*, 100.

36   Foucault, *Discipline and Punish*, 27.

37   Michel Foucault, *The Birth of Biopolitics, Lectures at the College de France, 1978–1979*, trans. Arnold I. Davidson (New York: Palgrave Macmillan, 2008), 144, 241.

38   Franco Berardi, *The Soul at Work: From Alienation to Autonomy* (Los Angeles: Semiotext(e), 2009), 139.

39   Maurizio Lazzarato, *The Making of the Indebted Man* (Los Angeles: Semiotext(e), 2012), 46.

40   Jacques Rancière, *Dissensus: On Politics and Aesthetics*, ed. and trans. Steven Corcoran (New York: Bloomsbury, 2015), 44, 114.

41   Stuart Hall, "Notes on Deconstructing 'the Popular,'" in *Essential Essays, Vol. 1: Foundations of Cultural Studies*, ed. David Morley (Durham, NC: Duke University Press, 2019), 518.

42   Stuart Hall, "Cultural Identity," in *Identity: Community, Culture, Difference*, ed. Jonathan Rutherford (London: Lawrence and Wishart, 1990), 236–37.

43   A vast literature has emerged regarding the important ways in which activist media making is used for collective organizing. Some of the most important are Alexandra Juhasz, *AIDS TV: Identity, Community, and Alternative Video* (Durham, NC: Duke University Press, 1995); Clemencia Rodríguez, *Citizens' Media against Armed Conflict: Disrupting Violence in Colombia* (Minneapolis: University of Minnesota Press, 2011); Todd Wolfson, *Digital Rebellion: The Birth of the Cyber Left* (Chicago: Chicago University Press, 2014); Maple Razsa, *Bastards of Utopia: Living Radical Politics after Socialism* (Bloomington: Indiana University Press, 2015); Chris Robé, *Breaking the Spell: A History of Anarchist Filmmakers, Videotape Guerrillas, and Digital Ninjas* (Oakland, CA: PM Press, 2017); Angela Aguayo, *Documentary Resistance: Social Change and Participatory Media* (Oxford: Oxford University Press, 2019); Peter Snowdon, *The People Are Not an Image: Vernacular Video after the Arab Spring* (New York: Verso, 2020); Chris Robé and Stephen Charbonneau, eds. *Insurgent Media from the Front: A Media Activism Reader* (Bloomington: Indiana University Press, 2020); Ryan Watson, *Radical Documentary and Global Crises: Militant Evidence in the Digital Age* (Bloomington: Indiana University Press, 2021); and Gino Canella, *Activist Media: Documenting Movements and Networked Solidarity* (New Brunswick, NJ: Rutgers University Press, 2022).

44   I place "social" in quotes here since I consider this descriptor nothing more than a marketing ploy used by corporations to data mine our information and surveil us. Although one might argue that such platforms have a social component, depending on how you define "the social," this is a secondary concern to the extraction of information, surveillance, and conditioning of our actions to act in accord with the ways of capital.

45   Paolo Gerbaudo, *Tweets and the Streets: Social Media and Contemporary Activism* (London: Pluto Press, 2012), 14.

46   Peter Snowdon, *The People Are Not an Image: Vernacular Video after the Arab Spring* (New York: Verso, 2020) 2.

47   Thomas Poell and José van Dijck, "Social Media and Activist Communication," in *The Routledge Companion to Alternative and Community Media*, ed. Chris Atton (New York: Routledge, 2015), 532.

48   W. Lance Bennett and Alexandra Segerberg, *The Logic of Connective Action Digital Media and the Personalization of Contentious Politics* (New York: Cambridge University Press, 2013).

49   Jeffrey S. Juris, "Reflections on #Occupy Everywhere: Social Media, Public Space, and Emerging Logics of Aggregation," *American Ethnologist* 19, no. 2 (2012): 259–79.

50   Luke Mogelson, *The Storm Is Here: An American Crucible* (New York: Penguin Press, 2022), 53.

51   Mogelson, *Storm*, 53.

CHAPTER 1 Seeing Past the Walls of Slaughterhouses

1   Amy Meyer, interview by author, June 3, 2020.

2 Charges quickly got dropped, however, once Meyer made her story public. Twenty-four hours after Will Potter, a well-respected animal rights and environmental journalist, posted Meyer's episode to his blog and it was picked up by a series of progressive news outlets, the state prosecutor called her attorney to say that her video evidence, which the state had been sitting on for many weeks, backed up Meyer's claim.

3 Alleen Brown, "The Green Scare," *The Intercept*, March 23, 2019, https://theintercept.com/2019/03/23/ecoterrorism-fbi-animal-rights.

4 Scott David, interview by author, August 21, 2020.

5 Taylor Radig, interview by author, June 25, 2020.

6 Caroline Abels, "Going Undercover in the American Factory Farm," *Grist*, November 26, 2012, https://grist.org/food/going-undercover-in-the-american-factory-farm.

7 Michel Foucault, *Discipline and Punish: The Birth of the Prison*, trans. Alan Sheridan (New York: Vintage Books, 1977), 215.

8 Timothy Pachirat, *Every Twelve Seconds: Industrialized Slaughter and the Politics of Sight* (New Haven: Yale University Press, 2011), 14.

9 Peter Snowdon, *The People Are Not an Image: Vernacular Video after the Arab Spring* (New York: Verso, 2020), 52–53.

10 Steven Best and Anthony J. Nocella II, "Behind the Mask: Uncovering the Animal Liberation Front," in *Terrorists or Freedom Fighters? Reflection on the Liberation of Animals*, ed. Steven Best and Anthony J. Nocella II (New York: Lantern Books, 2004), 19.

11 Best and Nocella, "Behind the Mask," 20.

12 Best and Nocella, "Behind the Mask," 21.

13 Ingrid Newkirk, *Free the Animals: The Amazing True Story of the Animal Liberation Front in North America* (New York: Lantern Books, 2012), 192.

14 Newkirk, *Free*, 198.

15 Jaimie Baron, *Reuse, Misuse, Abuse: The Ethics of Audiovisual Appropriation* (New Brunswick, NJ: Rutgers University Press, 2021), 129.

16 Baron, *Reuse*, 137.

17 Baron, *Reuse*, 134.

18 Newkirk, *Free*, 199.

19 Newkirk, *Free*, 200.

20 Newkirk, *Free*, 205.

21 David Cahn, "Penn Accused of Inflicting Animal Injuries," *Daily Pennsylvanian*, February 11, 2015, https://www.thedp.com/article/2015/02/animal-injuries-in-penn-labs.

22 Newkirk, *Free*, 205.

23 Newkirk, *Free*, 206.

24 Christina Lobrutto, "Penn Cited for Animal Abuse in Research," *Philly Voice*, March 4, 2015, https://www.phillyvoice.com/penn-cited-animal-abuse-research.

25 Cahn, "Penn Accused."

26 Snowdon, *People*, 2.

27 For in-depth coverage of media activism emerging from Eugene, Oregon, during this time period, see Chris Robé, "From the Forest to the Streets: Eco-Video Activism and Indymedia," in *Breaking the Spell: A History of Anarchist Filmmakers, Videotape Guerrillas, and Digital Ninjas* (Oakland, CA: PM Press, 2017).

28   Will Potter, *Green Is the New Red: An Insider's Account of a Social Movement under Siege* (San Francisco: City Lights Books, 2011), 55.

29   Potter, *Green*, 122.

30   Thomas Harding, *The Video Activist Handbook*, 2nd ed. (London: Pluto Press, 2001), 199.

31   Harding, *Video*, 199.

32   Josh Harper, interview by author, May 7, 2020.

33   Joshua Kielas, interview by author, June 9, 2020.

34   This account is derived from my interviews of Harper and Kielas.

35   We will witness similar anarchist humor in chapter 2 regarding the RNC Welcoming Committee's video "We're Getting Ready," suggesting a common through line of humor among many anarchist-inspired groups.

36   Andy Stepanian, interview by author, March 26, 2020.

37   For excellent analysis of the SHAC campaign, see Potter, *Green*.

38   "Forum on Direct Action for Animals," United Poultry Concerns, June 26–27, 2019, https://www.upc-online.org/99daa_review.html.

39   Karen Davis, "Open Rescues: Putting a Face on the Rescuers and on the Rescued," in Best and Nocella, *Terrorists*, 202–12.

40   Davis, "Open Rescues," 207.

41   Lori Gruen, *Entangled Empathy: An Alternative Ethic for Our Relationships with Animals* (New York: Lantern Books, 2015), 64.

42   Elizabeth Cowie, "The Spectacle of Actuality," in *Collecting Visible Evidence*, ed. Jane M. Gaines and Michael Renov (Minneapolis: University of Minnesota Press, 1999), 32.

43   Cowie, "Spectacle," 32.

44   I am specifically referencing Marti Kheel's concept the "heroic ideal," which I will go into in depth later in this chapter. See Marti Kheel, "Direct Action and the Heroic Ideal: An Ecofeminist Critique," in *Igniting a Revolution: Voices in Defense of the Earth*, ed. Steven Best and Anthony J. Nocella II (Oakland, CA: AK Press, 2006), 306–18.

45   Davis, "Open Rescues," 210.

46   Davis, "Open Rescues," 210.

47   Cowie, "Spectacle," 32.

48   Jason Black and Jennifer Black, "The Rhetorical 'Terrorist': Implications of the USA Patriot Act on Animal Liberation," in Best and Nocella, *Terrorists*, 291.

49   Steven Best, "It's War! The Escalating Battle between Animal Activists and the Corporate-State Complex," in Best and Nocella, *Terrorists*, 307–8.

50   "Operation Backfire: Searching for Two Final Fugitives," FBI, updated August 10, 2018, https://www.fbi.gov/contact-us/field-offices/portland/news/stories/operation-backfire.

51   For excellent coverage of this, see Potter, *Green* and Kera Abraham's "Flames of Dissent" series for the *Eugene Weekly*, November 2, 2006: https://www.eugeneweekly.com/2006/11/02/flames-of-dissent.

52   Potter, *Green*, 104.

53   Potter, *Green*, 98.

54   *Animal Rights: Activism vs. Criminality: Hearing before the Committee on the Judiciary, United States Senate,* 108th Cong. 4 (2004).

55   Potter, *Green*, 128.

56   Kim McCoy, "The Animal Enterprise Terrorism Act: Protecting the Profits of Animal Enterprises at the Expense of the First Amendment," in *The Terrorization of Dissent: Corporate Repression, Legal Corruption, and the Animal Enterprise Terrorism Act*, ed. Jason Del Gandio and Anthony J. Nocella II (New York: Lantern Books, 2014), 8–9.

57   Nathan Runkle, with Gene Stone, *Mercy for Animals: One Man's Quest to Inspire Compassion and Improve the Lives of Farm Animals* (New York: Avery, 2017), 85.

58   Bas Sanders, "Global Animal Slaughter Statistics and Charts: 2020 Update," Faunalytics, July, 29, 2020, https://faunalytics.org/global-animal-slaughter-statistics-and-charts-2020-update.

59   Foer, *Eating Animals* (New York: Back Bay Books, 2009), 146.

60   Pachirat, *Every Twelve*, 207.

61   Taylor Radig, interview by author, June, 25, 2020.

62   Pete Paxton with Gene Stone, *Rescue Dogs: Where They Come from, Why They Act the Way They Do, and How to Love Them Well* (New York: TarcherPerigee, 2019), 2. "Pete" is an alias since he is still working in the field.

63   "Astrid," interview by author, September 8, 2020.

64   Scott David, interview by author, August 21, 2020.

65   Bob Guilfoyle, interview by author, September 18, 2020.

66   Chrystal Ferber, interview by author, August, 6, 2020.

67   Deb Olin Unferth, *Barn 8* (Minneapolis: Minnesota: Greywolf Press, 2020), 146.

68   Jill Ettinger, "This Is What It's Like Being an Undercover Animal Rights Investigator," Medium, July 27, 2018, https://medium.com/@jillettinger/this-is-what-its-like-being-an-undercover-animal-rights-investigator-eabc1b2832f5. Punk rock served as a particularly important venue for people to get involved with animal rights. Seven out of the twenty-seven people I interviewed for this chapter mentioned punk rock as playing a central role in their becoming involved with animal rights. Most of the people who had mentioned a punk influence were in their thirties and forties. Only one in their late twenties mentioned punk as an influence.

69   Mary Beth Sweetland, interview by author, October 7, 2020.

70   Sean Thomas, interview by author, August 10, 2020.

71   Paxton with Stone, *Rescue Dogs*, 22.

72   Abels, "Going Undercover."

73   Pete, interview by author, August 28, 2020.

74   Sean Thomas, interview by author, August 10, 2020.

75   Lindsay Patton, "The Human Victims of Factory Farming," One Green Planet, accessed October 31, 2022, https://www.onegreenplanet.org/environment/the-human-victims-of-factory-farming.

76   Scott David, interview by author, August 21, 2020.

77   Chickens are often bred to such large sizes that it is not uncommon for them to be unable to support their own weight and become lame in the process.

78   "Radish," interview by author, August 2020. "Radish" is an alias.

79   Carol J. Adams, *The Sexual Politics of Meat: A Feminist-Vegetarian Critical Theory* (New York: Bloomsbury, 2015), 22.

80   Bill Nichols, *Representing Reality: Issues and Concepts in Documentary* (Bloomington: Indiana University Press, 1991), 154.

81   Lisa Stark, Jessica Hoffman, and Imaeyen Ibanga, "Undercover Video Prompts Nation's Largest Beef Recall," *ABC News*, February 9, 2009, https://abcnews.go.com/GMA/story?id=4305151&page=1.

82   Matthew L. Wald, "Meat Packer Admits Slaughter of Sick Cows," *New York Times*, March 13, 2008, https://www.nytimes.com/2008/03/13/business/13meat.html.

83   Andrew Martin, "Agriculture Dept. Vows to Improve Animal Welfare," *New York Times*, February 29, 2008, https://www.nytimes.com/2008/02/29/business/29food.html.

84   Michael Winter, "Calif. Meat Packer to Pay $317 M over Abuse, Recall," *USA Today*, November 16, 2012, https://www.usatoday.com/story/news/nation/2012/11/16/california-slaughterhouse-fraud-settlement-beef-recall/1710693.

85   Matthew Liebman, interview by author, July 28, 2020.

86   Runkle with Stone, *Mercy*, 229.

87   Mercy for Animals, "Burger King Cruelty – Video Exposes Horrific Abuse at a Burger King Dairy," YouTube video, 3:12, October 10, 2012: https://www.youtube.com/watch?app=desktop&v=lN_YcWOuVqk&has_verified=1.

88   Associated Press, "Idaho Workers Charged with Animal Cruelty at Bettencourt Dairies' Dry Creek Farm," *Daily News*, October 11, 2012, https://www.nydailynews.com/news/national/watch-animal-cruelty-filmed-idaho-dairy-article-1.1180094.

89   Claire Rasmussen, "Pleasure, Pain, and Place: Ag-gag, Crush Videos, and Animal Bodies on Display," in *Critical Animal Geographies: Politics, Intersections, and Hierarchies in a Multispecies World*, ed. Kathryn Gillespie and Rosemary-Claire Collard (London: Routledge, 2017), 58.

90   Justin Marceau, *Beyond Cages: Animal Law and Criminal Punishment* (Cambridge: Cambridge University Press, 2019), 7.

91   Rasmussen, "Pleasure," 59.

92   Cindy Galli, "Idaho Bill Would Jail Animal Activists Caught Using Hidden Cameras," *ABC News*, February 20, 2014, https://abcnews.go.com/Blotter/idaho-bill-jail-animal-activists-caught-hidden-cameras/story?id=22599192.

93   All of this is information is based on my interview with Pete.

94   Nichols, *Representing*, 85.

95   Nichols, *Representing*, 87.

96   Mike Hale, "How These Piggies Went to Market," *New York Times*, March 15, 2009, https://www.nytimes.com/2009/03/16/arts/television/16farm.html.

97   Matthew Liebman, interview by author, July 28, 2020.

98   Jessica Miller, "Federal Judge Strikes Down Utah's Ag-Gag Law as Unconstitutional," *Salt Lake Tribune*, July 8, 2017, https://archive.sltrib.com/article.php?id=5485584&itype=CMSID.

99   Reason TV, "Stossel: No Filming on Farms," YouTube video, 5:33, July 16, 2019, https://www.youtube.com/watch?v=OUf4DCfAeEw.

100   Will Potter, "Charges Dropped against Investigator Who Filmed Animal Cruelty," *Green Is the New Red* (blog), January 11, 2014, http://www.greenisthenewred.com/blog/taylor-radig-charges-dropped/7492.

101   F.R. Furtney, *This Is Hormel* (1964), 30:01, Internet Archive, accessed February 28, 2023, https://archive.org/details/this_is_hormel.

102   Davis, "Open Rescues," 210.

103   Jan Dutkiewicz, "Transparency and the Factory Farm: Agritourism and Counter-Activism at Fair Oak Farms," *Gastronomica: Journal of Critical Food Studies* 18, no. 2 (2018): 20.

104   Runkle with Stone, *Mercy*, 76; Sharon Núñez, interview by author, August 20, 2020.

105　For a Facebook group that critiques DxE as a cult, see https://www.facebook.com/ notes/sf-vegans/whats-wrong-with-direct-action-everywherewhy-dxe-isnt-allowed-in-this-groupdxe-i/1326734314036928. For a chronicle of many of the accusations against the group, see Dismantle DxE, "It's Not Intersectional, It's DxE: An Exposé Written by DxE's Victims," accessed February 28, 2023, https:// dismantledxe.wordpress.com/; and "Is DxE a Cult? You Decide," accessed March 21, 2023, https://isdxeacult.wordpress.com.

106　Carol J. Adams, "Why I Am Boycotting Events if DxE Is Also an Invited Speaker," *Carol J. Adams* (blog), April 21, 2018, https://caroljadams.com/carol-adams-blog/ why-i-am-boycotting-events-if-dxe-is-also-an-invited-speaker.

107　Frances Dinkelspiel, "Wayne Hsiung, Who Has Put His Freedom on the Line to Rescue Animals, Wants to Be Berkeley's Next Mayor," Berkeleyside, October 7, 2020, https://www.berkeleyside.org/2020/10/07/wayne-hsiung-dxe-berkeley-ca-mayor.

108　Wayne Hsiung, "On the Shoulders of Giants," DxE, December 1, 2014, https://www. directactioneverywhere.com/theliberationist/2014–11–24-on-the-shoulders-of-giants.

109　Almira Tanner, interview by author, July 9, 2020.

110　Lewis Bernier, interview by author, July 15, 2020.

111　Justin Wm. Moyer, "Animal Rights Activists Who Removed Two Piglets from Factory Farm Charged after FBI Raids," *Washington Post*, May 25, 2018, https:// www.washingtonpost.com/news/animalia/wp/2018/05/25/animal-rights-activists-who-removed-two-piglets-from-factory-farm-charged-after-fbi-raids/; Andrew Jacobs, "Stealing Lauri," *New York Times*, August 4, 2019, https://www. nytimes.com/2019/08/04/science/stealing-lauri.html; Andy Greenberg, "Meet the Activists Risking Prison to Film VR in Factory Farms," *Wired*, December 5, 2019, https://www.wired.com/story/direct-action-everywhere-virtual-reality-exposing-factory-farms/; and "They Rescued Pigs and Turkeys from Factory Farms—And Now Face Decades in Prison," *The Intercept*, December 23, 2018: https://theintercept. com/2018/12/23/dxe-animal-rights-factory-farms.

112　Leighton Woodhouse, interview by author, June 30, 2020.

113　Judith Butler, *Notes Toward A Performative Theory of Assembly* (Cambridge, MA: Harvard University Press, 2015), 165.

114　Butler, *Notes*, 94.

115　Emily Steel, "At Vice, Cutting-Edge Media and Allegations of Old-School Sexual Harassment," *New York Times*, December 23, 2017, https://www.nytimes. com/2017/12/23/business/media/vice-sexual-harassment.html.

116　Eriq Gardner, "Vice Media Agrees to $1.87 Million Settlement for Paying Female Staffers Less Than Men," *Hollywood Reporter*, March 27, 2019: https://www.hollywoodreporter.com/business/business-news/ vice-media-agrees-187-million-settlement-paying-female-staffers-men-1197427.

117　Adam Leith Gollner, "The Secret History of Gavin McInnes," *Vanity Fair*, June 29, 2021, https://www.vanityfair.com/news/2021/06/the-secret-history-of-gavin-mcinnes.

118　Cassie King, interview by author, July 20, 2020.

119　Vice Video, "Animal Rights Extremists: Terrorism or Protest?," 16:59, accessed January 17, 2012, https://video.vice.com/en_us/video/animal-rights-extremists-terrorism-vs-protests-dxe/5b107772f1cdb33f9a35cea6.

120   Direct Action Everywhere, "DxE's Wayne Hsiung Responds to 'VICE—Animal Rights Extremists: Trespassing to Rescue Chickens,'" November 3, 2019, YouTube video, 44:14, https://www.youtube.com/watch?v=_QmpdXaZyqw.

121   King, interview.

122   Direct Action Everywhere, "The Next Pandemic Could Come From a US Factory Farm," Facebook Watch video, 7:48, December 11, 2020, https://m.facebook.com/directactioneverywhere/videos/456026289128757/?refsrc=deprecated&_rdr.

123   Wayne Hsiung, "With Trial Approaching, I'm Stepping Down from All Leadership Positions at DxE. Here's Why That's a Good Thing," DxE, August 7, 2019, https://www.directactioneverywhere.com/theliberationist/2019–8–6-with-trial-approaching-im-stepping-down-from-all-leadership-positions-at-dxe-heres-why-thats-a-good-thing.

124   Tanner, interview.

125   King, interview.

126   DxE, "DxE's Roadmap to an Animal Bill of Rights," Google Doc, published September 2016, updated February 2021, https://docs.google.com/document/d/1YN7KpuShiZItqVuQtWv6ykrjrNv6rAnmjVOcsofRj0I/edit.

127   An excellent book that charts the hyperbole and overstatement attached to digital technologies in general is Vincent Mosco's *The Digital Sublime: Myth, Power, and Cyberspace* (Cambridge, MA: MIT Press, 2004).

128   Adi Robertson and Michael Zelenko, comps., "Voices from the Past: An Oral History of a Technology Whose Time Has Come Again," accessed February 28, 2023, https://www.theverge.com/a/virtual-reality/oral_history.

129   Jose Valle, interview by author, September 2, 2020; Kenneth Montville, interview by author, April 28, 2020; an excellent overview of VR in animal rights can be found in Andy Greenberg, "Meet the Activists Risking Prison to Film VR in Factory Farms," *Wired,* December 5, 2019, https://www.wired.com/story/direct-action-everywhere-virtual-reality-exposing-factory-farms.

130   Sam Heft-Luthy, "The Myth of the 'Empathy Machine,'" The Outline, August 28, 2019, https://theoutline.com/post/7885/virtual-reality-empathy-machine.

131   Kate Nash, "Virtual Reality Witness: Exploring the Ethics of Mediated Presence," *Studies in Documentary Film* 12, no. 2 (2018): 124.

132   Nash, "Virtual," 124–25.

133   Sara Ahmed, *The Cultural Politics of Emotion* (Edinburgh: Edinburgh University Press, 2014), 22.

134   Wayne Hsiung, "This Technology Is About to Smash Through Every Factory Farm's Closed Doors," *HuffPost*, January 19, 2017, https://www.huffpost.com/entry/this-technology-is-about-to-smash-through-every-factory_b_588110a3e4b0111ea60b940b.

135   Nichols, *Representing*, 152.

136   Dale Hudson, and Patricia R. Zimmermann, *Thinking through Digital Media: Transnational Environments and Locative Places* (New York: Palgrave Macmillan, 2015), 3.

137   Hsiung, "This Technology."

138   See Mila Bujić, Mikko Salminen, Joseph Macey, and Juho Hmari, "'Empathy Machine': How Virtual Reality Affects Human Rights Attitudes," *Internet Research* 30, no. 5 (2020): 1407–25; and Nicola S. Schutte and Emma J. Stilinović, "Facilitating Empathy through Virtual Reality," *Motivation and Emotion* 41, no. 6 (2017): 708–12.

139   See Harry Farmer, "A Broken Empathy Machine? Can Virtual Reality Increase Pro-Social Behaviour and Reduce Prejudice?," *Immerse* September 30, 2019, https://immerse.news/a-broken-empathy-machine-can-virtual-reality-increase-pro-social-behaviour-and-reduce-prejudice-cbcefb30525b.

140   Animal Equality press release, "Study Shows Video Outreach Improves Attitudes and Behavior," Animal Equality, November 19, 2017, https://faunalytics.org/wp-content/uploads/2017/12/Animal-Equality-Report-Final.pdf.

141   Donghee Shin, "Empathy and Embodied Experience in Virtual Environment: To What Extent Can Virtual Reality Stimulate Empathy and Embodied Experience?" *Computers in Human Behavior* 78 (January 2018): 70.

142   Stuart Hall most famously makes such an argument in "Encoding and Decoding in the Television Discourse," in *Essential Essays, Vol. 1: Foundations of Cultural Studies*, ed. David Morley (Durham, NC: Duke University Press, 2019), 257–76.

143   Sharon Núñez, interview by author, August 20, 2020.

144   Linda Williams, "Film Bodies: Gender, Genre, and Excess," *Film Quarterly* 44, no. 4 (1991): 4.

145   Williams, "Film Bodies," 4.

146   Kate Chopin, *The Awakening* (New York: Dover, 1993).

147   The classic maternal melodrama is *Stella Dallas*, directed by King Vidor (1937), a tear-jerker if there ever was one.

148   Ian Kullgren, "Female Employees Allege Culture of Sexual Harassment at Humane Society," *Politico Magazine*, January 30, 2018, https://www.politico.com/magazine/story/2018/01/30/humane-society-sexual-harassment-allegations-investigation-216553/; and Marc Gunther, "The Animal Welfare Movement's #MeToo Problem," *Nonprofit Chronicles*, January 26, 2018: https://nonprofitchronicles.com/2018/01/26/the-animal-welfare-movements-metoo-problem.

149   Lisa Kemmerer, "Evidence of Sexism and Male Privilege in the Animal Liberation/Rights Movement," *Between the Species* 21, no. 1 (Spring 2018): 243–86.

150   Paul Gorski, Stacy Lopresti-Goodman, and Dallas Rising, "'Nobody's Paying Me to Cry': The Causes of Activist Burnout in the United States Animal Rights Activists," *Social Movement Studies* 18, no. 3 (2019): 373.

151   Marceau, *Beyond Cages*, 2.

152   John Seber, interview by author, September 2, 2020.

153   pattrice jones, interview by author, February 23, 2021.

154   Carol J. Adams, interview by author, September 30, 2020.

155   Carol J. Adams, interview by author, November 7, 2020.

156   "David Lynch's Banned Bovine," *ABC News*, February 24, 2006: https://abcnews.go.com/Entertainment/WolfFiles/story?id=95752&page=1.

157   Lauren Ornelas, interview by author, March 3, 2021.

158   pattrice jones, interview by author, February 23, 2021.

159   Carol J. Adams, interview, November 7, 2020.

160   A. Breeze Harper, "Social Justice Beliefs and Addition to Uncompassionate Consumption," in *Sistah Vegan: Black Female Vegans Speak on Food, Identity, Health and Society*, ed. A. Breeze Harper (Brooklyn, NY: Lantern Books, 2010), 20.

161   Harper, "Social," 35.

162   Direct Action Everywhere–SF Bay Area, "How to Change the World in One Generation—DxE Intro Workshop," Facebook online event, April 24, 2021.

163   "Plant Based Meals in Prison K–12 and Hospitals," NAACP, 2019, https://naacp.org.

164   Harper, "Social," 29.

165   Harper, "Social," 29.

166   Centers for Disease Control and Prevention, "Leading Causes of Death – Males – Non-Hispanic Black – United States, 2017," last reviewed November 20, 2019, https://www.cdc.gov/healthequity/lcod/men/2017/nonhispanic-black/index.htm.

167   Sunaura Taylor, *Beasts of Burden: Animal and Disability Liberation* (New York: The New Press, 2017), 59.

168   Taylor, *Beasts*, 60.

169   Taylor, *Beasts*, 61.

170   Taylor, *Beasts*, 63.

CHAPTER 2 **Here Come the Anarchists**

1   See Alexei Wood, "Livestream Capture of Anarchist, Anti-Fascist, and Anti-Capitalism March in DC on January 20th, 2017 before Trump's Inauguration," Vimeo video, 42:18, accessed February 28, 2023, https://vimeo.com/218671216.

2   Jaclyn Peiser, "Journalist Charged with Rioting at Inauguration Day Protest Goes Free," *New York Times*, December 21, 2017, https://www.nytimes.com/2017/12/21/business/media/journalist-inauguration-day-protest-not-guilty-rioting.html.

3   "Stoked! Journalist Alexei Wood & First J20 Defendants Found 'Not Guilty' as 188 Still Face Trial," *Democracy Now!*, December 22, 2017, https://www.democracynow.org/2017/12/22/stoked_journalist_alexei_wood_first_j20 .

4   Chip Gibbons, "The Prosecution of Inauguration-Day Protesters Is a Threat to Dissent," *The Nation*, October 20, 2017, https://www.thenation.com/article/archive/the-prosecution-of-inauguration-day-protesters-is-a-threat-to-dissent.

5   Lesley J. Wood, *Crisis and Control: The Militarization of Protest Policing* (London: Pluto Press, 2014), 14–16; and Donatella Della Porta and Olivier Fillieule, "Policing Social Protest," in *The Blackwell Companion to Social Movements,* ed. David A. Snow, Sarah A. Soule, and Hanspeter Kriesi (Malden, MA: Blackwell Publishing, 2004), 225–26.

6   Michel Foucault, *Security, Territory, Population: Lectures at the College de France, 1977–1978* (New York: Picador, 2007), 117.

7   Foucault, *Security*, 118.

8   Wood, *Crisis*, 127–29; and Kristian Williams, "The Other Side of COIN: Counterinsurgency and Community Policing," *Interface: A Journal for and about Social Movements* 3, no. 1 (2011): 91–92.

9   K. Williams, "Other Side," 91.

10   Petra Bartosiewicz, "Beyond the Broken Window," *Harper's Magazine* (May 2015), 56. With this said, there has never been a hard line that divided the military from the police. The police were always militarized, but the forms of this militarization changed during different historical periods.

11   Christian Parenti, *Lockdown America: Police and Prisons in the Age of Crisis* (New York: Verso, 2000), 113, 127.

12   Wood, *Crisis*, 126.

13   Loïc Wacquant, *Punishing the Poor: The Neoliberal Government Social Insecurity* (Durham, NC: Duke University Press, 2009), 160.

14   Wacquant, *Punishing*, 305.

15   Maurizio Lazzarato, *The Making of the Indebted Man* (Los Angeles: Semiotext(e), 2012), 51.

16   Ben Hayes, "The Surveillance-Industrial Complex," in *Routledge Handbook of Surveillance Studies*, ed. Kirstie Ball, Kevin D. Haggerty, and David Lyon (New York: Routledge, 2012), 168.

17   Will Potter, *Green Is the New Red: An Insider's Account of a Social Movement under Siege* (San Francisco: City Lights Books, 2011), 37.

18   Wood, *Crisis*, 134, 139, 119.

19   John Fiske, "Surveilling the City: Whiteness, the Black Man and Democratic Totalitarianism," *Theory, Culture & Society* 15, no. 2 (1998): 69.

20   Michel Foucault, *Discipline and Punish: The Birth of the Prison*, trans. Alan Sheridan (New York: Vintage Books, 1977), 184.

21   I am employing the idea of the counterpublic sphere as defined by Oskar Negt and Alexander Kluge in *Public Sphere and Experience: Analysis of the Bourgeois and Proletarian Public Sphere* (New York: Verso, 2016), 266.

22   Todd Wolfson, *Digital Rebellion: The Birth of the Cyber Left* (Chicago: University of Illinois Press, 2014), 63.

23   Jeff Perlstein, interview by Miguel Bocanegra, Center for Labor Studies, October 15, 2000, http://depts.washington.edu/wtohist/interviews/Perlstein.pdf.

24   Even Henshaw-Plath, interview by author, September 23, 2010.

25   Quoted in Tish Stringer, "Move! Guerrilla Films, Collaborative Modes, and the Tactics of Radical Media-making" (PhD dissertation, Rice University, 2006), 64.

26   Dorothy Kidd, "Indymedia.org: A New Communications Commons," in *Cyberactivism: Online Activism in Theory and Practice*, ed. Martha McCaughey and Michael D. Ayers (New York: Routledge, 2003), 47–69; Graham Meikle, *Future Active: Media Activism and the Internet* (New York: Routledge, 2002); and James F. Hamilton, "Critical Celebrations of Independent Media Centers 20 Years On," *Media, Culture & Society* 42, no. 6 (2020): 1019–23, https://journals.sagepub.com/doi/10.1177/0163443720926048.

27   Pearlstein, interview.

28   Manuel Castells, *The Internet Galaxy: Reflections on the Internet, Business, and Society* (Oxford: Oxford University Press, 2002), 248.

29   Castells, *Internet*, 249.

30   Eric Galatas, interview by author, January 19, 2011.

31   For a detailed account of these tensions, see chapter 4 in Chris Robé, *Breaking the Spell: A History of Anarchist Filmmakers, Videotape Guerrillas, and Digital Ninjas* (Oakland, CA: PM Press, 2017).

32   Wood, *Crisis*, 26.

33   Frances Kennedy, "Genoa Summit: Dozens Injured in Midnight Battle with Police at Anarchists' Hide-Out," *The Independent,* July 23, 2001, 2.

34   Ramor Ryan, "And Balanced with This Life, This Death: Genoa, the G8 and the Battle in the Streets," in *Confronting Capitalism: Dispatches from a Global Movement*, ed. Eddie Yuen, Daniel Burton-Rose, and George Katsiaficas (Brooklyn, NY: Soft Skull Press, 2004), 139.

35   Silvia Federici and George Caffentzis, "Genoa and the Antiglobalization Movement," in Yuen, Burton-Rose, and Katsiaficas, *Confronting*, 143.

36   Kennedy, "Genoa Summit," 2.

37   Tamara Lush, "Miami Warily Awaits Protest," *St. Petersburg Times,* November 20, 2003.

38   Naomi Klein, "America's Enemy Within," *The Guardian*, November 26, 2003. Timoney also has the notoriety of being one of the central architects of escalating police

repression against protesters from his time as deputy inspector of the NYPD, when he oversaw the police riot at Tompkins Square Park in 1988, to his time as police commissioner in Philadelphia, when he accompanied police while they harassed protesters during the 2000 RNC.

39   Francesca Polletta, *Freedom Is an Endless Meeting: Democracy in American Social Movements* (Chicago: University of Chicago Press, 2002); Barbara Epstein, *Political Protest and Cultural Revolution: Nonviolent Direct Action in the 1970s and 1980s* (Berkeley: University of California Pres, 1991); and Andrew Cornell, *Unruly Equality: U.S. Anarchism in the Twentieth Century* (Berkeley: University of California Press, 2016).

40   Fiske, *Surveilling*, 83.

41   There are countless scholarly resources on anti-Black racism and television. A few notable sources are Robin B. Boylorn, "As Seen on TV: An Autoethnographic Reflection on Race and Reality Television," *Critical Studies in Media Communication* 25, no. 4 (2008): 413–33; Mark P. Orbe, "Representations of Race on Reality TV: Watch and Discuss," *Critical Studies in Media Communication* 25, no. 4 (2008): 345–52; Tia Tyree, "African American Stereotypes in Reality Television," *Howard Journal of Communication* 22 (2011): 394–413; and Robert M. Entman, "Modern Racism and the Images of Blacks in Local Television News," *Cultural Studies in Mass Communication* 7 (1990): 332–45.

42   Greg Elmer and Andy Opel, *Preempting Dissent: The Politics of an Inevitable Future* (Winnipeg: Arbeiter Ring, 2008), 30–31. With regard to undercover informants, see Andrea Todd, "The Believers," *Elle* (April 2008): 266–72, 323–25.

43   Foucault, *Discipline*, 272.

44   Klein, "America's."

45   Sasha Costanza-Chock, interview by author, November 14, 2011.

46   These restrictive assembly laws were later deemed unconstitutional in February 2004 during the case of *Lake Worth for Global Justice v. City of Miami*.

47   Foucault, *Security*, 109, 358.

48   Foucault, *Security*, 201.

49   Sarahjane Blum, Jay Johnson, and Ryan Shapiro, "Blum v. Holder," in *The Terrorization of Dissent: Corporate Repression, Legal Corruption, and the Animal Enterprise Terrorism Act*, ed. Jason Del Gandio and Anthony J. Nocella II (New York: Lantern Books, 2014), 300–306.

50   Mara H. Gottfried and Jason Hoppin, "St. Paul Police Detail Spending of $50M Grant for RNC Security," *St. Paul Pioneer Press*, August 6, 2008, http://www.twincities.com/politics/ci_10109006.

51   Anastasia Loukaitou-Sideris and Renia Ehrenfeucht, *Sidewalks: Conflict and Negotiation over Public Space* (Cambridge, MA: MIT Press, 2011), 119–-20.

52   Emily Gurnon, "Last 'RNC 8' Protesters Admit Guilt—But Remain Defiant," *St. Paul Pioneer Press*, October 19, 2010, http://www.twincities.com/news/ci_16382084.

53   Crass Zine Working Group, *Untitled, or What to Do When Everyone Gets Arrested: A CRASS Course in Providing Arrestee Support*, 4, accessed May 12, 2015, https://ia601403.us.archive.org/27/items/UntitledOrWhatToDoWhenEveryoneGets Arrested/untitled_or-print.pdf.

54   RNC Review Commission, *Report of the Republican National Convention Public Safety Planning and Implementation Review Commission*, January 14, 2009, https://www.stpaul.gov.

55   Human Iterations, "We're Getting Ready! RNC Welcoming Committee Trailer," YouTube video, 3:11, accessed March 1, 2023, https://www.youtube.com/watch?v=j6PLwOt0Bls&feature=emb_logo.

56   Gus Ganley, interview by author, April 17, 2016.

57   Brendan McQuade, *Pacifying the Homeland: Intelligence Fusion and Mass Supervision* (Berkeley: University of California Press, 2019), 121.

58   State of Minnesota, County of Ramsey District Court, Application for Search Warrant and Supporting Affidavit, September 2, 2008: 5.

59   Mara H. Gottfried and Elizabeth Mohr, "Houses Raided, 5 Arrested, Critics Decry Crackdown," *St. Paul Pioneer Press,* August 30, 2008, http://www.twincities.com/ci_10346122.

60   David Solnit and Rebecca Solnit, *The Battle of the Story of the Battle of Seattle* (Oakland, CA: AK Press, 2009), 42.

61   Wood, *Crisis*, 159.

62   Crass, *Untitled*, 72.

63   Tad Vezner and Dave Orrick, "3 N.Y. Videographers in Town for RNC Claim Police Harassment in Minneapolis," *St. Paul Pioneer Press,* August 26, 2008, http://www.twincities.com/localnews/ci_10311346?nclick_check=1.

64   Amy Goodman, "Why We Were Falsely Arrested," *Democracy Now!,* September 3, 2008, accessed May 1, 2015, https://www.democracynow.org/2008/9/3/amy_goodmans_new_column_why_we_were_falsely_arrested.

65   Randy Furst, "Fallout from RNC Lawsuits: $175,000 so far in Settlements," *Star Tribune,* June 3, 2011.

66   Chao Xiong, "3 Journalists Settle with Cities in 2008 RNC Arrests," *Star Tribune,* October 4, 2011.

67   Crass, *Untitled*, 7.

68   Crass, *Untitled*, 44–54.

69   Vlad Teichberg, interview by author, November 23, 2010.

70   Michelle Gross, interview by author, April 14, 2016.

71   Dan Feidt, interview by author, December 9, 2010.

72   Patricia Zimmermann, *States of Emergency: Documentaries, Wars, Democracies* (Minneapolis: University of Minnesota Press, 2000), 91.

73   Jane M. Gaines, "Political Mimesis," in *Collecting Visible Evidence*, ed. Jane M. Gaines and Michael Renov (Minneapolis: University of Minnesota Press, 1999), 91.

74   Zimmermann, *States*, 98.

75   Gus Ganley, interview by author, April 17, 2016.

76   Melissa Hill, interview by author, April 8, 2016.

77   Melissa Hill, interview by author, December 3, 2010.

78   Crass, *Untitled*, 51.

79   Gross, interview.

80   Gross, interview. See also Sheila Regan, "Lights, Cameras—But No Action for St. Paul Police," *Twin Cities Daily Planet,* October 30, 2008, http://www.tcdailyplanet.net/lights-cameras-no-action-st-paul-police.

81   Michel Foucault, *The Punitive Society, Lectures at the College de France, 1972–1973* (New York: Picador, 2015), 100.

82   Foucault, *Discipline*, 296.

83   Foucault, *Discipline*, 176.

84   Foucault, *Discipline*, 281.

85 Trevor Aaronson, *The Terror Factory: Inside the FBI's Manufactured War on Terrorism* (Brooklyn, NY: IG Publishing, 2014), 44.

86 John Slade, interview by author, February 1, 2012.

87 Jeff Keating, interview by author, July 20, 2010.

88 Of course, there were a few community-oriented Indymedia chapters like those found in Los Angeles, Urbana-Champaign, and more recently in sub-Saharan Africa.

89 For Anna's story, see Elle Reader Investigation, "The Believers," *Elle* (April 2008): 266–72, 323–25; and Trevor Aaronson and Katie Galloway, "Manufacturing Terror: An FBI Informant Seduced Eric McDavid into a Bomb Plot, Then the Government Lied About it," *The Intercept*, November 19, 2015, https://theintercept.com/2015/11/19/an-fbi-informant-seduced-eric-mcdavid-into-a-bomb-plot-then-the-government-lied-about-it/.

90 Aaronson and Galloway, "Manufacturing."

91 Aaronson and Galloway, "Manufacturing," 30.

92 Brian Bailitz, interview by author, March 23, 2011.

93 For more on this, see Potter, *Green*; and Chris Robé, *Breaking the Spell: A History of Anarchist Filmmakers, Videotape Guerrillas, and Digital Ninjas* (Oakland, CA: PM Press, 2017).

94 Foucault, *Punitive*, 262.

95 Much of this information is from Josh Harkinson, "How a Radical Leftist Became an FBI's BFF," *Mother Jones*, July 29, 2011, http://www.motherjones.com/politics/2011/08/brandon-darby-anarchist-fbi-terrorism.

96 Specktor quoted in *Conspiracy to Riot in Furtherance of Terrorism: The Collective Autobiography of the RNC 8*, ed. Leslie James Pickering (Portland, OR: Arissa Media Group, 2011), 315.

97 Guillén-Givins quoted in Pickering, *Conspiracy*, 235.

98 Bicking quoted in Pickering, *Conspiracy*, 298.

99 Gross, interview.

100 Foucault, *Punitive*, 210.

101 Foucault, *Punitive*, 211.

102 Kris Hermes, *Crashing the Party: Legacies and Lessons from the RNC 2000* (Oakland, CA: PM Press, 2015), 67–90.

103 Hermes, *Crashing*, 223.

104 Fitzgerald quoted in Pickering, *Conspiracy*, 388.

105 Fitzgerald quoted in Pickering, *Conspiracy*, 388.

106 Hermes, *Crashing*, 275.

107 Gross, interview.

108 Guillén-Givins quoted in Pickering, *Conspiracy*, 380.

109 Guillén-Givins quoted in Pickering, *Conspiracy*, 388.

110 RNC Review Commission, *Report*, 74.

111 RNC Review Commission, *Report*, 8.

112 RNC Review Commission, *Report*, 72.

113 RNC Review Commission, *Report*, 76.

114 Alessandra Renzi and Greg Elmer, *Infrastructure Critical: Sacrifice at Toronto's G8/G20 Summit* (Winnipeg: Arbeiter Ring Publishing, 2012), 55.

115 Renzi and Elmer, *Infrastructure*, 47.

116 "G8-G20 $1B Price Tag Sparks Audit Calls, Hard Questions from Angry Opposition," *Waterloo Chronicle*, May 27, 2010.

117   Renzi and Elmer, *Infrastructure*, 68.

118   Melissa Hill, interview by author, December 3, 2010.

119   Dawn Paley, interview by author, March 9, 2015.

120   Jennifer Pagliaro, "Tally of Dropped G20 Charges Rise," *Toronto Star,* December 21, 2011.

121   Renzi and Elmer, *Infrastructure*, 12–13.

122   Naomi Klein, *The Shock Doctrine* (New York: Picador, 2008), 13.

123   Torin Monahan, "Surveillance and Terrorism," in Ball, Haggarty, and Lion, *Routledge Handbook*, 288.

124   Keith Morelli, "Anarchists' Game Plan for Tampa RNC Unclear," *Tampa Tribune*, June 17, 2012, http://tbo.com/ap/politics/anarchist--game-plan-for-tampa-rnc-unclear-416976 (site discontinued).

125   Kevin Wiatrowski, "Tampa May Be Caught between Anarchy, Rights," *Tampa Tribune*, February 12, 2012.

126   "Conventional Wisdom," *RNC '08 Report*, accessed May 13, 2015, currently not available, http://rnc08report.org/archive/1457.shtml,.

127   Kevin Wiatrowski, "Tampa Council Tentatively Passes RNC Event Zone Ordinance," *Tampa Tribune*, May 3, 2012, accessed May 13, 2015, http://tbo.com/news/politics/tampa-council-passes-rnc-event-zone-ordinance-399432?referer=None&shortu rl=http%3A%2F%2Ftbo.ly%2FJPPeT8 (site discontinued).

128   Ray Reyes and Rob Shaw interview with Jane Castor, "Castor Shares 'Golden Rule' for RNC," *Tampa Tribune*, September 1, 2012.

129   Nicholas Fandos, "Trump Inauguration Security Planners Brace for Wave of Protesters," *New York Times*, December 27, 2016, https://www.nytimes.com/2016/12/27/us/politics/donald-trump-inauguration-security.html.

130   Sarah Frostenson, "A Crowd Scientist Says Trump's Inauguration Attendance Was Pretty Average," Vox, January 24, 2017, https://www.vox.com/policy-and-politics/2017/1/24/14354036/crowds-presidential-inaugurations-trump-average.

131   Associated Press, "Government Drops Charges against All Inauguration Protesters," *NBC News*, July 6, 2018, https://www.nbcnews.com/news/us-news/government-drops-charges-against-all-inauguration-protesters-n889531.

132   Michelle Stoddart, "Washington to Pay $1.6M to Settle Lawsuits After Protests at Trump's 2017 Inauguration," *ABC News*, April 26, 2021, https://abcnews.go.com/Politics/washington-pay-16m-settle-lawsuits-protests-trumps-2017/story?id=77324117.

133   Monahan, "Surveillance and Terrorism," 288.

134   See David Graeber, *Direct Action: An Ethnography* (Oakland, CA: AK Press, 2009); and Jeffrey S. Juris, *Networking Futures: The Movements against Corporate Globalization* (Durham, NC: Duke University Press, 2008).

CHAPTER 3 **Documenting the Little Abuses**

1   Such imagery also overlooks how police violence and harassment disproportionately impacts transgender working-class people of color. For more information, see Joey L. Mogul, Andrea J. Ritchie, and Kay Whitlock, *Queer (In)justice: The Criminalization of LGBT People in the United States* (Boston: Beacon Press, 2011).

2   Susan Sontag, *On Photography* (New York: Delta, 1977), 178.

3   See Peter N. Funke, Chris Robé, and Todd Wolfson, "Suturing Working Class Subjectivities: Media Mobilizing Project and the Role of Media Building a Class-Based Social Movement," *tripleC* 10, no. 1 (2012): 16–29; Jesse Drew, *A Social History of Contemporary Democratic Media* (New York: Routledge, 2013); and Angela Aguayo, *Documentary Resistance: Social Change and Participatory Media* (Oxford: Oxford University Press, 2019).

4   For good analysis regarding the problems of neoliberalism, see David Harvey, *A Brief History of Neoliberalism* (Oxford: Oxford University Press, 2005).

5   Kevin Howley, *Community Media: People, Places, and Communication Technologies* (Cambridge: Cambridge University Press, 2005), 40.

6   Jeremiah Moss, *Vanishing New York: How a Great City Lost Its Soul* (New York: Dey St, 2017), 76–77; and Peter Moskowitz, *How to Kill a City: Gentrification, Inequality, and The Fight for the Neighborhood* (New York: Nation Books, 2017), 191–93.

7   Moss, *Vanishing*, 310.

8   See Loïc Wacquant, *Punishing the Poor: The Neoliberal Government of Social Insecurity* (Durham, NC: Duke University Press, 2009); and Brendan McQuade, *Pacifying the Homeland: Intelligence Fusion and Mass Supervision* (Berkeley: University of California Press, 2019).

9   Paul Gilroy, *The Black Atlantic: Modernity and Double Consciousness* (Cambridge, MA: Harvard University Press, 1993); and Stuart Hall, *The Fateful Triangle: Race, Ethnicity, Nation*, ed. Kobena Mercer (Cambridge, MA: Harvard University Press, 2017).

10   Wacquant, *Punishing*, 160.

11   In NYPD jargon, such infractions are called "quality-of-life misdemeanors."

12   Marc Lamont Hill, *Nobody: Casualties of America's War on the Vulnerable, from Ferguson to Flint and Beyond* (New York: Atria Books, 2016), 45.

13   Police Reform Organizing Project, "The Case against the NYPD's Quota-Driven 'Broken Windows' Policing," accessed February 1, 2023, http://www.policereformorganizingproject.org/wp-content/uploads/2012/09/Case_Against_Broken_Windows.pdf.

14   Josmar Trujillo, "Militarized Policing, Gentrifying City: Doubting NYPD Reforms," *City Limits*, June 3, 2014, http://citylimits.org/2014/06/03/militarized-policing-gentrifying-city-doubting-nypd-reforms.

15   George Joseph, "Developers Are 'Very, Very Excited to Pioneer' New Neighborhoods Under De Blasio's Affordable Housing Plan," *Gothamist*, March 22, 2016, http://gothamist.com/2016/03/22/pioneering_brooklyn_east_ny.php.

16   Neil Smith, *The New Urban Frontier: Gentrification and the Revanchist City* (New York: Routledge, 1996), 211.

17   Moss, *Vanishing*, 159; and Moskowitz, *How*, 171–89.

18   Moss, *Vanishing*, 310.

19   See Katie Glueck and Ashley Southall, "As Adams Toughens on Crime, Some Fear a Return to '90s Era Policing," *New York Times*, March 26, 2022, https://www.nytimes.com/2022/03/26/nyregion/broken-windows-eric-adams.html; and Josmar Trujillo, "The Black Giuliani," Copwatch Media, March 28, 2022, https://copwatch.media/2022/03/the-black-giuliani.

20   For more on primitive accumulation see Robin D.G. Kelley, "Thug Nation: On State Violence and Disposability" in *Policing the Planet: Why the Policing Crisis Led to Black Lives Matter*, ed. Jordan T. Camp and Christina Heatherton (New York: Verso, 2016), 29–30; and George Karandinos, Laurie Kain Hart, Fernando Montero Castrillo, and

Philippe Bourgois, "The Moral Economy of Violence in the US Inner City," in *Violence at the Urban Margins*, ed. Javier Auyero, Philippe Bourgois, and Nancy Scheper-Hughes (Oxford: Oxford University Press, 2015), 41–72.

21   Josmar Trujillo, interview by author, August 16, 2016.

22   Lipsitz, "Policing Place and Taxing Time on Skid Row," in *Policing the Planet: Why the Policing Crisis Led to Black Lives Matter*, ed. Jordan T. Camp and Christina Heatherton (New York: Verso, 2016), 131.

23   Lipsitz, "Policing," 135.

24   Queens Neighborhood United, "End of Year Report: January 2015," accessed February 1, 2023, http://www.queensneighborhoodsunited.org/wp-content/uploads/2014/12/QNU_EndofYearReport_2014.pdf.

25   Yul-San Liem, interview by author, June 24, 2016.

26   Sarah Maslin Nir, "Roosevelt Avenue, a Corridor of Vice," *New York Times*, October, 12, 2012, http://www.nytimes.com/2012/10/14/nyregion/on-roosevelt-avenue-in-queens-vice-remains-a-stubborn-presence.html.

27   The entire film was thought to be lost until the Communist Party USA donated a copy to the Tamiment Library at New York University in 2007. A full version can be seen on YouTube https://youtu.be/b0gr8H-VHyQ. For more information, see Kevin Brownlow, *Behind the Mask of Innocence* (Berkeley: University of California Press, 1990), 498–508. For more on the Passaic Textile Strike, see Jacob A. Zumoff, *The Red Thread: The Passaic Textile Strike* (New Brunswick, NJ: Rutgers University Press, 2021).

28   For more on the Black Panthers, see Joshua Bloom, *Black against Empire: The History and Politics of the Black Panther Party* (Berkeley: University of California Press, 2016). For more on the Young Lords, see the Young Lords, *Palante: Voices and Photographs of the Young Lords, 1969–1971* (Chicago: Haymarket Books, 1971).

29   Catherine Saalfield, "On the Make: Activist Video Collectives," in *Queer Looks: Perspectives on Lesbian and Gay Film and Video*, ed. Martha Geever, John Greyson, and Pratibha Parmar (New York: Routledge, 1993), 21–27.

30   Andrea Pritchett, interview by author, March 4, 2016.

31   "Jacob Crawford Interview, Photography Is Not a Crime," May 12, 2015, http://photographyisnotacrime.com/2015/05/12/wecopwatch-veteran-jacob-crawford-empowers-communities-after-police-tragedies/ (site discontinued).

32   Mary D. Fan, *Camera Power: Proof, Policing, Privacy, and Audiovisual Big Data* (Cambridge: Cambridge University Press, 2019), 35.

33   Dennis Flores, interview by author, August 24, 2016.

34   Monifa Bandele, interview by author, August 19, 2016.

35   Dennis Flores, interview by author, February 15, 2016.

36   Jason Del Aguila, interview by author, April 11, 2016. Subsequent quotations of Del Aguila are from this interview unless otherwise noted.

37   Claudio Gaeta-Tapia, interview by author, April 13, 2016. Subsequent quotations of Gaete-Tapia are from this interview unless otherwise noted.

38   Gilroy, *Black Atlantic*, 45.

39   Hall, *Fateful Triangle*, 123.

40   C.J. Hughes, "Sunset Park, Brooklyn: Not Quite Trendy," *New York Times*, January 20, 2016, https://www.nytimes.com/2016/01/24/realestate/sunset-park-brooklyn-not-quite-trendy.html?_r=0.

41   NYU Furman Center, *State of New York City's Housing and Neighborhoods in 2015* (New York: NYU Furman Center, 2016), 94.

42   Chon A. Noriega, *Shot in America: Television, the State, and the Rise of Chicano Cinema* (Minneapolis: University of Minnesota Press, 2000).

43   Chon A. Noriega, "Imagined Borders: Locating Chicano Cinema in America/ América," in *The Ethnic Eyes: Latino Media Arts*, ed. Chon A. Noriega and Ana M. Lopez (Minneapolis: University of Minnesota Press, 1996), 14.

44   Cynthia A. Young, *Soul Power: Culture, Radicalism, and the Making of a U.S. Third World Left* (Durham, NC: Duke University Press, 2006), 119.

45   For recent excellent analysis on *Rompiendo Puertas*, see Morgan Adamson, "*Rompiendo Puertas/Break and Enter* (1971), Residential Autonomy: Economies of Dispossession and Their Undoing," *Jump Cut* no. 61 (2022), https://www.ejumpcut. org/currentissue/MorganAdamson/index.html.

46   Young, *Soul*, 16.

47   See Francisco X. Camplis, "Toward the Development of Raza Cinema," in *Chicanos and Film: Representation and Resistance*, ed. Chon A. Noriega (Minneapolis: University of Minnesota Press, 1992), 284–302.

48   Chon A. Noriega, "Between a Weapon and a Formula: Chicano Cinema and Its Contexts," in Noriega, *Chicanos and Film*, 50–51.

49   Mark Morales, "Sunset Park Tenants Use Their Own Photos of Shoddy Conditions of Their Apartment Buildings as Subjects for Art Show," *New York Daily News*, August 2, 2012, http://www.nydailynews.com/new-york/brooklyn/sunset-park- tenants-photos-shoddy-conditions-apartment-buildings-subjects-art-show- article-1.1127828.

50   Morales, "Sunset Park."

51   The webpage, https://www.facebook.com/RentStrikeSolidarity/, is no longer available.

52   Tina Askanius, "Protest Movements and Spectacles of Death: From Urban Places to Video Spaces," in *Advances in the Visual Analysis of Social Movements*, ed. Nicole Doerr, Alice Mattoni, and Simon Teune (Bingley, UK: Emerald Group Publishing, 2013), 114.

53   Paolo Gerbaudo, *Tweets and the Streets: Social Media and Contemporary Activism* (London: Pluto Press, 2012), 14.

54   El Grito, "Sunset Park Rent Strikers (The Basement)," YouTube video, accessed February 1, 2023, https://www.youtube.com/watch?v=9J5R7ZJ8g9w.

55   Patricia Zimmermann, *States of Emergency: Documentaries, Wars, Democracies* (Minneapolis: University of Minnesota Press, 2000), 63–64.

56   Sara Ahmed, *The Cultural Politics of Emotion* (Edinburgh: Edinburgh University Press, 2014), 10.

57   Ahmed, *Cultural*, 105.

58   Kevin DeLuca, Sean Lawson, and Ye Sun, "Occupy Wall Street on the Public Screens of Social Media: The Many Framings of the Birth of a Protest Movement," *Communication, Culture & Critique* 5, no. 4 (2012): 483–509.

59   Smith, *New Urban*, 23.

60   Dennis Flores Miranda, "7-19–2012 COPWATCH Films NYPD Transit Cop Assaulting," YouTube video, 4:12, accessed February 1, 2023, https://www.youtube.com/ watch?v=iarUHZJ9sCk.

61　Police Reform Organizing Project, "Nearly 1,800,000 Per Year Punitive Interactions between NYPD and New Yorkers," (October 2016), 6, http://www.policereformorganizingproject.org/wp-content/uploads/2012/09/Nearly_1.8million_a_year_PROP_report.pdf.

62　As the increasing prevalence of cloud technology enables copwatchers to upload their footage, the value of the two-camera approach has shifted from preserving footage toward offering multiple perspectives of the incident while also lending some protection to those copwatchers closest to the police.

63　Zimmermann, *States of Emergency*, 95.

64　Flores, interview, February 15, 2016.

65　Susan Sontag, *Regarding the Pain of Others* (New York: Picador, 2003), 26–27.

66　Bill Nichols, *Representing Reality: Issues and Concepts in Documentary* (Bloomington: Indiana University Press, 1991), 117.

67　Nichols, *Representing*, 151.

68　Jeffrey S. Juris, "Reflections on #Occupy Everywhere: Social Media, Public Space, and Emerging Logics of Aggregation," *American Ethnologist* 39, no. 2 (2012): 266.

69　Jason Del Aguila and Dennis Flores, interview by author, November 21, 2016.

70　Stuart Hall, Charles Critcher, Tony Jefferson, John Clarke, and Brian Roberts, *Policing the Crisis: Mugging, the State, and Law and Order* (London: Macmillan, 1978), 388.

71　Murray Bookchin, *Post-Scarcity Anarchism* (Oakland, CA: AK Press, 2004), 15.

72　El Grito, "Copwatch June 8th 2014," YouTube video, 3:27, accessed February 1, 2023, https://www.youtube.com/watch?v=SjpDYFAsuC4.

73　Walter Benjamin, *Illuminations*, ed. Hannah Arendt (New York: Schocken Books, 1968), 236.

74　John Surico, "On Patrol with the Copwatchers Who Film the NYPD," *Vice News*, August 21, 2015, https://www.vice.com/en_us/article/wd7xvq/we-spent-a-night-copwatching-in-brooklyn-821; Josmar Trujillo, "Puerto Rican Pride as Sunset Park Fights Off Police Brutality," *Huffington Post*, December 6, 2017, https://www.huffingtonpost.com/josmar-trujillo/puerto-rican-pride-as-sun_b_7540022.html; and Andrew Breiner, "Brooklyn Teen Was Charged with Assaulting A Cop Until This Video Proved That The Police Were Lying," *ThinkProgress*, March 5, 2015, https://thinkprogress.org/brooklyn-teen-was-charged-with-assaulting-a-cop-until-this-video-proved-the-police-were-lying-486c0aeb549c.

75　Max Jaeger, "Charges Dropped against Sunset Park Teen After Video Shows Cops Lied," *Brooklyn Paper*, March 5, 2015, https://www.brooklynpaper.com/stories/38/10/br-sunset-park-video-exoneration-2015-03-06-bk_38_10.html.

76　*Russia Today America*, March 11, 2015, https://www.youtube.com/watch?v=9Ux8Mb_cqP0 (unavailable in US). I only cite *Russia Today* with caution since it is, after all, a Russian propaganda media organization.

77　Max Jaeger, "Teen Falsely Accused of Bashing Cops Fights Back in Court," *Brooklyn Paper*, April 20, 2015, https://www.brooklynpaper.com/teen-falsely-accused-of-bashing-cops-fights-back-in-court/; and Flores, interview, February 2, 2016.

78　Nichols, *Representing Reality*, 152; for more information on the use of the Rodney King footage, see Mike Mashon, "Losing Control: Popular Reception(s) of the Rodney King Video," *Wide Angle* 15, no. 2 (1993), 7–18.

79　Dennis Flores Miranda, "El Grito de Sunset Park June 9th 2013," YouTube video, 2:28, accessed February 20, 2023, https://www.youtube.com/watch?v=kOT4Fu0wap0&t=2s.

80   Raquel Z. Rivera, "New York Afro-Puerto Rican and Afro-Dominican Roots Music: Liberation Mythologies and Overlapping Diasporas," *Black Music Research Journal* 32, no. 2 (2012): 3–24.

81   It is not coincidental that when I walked into Dennis Flores's apartment a series of congas were prominently displayed by its entrance thus punctuating how music and activism serve interrelated roles for him as well.

82   Stacy L. Smith, Marc Choueiti, and Katherine Pieper, *Inclusion of Invisibility? Comprehensive Annenberg Report on Diversity in Entertainment* (Los Angeles: Institute for Diversity and Empowerment at Annenberg, 2016), 16.

83   Leo R. Chavez, *The Latino Threat: Constructing Immigrants, Citizens and the Nation* (Stanford, CA: Stanford University Press, 2013).

84   Mary Beltran, "Fast and Bilingual: *Fast & Furious* and the Latinization of Racelessness," *Cinema Journal* 53, no. 1 (Fall 2013): 85–86.

85   Dennis Flores, interview by author, August 27, 2021, and email from Dennis Flores, March 19, 2023.

86   See Ross Tuttle and Quinn Rose Schneider, "Stopped-and-Frisked: 'For Being a F**cking Mutt,'" *The Nation*, October 8, 2012, https://www.thenation.com/article/stopped-and-frisked-being-fking-mutt-video.

87   Jose LaSalle, interview by author, July 19, 2016. Henceforth LaSalle is quoted from this interview unless otherwise noted.

88   Kim Ortiz, interview by author, August 19, 2016. Additional quotations from Ortiz are from this interview unless otherwise noted.

89   See NYPD CompStat, https://compstat.nypdonline.org/2e5c3f4b-85c1–4635-83c6–22b27fe7c75c/view/89.

90   T.V. Reed, *The Art of Protest: Culture and Activities from the Civil Rights Movement to the Streets of Seattle* (Minneapolis: University of Minnesota Press, 2005), 53.

91   See CPU's YouTube page https://www.youtube.com/user/endstopandfrisknowjl/videos.

92   Sasha Costanza-Chock, *Out of the Shadows, Into the Streets!: Transmedia Organizing and the Immigrant Rights Movement* (Cambridge, MA: MIT Press, 2014), 80.

93   George Joseph, "Undercover Police Have Regularly Spied on Black Lives Matter Activists in New York," *The Intercept*, August 18, 2015, https://theintercept.com/2015/08/18/undercover-police-spied-on-ny-black-lives-matter.

94   Dean Meminger, "Activist, Who Says NYPD Officers Tried to Frame Him, Gets $860,000 Settlement," *Spectrum News: NY1*, 2:18, March 28, 2019, https://www.ny1.com/nyc/all-boroughs/news/2019/03/29/jose-lasalle-copwatch-patrol-unit-gets-settlement-nyc-nypd-says-officers-wrongfully-arrested-him#.

95   The amount of articles documenting NYPD surveillance of social movements is mountainous. For representative examples see George Joseph, "NYPD Officers Accessed Black Lives Matter Activists' Texts, Documents Show," *The Guardian*, April 4, 2017: https://www.theguardian.com/us-news/2017/apr/04/nypd-police-black-lives-matter-surveillance-undercover; Associated Press, "Docs Show NYPD Infiltrated Liberal Groups," *CBS News*, March 23, 2013: https://www.cbsnews.com/news/docs-show-nypd-infiltrated-liberal-groups/; and Sahil Singhvi, "Police Infiltration of Protests Undermines the First Amendment," *Brennan Center for Justice*, August 4, 2020, https://www.brennancenter.org/our-work/analysis-opinion/police-infiltration-protests-undermines-first-amendment.

96 Christian Fuchs, *Culture and Economy in the Age of Social Media* (New York: Routledge, 2015), 294.

97 Copwatch Patrol Unit, "TD 20-No CPR, These Officers Should be Fired (The Case of the Churros)," YouTube video, 0:26, accessed February 18, 2023, https://www.youtube.com/watch?v=cJWqZsdaJu4.

98 Robert Gangi, interview by author, June 28, 2016. Additional quotations from Gangi are from this interview unless otherwise noted.

99 Legislation passed in early 2021 to increase the number of vendor licenses available, something that vendors have demanded for decades. But as of March 2023, the time of this writing, the access to such new licenses has been held up. As a result, vendors have been holding protests since September 2022 to expedite the process as well as reduce harassment against them. For more, see Emma Seiwell and Leonard Greene, "Struggling NYC Street Vendors Rally for Changes in Enforcement Law," *Daily News*, March 16, 2023, https://www.nydailynews.com/new-york/ny-vendors-rally-enforcement-legislation-20230316-xkybvfzoordghi3w6t6xlp7mfu-story.html.

100 Josmar Trujillo, "'WE LIVE HERE': How the NYPD Turned a Shrine into an Occupation," *Huffington Post*, April 1, 2016, updated December 6, 2017, http://www.huffingtonpost.com/josmar-trujillo/we-live-here-how-the-nypd_b_9592834.html.

101 NYPD Exposed, "46 Pct v. Copwatch Patrol Unit (Harassing the Community & Interfering with Recording)," YouTube video, 7:08, accessed February 20, 2023, https://www.youtube.com/watch?v=RL0K6kbye6c.

102 Nichols, *Representing*, 157.

103 Nichols, *Representing*, 159.

104 Ahmed, *Cultural*, 175.

105 Ahmed, *Cultural*, 176.

106 Darrel Wanzer-Serrano, *The New York Young Lords and the Struggle for Liberation* (Philadelphia: Temple University Press, 2015), 52.

107 Wanzer-Serrano, *New York* , 95.

108 Solanas and Getino, "Third Cinema," 278.

109 Anna, "The Feministing Five: Andrea Pritchett," *Feministing*, accessed February 1, 2023, http://feministing.com/2011/09/17/the-feministing-five-andrea-prichett. As I have documented elsewhere, this gendered division of labor plagues much media activism. See Chris Robé, *Breaking the Spell*.

110 Copwatch Patrol Unite, "30 Pct. – Police Try to arrest 2 Young Girls and The Community Did Not Allow It," YouTube video, 8:16, accessed February 2, 2023, https://www.youtube.com/watch?v=M9FQP-8OAJE.

111 Molly Crabapple, "Nine Months After He Filmed Eric Garner's Killing, the Cops Are Trying to Put Ramsey Orta behind Bars," Vice, April 24, 2015, http://www.vice.com/read/nine-months-after-he-filmed-eric-garners-killing-the-cops-are-trying-to-put-ramsey-orta-behind-bars.

112 International Documentary Association, "Statement in Support of #RightToRecord," August 9, 2016, http://www.documentary.org/righttorecord (site discontinued); and Jamiles Lartey, "Film-Makers Demand Inquiry into 'Targeting' of People Who Record Police," *The Guardian*, August 11, 2016, https://www.theguardian.com/film/2016/aug/10/filmmakers-citizen-journalists-justice-department-investigation.

113 *Swiping* is the action of sliding one's Metrocard through the scanner to gain access through the turnstile.

114 Rocco Parascandola and Graham Rayman, "NYPD Arrests Mostly People of Color for Fare Beating, Stats Show," *New York Daily News*, February 12, 2016, http://www.nydailynews.com/new-york/nypd-arrests-people-color-fare-beating-stats-article-1.2528320.

115 New York City Department of Investigation, Office of the Inspector General for NYPD, *An Analysis of Quality-of-Life Summonses, Quality-of-Life Misdemeanor Arrests, and Felony Crime in New York City, 2010–2015* (OIG-NYPD), June 22, 2016: http://www1.nyc.gov/assets/oignypd/downloads/pdf/Quality-of-Life-Report-2010–2015.pdf.

116 Paul Notice II, "Fare Beating: The Controversy Behind the NYPD's Number One Reason for Arrest," Elite Daily, video, 2.27, May 13, 2016, http://elitedaily.com/news/fare-beating-new-york-subway/1492339.

117 John Fiske, "Surveilling the City: Whiteness, the Black Man and Democratic Totalitarianism," *Theory, Culture & Society* 15, no. 2 (1998): 69.

118 Zimmermann, *States of Emergency*, 98.

119 McKenzie Funk, "Should We See Everything a Cop Sees?" *New York Times Magazine*, October 18, 2016, http://www.nytimes.com/2016/10/23/magazine/police-body-cameras.html.

120 Funk, "Should We"; and Myra Frazier, "A Camera on Every Cop," *Harper's Magazine* (August 2015): 62.

121 Funk, "Should We."

122 See Bill Hutchinson, "Recent High-Profile Deaths Put Police Body Cameras under New Scrutiny," *ABC News*, March 5, 2023, https://abcnews.go.com/US/recent-high-profile-deaths-put-police-body-cameras/story?id=96848683; and National Institute of Justice, "Research on Body-Worn Cameras and Law Enforcement," January 7, 2023, https://nij.ojp.gov/topics/articles/research-body-worn-cameras-and-law-enforcement.

123 Frazier, "Camera," 62–63.

124 Ethan Geringer-Sameth, "Initial Report Shows Benefits and Challenges of NYPD Body Camera Program from Police Watchdog," *Gotham Gazette*, February 27, 2020, https://www.gothamgazette.com/city/9167-initial-report-shows-benefits-and-challenges-of-nypd-body-camera-program-for-watchdog-agency.

125 Andrew Padilla quoted in Raven Rakia, "The Cops Hate Being Filmed. So Why are They Okay with Body worn cameras?" *The Nation,* December 19, 2014, http://www.thenation.com/article/cops-hate-being-filmed-so-why-are-they-ok-body-cameras.

126 Fiske, "Surveilling," 69.

127 Rakia, "Cops Hate."

128 Geringer-Sameth, "Initial Report."

129 Jennifer I. Mnookin, "Can a Jury Believe What It Sees?" *New York Times*, July 13, 2014, http://www.nytimes.com/2014/07/14/opinion/videotaped-confessions-can-be-misleading.html.

130 Alison Banville, "Embedded War Reporting Cannot Escape Its Own Bias," *The Guardian*, April 18, 2010, https://www.theguardian.com/commentisfree/2010/apr/18/embedded-war-reporting-iraq-afghanistan.

131 Ben Austen, "Chicago on the Edge," *New York Times Magazine* (April 24, 2016): 47–52, 55–56.

132 Center for Constitutional Rights, "Re: Floyd Submission Regarding NYPD BWC Impact and Use Policy," February 25, 2021, https://ccrjustice.org/sites/default/files/attach/2021/02/BWC%20Submission%20BLH%20CCR%202-25-21.pdf.

133   Dennis Flores and Jason Del Aguila, interview by author, November 21, 2016.

134   Courtney Gross, "NYPD Body Cam Footage Given to NY1 Raises Transparency Questions," *Spectrum News NY1*, January 24, 2018, https://www.ny1.com/nyc/all-boroughs/politics/2018/01/25/nypd-body-camera-footage-released-to-ny1-raises-questions-transparency-of-body-camera-pilot-program, and Julia Marsh, "Network Sues NYPD over Charging $36K for Body Cam Footage," *New York Post*, January 14, 2016, http://nypost.com/2016/01/14/network-sues-nypd-over-charging-36k-for-body-cam-footage.

135   Samantha Ketterer, "Police Will Charge for Body Camera Footage under New State Rule," *Dallas Morning News*, November 21, 2016, https://www.dallasnews.com/news/politics/2016/11/21/police-will-charge-for-body-camera-footage-under-new-state-rule.

136   Elaina Athans, "New Law Makes Police Cam Footage Off Limits to Public," *11 Eyewitness News*, July 12, 2016, http://abc11.com/1422569.

137   Anne Sparaco, "North Carolina Leaders Push New Bill on Police Body Camera Footage in Wake of Andrew Brown Jr's Shooting Death," *13 News Now*, April, 27, 2021, https://www.13newsnow.com/article/news/politics/north-carolina-leaders-push-new-bill-on-police-body-camera-footage-in-wake-of-andrew-brown-jrs-shooting-death/291–3c8a2132–4189–47ca-82a8-c1ad88db08b3.

138   Lindsey Van Ness, "Body Cameras May Not Be the Easy Answer Everyone Was Looking For," Pew Stateline, January 14, 2020, https://www.pewtrusts.org/en/research-and-analysis/blogs/stateline/2020/01/14/body-cameras-may-not-be-the-easy-answer-everyone-was-looking-for.

139   Jose LaSalle, interview by author, February 11, 2020.

140   Kim Ortiz, interview, February 20, 2020.

141   "Atlanta Police Officer Resigns after Premiere of Police Brutality Docuseries Copwatch America Airs on BET," *BlackNews.com*, November 12, 2019, https://www.blacknews.com/news/atlanta-police-officer-resigns-after-premiere-police-brutality-docuseries-copwatch-america-airs-bet.

142   "Atlanta Police."

143   I made multiple attempts to contact BET executives but never received a response.

144   LaSalle, interview.

145   Dennis Flores, interview by author, July 12, 2018.

146   See El Grito, "Environmental Conservation in Puerto Rico," accessed February 1, 2023, https://elgrito.org/boriken-forest-reservation-project.

147   Dennis Flores, interview by author, August 27, 2021.

148   See "The People's Database for Community-Based Police Accountability: A Berkeley Copwatch + WITNESS Initiative," accessed February 1, 2023, https://lab.witness.org/berkeley-copwatch-database/#download. See also El Grito, "Profiling the Police," accessed February 1, 2023, https://elgrito.witness.org.

149   See Copwatch Media, "About Copwatch," accessed February 1, 2023, https://copwatch.media/about.

150   I heard much about these events through various New York City activists I know. To learn more, see Nabil Hassein, "A Personal Statement on Why Accountability and Take Back the Bronx," accessed February 1, 2023, https://nabilhassein.github.io/blog/wa-tbbx-statement.

151   Isaac Ortega, interview by author, September 15, 2021.

CHAPTER 4 **Somali American Narratives and Suspect Communities**

1   Rachel Weiner, "Fox News Commentator Who Feds Say Faked a CIA Career Sentenced to 33 Months in Prison," *Washington Post*, July 15, 2016.

2   It is now named the Clarion Project. "Anti-Muslim," *Southern Poverty Law Center*, accessed July 2, 2019: https://www.splcenter.org/fighting-hate/extremist-files/ideology/anti-muslim.

3   Ali Gharib and Eli Clifton, "Meet the Donors Behind The Clarion Fund's Islamophobic Documentary *The Third Jihad*," *Think Progress*, January 24, 2012: https://thinkprogress.org/meet-the-donors-behind-the-clarion-funds-islamophobic-documentary-the-third-jihad-2d6a4ee930a6.

4   Tom Robbins, "NYPD Cops' Training Included an Anti-Muslim Horror Flick," *Village Voice*, January 19, 2011, https://www.villagevoice.com/2011/01/19/nypd-cops-training-included-an-anti-muslim-horror-flick.

5   Michael Powell, "In Police Training, a Dark Film on U.S. Muslims," *New York Times*, January 23, 2012.

6   Diala Shamas and Nermeen Arastu, *Mapping Muslims: NYPD Spying and Its Impact on American Muslims* (Long Island City, NY: Muslim American Civil Liberties Coalition, and Creating Law Enforcement Accountability and Responsibility Project, 2013); and Matt Apuzzo and Adam Goldman, *Enemies Within: Inside the NYPD's Secret Spying Unit and bin Laden's Final Plot Against America* (New York: Touchstone, 2013).

7   See Mitchell D. Silber and Arvin Bhatt, *Radicalization in the West: The Homegrown Threat* (New York City Police Department, 2007), https://www.judicialwatch.org/wp-content/uploads/2016/01/NYPD_Report-Radicalization_in_the_West.pdf.

8   Rick Rojas, "They Create a Muslim Enclave in Upstate N.Y. Then Came the Online Conspiracies," *New York Times*, January 28, 2019: https://www.nytimes.com/2019/01/28/nyregion/islamberg-ny-attack-plot.html.

9   Regarding limited representations of Muslims on screen, see Jack G. Shaheen, *Guilty: Hollywood's Verdict on Arabs after 9/11* (Northampton, MA: Olive Branch Press, 2008); and Edward W. Said, *Covering Islam: How the Media and the Experts Determine How We See the Rest of the World* (New York: Vintage, 1997). The concepts of Orientalism and Islamophobia have been developed by many, but some notable works include Edward W. Said, *Orientalism* (New York: Vintage Books, 1994), Waïl S. Hassan, *Immigrant Narratives: Orientalism and Cultural Translation in Arab American and Arab British Literature* (Oxford: Oxford University Press, 2011), Deepa Kumar, *Islamophobia and the Politics of Empire* (Chicago: Haymarket Books, 2012); Arun Kundnani, *The Muslims Are Coming! Islamophobia, Extremism, and the Domestic War on Terror* (New York: Verso, 2015); and Erik Love, *Islamophobia and Racism in America* (New York: New York University, 2018).

10   CAIR, *The Empowerment of Hate: Civil Rights Report 2017*, accessed February 1, 2023, https://ca.cair.com/wp-content/uploads/2018/03/2017-Empowerment-of-Fear-Final1.pdf.

11   Adam Liptak, "'There's No Reason to Apologize' for Muslim Ban Remarks, Trump Says," *New York Times*, April 30, 2018, https://www.nytimes.com/2018/04/30/us/politics/trump-supreme-court-muslim-ban.html; Caitlin Dickerson, "'There is a Stench': Soiled Clothes and No Baths for Migrant Children at a Texas Center," *New York Times*, June 21, 2019, https://www.nytimes.com/2019/06/21/us/migrant-children-border-soap.html; Felicia Sonmez and Ashley Parker, "As Trump Stands by Charlottesville Remarks, Rise of White-Nationalists Violence Becomes an

Issue in 2020 Presidential Race," *Washington Post*, April 28, 2019. https://www. washingtonpost.com/politics/as-trump-stands-by-charlottesville-remarks-rise-of-white-nationalist-violence-becomes-an-issue-in-2020-presidential-race/2019/04/28/83aaf1ca-69c0–11e9-a66d-a82d3f3d96d5_story.html?utm_term=. b256ff31d3b3; and Julie Hirschfeld Davis and Michael D. Shear, *Border Wars: Inside Trump's Assault on Immigration* (New York: Simon & Schuster, 2019).

12   Yochai Benkler, Robert Faris, and Hal Roberts, *Network Propaganda: Manipulation, Disinformation, and Radicalization in American Politics* (Oxford: Oxford University Press, 2018), 105–44.

13   Ella Shohat and Robert Stam, *Unthinking Eurocentrism: Multiculturalism and the Media* (New York: Routledge, 1994), 198.

14   Lori Kido Lopez, *Asian American Media Activism: Fighting for Cultural Citizenship* (New York: New York University Press, 2016), 221.

15   Michel Foucault, *Discipline and Punish: The Birth of the Prison*, trans. Alan Sheridan (New York: Vintage Books, 1977), 187.

16   I want to be clear that I am not offering a conspiratorial notion of commercial media simply mimicking state propaganda. I will develop the subtle relations that operate between media and the government further in the chapter. But in our conspiracy-ridden world, I want to clearly state that I will have none of this framework.

17   Sohail Daulatzai, *Black Star, Crescent Moon: The Muslim International and Black Freedom beyond America* (Minneapolis: University of Minnesota Press, 2012), xviii.

18   Love, *Islamophobia and Racism*, 100–101.

19   Murtaza Hussain, "Complaints Describe Border Agents Interrogating Muslim Americans, Asking for Social Media Accounts," *The Intercept,* January 14, 2017, https:// theintercept.com/2017/01/14/complaints-describes-border-agents-interrogating-muslim-americans-asking-for-social-media-accounts/; and Cora Currier, "Revealed: The FBI's Secret Methods for Recruiting Informants at the Border," *The Intercept*, October 5, 2016, https://theintercept.com/2016/10/05/fbi-secret-methods-for-recruiting-informants-at-the-border.

20   Cora Currier, "Undercover FBI Agents Swarm the Internet Seeking Contact with Terrorists," *The Intercept*, January 31, 2017, https://theintercept.com/2017/01/31/ undercover-fbi-agents-swarm-the-internet-seeking-contact-with-terrorists.

21   Love, *Islamophobia and Racism*, 102; Kundnani, *Muslims*, 134.

22   Gino Canella, "Racialized Surveillance: Activist Media and the Policing of Black Bodies," *Communication, Culture & Critique* (July 27, 2018): 1–21; and Alanna Durkin Richer, "Report: Social Media Surveillance Unfairly Targeted Muslims," *Boston Herald,* February 7, 2018.

23   Kundnani, *Muslims*, 15; Alia Malek, ed., *Patriot Acts: Narratives of Post-9/11 Injustice* (San Francisco: McSweeney's Books, 2011), 351; and Human Rights Watch, *Illusions of Justice: Human Rights Abuses in US Terrorism Prosecutions* (2014), 61–67, https:// www.hrw.org/sites/default/files/reports/usterrorism0714_ForUpload_1_0.pdf.

24   Lesley J. Wood, *Crisis and Control: The Militarization of Protest Policing* (London: Pluto Press, 2014), 134; Azadeh Shahshahani, "Government Spying on Immigrants in America is Now Fair Game. What Next?," *The Guardian*, February 12, 2018, https://www. theguardian.com/commentisfree/2018/feb/12/government-spying-immigrants-america; and Mattathias Schwartz, "The Whole Haystack," *New Yorker*, January 26, 2015, https://www.newyorker.com/magazine/2015/01/26/whole-haystack.

25   Moustafa Bayoumi, *How Does It Feel to Be a Problem? Being Young and Arab in America* (New York: Penguin, 2008), 3.

26   "Hate Crimes Continue to Surge in America," *Arab Daily News*, November 13, 2018, https://thearabdailynews.com/2018/11/13/hate-crimes-continue-to-surge-in-america.

27   Adeel Hassan, "Hate-Crime Violence Hits 16-Year High, F.B.I. Reports," *New York Times* November 12, 2019, https://www.nytimes.com/2019/11/12/us/hate-crimes-fbi-report.html.

28   Scott Shane, Matthew Rosenberg, and Eric Lipton, "Trump Pushes Dark View of Islam to Center of U.S. Policy-Making," *New York Times*, February 1, 2017, https://www.nytimes.com/2017/02/01/us/politics/donald-trump-islam.html; and Peter Beinart, "The Denationalization of Muslims," *The Atlantic*, March 19, 2017, https://www.theatlantic.com/politics/archive/2017/03/frank-gaffney-donald-trump-and-the-denationalization-of-american-muslims/519954.

29   Franklin Foer, "How ICE Went Rogue," *The Atlantic* (September 2018): 56–70.

30   Based on its website, MPower Change has been dormant in 2023.

31   Linda Sarsour, interview by author, March 28, 2019.

32   Ishraq Ali, interview by author, April 16, 2019.

33   He stepped down from this position in 2019 to run for Congress.

34   Shahid Buttar, interview by author, February 4, 2019.

35   Kundnani, *Muslims*, 157.

36   Stefano Bonino, "*Prevent*-ing Muslimness in Britain: The Normalization of Exceptional Measures to Combat Terrorism," *Journal of Muslim Minority Affairs* 13, no. 3 (2013): 387.

37   Bonino, "*Prevent*-ing," 390.

38   Paddy Hillyard, *Suspect Community: People's Experience of the Prevention of Terrorism Act in Britain* (London: Pluto Press, 1993), 260.

39   Executive Office of the President of the United States, "Strategic Implementation Plan for Empowering Local Partners to Prevent Violent Extremism in the United States," (December 2011): https://obamawhitehouse.archives.gov/sites/default/files/sip-final.pdf.

40   Gaylene Armstrong, Douglas Derrick, Justin Hienz, Gina Ligon, and Errol Southers, *Characteristics of Homegrown Violent Extremist Radicalization* (Los Angeles, CA: National Center for Risk and Economic Analysis of Terrorism Events, 2019), 114.

41   "Letter: Establish New Countering Violent Extremism Department, Bad Idea," The Brennan Center for Justice, accessed July 10, 2015, https://www.brennancenter.org/analysis/letter-establish-new-countering-violence-extremism-department-bad-ideaartment-bad-idea.

42   Janet Reitman, "'I Helped Destroy People,'" *New York Times Magazine*, September 5, 2021, https://www.nytimes.com/2021/09/01/magazine/fbi-terrorism-terry-albury.html. 41.

43   Faiza Patel and Meghan Koushik, *Countering Violent Extremism* (New York: Brenan Center for Justice, 2017), 8.

44   Emmanuel Mauleón, "Black Twice: Policing Black Muslim Identities," 65 *U.C.L.A. Law Review* 1326 (2018): 1352–53.

45   National Counterterrorism Center (NCTC) *Homegrown Violent Extremism Mobilization Indicators*, 2019 ed., https://www.dni.gov/files/NCTC/documents/news_documents/NCTC-FBI-DHS-HVE-Mobilization-Indicators-Booklet-2019.pdf.

46   NCTC, *Homegrown Violent Extremism*, 10, 14, and 27.

47   "#ExOut Extremism: RIT students Win Global Anti-Terrorism Contest," Rochester Institute of Technology, July 7, 2016, https://www.rit.edu/showcase/index.php?id=333.

48   Layla Quran, "Rochester School Receives Federal Grant to Combat Extremism," *WNYC News*, March 15, 2017, https://www.wnyc.org/story/rochester-school-receives-federal-grant-combat-extremism.

49   Qaran, "Rochester School."

50   Fatema Ahmad and Shannon Al-Wakeel, interview by author, March 28, 2018. Al-Wakeel departed from the league in November 2019.

51   Lucinda Winter, interview by author, July 9, 2019.

52   Armstrong, et al., *Characteristics*, 103–4.

53   "University of Minnesota—Twin Cities," College Factual, accessed July 5, 2019, https://www.collegefactual.com/colleges/university-of-minnesota-twin-cities/student-life/diversity.

54   See "Cedar Riverside Neighborhood," Minnesota Compass, accessed July 5, 2019, https://www.mncompass.org/profiles/neighborhoods/minneapolis/cedar-riverside; and "Quick Facts: Minneapolis City, Minnesota," United States Census, accessed July 5, 2019, https://www.census.gov/quickfacts/minneapoliscityminnesota.

55   Alana Semuels, "Segregation in Paradise?," *The Atlantic*, July 12, 2016, https://www.theatlantic.com/business/archive/2016/07/twin-cities-segregation/490970.

56   "Augsburg Demographics and Diversity Report," Augsburg University, accessed July 5, 2019, https://www.collegefactual.com/colleges/augsburg-college/student-life/diversity/ (site has been substantially revised).

57   Armstrong, et al., *Characteristics*, 107; and Schwartz, "Whole Haystack."

58   Cora Currier, "How Community Outreach Programs to Muslims Blur Lines Between Outreach and Intelligence," *The Intercept*, January 21, 2015, https://theintercept.com/2015/01/21/spies-among-us-community-outreach-programs-muslims-blur-lines-outreach-intelligence/; and City of St. Paul Police Department, "African Immigrant Muslim Coordinated Outreach Program," The Brennan Center, accessed July 5, 2019: https://www.brennancenter.org/sites/default/files/analysis/FN%20120%20%28Saint%20Paul%20Police%20Dep%27t,%20Program%20Narrative--African%20Immigrant%20Muslim%20Coordinated%20Outreach%20Program%29.pdf.

59   Arun Kundnani, *The Muslims Are Coming! Islamophobia, Extremism, and the Domestic War on Terror* (New York: Verso, 2015), 212.

60   Armstrong, et al., *Characteristics*, 107–8.

61   Heather J Williams, Nathan Chandler, and Eric Robinson, *Trends in the Draw of Americans to Foreign Terrorist Organizations from 9/11 to Today* (Santa Monica, CA: RAND, 2018), ix.

62   Williams, Chandler, and Robinson, *Trends*, x.

63   Armstrong, et al., *Characteristics*, 108–9.

64   Armstrong, et al., *Characteristics*, 110.

65   Oliver Laughland, "Somalia Americans Divided as FBI Informant Testifies against Friends," *The Guardian*, May 27, 2016, https://www.theguardian.com/us-news/2016/may/27/somali-americans-trial-isis-fbi-informant-minneapolis.

66   Trevor Aaronson, *The Terror Factory: Inside the FBI's Manufactured War on Terrorism* (Brooklyn, NY: IG Publishing, 2014), 44.

67   Human Rights Watch, *Illusions of Justice*, 2.

68   Aaronson, *Terror Factory*, 211.

69   Stuart Hall, Charles Critcher, Tony Jefferson, John Clarke, and Brian Roberts, *Policing the Crisis: Mugging, the State, and Law and Order* (London: Macmillan, 1978), 38.

70   Peter Bergen, *United State of Jihad: Investigating America's Homegrown Terrorists* (New York: Crown Publishers, 2016), 17; and Williams, Chandler, and Robinson, *Trends*, 3.

71   Stephen Montemayor, "Appeals Court Upholds Sentences for Three Twin Cities Men in ISIS Case," *Star Tribune*, August 10, 2018, http://www.startribune.com/appeals-court-upholds-sentences-for-three-twin-cities-men-in-isis-trial/490564711.

72   United States Attorney's Office, District of Minnesota, "Twin Cities Somali Community Leaders, Government Officials and Private Partners Present Plan to Build Community Resilience," Department of Justice, accessed July 5, 2019, https://www.justice.gov/usao-mn/pr/twin-cities-somali-community-leaders-government-officials-and-private-partners-present.

73   "Grants Given to 6 Somali Groups in MN to Counter Violent Extremism," *Bring Me the News*, March 11, 2016, https://bringmethenews.com/news/grants-given-to-these-6-somali-groups-in-mn-to-counter-violent-extremism.

74   Ramla Bile, interview by the author, April 10, 2019.

75   Paul Gilroy, "Steppin' out of Babylon: Race, Class and Autonomy," in *The Empire Strikes Back: Race and Racism in 1970s Britain*, ed. Centre for Contemporary Cultural Studies (London: Hutchinson, 1982), 286.

76   Ayaan Dahir, interview by the author, April 12, 2019.

77   "Cedar Riverside Neighborhood," Minnesota Compass.

78   Amano Dube, interview by the author, July 9, 2018.

79   Burhan Israfael Isaaq, interview by the author, April 10, 2019.

80   Filsan Ibrahim, interview by author, July 7, 2018.

81   Star Tribune Editorial Board, "Countering Extremism in Minnesota: A Beautiful Goal, Barely Begun," *Star Tribune*, April 23, 2016, http://www.startribune.com/countering-extremism-in-minnesota-a-beautiful-goal-barely-begun/376797911.

82   "Cedar Riverside Neighborhood," Minnesota Compass.

83   Star Tribune Editorial Board, "Countering."

84   "Statement on the Somali Youth Development Fund Sources," Youthprise, accessed July 5, 2019, https://youthprise.org/wp-content/uploads/2015/12/SYDF-Statement-Final.pdf (site discontinued).

85   Bile, interview. Also, multiple attempts were made to interview representatives of Youthprise. No one responded.

86   Amano Dube, interview.

87   Burhan, interview.

88   Filsan, interview.

89   Ayaan Dahir, interview by author, March 23, 2018.

90   Su'ad Abdul Khabeer, *Muslim Cool: Race, Religion, and Hip Hop in the United States* (New York: New York University, 2016), 5.

91   Dahir, interview, March 23, 2018.

92   Judith Butler, *Precarious Life: The Powers of Mourning and Violence* (New York: Verso, 2004), xiv.

93   Butler, *Precarious*, xiv.

94   Jaylani Hussein, interview by author, April 16, 2018.

95   Hussein, interview.

96   Love, *Islamophobia and Racism*. 133.

97   Michelle Gross, interview by author, February 12, 2018.

98   Ramla Bile, Kadra Abdi, and anonymous person, interview by author, April 10, 2019.

99   This problematic relationship between the local #BLM and other organizations serves to reinforce the value for researchers of on-the-ground work that helps uncover the core activist organizations that might not receive the same press as #BLM but are nonetheless doing the heavy lifting on local campaigns.

100   Ayaan Dahir, interview, March 23, 2018; and Ahmad and Al-Wakeel, interview.

101   Judith Butler, *Frames of War: When Is Life Grievable?* (New York: Verso, 2010), 11.

102   Dahir, interview, March 23, 2018.

103   Editorial Board, "Countering Extremism In Minnesota: A Beautiful Goal, Barely Begun," *Star Tribune*, April 23, 2016, http://www.startribune.com/countering-extremism-in-minnesota/396170061.

104   Hall, et al., *Policing the Crisis*, 58.

105   Hall, et al., *Policing the Crisis*, 64.

106   Edward Said, *Covering Islam: How the Media and the Experts Determine How We See the Rest of the World* (New York: Vintage, 1997), 107.

107   Ahmad and Al-Wakeel, interview.

108   Dahir, interview, March 23, 2018.

109   Ahmad and Al-Wakeel, interview.

110   See Resisting Surveillance, accessed July 6, 2019, https://resistingsurveillance.org.

111   Niko Georgiades, interview by author, February 18, 2019. The discussion about Unicorn Riot is based upon this interview and the other times I have met with Niko to discuss Unicorn Riot, video activism, and organizing in general.

112   Chris Robé, *Breaking the Spell: A History of Anarchist Filmmakers, Videotape Guerrillas, and Digital Ninjas* (Oakland, CA: PM Press, 2017).

113   Vlad Teichberg, interview by author, November 23, 2010.

114   Flux Rostrum, written response to author's questions, April 23, 2011.

115   Erin Corbett, "Trump Defends His Comments on Deadly Charlottesville Rally," *Fortune*, April 26, 2019, https://fortune.com/2019/04/26/trump-defends-charlottesville-comments.

116   Eoin Higgins, "Confidential ICE Handbook Lays Out Paths for Investigators to Avoid Constitutional Challenges," *The Intercept*, February 23, 2018, https://theintercept.com/2018/02/23/ice-search-seizure-handbook-manual-secret.

117   Unicorn Riot, "Islamophobia & Anti-Blackness Confronted at #OurThreeBoys Rally," Unicorn Riot, March 2, 2016, https://unicornriot.ninja/2016/islamophobia-anti-blackness-confronted-ourthreeboys-rally.

118   Niko Georgiades, "Sharing Black History One Story at a Time: Festival Reaches 27 Years," Unicorn Riot, January 15, 2019, https://unicornriot.ninja/2019/sharing-black-history-one-story-at-a-time-festival-reaches-27-years.

119   Butler, *Frames of War*, 83.

120   Jack Healy and Matt Furber, "3 Somali-Americans Found Guilty of Trying to Join Islamic State," *New York Times*, June 3, 2016: https://www.nytimes.com/2016/06/04/us/somali-americans-verdict-minneapolis-isis.html.

121   Burhan, interview.

122   *The Grayzone*, "FBI Agents Attempt to 'Interview' Activist Burhan Mohamed," YouTube audio only, 2:56, August 29, 2016, https://www.youtube.com/watch?v=5Te9t3nDLUk.

123   Charlie Savage, "Loosening of FBI Rules Stirs Privacy Concerns," *New York Times*, October 28, 2009, https://www.nytimes.com/2009/10/29/us/29manual.html; Mike German, *Disrupt, Discredit and Divide: How the New FBI Damages Democracy* (New York: The New Press, 2019); and Reitman, "'I Helped.'"

124   Reitman, "'I Helped.'"

125   Joseph Sabroski, "Video of FBI Visit of Muslim Activist Highlights Disturbing Nature of Federal Counter-Extremism Programs," *AlterNet*, August 28, 2016, https://www.alternet.org/2016/08/video-fbi-visit-muslim-activist-highlights-disturbing-nature-federal-counter.

126   Charlie Savage and Mitch Smith, "Ex-Minneapolis FBI Agent is Sentenced to 4 Years in Leak Case," *The Intercept*, October 18, 2018, https://www.nytimes.com/2018/10/18/us/politics/terry-albury-fbi-sentencing.html.

127   Reitman, "'I Helped.'"

128   Alice Speri, "As FBI Whistleblower Terry Albury Faces Sentencing, His Lawyers Say He Was Motivated by Racism and Abuses at the Bureau," *The Intercept*, October 18, 2018, https://theintercept.com/2018/10/18/terry-albury-sentencing-fbi.

129   Reitman, "'I Helped.'"

130   Jamal Abdulahi, "Somalis in Minnesota: Still Misunderstood," *Star Tribune*, March 3, 2014, http://www.startribune.com/somalis-in-minnesota-still-misunderstood/247927831.

131   D.L. Mayfield, "Wrong Side of the Story: How Captain Phillips Affected a Somali Community," Christ Pop Culture, accessed February 1, 2023, https://christandpopculture.com/wrong-side-story-captain-phillips-somali-community.

132   Abdirizak Bihi, interview by author, April 15, 2019.

133   Ifrah Mansour, interview by author, April 10, 2019.

134   Barkhad Abdirahman, interview by author, April 12, 2019.

135   Eric Kohn, review of *Captain Phillips* by Dana Brunetti, Michael De Luca, Scott Rudin, Paul Greengrass, Billy Ray; and *A Hijacking* by Rene Ezra, Tomas Radoor, Tobias Lindholm, *Cineaste* 39, no. 1 (Winter 2013): 52.

136   Kohn, *Captain Phillips*.

137   Jim Walsh, "Does Feel-Good Captain Phillips Film Unfairly Depict Somali Plight?" *MinnPost*, October 16, 2013, https://www.minnpost.com/politics-policy/2013/10/does-feel-good-captain-phillips-film-unfairly-depict-somali-plight.

138   Jack Jones, "Inaccurate Quote," comment on Walsh, "Does Feel-Good," October 19, 2013.

139   Rosalind Kohls, "Regardless of Accuracy," comment on Walsh, "Does Feel-Good," October 16, 2013.

140   Daniel Kreps, "K'naan, Kathryn Bigelow Team for Jihadi Recruitment HBO Series," *Rolling Stone,* December 12, 2015, https://www.rollingstone.com/music/music-news/knaan-kathryn-bigelow-team-for-jihadi-recruitment-hbo-series-173464.

141   Lesley Goldberg, "Kathryn Bigelow Prepping Jihadi Recruitment Drama for HBO," *Hollywood Reporter*, December 11, 2015, https://www.hollywoodreporter.com/live-feed/kathryn-bigelow-prepping-jihadi-recruitment-848170.

142   Idil Osman, *Media, Diaspora and the Somali Conflict* (New York: Palgrave Macmillan, 2017), 85.

143   Adali, reply to "K'naan making MN Jihadi recruitment show for HBO," SomaliNet, December 22, 2015, https://www.somalinet.com/forums/viewtopic.php?f=18&t=371792.

144 Cherine, reply to "K'naan making MN Jihadi recruitment show for HBO," SomaliNet, December 22, 2015, https://www.somalinet.com/forums/viewtopic. php?f=18&t=371792&start=15.

145 Sara Ahmed, *The Cultural Politics of Emotion* (Edinburgh: Edinburgh University Press, 2014), 212.

146 Norm Coleman, "On Battling Recruitment in the Land of 10,000 Terrorists," *Star Tribune*, April 23, 2015, http://www.startribune.com/norm-coleman-on-battling-recruitment-in-the-land-of-10-000-terrorists/301153401.

147 Ben Jacobs and Alan Yuhas, "Somali Migrants Are 'Disaster' for Minnesota, Says Donald Trump," *The Guardian*, November 7, 2016, https://www.theguardian.com/ us-news/2016/nov/06/donald-trump-minnesota-somali-migrants-isis.

148 Barkhad, interview.

149 Burhan, interview.

150 InaSamaale, reply to "HBO Cancels K'naan Mogadishu, Minnesota Show," SomaliNet, September 4, 2017, https://www.somalinet.com/forums/viewtopic. php?f=18&t=386923&start=15.

151 "Is K'naan Selling Out the Somali Community?" YouTube video, September 25, 2016, (no longer available online; the author will supply a copy upon request).

152 Integration TV, "HBO: Who Controls the Somali Narrative?" YouTube video, 16:47, December 10, 2016, https://www.youtube.com/watch?v=01A1AzEOaHU.

153 Lucinda Winter, interview by author, July 9, 2019.

154 I reached out to HBO and K'naan for interviews. Neither answered any of my requests.

155 Greg M. Smith, "Blocking 'Blockade': Partisan Protest, Popular Debate, and Encapsulated Texts," *Cinema Journal* 36, no.1 (Autumn 1996): 20.

156 Avi Santo, "Para-Television and Discourses of Distinction," in *It's Not TV: Watching HBO in the Post-Television Era*, ed. Marc Leverette, Brain L. Ott, and Cara Louise Buckley (New York: Routledge, 2008), 24.

157 Ayaan Dahir, interview by author, April 12, 2019.

158 Some examples are "Sawina Sentenced to 39 Years for Dinkytown Shooting," Fox 9 Minneapolis-St. Paul, June 12, 2017, http://www.fox9.com/news/sawina-sentenced-to-39-years-for-dinkytown-shooting; Margaret Talbot, "The Story of a Hate Crime," *New Yorker*, June 15, 2015 https://www.newyorker.com/magazine/2015/06/22/ the-story-of-a-hate-crime; and "Indiana Man Charged in Muslim Man's Road Rage Shooting Death," *CBS News*, February 22, 2019, https://www.cbsnews.com/news/ dustin-passarelli-indiana-man-charged-road-rage-shooting-death-muslim-man-zahra-ayoubi-2019–02–22.

159 Burhan, interview.

160 Melena Ryzik, "Can Television Be Fair to Muslims?" *New York Times*, November 30, 2016, https://www.nytimes.com/2016/11/30/arts/television/can-television-be-fair-to-muslims.html.

161 Dahir, interview, April 12, 2019.

162 Elizabeth Wagmeister, "HBO Sets Cast for 'Mogadishu, Minnesota' Plot," *Variety*, September 29, 2016, https://variety.com/2016/tv/news/mogadishu-minnesota-cast-hbo-pilot-1201873269.

163 Mahmoud Mire, "The Problem with the Upcoming HBO Drama 'Mogadishu, Minnesota," *HuffPost*, updated January 13, 2017, https://www.huffpost.com/entry/

the-problem-with-the-upcoming-hbo-drama-mogadishu_b_5873f6b6e4b0a5e60
0a78dbd.

164   Arraweelo, "What Happened When K'naan Came to Cedar," *Maandeeq*, September 13, 2016, http://themaandeeq.com/what-happened-when-knaan-came-to-cedar (site discontinued).

165   Ayaan Dahir, "Despite Community Rejection of HBO TV Series, Public Officials Support the Ongoing Production," *Twin Cities Daily Planet*, October 13, 2016, https://www.tcdailyplanet.net/despite-community-rejection-of-hbo-tv-series-public-officials-support-the-ongoing-production.

166   Imran Siddiquee, "Why Are Brown Men So Infatuated with White Women Onscreen?" *BuzzFeed*, June 24, 2017, https://www.buzzfeednews.com/article/imransiddiquee/why-are-brown-men-so-infatuated-with-white-women-onscreen; Sopan Deb, "*The Big Sick*, South Asian Identity and Me," *New York Times*, July 23, 2017, https://www.nytimes.com/2017/07/23/movies/the-big-sick-south-asian-identity-and-marriage.html?login=email&auth=login-email.

167   Despite repeated attempts, K'naan never responded to my interview requests.

168   Filsan, interview.

169   Ramla, interview.

170   Winter, interview.

171   Ramla, interview.

172   Burhan, interview.

173   Integration TV, "HBO: Who Controls the Somali Narrative," YouTube video, December 10, 2016, https://www.youtube.com/watch?v=01A1AzEOaHU.

174   All the Rage News, "K'naan at Cedar Community Event Leaves as Protestors Demonstrate," YouTube video, 3:58, September 11, 2016, https://www.youtube.com/watch?v=uhU_LrMDobY.

175   Mansour, interview.

176   Associated Press, "HBO's Somali-American Family Drama Filming in Minneapolis (Except Here)," *Twin Cities Pioneer Press*, October 6, 2016, https://www.twincities.com/2016/10/06/hbos-request-to-film-show-in-minneapolis-building-rejected/; Allie Shah, "Public Housing Residents Object to On-Site Filming of HBO Series 'Mogadishu, Minnesota,'" *Star Tribune*, October 6, 2016: http://m.startribune.com/public-housing-resident-object-to-on-site-filming-of-mogadishu-minnesota/396095281.

177   Dahir, interview, April 12, 2019.

178   Mire, "The Problem."

179   Killakam, "Protest Sparked Over K'naan's HBO Series 'Mogadishu, Minnesota,'" OkayAfrica, September 15, 2016, https://www.okayafrica.com/knaan-hbo-mogadishu-minnesota-protests.

180   Chris O'Connor, "Protesters Arrive Shortly After Mogadishu, MN Wraps," YouTube video, October 28, 2016, https://www.youtube.com/watch?v=fWTiLOsb4xw (video unavailable).

181   Dahir, interview, March 23, 2018.

182   Ramla, interview.

183   Neal Justin, "The Hopes of Minnesota's Film Industry Ride on 'Mogadishu,'" *Star Tribune*, December 27, 2016, http://www.startribune.com/hopes-of-minnesota-s-film-industry-ride-on-mogadishu/408171916.

184 Vicki Mayer, *Almost Hollywood, Nearly New Orleans: The Lure of the Local Film Economy* (Berkeley: University of California Press, 2017), 2.

185 Sheila Regan, "Snowbate: The Vital Program Keeping Filmmaking Alive in Minnesota," The Growler, June 28, 2016, https://growlermag.com/snowbate-the-vital-program-keeping-filmmaking-alive-in-minnesota.

186 Mayer, *Almost Hollywood,* 57.

187 Robert Tannenwald, "State Film Subsidies: Not Much Bang for Too Many Bucks," Center on Budget and Policy Priorities, December 9, 2010, https://www.cbpp.org/research/state-film-subsidies-not-much-bang-for-too-many-bucks.

188 Integration TV, "Hanging Out with K'naan at the HBO Set," YouTube video, 13:05, October 3, 2016, https://www.youtube.com/watch?v=ZrK7hcizVAk. Similar lines are used in the puff piece Jeff Baenen, "HBO Show Would Tell the Somali Immigrant Experience, with Minneapolis Backdrop," *Twin Cities Pioneer Press*, November 1, 2016, https://www.twincities.com/2016/11/01/hbo-show-would-tell-the-somali-immigrant-experience-with-minneapolis-backdrop.

189 Dahir, interview, March 23, 2018.

190 Tennewald, "State Film Subsidies," 6.

191 Nina F. O'Brien and Christianne J. Lane, "Effects of Economic Incentives in the American Film Industry: An Ecological Approach," *Regional Studies* 52, no. 6 (2017): 873.

192 For valuable links to multiple 2019 studies regarding the problems with film tax credits, see Alex Muresianu, "Deceptive Data Make Georgia's Film Tax Credit Program Look Less Wasteful," *Reason* July 1, 2019, https://reason.com/2019/07/01/deceptive-data-make-georgias-film-tax-credit-program-look-less-wasteful.

193 Amelia Cruver, Matt Hauck, Micah Intermill, Leah Lundquist, and John Meyer, "Minnesota's Film and TV Future: Cultivating a Healthy Ecosystem," (master's thesis, University of Minnesota, 2012), 21.

194 Somali Minnesotans, "Ask HBO to Pull Drama Stereotyping Somali Minnesotans," petition on Change.org, accessed July 9, 2019, https://www.change.org/p/ask-hbo-to-pull-drama-stereotyping-somali-minnesotans.

195 All the Rage News, "K'naan at Cedar."

196 Filsan, interview.

197 Henry Jenkins, "Youth Voice, Media, and Political Engagement: Introducing Core Concepts," in *By Any Media Necessary: The New Youth Activism,* ed. Henry Jenkins, Sangita Shresthova, Liana Gamber-Thompson, Neta Kligler-Vilenchik, and Arely M. Zimmerman (New York: New York University Press, 2016), 26–27.

198 All the Rage News, "K'naan at Cedar."

199 Comment by "mahadalla" on "HBO Cancels K'naan's Mogadishu, Minnesota Show," September 4, 2017, SomaliNet Forums, https://www.somalinet.com/forums/viewtopic.php?f=18&t=386923&start=15. "HG" stands for Habar Gidir, a subclan of the Hawiye. Jerberti is a subclan of the Darod. There are four major Somali clans in Africa: Hawiye, Darod, Darod, and Isaaq. They control most of the socio-economic aspects of local regions within Africa.

200 Benkler, Faris, and Roberts, *Network Propaganda,* 105–44.

201 All the Rage News, "K'naan at Cedar."

202 All the Rage News, "K'naan at Cedar."

203 Nick Couldry, "The Myth of 'Us': Digital Networks, Political Change and the Production of Collectivity," *Information, Communication & Society* 18, no. 6 (2015): 622.

204 Osman, *Media, Diaspora*, 87.

205 Beatrice Dupuy, "HBO's Decision Not to Move Forward with 'Mogadishu, Minnesota' Draws Range of Local Reaction," *Star Tribune*, September 2, 2017, http://www.startribune.com/hbo-no-longer-moving-forward-with-tv-show-on-somali-life/442521993.

206 Sam Schaust, "Can Minnesota Reel in Hollywood Money?" *MinnPost*, January 8, 2016, https://www.minnpost.com/twin-cities-business/2016/01/can-minnesota-reel-hollywood-money.

207 Rod Hubbard, "Making movies in Minnesota May Get Boost from Tax Credit," Minnesota House of Representatives, March 28, 2019, https://www.house.leg.state.mn.us/SessionDaily/Story/13842.

208 Cruver, et al., *Minnesota's Film*, 7.

209 Although production of the series was halted in Minneapolis, *Mogadishu, Minnesota* has been listed on IMDB as a completed TV movie as of January 4, 2019. This suggests the possibility that HBO may yet find a way to circumvent community objections and release the movie in some form.

210 David James, *Allegories of Cinema: American Film in the 1960s* (Princeton, NJ: Princeton University Press, 1989), 5.

211 Jessica Lussenhop, "*A Stray*: Finding and Filming the Real Somali Immigrant Experience," *BBC News Magazine*, October 27, 2016, https://www.bbc.com/news/world-us-canada-37735113?ocid=socialflow_gplus.

212 Cat D. Hyeon, "Portrait of an Artist: Musa Syeed," *Harvard Crimson,* December 4, 2018.

213 Musa Syeed, interview by author, September 28, 2018.

214 Barkhad, interview.

215 Sangita Shresthova, "Between Storytelling and Surveillance: The Precarious Public of American Muslim Youth," in Jenkins, et al., *By Any Media Necessary*, 168.

216 Hyeon, "Portrait."

217 Shresthova, "Between Storytelling," 151.

218 Stuart Hall, "New Ethnicities," in *Black British Cultural Studies: A Reader*, ed. Houston A. Baker, Jr., Manthia Diawara, and Ruth H. Lindeborg (Chicago: University of Chicago Press, 1996): 164.

219 She periodically punctuates her thoughts with a contagious laugh and can't help but view life from a compassionate yet absurdist lens. After having recently participated at a rally at the state capitol to pass legislation that would allow undocumented residents to obtain a driver's license, she reflects, "I definitely feel like politics can be a place where, you know, souls go to die."

220 Julio García Espinosa, "For an Imperfect Cinema," in *Film and Theory: An Anthology*, ed. Robert Stam and Toby Miller (Malden, MA: Blackwell, 2000), 291.

221 I have written about *Muslim Youth Voices* in "Discovering Muslim Youth Voices: The Politics of Visibility in the Age of Islamophobia," *Cineaste* 44, no. 4 (Fall 2019): 32–36.

222 Stephen Gong, interview by author, February 19, 2019.

223 *Screened*, Muslim Youth Voices, 0:2:36, December 10, 2018, https://www.pbs.org/video/screened-qipcu5.

224 *Imagination*, Muslim Youth Voices, 0:3:9, December 10, 2018, https://www.pbs.org/video/imagination-nn3vyz.

225 *A Stray* has a snippet of this performance within it as well but from a different camera angle.

226 Hall, "New Ethnicities," 164.

227 Integration TV, "HBO."

228 Fernando Solanas and Octavio Getino, "Towards a Third Cinema," in Stam and Miller *Film and Theory*, 284.

229 Solanas and Getino, "Third Cinema," 284.

230 Solanas and Getino, "Third Cinema," 283.

231 Georgiades, interview.

232 Cora Currier, "Revealed: The FBI's Secret Methods for Recruiting Informants at the Border," *The Intercept*, October 5, 2016, https://theintercept.com/2016/10/05/fbi-secret-methods-for-recruiting-informants-at-the-border.

233 Dahir, interview, April 12, 2019.

234 Boundaoui's work with communities ultimately resulted in the Inverse Surveillance Project in 2022. For more information on the project, see Tashima Khan, "A Community Art Project Turns the Lens Back on Government Surveillance," *Next City*, July 6, 2022, https://nextcity.org/urbanist-news/a-community-art-project-turns-the-lens-back-on-government-surveillance.

235 Stuart Hall, "Notes on Deconstructing 'the Popular,'" in *Essential Essays, Vol. 1: Foundations of Cultural Studies*, ed. David Morley, (Durham, NC: Duke University Press, 2019), 509.

236 Dahir quoted in Arraweelo, "What Happened When K'naan Came to Cedar," *Maandeeq*, September 13, 2016, http://themaandeeq.com/what-happened-when-knaan-came-to-cedar/ (site discontinued).

Coda

1 Sarah Mervosh, "The Pandemic Hurt These Students the Most," *New York Times*, July 28, 2021, https://www.nytimes.com/2021/07/28/us/covid-schools-at-home-learning-study.html.

2 Molly Kinder and Martha Ross, "Reopening America: Low-Wage Workers Have Suffered Badly from COVID-19 So Policymakers Should Focus on Equity," Brookings Institute, June 23, 2020, https://www.brookings.edu/research/reopening-america-low-wage-workers-have-suffered-badly-from-covid-19-so-policymakers-should-focus-on-equity.

3 Mike Dorning and Bloomberg, "At Least 59,000 Meat Workers Got COVID-19 in Pandemic's First Year, Report Says," *Fortune*. October 27, 2021, https://fortune.com/2021/10/27/at-least-59000-meat-workers-got-covid-19-in-pandemic-first-year.

4 Taylor Telford, Kimberly Kindy, and Jacob Bogage, "Trump Orders Meat Plants to Stay Open in Pandemic," *Washington Post*, April 29, 2020, https://www.washingtonpost.com/business/2020/04/28/trump-meat-plants-dpa.

5 Kevin Weise, "Amazon's Profit Soars 220 Percent as Pandemic Drives Shopping Online," *New York Times*, April 20, 2021, https://www.nytimes.com/2021/04/29/technology/amazons-profits-triple.html.

6 Mike Isaac, "Facebook's Profit Surges 101 Percent on Strong Ad Sales," *New York Times*, July 28, 2021, https://www.nytimes.com/2021/07/28/business/facebook-q2-earnings.html.

7   Shoshana Zuboff, *The Age of Surveillance Capitalism: The Fight for a Human Future at the New Frontier of Power* (New York: Public Affairs, 2019), 449. Also see the film, *The Social Dilemma* (2022).

8   Zuboff, *Age*, 10.

9   Natasha Singer, "The Hot New Covid Tech is Wearable and Constantly Tracks You," *New York Times*, November 15, 2020, https://www.nytimes.com/2020/11/15/technology/virus-wearable-tracker-privacy.html.

10   Candace Bernd, "Pandemic Policing is Expanding the Use of Surveillance Technology," *Truthout*, May 14, 2020: https://truthout.org/articles/pandemic-policing-is-expanding-the-use-of-surveillance-technology.

11   Naomi Klein, "Screen New Deal," *The Intercept*, May 8, 2020, https://theintercept.com/2020/05/08/andrew-cuomo-eric-schmidt-coronavirus-tech-shock-doctrine.

12   Bernd, "Pandemic Policing"; and Meka Boyle, "Interest in Community Police Watch Training Soars as Courses Go Online," *San Francisco Public Press*, September 2, 2020, https://truthout.org/articles/pandemic-policing-is-expanding-the-use-of-surveillance-technology.

13   Larry Buchanan, Quoctrung Bui, and Jugal K. Patel, "Black Lives Matter May Be the Largest Movement in U.S. History," *New York Times*, July 3, 2020, https://www.nytimes.com/interactive/2020/07/03/us/george-floyd-protests-crowd-size.html?.

14   Jennifer Chudy and Hakeem Jefferson, "Support for Black Lives Matter Surged Last Year. Did It Last?" *New York Times*, May 22, 2021, https://www.nytimes.com/2021/05/22/opinion/blm-movement-protests-support.html.

15   Cassie King, interview by author, July 20, 2020.

16   Leto Sapunar and Jordan Miller, "Animal Rights Activists Found Not Guilty on All Charges after Two Piglets Were Taken from Circle Four Farms in Utah," *Salt Lake Tribune*, October 8, 2022, https://www.sltrib.com/news/2022/10/08/animal-rights-activists-charged.

17   Robert Rodriguez, "Former *Baywatch* actress Alexandra Paul 'Not Guilty' in Foster Farms Case in Merced," *Fresno Bee*, March 17, 2023, https://www.fresnobee.com/news/local/article273295350.html.

18   See Angela Nagle, *Kill All Normies: Online Culture Wars from 4Chan and Tumblr to Trump and the Alt-Right* (Washington: Zero Books, 2017).

19   Kevin Roose, "The Making of a YouTube Radical," *New York Times*, June 9, 2019, https://www.nytimes.com/interactive/2019/06/08/technology/youtube-radical.html.

20   Dan Barry, Alan Feuer, and Matthew Rosenberg, "90 Seconds of Rage," *New York Times*, October 16, 2021, https://www.nytimes.com/interactive/2021/10/16/us/capitol-riot.html; Bob Woodward and Robert Costa, *Peril* (New York: Simon & Schuster, 2021).

21   DeSantis, at the time of writing, has not officially announced he is running for president. But it is a well-known secret that it will be announced in the near future.

22   Ryan Devereaux, "Leaked Documents Show Police Knew Far-Right Extremists Were the Real Threat at Protests, not 'Antifa,'" *The Intercept*, July 16, 2020: https://theintercept.com/2020/07/15/george-floyd-protests-police-far-right-antifa.

23   National Security Council, *National Strategy for Countering Domestic Terrorism*, June 2021, https://www.whitehouse.gov/wp-content/uploads/2021/06/National-Strategy-for-Countering-Domestic-Terrorism.pdf.

24   Andrea Miller and Lisa Bhungalia, "The Fungible Terrorist: Abject Whiteness, Domestic Terrorism, and the Multicultural Security State," *Small Wars and Insurgencies* 33, no. 25: 902–25.

25   See Defend the Atlanta Forest, https://defendtheatlantaforest.org.

26   Alex Binder, "Manuel 'Tortuguita' Terán's Independent Autopsy Report Released at Press Conference," Unicorn Riot, March 13, 2023: https://unicornriot.ninja/2023/manuel-tortuguita-terans-independent-autopsy-report-released-at-press-conference.

Selected Bibliography

Aaronson, Trevor. *The Terror Factory: Inside the FBI's Manufactured War on Terrorism.* Brooklyn, NY: IG Publishing, 2014.

Adams, Carol J. *The Sexual Politics of Meat: A Feminist-Vegetarian Critical Theory.* New York: Bloomsbury, 2015.

Aguayo, Angela. *Documentary Resistance: Social Change and Participatory Media.* Oxford: Oxford University Press, 2019.

Ahmed, Sara. *The Cultural Politics of Emotion.* Edinburgh: Edinburgh University Press, 2014.

Baron, Jaimie. *Reuse, Misuse, Abuse: The Ethics of Audiovisual Appropriation.* New Brunswick, NJ: Rutgers University Press, 2021.

Bayoumi, Moustafa. *How Does It Feel to Be a Problem? Being Young and Arab in America.* New York: Penguin, 2008.

Bennett, W. Lance, and Alexandra Segerberg. *The Logic of Connective Action Digital Media and the Personalization of Contentious Politics.* New York: Cambridge University Press, 2013.

Best, Steven, and Anthony J. Nocella II., eds. *Terrorists or Freedom Fighters? Reflection on the Liberation of Animals.* New York: Lantern Books, 2004.

Bloom, Joshua. *Black against Empire: The History and Politics of the Black Panther Party.* Berkeley: University of California Press, 2016.

Browne, Simone. *Dark Matters: On The Surveillance of Blackness.* Durham, NC: Duke University Press, 2015.

Butler, Judith. *Frames of War: When Is Life Grievable?* New York: Verso, 2010.

———. *Notes Toward A Performative Theory of Assembly.* Cambridge, MA: Harvard University Press, 2015.

———. *Precarious Life: The Powers of Mourning and Violence.* New York: Verso, 2004.

Camp, Jordan T. *Incarcerating the Crisis: Freedom Struggles and the Rise of the Neoliberal State.* Berkeley: University of California Press, 2016.

Canella, Gino. "Racialized Surveillance: Activist Media and the Policing of Black Bodies," *Communication, Culture & Critique* (July 27, 2018): 1–21.

Chavez, Leo R. *The Latino Threat: Constructing Immigrants, Citizens and the Nation.* Stanford, CA: Stanford University Press, 2013.

Cornell, Andrew. *Unruly Equality: U.S. Anarchism in the Twentieth Century*. Berkeley: University of California Press, 2016.

Costanza-Chock, Sacha. *Out of the Shadows, Into the Streets! Transmedia Organizing and the Immigrant Rights Movement*. Cambridge, MA: MIT Press, 2014.

Cowie, Elizabeth. "The Spectacle of Actuality." In *Collecting Visible Evidence*, edited by Jane M. Gaines and Michael Renov, 19–45. Minneapolis: University of Minnesota Press, 1999.

Daulatzai, Sohail. *Black Star, Crescent Moon: The Muslim International and Black Freedom beyond America*. Minneapolis: University of Minnesota Press, 2012.

Elmer, Greg, and Andy Opel. *Preempting Dissent: The Politics of an Inevitable Future*. Winnipeg: Arbeiter Ring Publishing, 2008.

Epstein, Barbara. *Political Protest and Cultural Revolution: Nonviolence Direct Action in the 1970s and 1980s*. Berkeley: University of California Press, 1991.

Fan, Mary D. *Camera Power: Proof, Policing, Privacy, and Audiovisual Big Data*. Cambridge: Cambridge University Press, 2019.

Fiske, John. "Surveilling the City: Whiteness, the Black Man and Democratic Totalitarianism," *Theory, Culture & Society* 15, no. 2 (1998): 67–88.

Foucault, Michel. *The Birth of Biopolitics, Lectures at the College de France, 1978–1979*. Translated by Arnold I. Davidson. New York: Palgrave Macmillan, 2008.

———. *Discipline and Punish*. Translated by Alan Sheridan. New York: Vintage Books, 1977.

———. *The Punitive Society, Lectures at the College de France, 1972–1973*, Translated by Graham Burchell. Picador: New York, 2015.

———. *Security, Territory, Population, Lectures at the College de France, 1977–1978*. Translated by Graham Burchell. New York: Picador, 2007.

Gerbaudo, Paolo. *Tweets and the Streets: Social Media and Contemporary Activism*. London: Pluto Press, 2012.

German, Mike. *Disrupt, Discredit and Divide: How the New FBI Damages Democracy*. New York: The New Press, 2019.

Gilroy, Paul. *The Black Atlantic: Modernity and Double Consciousness*. Cambridge, MA: Harvard University Press, 1993.

———. "Steppin' Out of Babylon: Race, Class and Autonomy." In *The Empire Strikes Back: Race and Racism in '70s Britain*, edited by the Centre for Contemporary Cultural Studies, 276–314. London: Hutchinson, 1982.

Gorski, Paul, Stacy Lopresti-Goodman, and Dallas Rising, "'Nobody's Paying Me to Cry': The Causes of Activist Burnout in United States Animal Rights Activists," *Social Movement Studies* 18, no. 3 (2019): 364–80.

Gruen, Lori. *Entangled Empathy: An Alternative Ethic for Our Relationships with Animals*. New York: Lantern Books, 2015.

Hall, Stuart. *The Fateful Triangle: Race, Ethnicity, Nation*, edited by Kobena Mercer. Cambridge, MA: Harvard University Press, 2017.

———. "New Ethnicities." In *Black British Cultural Studies: A Reader*, edited by Houston A. Baker Jr., Manthia Diawara, and Ruth H. Lindeborg, 163–72 Chicago: University of Chicago Press, 1996.

———. "Notes on Deconstructing 'the Popular.'" In *Essential Essays, Vol. 1: Foundations of Cultural Studies*, edited by David Morley, 347–61. Durham, NC: Duke University Press, 2019.

Hall, Stuart, Charles Critcher, Tony Jefferson, John Clarke, and Brian Roberts, *Policing the Crisis: Mugging, the State, and Law and Order*. London: Macmillan, 1978.

Harper, A. Breeze, ed. *Sistah Vegan: Black Female Vegans Speak on Food, Identity, Health, and Society*. New York: Lantern Books, 2010.

Harvey, David. *A Brief History of Neoliberalism*. Oxford: Oxford University Press, 2005.

Hayes, Ben. "The Surveillance-Industrial Complex." In *Routledge Handbook of Surveillance Studies*, edited by Kirstie Ball, Kevin D. Haggerty, and David Lyon, 167–75. New York: Routledge, 2012.

Hermes, Kris. *Crashing the Party: Legacies and Lessons from the RNC 2000*. Oakland, CA: PM Press, 2015.

Hillyard, Paddy. *Suspect Community: People's Experience of the Prevention of Terrorism Act in Britain*. London: Pluto Press, 1993.

Hinton, Elizabeth. *America on Fire: The Untold History of Police Violence and Black Rebellion Since the 1960s*. New York: Liveright, 2021.

———. *From the War on Poverty to the War on Crime: The Making of Mass Incarceration in America*. Cambridge, MA: Harvard University Press, 2016.

Hudson, Dale, and Patricia R. Zimmermann. *Thinking Through Digital Media: Transnational Environments and Locative Places*. New York: Palgrave Macmillan, 2015.

Jenkins, Henry, Sangita Shresthova, Liana Gamber-Thompson, Neta Kligler-Vilenchik, and Arely M. Zimmerman. *By Any Media Necessary: The New Youth Activism*. New York: New York University Press, 2016.

Juris, Jeffrey S. "Reflections on #Occupy Everywhere: Social Media, Public Space, and Emerging Logics of Aggregation." *American Ethnologist* 19, no. 2 (2012): 259–79.

Kemmerer, Lisa. "Evidence of Sexism and Male Privilege in the Animal Liberation/Rights Movement." *Between the Species* 21, no. 1 (Spring 2018): 243–86.

Khabeer, Su'ad Abdul. *Muslim Cool: Race, Religion, and Hip Hop in the United States*. New York: New York University, 2016.

Kheel, Marti. "Direct Action and the Heroic Ideal: An Ecofeminist Critique." In *Igniting a Revolution: Voices in Defense of the Earth*, edited by Steven Best and Anthony J. Nocella, II, 306–18 Oakland, CA: AK Press, 2006.

Klein, Naomi. "Screen New Deal." *The Intercept*, May 8, 2020, https://theintercept.com/2020/05/08/andrew-cuomo-eric-schmidt-coronavirus-tech-shock-doctrine/.

Ko, Aph, and Syl Ko. *Aphro-ism: Essays on Pop Culture and Black Veganism from Two Sisters*. New York: Lantern Books, 2017.

Kumar, Deepa. *Islamophobia and the Politics of Empire*. Chicago: Haymarket Books, 2012.

Kundnani, Arun. *The Muslims Are Coming! Islamophobia, Extremism, and the Domestic War on Terror*. New York: Verso, 2015.

Lazzarato, Maurizio. *The Making of the Indebted Man*. Translated by Joshua David Jordan. Los Angeles: Semiotext(e), 2012.

Love, Erik. *Islamophobia and Racism in America*. New York: New York University, 2018.

Marceau, Justin. *Beyond Cages: Animal Law and Criminal Punishment*. Cambridge: Cambridge University Press, 2019.

Mayer, Vicki. *Almost Hollywood, Nearly New Orleans: The Lure of the Local Film Economy*. Berkeley: University of California Press, 2017.

McQuade, Brendan. *Pacifying the Homeland: Intelligence Fusion and Mass Supervision*. Berkeley: University of California Press, 2019.

Mogul, Joey L., Andrea J. Ritchie, and Kay Whitlock. *Queer (In)justice: The Criminalization of LGBT People in the United States*. Boston: Beacon Press, 2011.

Moskowitz, Peter. *How to Kill a City: Gentrification, Inequality, and the Fight for the Neighborhood*. New York: Nation Books, 2017.

Moss, Jeremiah. *Vanishing New York: How a Great City Lost Its Soul*. New York: Dey St., 2017.

Neocleous, Mark. *A Critical Theory of Police Power*. New York: Verso, 2021.

Newkirk, Ingrid. *Free the Animals: The Amazing True Story of the Animal Liberation Front in North America*. New York: Lantern Books, 2012.

Nichols, Bill. *Representing Reality: Issues and Concepts in Documentary*. Bloomington: Indiana University Press, 1991.

Noriega, Chon A., and Ana M. Lopez, eds. *The Ethnic Eyes: Latino Media Arts*. Minneapolis: University of Minnesota Press, 1996.

Osman, Idil. *Media, Diaspora and the Somali Conflict*. New York: Palgrave Macmillan, 2017.

Pachirat, Timothy. *Every Twelve Seconds: Industrialized Slaughter and the Politics of Sight*. New Haven, CT: Yale University Press, 2011.

Parenti, Christian. *Lockdown America: Police and Prisons in the Age of Crisis*. New York: Verso, 2000.

Paxton, Pete, with Gene Stone. *Rescue Dogs: Where They Come From, Why They Act the Way They Do, and How to Love Them Well*. New York: TarcherPerigee, 2019.

Pickering, Leslie James, ed. *Conspiracy to Riot in Furtherance of Terrorism: The Collective Autobiography of the RNC 8*. Portland, OR: Arissa Media Group, 2011.

Poell, Thomas, and José van Dijck, "Social Media and Activist Communication." In *The Routledge Companion to Alternative and Community Media*, edited by Chris Atton, 527–37. New York: Routledge.

Potter, Will. *Green Is the New Red: An Insider's Account of a Social Movement under Siege*. San Francisco: City Lights Books, 2011.

Rancière, Jacques. *Dissensus: On Politics and Aesthetics*. Edited and translated by Steven Corcoran. New York: Bloomsbury, 2015.

Robé, Chris. *Breaking the Spell: A History of Anarchist Filmmakers, Videotape Guerrillas, and Digital Ninjas*. Oakland, CA: PM Press, 2017.

Runkle, Nathan, with Gene Stone. *Mercy for Animals: One Man's Quest to Inspire Compassion and Improve the Lives of Farm Animals*. New York: Avery, 2017.

Said, Edward W. *Covering Islam: How the Media and the Experts Determine How We See the Rest of the World*. New York: Vintage, 1997.

Snowdon, Peter. *The People Are Not an Image: Vernacular Video after the Arab Spring*. New York: Verso, 2020.

Wacquant, Loïc. *Punishing the Poor: The Neoliberal Government of Social Insecurity*. Durham, NC: Duke University Press, 2009.

Williams, Kristian. *Our Enemies in Blue: Police and Power in America*. Oakland, CA: AK Press, 2015.

Wolfson, Todd. *Digital Rebellion: The Birth of the Cyber Left*. Chicago: University of Illinois Press, 2014.

Wood, Lesley J. *Crisis and Control: The Militarization of Protest Policing*. London: Pluto Press, 2014.

Young, Cynthia A. *Soul Power: Culture, Radicalism, and the Making of a U.S. Third World Left*. Durham, NC: Duke University Press, 2006.

Zimmermann, Patricia. *States of Emergency: Documentaries, Wars, Democracies*. Minneapolis: University of Minnesota Press, 2000.

Zuboff, Shoshana. *The Age of Surveillance Capitalism: The Fight for a Human Future at the New Frontier of Power*. New York: Public Affairs, 2019.

Index

Page numbers in *italic* refer to illustrations. "Passim" (literally "scattered") indicates intermittent discussion of a topic over a cluster of pages.

Aaronson, Trevor, 114

Abdi, Barkhad, 221

Abdi, Iqbal, 225, 231, 236

Abdi, Kadra, 207, 208, 256

Abdikadir, Roodo: *Imagination*, 249

Abdirahman, Barkhad, 221, 224, 230–31, 240, 242, 246, 252

Abdulahi, Jamal, 219

ableism, 85

absent referent: meat-eating and, 54, 63

"accusatory gaze" (Baron), 27

ACLU, 15, 154, 157

Adams, Carol J., 54, 66, 81, 82–83, 84

African Immigrant Muslim Coordinated Outreach Program, 196

agents provocateurs. *See* informers and agents provocateurs

"ag-gag" laws, 20, 59, 62–63

agriculture, industrial. *See* factory farms and farming

Ahmad, Fatema, 211–12

Ahmed, Sara, 75, 163, 223

Alba, Vicente "Panama," 134

Albury, Terry, 218–19

ALF. *See* Animal Liberation Front (ALF)

Ali, Ishraq, 188

Ali, Muhammad, 249

Allen, Taisha, 169

Al-Shabaab, 196, 219

Al-Wakeel, Shannon, 192, 209, 212, 256

Amazon, *10*, 261–62

American Civil Liberties Union. *See* ACLU

Animal Enterprise Protection Act (AEPA), 30, 39–40, 100

Animal Enterprise Terrorism Act (AETA), 39–40, 100

Animal Equality: open rescues, 36, 66; VR, 74, 76–77; *With My Own Eyes*, 80–81

American Legislative Exchange Council (ALEC), 39

Animal Liberation Front (ALF), 23, 33–40 passim

Animal Liberation Victoria (ALV), 36–37

American Meat Institute: Glass Walls Project, 63–66

anarchists: fear of, 96, 110; labeling and demonization of, 8, 93, 96, 97, 109, 120, 124

Animal Outlook, 42, 43; *Beyond Lies*, 52

animal welfare and animal rights activism, 17–87 passim, 263–64;

"open rescue," 21, 36, 66–71 passim, 79, 263, 264; punk rock and 273n68
anti-Muslim sentiment and action. *See* Islamophobia
Atchison, Jimmy, 177
Atlanta, 176–78 passim, 266–67

Bailitz, Brian, 114–15
Baird, John, 121
Bandele, Monifa, 134, 169
Baron, Jaimie, 25, 26, 27
Bartosiewicz, Petra, 91
Bashir, Abdirahman, 197
Berardi, Franco, 10–11
Berkeley Copwatch, 180
Berlusconi, Silvio, 96
Bernier, Lewis, 67, 75
Bettencourt Dairy Farm, 57–58
Bicking, Monica, 104, 109, 112, 117, 119
Bigelow, Kathryn, 222–25 passim, 236
Bihi, Abdirizak, 219–22, 251
Bile, Ramla, 198, 201, 207–9 passim, 230–36 passim
Billoo, Zahra, 188
black blocs, 102, 124
Black Entertainment Television (BET): *Copwatch America*, 176–78
Black Lives Matter, 181, 188, 208, 263
Black Panthers, 132, 134, 153, 155
Black Storytellers Alliance (BSA), 216
Blount, Roy, 124
body-worn cameras (BWC), 173–76
Bookchin, Murray, 146–47
Boston, 187, 190, 212, 213
Boundaoui, Assia: *The Feeling of Being Watched*, 254–58
Bradford, Javaris, 215
Bratton, William, 128, 130–31, 157, 159
Breaking Free Video Magazine, 31–35
Brian Coyle Community Center, Minneapolis, 199, 200, 202, 219, 223
Britain, 189, 210
broken windows policing, 5, 128–32 passim, 152, 156, 159, 164, 170
Brown, Michael, 133
Browne, Simone, 7
Buckthorn, Bob, 122

Building Community Resilience. *See* Countering Violent Extremism program (CVE)
Burger King, 58
business improvement districts (BIDs), 132
Butler, Judith, 68–69, 204, 210, 217
Buttar, Shahid, 188–89

CAAM. *See* Center for Asian American Media (CAAM)
Caffentzis, George, 96
CAIR. *See* Council on American-Islamic Relations (CAIR)
camcorders, 30, 31, 153
Canadian film tax credits. *See* Snowbate
Canals, Nelson W., 179–80
Canfield Watchmen, 133
Captain Phillips, 221–22
Carlson, Cody, 43, 44
Castile, Philando, 15, 126, 169
Castor, Jane, 122, 123
Cedar-Riverside, Minneapolis, 193–207, 219–24 passim, 232–33; in *A Stray*, 246, 247
Center for Asian American Media (CAAM), 248
Chauvin, Derek, 126
Chicago, 123; DNC 1968, 91, 118; DNC, 1996, 93; *The Feeling of Being Watched*, 254, 257; NATO summit protests (2012), 123; police killings, 175
Chicano/a movement, 136–37
Choudhury, Nusrat, 157
Clarion Fund, 183
Clark, Jamar, 15, 209
Cleveland Police Department, 174
Coleman, Norm, 224
commercial media, 97, 103, 105, 141, 183, 210–11
Common Ground (New Orleans), 116
Communities United Against Police Brutality (CUAPB), 105, 206
CompStat, 155
Copwatch America, 176–78
copwatching, 132–36, 142–81 passim
Copwatch Media, 180

Copwatch Patrol Unit (COU), 127, 129, 153–68
Couldry, Nick, 237–38
Council on American-Islamic Relations (CAIR), 187, 188, 198, 205–6, 206–7, 253
Countering Violent Extremism program (CVE), 5, 189–92 passim, 198–212, 229, 252, 259
counter-summit protests, 94–100 passim, 113, 121–24 passim
COVID-19 pandemic, 261–64
Cowie, Elizabeth, 37, 38
CRASS (Community RNC Arrestee Support Structure), 104, 118
Crawford, Jacob, 133
Crimes of Hallmark/Westland Meat Company, 54–55
Crowder, Bradley, 116
CVE. See Countering Violent Extremism program (CVE)
Czernik, Rob, 104, 109, 112

Dahir, Ayaan, 199, 204, 205, 210, 212, 226–29 passim, 233, 235, 255–60 passim; Unicorn Riot and, 216
dairy industry, 48, 55, 57–58, 59, 63, 75, 85
Darby, Brandon, 116
Darst, Andrew, 116
Daulatzai, Sohail, 186
David, Scott, 21, 42, 43, 46, 49, 53
Davis, Karen, 35, 36, 37, 64
Dealing Dogs, 49, 59
Death on a Factory Farm, 59, 60
De Blasio, Bill, 129, 130, 141, 159
dehumanization, 8, 48, 103, 172, 227
Del Aguila, Jason, 134–36 passim, 146, 152, 168, 179
Delaney, Ben, 74
Del Rosario, Enrique, 147–50 passim
Democracy Now!, 97, 103–4
Democratic National Convention: 1968 (Chicago), 118; 1996 (Chicago), 93
DeSantis, Ron, 265
Didion, Joan, 1, 11
diet: African Americans and, 85
Dijck, José van, 13

Direct Action Everywhere (DxE), 66–73, 85, 262–64 passim; Piglet Refuses to Give Up, 79–80
disability studies, 85
Discipline and Punish (Foucault), 112, 185
Disrupt J20 protests, Washington, DC, 2017, 88–89, 123–24
Doggart, Robert, 184
Dube, Amano, 199, 201, 202
Dugger, Chris, 116
Dutkiewicz, Jan, 66

Earth Liberation Front (ELF), 33, 39, 115
Earthlings (Monson), 29, 43
"Eat My Fear" (Lynch), 83
Electronic Frontier Federation, 188–89
ELF. See Earth Liberation Front (ELF)
El Grito de Sunset Park, 127–28, 133–53 passim, 157, 165, 168–69, 175, 179–82; CPU compared, 159, 162
entrapment, 114, 116, 197
"extractive gaze" (Baron), 27

Facebook, 158, 262, 264; El Grito, 138–39; YMC, 215
factory farms and farming, 9, 40, 47, 59, 63–75 passim, 81–86 passim, 261; Death on a Factory Farm, 59, 60
FBI, 30, 92, 114–17 passim, 130, 197; COINTELPRO, 2; in films, 239–42 passim, 253, 254–55; Minneapolis, 196, 212, 217–19; Muslim Americans and, 187; Operation Backfire, 39, 115; RNC (2008), 102
Federici, Silvia, 96
The Feeling of Being Watched (Boundaoui), 254–58
Feidt, Dan, 105
Ferber, Chrystal, 43, 47–53 passim
Ferguson, Missouri, 133, 213, 249
films, 221–27 passim, 238–58 passim; Minnesota, 193. See also Snowbate
Fiske, John, 6, 7, 92, 96–97
Fitzgerald, Garrett, 104, 112, 119
Flores, Dennis, 134–39 passim, 142, 144, 150–51, 164, 175, 179–82 passim
Floyd, George, 15, 126, 176, 180, 214, 268
Fonseca, Nico, 165

Food Empowerment Project, 83
food vendors, harassment and beating
    by police, 160–61, 175
forest defenders: Atlanta, 266–67
For Our Liberation, 182
Foucault, Michel, 3, 9, 10, 22, 90, 92, 97,
    99, 118; *Discipline and Punish*, 112, 185;
    "new optics," 115
Free Trade Area of the Americas (FTAA)
    protests, Miami, 2003, 94–100 passim,
    113

Gaertner, Susan, 111
Gaete-Tapia, Claudio, 135, 137–38, 146, 152
Gaines, Jane, 108
Galatas, Eric, 95
Galloway, Katie, 114
Gangi, Bob, 160, 170
Ganley, Gus, 101, 102, 110, 115–16, 118
García Espinosa, Julio, 247
Garner, Eric, 168, 169, 181
Garrett, Steve, 43
G8 protests and G20: 2001 (Genoa),
    95–96; 2010 (Toronto), 121
Gennarelli, Thomas, 24–25, 29
gentrification, 129–32 passim, 136–42
    passim; resistance to, 150
Georgiades, Niko, 213, 214, 254, 255
Gerbaudo, Paolo, 139
German, Mike, 252
Getino, Octavio, 165, 253
Gilroy, Paul, 135, 198
Giuliani, Rudy, 130, 159
Glass Bead Collective, 103, 104, 105, 214
Glass Walls Project, 63–66
Global Revolution, 214
Gong, Stephen, 248
Goodman, Amy, 103–4
Goodman, Cliff, 23
Graham, Ramarley, 153
Grandin, Temple, 63–65
Gray, Freddie, 169
Great Britain. *See* Britain
Greiling, Tom, 106
Gross, Michelle, 105, 111, 117, 119, 206
Gruen, Lori, 36
Guilfoyle, Bob, 42–52 passim

Guillén-Givins, Luce, 104, 109, 112, 117,
    119–20

Hall, Stuart, 12, 135, 197, 210, 211, 244, 252,
    259
Hallmark/Westland Meat Packing
    Company, 51, 55, 57
Harding, Thomas, 30–31
Harper, Breeze, 84, 85
Harper, Josh, 31–35
Harrington, John, 104
Hassan, Hodan, 198
hate crimes: anti-Arab and anti-Muslim,
    185, 187–88
HBO: *Mogadishu, Minnesota* (proposed
    series), 219–35 passim, 242, 252–53,
    259
Heckler, Margaret, 29
Hedstrom, Marilyn, 116
Heinegg, Rebecca, 148, 149
Henshaw-Plath, Evan, 94
Hermes, Kris, 119
Hill, Melissa, 110–11, 121
Hillyard, Paddy, 189–90
Hinton, Elizabeth, 6
Hog Production at Smithfield, 63
Homeland Security Department. *See* US
    Department of Homeland Security
    (DHS)
housing: government spending, 128;
    New York City, 129, 136–42 passim,
    161–62
Howley, Kevin, 127
Hsiung, Wayne, 66–72 passim, 79–80,
    263–64
Hudson, Dale, 76
Humane Methods of Slaughter Act of
    1958, 40
Human Society of the United States
    (HSUS), 42, 43, 51, 54–55
Huntington Life Science, 34, 35
Hussein, Jaylani, 188, 205, 210, 211, 215–16

Ibrahim, Filsan, 200–205 passim, 209–10,
    229–31 passim, 236, 237, 255, 258
Imagination (Abdikadir), 249
immigrants, Somali. *See* Somali
    Americans

Immigration and Customs Enforcement (ICE). See US Immigration and Customs Enforcement (ICE)

Independent Media Center (IMC). *See* Indymedia (IMC)

industry videos, 63–66

Indymedia (IMC), 93–96 passim; 112–15 passim; Miami, 113; Portland, 114; Twin Cities, 15, 104, 105, 112–13, 213

informers and agents provocateurs, 112–17 passim, 121, 197; in films, 239, 240, 253; Muslim Americans and Somali Americans, 187, 197, 212, 218, 239

The Intercept, 157, 254; *They Rescued Pigs and Turkeys from Factory Farms*, 68, 69, 71

interrogation videos, 175

I, Orca, 75, 78

Ireland, 189

Isaac, Najieb, 180

Isaaq, Burhan Israfael, 200–205 passim, 216–18 passim, 224–31 passim, 240–43 passim, 252, 255, 258, 259

ISIS/ISIL (Islamic State), 192, 196, 197, 198, 208, 217, 224

Islamberg, New York, 184

Islamophobia, 183–92 passim, 203–11 passim, 223–27 passim, 237, 244–45, 252–53, 258–60 passim; anti-Arab and anti-Muslim hate crimes, 185, 187–88

I-Witness Video, 103

James, David, 239

Jenkins, Henry, 236–37

Jensen, Dennis, 196

Jensen, Zach, 114

Johnson, Jeh, 200, 202

Jones, Jack, 222

Jones, Miriam, 83

jones, pattrice, 82, 83–84

Juris, Jeffrey, 145–46

Justice Coalition, 253, 259

Justice Committee, 132, 176, 262

Keating, Jeff, 113

Kelly, Ray, 183–84

Khabeer, Su'ad Abdul, 204

Kielas, Joshua, 31–32, 34

Kim, Claire Jean, 8

King, Cassie, 69–73 passim, 85, 263

Klein, Naomi, 97, 122, 262

K'naan, 222–25 passim, 229–37 passim, 252

Ko, Syl, 8–9

Kohls, Rosalind, 222

Kohn, Eric, 221–22

Kundnani, Arun, 196

LaSalle, Jose, 153–64 passim, 175–78 passim

Last Chance for Animals, 43, 59, 60

Latinx copwatchers: New York City, 132–36, 142–81 passim

Lazzarato, Mauricio, 11, 91–92

LeDay, Chris, 169

Lee, Ronnie, 23

Lewis, John E., 39

Liebman, Matthew, 57

Liem, Yul-San, 132, 176

Lipsitz, George, 131

Los Angeles, 131; CVE, 190, 212; police, 150, 174

Luger, Andrew, 197, 208

Luger, Ellen Goldberg, 208

Lynch, David: "Eat My Fear," 83

Malcolm X Grassroots Movement, 134, 169

Mansour, Ifrah, 220, 223, 232, 240, 245, 251, 252; *How to Have Fun in a Civil War*, 220, 243

Marceau, Justin, 58, 82

Marin, André, 122

Mark, Patty, 36

mass media. *See* commercial media

maternal melodrama in animal rights videos, 77–80

Mauleón, Emanuel, 191

Maxamed, Iqbal: *Screened*, 249

Mayer, Vicki, 234

McCartney, Paul, 21

McDavid, Eric, 114

McDonald, Laquan, 175

McKay, David, 116

McQuade, Brendan, 10

meatpackers and meatpacking, 51, 55, 57, 63, 64, 261. *See also* slaughterhouses
Meet Your Meat (PETA), 43
Mercy for Animals, 58, 82, 84–85; open rescues, 36, 66
Meyer, Amy, 17–21, 62, 74
Miami FTAA protests, 2003. *See* Free Trade Area of the Americas (FTAA) protests, Miami, 2003
Miami Model, 98–99, 105
Minneapolis, 15, 188, 192–259 passim
Minneapolis Foundation, 208
Minnesota, 186; Film and Television Board, 193; Somali American population, 193; in *A Stray*, 246. *See also* Twin Cities
Mire, Mahmoud, 228, 229
Mogadishu, Minnesota (proposed HBO series), 219–35 passim, 242, 252–53, 259
Mogelson, Luke, 15
Mohaud, Mohammed, 202
Molotov cocktails, 101–2, *101*, 116
Monson, Shaun, 29, 43
Montville, Kenneth, 77
Moore, Kevin, 169
Morales, Iris, 164
MPower Change, 188, 256
Muflahi, Abdullah, 169
Mukhtar, Abdirahman, 248
Muslim Americans, 183–260 passim
Muslim Justice League, 188, 192, 209, 212, 213, 253, 256
Muslims, repression of. *See* Islamophobia
Muslim Youth Voices, 248

NAACP, 85
Nash, Kate, 74–75
National Security Agency (NSA), 2, 189
NATO summit protests, Chicago, 2012, 123
Neocleous, Mark, 3
Newkirk, Ingrid, 24, 25–26
New Orleans, 116
New York City, 127–82 passim; gentrification, 129–32 passim, 136–42 passim; police Islamophobia, 183–84,

187; Occupy Wall Street, 141, 214; police killings, 153, 168; Puerto Rican Day Parade, 147–50 passim; rent strikes, 137–42 passim; RNC (2004), 103; transit police and fare evasion, 170–73 passim
Nichols, Bill, 56, 59, 60, 76, 144, 145, 150, 163
Noor, Mohamud, 233
Núñez, Sharon, 77

Occupy Wall Street, 141, 214
Ornelas, Lauren, 83, 84
Orta, Ramsey, 168–69, 181
Ortega, Isaac, 181, 182
Ortiz, Kim, 154, 168, 177, 178
Oseland, Erik, 104, 109, 111–12, 119
Osman, Idil, 223, 238

Pacheco, Alex, 24, 28–29
Pachirat, Timothy, 22–23; *Every Twelve Seconds*, 55
Padilla, Andrew, 174
Paley, Dawn, 121
Pantaleo, Daniel, 168, 169
Patriot Act. *See* USA Patriot Act
Paul, Alexandra, 264
People for the Ethical Treatment of Animals (PETA), 24, 28–29, 34–43 passim, 66, 74; "Got Autism" campaign, 85; *Meet Your Meat*, 43; VR documentaries, 75
Perez, Richie, 134
Petito, Orazio, 141, 142
Picklesimer, Paul Darwin, 264
Piglet Refuses to Give Up, 79–80
Poell, Thomas, 13
police and policing, 3, 11, 15, 90–108 passim, 114–23 passim, 262; body-worn cameras, 173–76; Cleveland, 174; harassment of food vendors, 160–61, 175; Los Angeles, 150, 174; militarization, 91, 92, 121; New York City, 127–82 passim; search warrants, 106–7; targeting of media, 121. *See also* broken windows policing; Communities United Against Police Brutality (CUAPB); copwatching;

entrapment; stop-and-frisk policing; transit police

police, killings by: 95, 126, 214; Atlanta, 177, 266; Chicago, 175; New York City, 153, 168; Twin Cities, 105

Police Reform Organizing Project (PROP), 160, 164, 170, 176

Potter, Will, 21, 30, 39

Pritchett, Andrea, 133, 165

PROP. *See* Police Reform Organizing Project (PROP)

public housing, 91, 128, 233

Puerto Rican Day Parade, New York City, 147–50 passim

Puerto Rico, 135, 179–80

Quanah Cattle Company, 63

Queens Neighborhood United (QNU), 131

racial capitalism, 7

racial Other, 6–9 passim

racial profiling, 129, 191

racism and speciesism, 8–9

Radig, Taylor, 21–22, 41–52 passim, 63

Rancière, Jacques, 11

Rasmussen, Claire, 58

The Recruiters (proposed HBO series). *See Mogadishu, Minnesota* (proposed HBO series)

Reed, T.V., 155

rent strikes: New York City, 137–42 passim

Republican National Convention (RNC): 2000 (Philadelphia), 118; 2004 (New York), 103; 2008 (Twin Cities), 89, 100–112, 116–22 passim; 2012 (Tampa), 122–23

Revolutionary Anarchist Bowling League (RABL), 102

Reynolds, Diamond, 169

RNC 8 case, 103–5 passim, 109–12 passim

Robinson, Cedric, 7

Rochester Institute of Technology (RIT), 191–92

Said, Edward, 211

Sand, Jay, 94

Sanders, Alfred "Abuka," 105

Santo, Avi, 226

Santurio, Alicia, 264

Sarsour, Linda, 188, 256

#SayNOtoHBO, 236–38 passim, 250

Screened (Maxamed), 249

search warrants, 102, 106–7

Seattle WTO protests, 1999. *See* World Trade Organization (WTO) protests, Seattle, 1999

Seber, John, 82, 84

Secor, Nathanael, 104, 112

September 11, 2001, terrorist attacks, 1–3, 112, 160, 185

sexism, 81–82

sexual harassment, 50–51, 69, 81

The Sexual Politics of Meat (Adams), 82

SHAC. *See* Stop Huntington Animal Cruelty (SHAC)

Shadowbox Studios, 266

Shin, Donghee, 76–77

Showdown in Seattle, 94–95

Shresthova, Sangita, 244

Simmons, Wayne, 183

Slade, John, 113

slaughterhouses, 21, 22, 40–41, 48–58 passim, 63–66 passim, 74, 75, 83

slavery, 5–7

Slotkin, Richard, 1

Smith, Greg M., 226

Smith, Neil, 142

Smithfield Foods, 63, 67

SNC-Lavalin, 121

Snowbate, 234, 235, 238

Snowdon, Peter, 13

social media, 13, 93, 139, 158–59, 236–38 passim, 262, 264. *See also* Facebook; YouTube

Solanas, Fernando, 164–65, 253

Somali Americans, 193–260 passim

Sontag, Susan, 127, 144

sousveillance, 9

speciesism and racism. *See* racism and speciesism

Specktor, Max, 104, 109, 112, 116–17

Spiegel, Marjorie, 8

Star Tribune, 210–11

Sterling, Alton, 169

sting operations, 114, 197

stop-and-frisk policing, 129, 154, 169, 174
Stop Huntington Animal Cruelty (SHAC), 34, 35, 39
Stossel, John, 62
A Stray (Syeed), 238–52
Sweetland, Mary Beth, 22, 43, 51–52
Syeed, Musa, 239, 242–43; *A Stray*, 238–52

Tanner, Almira, 67, 73, 85, 262, 263
Tavarez, Juwan "Chico," 161
Taylor, Breonna, 180, 214, 263
Taylor, Sunaura, 85–86
Teichberg, Vlad, 104–5, 214
television, 96, 175, 192–93, 231, 248; Chicano/a, 136; *Copwatch America*, 176–78; DNC, 1968 (Chicago), 91; in *Imagination* and *Screened*, 249. See also *Mogadishu, Minnesota* (proposed HBO series)
Tennewald, Robert, 235
Terán, Manuel "Tortuguita," 266
(T)error, 212, 253–55 passim
terrorism and counterterrorism: al-Shabaab, 196; animal rights activism criminalization, 30, 39–40, 70–71; Biden policy, 265; in films and TV, 226–31 passim; political dissent criminalization, 89–92 passim, 96–114 passim, 118, 214; Somali and Muslim American criminalization, 183–92 passim, 196–201 passim, 208–11 passim, 216–31 passim, 252, 254, 266
terrorism-related legislation, 187; Britain, 189. See also Animal Enterprise Terrorism Act (AETA); USA Patriot Act
Terrorizing Dissent, 104–11, 214
Théard, Noelle, 138
They Rescued Pigs and Turkeys from Factory Farms, 68
Third Cinema, 137, 164–65, 247–48, 253
The Third Jihad: Radical Islam's Vision for America, 183–84
This Is Hormel, 63
Thomas, Sean, 43, 44, 46, 52–57 passim
Timoney, John, 96, 279–80n68
transit police, 142–45, 170–73 passim

Trimmer, Eryn, 104, 112
Trujillo, Josmar, 129, 130, 156, 157, 161, 168–74 passim, 180
Trump, Donald, 4, 185, 188, 224, 237, 238, 261–65 passim. See also Disrupt J20 protests, Washington, DC, 2017
Twin Cities: Indymedia, 104, 105, 112–13, 213; policing, 15. See also Minneapolis; Republican National Convention (RNC), 2008
Twitter, 93, 236, 262, 264

Unicorn Riot, 213–17, 254, 259, 266
United Kingdom. See Britain
Unite the Right, Charlottesville, Virginia, August 2017, 184, 196, 214
Unnecessary Fuss (1984 video), 24–29
USA Patriot Act, 38, 92, 100, 104, 187
US Department of Agriculture (USDA), 41, 57
US Department of Homeland Security (DHS), 190, 191, 200, 201, 265
US Immigration and Customs Enforcement (ICE), 188, 214

Valle, Jose, 74
van Dijck, José. See Dijck, José van
Vice Media, 69–72 passim
The Video Activist Handbook, 30–31
videos, activist, 13, 88–111 passim, 116, 122, 125; in AIDS activism, 132; in animal welfare and rights movement, 17–87 passim; George Floyd killing, 126; New York City, 127, 128, 136–52 passim, 156–75 passim, 180–82 passim. See also Unicorn Riot
virtual reality (VR), 73–78 passim

Wacquant, Loïc, 91
Wakeel, Shannon al-. See Al-Wakeel, Shannon
Washington, DC, inauguration protests, 2017. See Disrupt J20 protests, Washington, DC, 2017
Weah, Wokie, 198
Weber, Mike, 70–71
WeCopwatch, 133
Weiner, Lauren, 114

West Bank, Minneapolis. *See* Cedar-
   Riverside, Minneapolis
West Bank Community Coalition
   (Minneapolis), 198, 202–8 passim, 232
We're Getting Ready, 100–103
Whitt, David, 133
Williams, Kristian, 6
Williams, Linda, 77–78
Winter, Lucinda, 193, 225–26, 230, 231–32,
   238
With My Own Eyes, 80–81
WITNESS, 180
Wood, Alexei, 88–89
Wood, Lesley J., 103
Woodhouse, Leighton, 75
World Trade Organization (WTO)
   protests, Seattle, 1999, 94–95, 98, 124
Wyngaarden, James, 29

Young Lords, 132, *133*, 134, 137; machismo,
   164
Young Muslim Collective (YMC), 198,
   203–8 passim, 212–17 passim, 242, 255
Youthprise, 198, 201
YouTube, 213, 218, 237, 264; copwatching
   videos, 142–47 passim, 156–59
   passim, *156*, 166–67, 178–79; Somali
   Americans, 225, 236, 237

Zimmermann, Patricia, 76, 107–8, 141,
   143, 172

About the Author

Chris Robé is a professor of film and media studies in the School of Communication and Multimedia Studies at Florida Atlantic University. He primarily writes about how various communities and social movements employ media making in their activism. He has written several books including *Left of Hollywood: Cinema, Modernism, and the Emergence of U.S. Radical Film Culture* (2010) and *Breaking the Spell: A History of Anarchist Filmmakers, Videotape Guerrillas, and Digital Ninjas* (2017). He coedited the collection *Insurgent Media from the Front: A Media Activism Reader* (2020) with Stephen Charbonneau. He has long been involved with his faculty union in pursuit of creating an accessible and quality public higher education for all who desire it.

ABOUT PM PRESS

PM Press is an independent, radical publisher of books and media to educate, entertain, and inspire. Founded in 2007 by a small group of people with decades of publishing, media, and organizing experience, PM Press amplifies the voices of radical authors, artists, and activists. Our aim is to deliver bold political ideas and vital stories to people from all walks of life and arm the dreamers to demand the impossible. We have sold millions of copies of our books, most often one at a time, face to face. We're old enough to know what we're doing and young enough to know what's at stake. Join us to create a better world.

PM Press
PO Box 23912
Oakland, CA 94623
www.pmpress.org

PM Press in Europe
europe@pmpress.org
www.pmpress.org.uk

FRIENDS OF PM PRESS

These are indisputably momentous times—the financial system is melting down globally and the Empire is stumbling. Now more than ever there is a vital need for radical ideas.

In the many years since its founding—and on a mere shoestring—PM Press has risen to the formidable challenge of publishing and distributing knowledge and entertainment for the struggles ahead. With hundreds of releases to date, we have published an impressive and stimulating array of literature, art, music, politics, and culture. Using every available medium, we've succeeded in connecting those hungry for ideas and information to those putting them into practice.

Friends of PM allows you to directly help impact, amplify, and revitalize the discourse and actions of radical writers, filmmakers, and artists. It provides us with a stable foundation from which we can build upon our early successes and provides a much-needed subsidy for the materials that can't necessarily pay their own way. You can help make that happen—and receive every new title automatically delivered to your door once a month—by joining as a Friend of PM Press. And, we'll throw in a free T-shirt when you sign up.

Here are your options:

- **$30 a month** Get all books and pamphlets plus a 50% discount on all webstore purchases

- **$40 a month** Get all PM Press releases (including CDs and DVDs) plus a 50% discount on all webstore purchases

- **$100 a month** Superstar—Everything plus PM merchandise, free downloads, and a 50% discount on all webstore purchases

For those who can't afford $30 or more a month, we have **Sustainer Rates** at $15, $10, and $5. Sustainers get a free PM Press T-shirt and a 50% discount on all purchases from our website.

Your Visa or Mastercard will be billed once a month, until you tell us to stop. Or until our efforts succeed in bringing the revolution around. Or the financial meltdown of Capital makes plastic redundant. Whichever comes first.

Breaking the Spell: A History of Anarchist Filmmakers, Videotape Guerrillas, and Digital Ninjas

Chris Robé

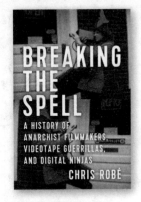

ISBN: 978-1-62963-233-9
$26.95   480 pages

Breaking the Spell offers the first full-length study that charts the historical trajectory of anarchist-inflected video activism from the late 1960s to the present. Two predominant trends emerge from this social movement-based video activism: 1) anarchist-inflected processes increasingly structure its production, distribution, and exhibition practices; and 2) video does not simply represent collective actions and events, but also serves as a form of activist practice in and of itself from the moment of recording to its later distribution and exhibition. Video plays an increasingly important role among activists in the growing global resistance against neoliberal capitalism. As various radical theorists have pointed out, subjectivity itself becomes a key terrain of struggle as capitalism increasingly structures and mines it through social media sites, cell phone technology, and new "flexible" work and living patterns. As a result, alternative media production becomes a central location where new collective forms of subjectivity can be created to challenge aspects of neoliberalism.

Chris Robé's book fills in historical gaps by bringing to light unexplored video activist groups like the Cascadia Forest Defenders, eco-video activists from Eugene, Oregon; Mobile Voices, Latino day laborers harnessing cell phone technology to combat racism and police harassment in Los Angeles; and Outta Your Backpack Media, indigenous youth from the Southwest who use video to celebrate their culture and fight against marginalization. This groundbreaking study also deepens our understanding of more well-researched movements like AIDS video activism, Paper Tiger Television, and Indymedia by situating them within a longer history and wider context of radical video activism.

"Christopher Robé's meticulously researched Breaking the Spell *traces the roots of contemporary, anarchist-inflected video and Internet activism and clearly demonstrates the affinities between the anti-authoritarian ethos and aesthetic of collectives from the '60s and '70s—such as Newsreel and the Videofreex—and their contemporary descendants. Robé's nuanced perspective enables him to both celebrate and critique anarchist forays into guerrilla media.* Breaking the Spell *is an invaluable guide to the contemporary anarchist media landscape that will prove useful for activists as well as scholars."*
—Richard Porton, author of *Film and the Anarchist Imagination*

Surviving the Future: Abolitionist Queer Strategies

Edited by Scott Branson, Raven Hudson, and Bry Reed with a Foreword by Mimi Thi Nguyen

ISBN: 978-1-62963-971-0
$22.95   328 pages

Abolish the Police
Abolish Prisons
Abolish the State
Abolish Identity
Abolish the Family
Abolish Racial Capitalism
Abolish Settler Colonialism
Abolish Society

Surviving the Future

Abolitionist Queer Strategies

Edited by Scott Branson, Raven Hudson, and Bry Reed
Foreword by Mimi Thi Nguyen

Surviving the Future is a collection of the most current ideas in radical queer movement work and revolutionary queer theory. Beset by a new pandemic, fanning the flames of global uprising, these queers cast off progressive narratives of liberal hope while building mutual networks of rebellion and care. These essays propose a militant strategy of queer survival in an ever-precarious future. Starting from a position of abolition—of prisons, police, the State, identity, and racist cisheteronormative society—this collection refuses the bribes of inclusion in a system built on our expendability. Though the mainstream media saturates us with the boring norms of queer representation (with a recent focus on trans visibility), the writers in this book ditch false hope to imagine collective visions of liberation that tell different stories, build alternate worlds, and refuse the legacies of racial capitalism, anti-Blackness, and settler colonialism. The work curated in this book spans Black queer life in the time of COVID-19 and uprising, assimilation and pinkwashing settler colonial projects, subversive and deviant forms of representation, building anarchist trans/queer infrastructures, and more. Contributors include Che Gossett, Yasmin Nair, Mattilda Bernstein Sycamore, Adrian Shanker, Kitty Stryker, Toshio Meronek, and more.

"Surviving the Future *is a testament that otherwise worlds are not only possible, our people are making them right now—and they are queering how we get there through organizing and intellectual work. Now is the perfect time to interrogate how we are with each other and the land we inhabit. This collection gives us ample room to do just that in a moment of mass uprisings led by everyday people demanding safety without policing, prisons and other forms of punishment.*
—Charlene A. Carruthers, author of *Unapologetic: A Black, Queer, and Feminist Mandate for Radical Movements*

"Surviving the Future *is not an anthology that simply includes queer and trans minorities in mix of existing abolitionist thought. Rather, it is a transformative collection of queer/trans methods for living an abolitionist life. Anyone who dreams of dismantling the prison-industrial complex, policing, borders and the surveillance state should read this book. Frankly, everybody who doesn't share that dream should read it, too, and maybe they'll start dreaming differently."*
—Susan Stryker, author of *Transgender History: The Roots of Today's Revolution*

It Did Happen Here: An Antifascist People's History

Edited by Moe Bowstern, Mic Crenshaw, Alec Dunn, Celina Flores, Julie Perini, Erin Yanke

ISBN: 978-1-62963-351-0
$21.95   304 pages

Portland, Oregon, 1988: the brutal murder of Ethiopian immigrant Mulugeta Seraw by racist skinheads shocked the city. In response disparate groups quickly came together to organize against white nationalist violence and right-wing organizing throughout the Rose City and the Pacific Northwest.

It Did Happen Here compiles interviews with dozens of people who worked together during the waning decades of the twentieth century to reveal an inspiring collaboration between groups of immigrants, civil rights activists, militant youth, and queer organizers. This oral history focuses on participants in three core groups: the Portland chapters of Anti-Racist Action and Skinheads Against Racial Prejudice, and the Coalition for Human Dignity.

Using a diversity of tactics—from out-and-out brawls on the streets and at punk shows, to behind-the-scenes intelligence gathering—brave antiracists unified on their home ground over and over, directly attacking right-wing fascists and exposing white nationalist organizations and neo-Nazi skinheads. Embattled by police and unsupported by the city, these citizen activists eventually drove the boneheads out of the music scene and off the streets of Portland. This book shares their stories about what worked, what didn't, and ideas on how to continue the fight.

"By the time I moved my queer little family to Portland at the turn of the millennium, the city had a reputation as a homo-friendly bastion of progressive politics, so we were somewhat taken aback when my daughter's racially diverse sports team was met with a burning cross at a suburban game. So much progress had been made yet, at times, it felt like the past hadn't gone anywhere. If only we'd had It Did Happen Here. *This documentary project tells the forgotten history of Portland's roots as a haven for white supremacists and recounts the ways anti-racists formed coalitions across subcultures to protect the vulnerable and fight the good fight against Nazi boneheads and the bigoted right. Through the voices of lived experience,* It Did Happen Here *illuminates community dynamics and lays out ideas and inspiration for long-term and nonpolice solutions to poverty and hatred."*
—Ariel Gore, author of *We Were Witches*

Jackson Rising Redux: Lessons on Building the Future in the Present

Edited by Kali Akuno & Matt Meyer
with a Foreword by Richard D. Wolff

ISBN: 978-1-62963-928-4 (paperback)
   978-1-62963-864-5 (hardcover)
$24.95/$59.95   584 pages

Mississippi is the poorest state in the US, with the highest percentage of Black people and a history of vicious racial terror. Black resistance at a time of global health, economic, and climate crisis is the backdrop and context for the drama captured in this new and revised collection of essays. Cooperation Jackson, founded in 2014 in Mississippi's capital to develop an economically uplifting democratic "solidarity economy," is anchored by a network of worker-owned, self-managed cooperative enterprises. The organization developed in the context of the historic election of radical Mayor Chokwe Lumumba, lifetime human rights attorney. Subsequent to Lumumba's passing less than one year after assuming office, the network developed projects both inside and outside of the formal political arena. In 2020, Cooperation Jackson became the center for national and international coalition efforts, bringing together progressive peoples from diverse trade union, youth, church, and cultural movements. This long-anticipated anthology details the foundations behind those successful campaigns. It unveils new and ongoing strategies and methods being pursued by the movement for grassroots-centered Black community control and self-determination, inspiring partnership and emulation across the globe.

"Jackson is one of the epicenters of resistance for all of us to emulate; this book lays the scene."
—Chris Hedges, journalist, Presbyterian minister, and Princeton University lecturer; author of *War Is a Force That Gives Us Meaning*

"Jackson Rising is the rarest of things: a real strategic plan. You will not find a simple wish list that glosses over the hard questions of resources, or some disembodied manifesto imploring the workers forward, but a work in progress building the capacity of people to exercise power."
—Richard Moser, author of *The World the Sixties Made*